ACCELERATING DISCOVERY

MINING UNSTRUCTURED INFORMATION FOR HYPOTHESIS GENERATION

Chapman & Hall/CRC
Data Mining and Knowledge Discovery Series

SERIES EDITOR

Vipin Kumar

University of Minnesota
Department of Computer Science and Engineering
Minneapolis, Minnesota, U.S.A.

AIMS AND SCOPE

This series aims to capture new developments and applications in data mining and knowledge discovery, while summarizing the computational tools and techniques useful in data analysis. This series encourages the integration of mathematical, statistical, and computational methods and techniques through the publication of a broad range of textbooks, reference works, and handbooks. The inclusion of concrete examples and applications is highly encouraged. The scope of the series includes, but is not limited to, titles in the areas of data mining and knowledge discovery methods and applications, modeling, algorithms, theory and foundations, data and knowledge visualization, data mining systems and tools, and privacy and security issues.

PUBLISHED TITLES

ACCELERATING DISCOVERY: MINING UNSTRUCTURED INFORMATION FOR HYPOTHESIS GENERATION
Scott Spangler

ADVANCES IN MACHINE LEARNING AND DATA MINING FOR ASTRONOMY
Michael J. Way, Jeffrey D. Scargle, Kamal M. Ali, and Ashok N. Srivastava

BIOLOGICAL DATA MINING
Jake Y. Chen and Stefano Lonardi

COMPUTATIONAL BUSINESS ANALYTICS
Subrata Das

COMPUTATIONAL INTELLIGENT DATA ANALYSIS FOR SUSTAINABLE DEVELOPMENT
Ting Yu, Nitesh V. Chawla, and Simeon Simoff

COMPUTATIONAL METHODS OF FEATURE SELECTION
Huan Liu and Hiroshi Motoda

CONSTRAINED CLUSTERING: ADVANCES IN ALGORITHMS, THEORY, AND APPLICATIONS
Sugato Basu, Ian Davidson, and Kiri L. Wagstaff

CONTRAST DATA MINING: CONCEPTS, ALGORITHMS, AND APPLICATIONS
Guozhu Dong and James Bailey

DATA CLASSIFICATION: ALGORITHMS AND APPLICATIONS
Charu C. Aggarawal

DATA CLUSTERING: ALGORITHMS AND APPLICATIONS
Charu C. Aggarawal and Chandan K. Reddy

DATA CLUSTERING IN C++: AN OBJECT-ORIENTED APPROACH
Guojun Gan

DATA MINING FOR DESIGN AND MARKETING
Yukio Ohsawa and Katsutoshi Yada

DATA MINING WITH R: LEARNING WITH CASE STUDIES
Luís Torgo

FOUNDATIONS OF PREDICTIVE ANALYTICS
James Wu and Stephen Coggeshall

GEOGRAPHIC DATA MINING AND KNOWLEDGE DISCOVERY, SECOND EDITION
Harvey J. Miller and Jiawei Han

HANDBOOK OF EDUCATIONAL DATA MINING
Cristóbal Romero, Sebastian Ventura, Mykola Pechenizkiy, and Ryan S.J.d. Baker

HEALTHCARE DATA ANALYTICS
Chandan K. Reddy and Charu C. Aggarwal

INFORMATION DISCOVERY ON ELECTRONIC HEALTH RECORDS
Vagelis Hristidis

INTELLIGENT TECHNOLOGIES FOR WEB APPLICATIONS
Priti Srinivas Sajja and Rajendra Akerkar

INTRODUCTION TO PRIVACY-PRESERVING DATA PUBLISHING: CONCEPTS AND TECHNIQUES
Benjamin C. M. Fung, Ke Wang, Ada Wai-Chee Fu, and Philip S. Yu

KNOWLEDGE DISCOVERY FOR COUNTERTERRORISM AND LAW ENFORCEMENT
David Skillicorn

KNOWLEDGE DISCOVERY FROM DATA STREAMS
João Gama

MACHINE LEARNING AND KNOWLEDGE DISCOVERY FOR ENGINEERING SYSTEMS HEALTH MANAGEMENT
Ashok N. Srivastava and Jiawei Han

MINING SOFTWARE SPECIFICATIONS: METHODOLOGIES AND APPLICATIONS
David Lo, Siau-Cheng Khoo, Jiawei Han, and Chao Liu

MULTIMEDIA DATA MINING: A SYSTEMATIC INTRODUCTION TO CONCEPTS AND THEORY
Zhongfei Zhang and Ruofei Zhang

MUSIC DATA MINING
Tao Li, Mitsunori Ogihara, and George Tzanetakis

NEXT GENERATION OF DATA MINING
Hillol Kargupta, Jiawei Han, Philip S. Yu, Rajeev Motwani, and Vipin Kumar

RAPIDMINER: DATA MINING USE CASES AND BUSINESS ANALYTICS APPLICATIONS
Markus Hofmann and Ralf Klinkenberg

RELATIONAL DATA CLUSTERING: MODELS, ALGORITHMS, AND APPLICATIONS
Bo Long, Zhongfei Zhang, and Philip S. Yu

SERVICE-ORIENTED DISTRIBUTED KNOWLEDGE DISCOVERY
Domenico Talia and Paolo Trunfio

SPECTRAL FEATURE SELECTION FOR DATA MINING
Zheng Alan Zhao and Huan Liu

STATISTICAL DATA MINING USING SAS APPLICATIONS, SECOND EDITION
George Fernandez

SUPPORT VECTOR MACHINES: OPTIMIZATION BASED THEORY, ALGORITHMS, AND EXTENSIONS
Naiyang Deng, Yingjie Tian, and Chunhua Zhang

TEMPORAL DATA MINING
Theophano Mitsa

TEXT MINING: CLASSIFICATION, CLUSTERING, AND APPLICATIONS
Ashok N. Srivastava and Mehran Sahami

THE TOP TEN ALGORITHMS IN DATA MINING
Xindong Wu and Vipin Kumar

UNDERSTANDING COMPLEX DATASETS: DATA MINING WITH MATRIX DECOMPOSITIONS
David Skillicorn

ACCELERATING DISCOVERY

MINING UNSTRUCTURED INFORMATION FOR HYPOTHESIS GENERATION

Scott Spangler

IBM Research

San Jose, California, USA

CRC Press is an imprint of the
Taylor & Francis Group, an **informa** business
A CHAPMAN & HALL BOOK

The views expressed here are solely those of the author in his private capacity and do not in any way represent the views of the IBM Corporation.

CRC Press
Taylor & Francis Group
6000 Broken Sound Parkway NW, Suite 300
Boca Raton, FL 33487-2742

First issued in paperback 2020

ISBN 13: 978-0-367-57547-2 (pbk)
ISBN 13: 978-1-4822-3913-3 (hbk)

Library of Congress Cataloging-in-Publication Data

Spangler, Scott.
Accelerating discovery : mining unstructured information for hypothesis generation / Scott Spangler.
pages cm. -- (Chapman & Hall/CRC data mining and knowledge discovery series ; 37)
Includes index.
ISBN 978-1-4822-3913-3
1. Data mining. 2. Science--Information resources. 3. Science--Methodology. I. Title.

QA76.9.D343S6829 2016
006.3'12--dc23 2015016373

Visit the Taylor & Francis Web site at
http://www.taylorandfrancis.com

and the CRC Press Web site at
http://www.crcpress.com

To Karon, my love

Contents

Preface

A FEW YEARS AGO, HAVING spent more than a decade doing unstructured data mining of one form or another, in domains spanning helpdesk problem tickets, social media, and patents, I thought I fully understood the potential range of problems and likely areas of applicability of this mature technology. Then, something happened that completely changed how I thought about what I was doing and what its potential really was.

The change in my outlook began with the Watson Jeopardy challenge. Seeing a computer learn from text to play a game I had thought was far beyond the capabilities of any artificial intelligence opened my eyes to new possibilities. And I was not alone. Soon many customers were coming forward with their own unique problems—problems I would have said a few years ago were just too hard to solve with existing techniques. And now, I said, let's give it a try.

This wasn't simply a straightforward application of the algorithms used to win Jeopardy in a different context. Most of the problems I was being asked to solve weren't really even question-answering problems at all. But they all had a similar quality in that they forced us to digest all of the information in a given area and find a way to synthesize a new kind of meaning out of it. This time the problem was not to win a game show, but (to put it bluntly) to advance human scientific knowledge. More than once in the early going, before we had any results to show for our efforts, I wondered if I was out of my mind for even trying this. Early on, I remember making more than one presentation to senior executives at my company, describing what I was doing, half expecting they would tell me to cease immediately, because I was attempting something way too hard for current technology and far outside the bounds of a reasonable business opportunity. But fortunately, no one ever said that, and I kept on going.

Somewhere along the way (I can't say just when), I lost all doubt that I was really onto something very important. This was more than another new application of unstructured data mining. And as each new scientific area came forward for analysis, the approach we were using began to solidify into a kind of methodology. And then, just as this was happening, I attended the ACM Knowledge Discovery and Data Mining Conference in 2013 (KDD13); I met with CRC Press in a booth at the conference and told them about my idea. Shortly thereafter, I was signed up to write a book.

I knew at the time that what would make this book especially challenging is that I was still proving the methodology and tweaking it, even as I was writing out the description of that method. This was not ideal, but neither could it be avoided if I wanted to broaden the application of the method beyond a small team of people working in my own group. And if it could not be broadened, it would never realize its full potential.

Data science is a new discipline. It lacks a curriculum, a set of textbooks, a fundamental theory, and a set of guiding principles. This is both regrettable and exciting. It must be rectified if the discipline is to become established. Since I greatly desire that end, I write this book in the hopes of furthering it.

Many years ago, I remember stumbling across a book by the statistician John Tukey called *Exploratory Data Analysis*. It was written 30 years before I read it, and the author was no longer living; yet it spoke to me as if I were his research collaborator. It showed me how the ideas I had been grappling with in the area of unstructured text had been similarly addressed in the realm of structured data. Reading that book gave me renewed confidence in the direction I was taking and a larger vision for what the fulfillment of that vision might one day accomplish.

This book is one more step on that journey. The journey is essentially my life's work, and this book is that work's synthesis thus far. It is far from perfect, as anything that is real will always be a diminishment from what is merely imagined. But I hope even in its imperfect state it will communicate some part of what I experience on a daily basis working through accelerated discovery problems as a data scientist. I think it is unquestionably the most rewarding and exciting job in the world. And I dare to hope that 30 years from now, or maybe even sooner, someone will pick up this book and see their own ideas and challenges reflected in its pages and feel renewed confidence in the direction they are heading.

At the same time, I fear that one or two readers (at least) will buy this book and immediately be disappointed because it is not at all what they were expecting it would be. It's not a textbook. It's not a business book. It's not a popular science book. It doesn't fit well in any classification. I can only say this: I wrote it for the person I was a few years back. Read it with an open mind: you might find you get something useful out of it, regardless of the failure to meet your initial expectations. It took me a long time to get to this level of proficiency in knowing how to address accelerated discovery problems. I've tried my best to capture exactly how I go about it, both from a systematic perspective and from a practical point of view. This book provides motivation, strategy, tactics, and a heterogeneous set of comprehensive examples to illustrate all the points I make. If it works as I have intended it to, it will fill an important gap left by the other types of books I have mentioned…the ones you thought this might be. You can still buy those other books as well, but keep this one. Come back to it later when you have started to put in practice the theories that you learned in school to solve real-world applications. You may find then that the book has more to say to you than you first thought.

Today, I go into each new problem domain with complete confidence that I know how to get started; I know the major steps I need to accomplish, and I have a pretty good idea what the final solution will look like (or at least I know the range of things it might look like when we first deliver a useful prototype). It wasn't always that way. Those first few customer engagements of this type that I did, I was mostly winging it. It was exciting, no doubt, but I would have really loved to have this book on my desk (or in my e-reader) to look over after each meeting and help me figure out what I should do next. If you are fortunate enough to do what I do for a living, I think you will (eventually) find this book worthwhile.

Acknowledgments

THERE WERE MANY PEOPLE who were instrumental in the creation of this methodology and in the process of writing the book that explains it. First, the team at IBM Watson Innovations, who made it all possible: Ying Chen, Meena Nagarajan, Qi He, Linda Kato, Ana Lelescu, Jacques LaBrie, Cartic Ramakrishnan, Sheng Hua Boa, Steven Boyer, Eric Louie, Anshu Jain, Isaac Cheng, Griff Weber, Su Yan, and Roxana Stanoi. Also instrumental in realizing the vision were the team at Baylor College of Medicine, led by Olivier Lichtarge, with Larry Donehower, Angela Dawn Wilkins, Sam Regenbogen, Curtis Pickering, and Ben Bachman.

Jeff Kreulen has been a collaborator for many years now and continues to be a big supporter and contributor to the ideas described here. Michael Karasick and Laura Haas have been instrumental in consistently supporting and encouraging this work from a management perspective at IBM. John Richter, Meena Nagarajan, and Peter Haas were early reviewers of my first draft, and I appreciate their input. Ying Chen helped write the chapter on Why Accelerate Discovery?, for which I am most grateful. Pat Langley provided some very good advice during the planning phase for the book, which I profited from.

Finally, and most importantly, my wife, Karon Barber, who insisted that I finish this project, at the expense of time that I would rather have spent with her. Nothing I've accomplished in life would have happened without her steadfast faith and love.

CHAPTER 1

Introduction

THIS BOOK IS ABOUT discovery in science and the importance of heterogeneous data analytics in aiding that discovery. As the volume of scientific data and literature increases exponentially, scientists need ever-more powerful tools to process and synthesize that information in a practical and meaningful way. But in addition, scientists need a methodology that takes all the relevant information in a given problem area—all the available evidence—and processes it in order to propose the set of potential new hypotheses that are most likely to be both true and important. This book describes a method for achieving this goal.

But first, I owe the reader a short introduction and an explanation of why I am the one writing this book. The short answer is a lucky accident (lucky for me anyway; for you it remains to be seen). I stumbled into a career doing the most exciting and rewarding work I can imagine. I do not know it for a fact, but I suspect that I have done more of this kind of work and for a longer period of time than anyone else now alive. It is this experience that I now feel compelled to share, and it is that experience that should make the book interesting reading for those who also see the potential of the approach but do not know how to get started applying it.

It all started out with a love of mathematics, in particular discreet mathematics, and to be even more specific: combinatorics. Basically this is the study of how to count things. I was never happier than when I found this course in college. The discovery of a discipline devoted precisely to what one instinctively loves is one of life's greatest joys. I was equally disappointed to find there was no such thing as a career in combinatorics, outside of academia—at least, not at that time.

But I wandered into computer science, and from there into machine learning and from there into text mining, and suddenly I became aware that the skill and practice of knowing how to count things had a great deal of practical application after all. And now 30 years have passed since I finished that combinatorics course, and with every passing year the number, variety, importance, and fascination of the problems I work on are still increasing.

Nothing thrills me more than to have a new data set land in my inbox. This is especially so if it is some kind of data I have never seen before, better still if analyzing it requires me to learn about a whole new field of knowledge, and best yet if the result will somehow make a difference in the world. I can honestly say I have had the privilege of working on such problems, not once, not twice, but more times than I can reckon. I do not always succeed, but I do make progress often enough that more and more of these problems seem to find their way to me. At some level I wish I could do them all, but that would be selfish (and not very practical). So I am writing this book instead. If you love working with unstructured, heterogeneous data the way I do, I believe this book will have a positive impact on your career, and that you will in turn have a positive impact on society.

This book is an attempt to document and teach Accelerated Discovery to the next generation of data scientists. Once you have learned these techniques and practiced them in the lab, your mission will be to find a scientist or an engineer struggling with a big data challenge and help them to make a better world. I know these scientists and engineers exist, and I know they have these challenges, because I have talked to them and corresponded with them. I have wished there were more of me to go around so that I could help with every one of them, because they are all fascinating and all incredibly promising and worthy efforts. But there are only so many hours in a week, and I can only pick a few of the most promising to pursue, and every one of these has been a rewarding endeavor. For the rest and for those problems that will come, I have written this book.

This book is not a data-mining manual. It does not discuss how to build a text-classification engine or the ins and outs of writing an unsupervised clustering implementation. Other books already do this, and I could not surpass these. This book assumes you already know how to process data using the basic bag of tools that are now taught in any good data-mining or machine-learning course. Where those courses leave off, this book begins. The question this book answers is how to use unstructured mining approaches to solve a really complex problem in a given scientific domain. How do you create a system that can reason in a sophisticated way about a complex problem and come up with solutions that are profound, nonobvious, and original?

From here on, this book is organized in a more or less top-down fashion. The next chapter discusses the importance of the Accelerated Discovery problem space and why the time has come to tackle it with the tools we currently have available. Even if you are already motivated to read the book, do not skip this chapter, because it contains some important material about how flexibly the technology can be applied across a wide swath of problems.

What follows immediately thereafter is a set of five chapters that describe the method at a fairly high level. These are the most important chapters of the book, because they should be in the front of your mind each time you face a new analytics challenge in science. First there is a high-level description of our method for tackling these problems, followed by four detailed chapters giving a general approach to arriving at a solution. When put together, these five chapters essentially cover our method for accelerating discovery. Not every problem you encounter will use every step of this method in its solution, but the basic approach can be applied in a more or less universal way.

The next section brings the level of detail down to specific technologies for implementing the method. These are less universal in character but hopefully will make the method more concrete. This set of four chapters goes into greater detail about the tools and algorithms I use to help realize the approach in practice. It is not complete, but hopefully it will be illustrative of the kinds of techniques that can make the abstract process a reality.

The rest of the book is made up of sample problems or examples of how this really works in practice. I included ten such examples because it was a nice round number, and I think the examples I have selected do provide a good representative sample of this kind of engagement. All of these examples are from real scientists, are based on real data, and are focused on important problems in discovery. The examples all come from the life-sciences area, but that is not meant to be the only area where these techniques would apply; in fact, I have applied them in several other sciences, including materials and chemistry. But my best physical science examples are not publishable due to proprietary concerns, so for this book I have chosen to focus on the science of biology.

That is how the book is organized, but do not feel you have to read it this way. You could just as well start with the examples and work your way back to the earlier chapters when you want to understand the method in more detail. You will quickly notice that not every problem solution employs every step of the methodology anyway. The methodology is a flexible framework on which to assemble the components of your solution, as you need them, and where they make sense. And it is meant to be iterative and to evolve as you get deeper into the information complexity of each new domain.

As you read the book, I hope that certain core principles of how to be a good data scientist will naturally become apparent. Here is a brief catalogue of those principles to keep in mind each time you are faced with a new problem.

- The whole is greater than the sum of the parts: As scientists we naturally tend toward reductionism when we think about how to solve a problem. But in data science, it is frequently the case that, by considering all the relevant data at once, we can learn something that we cannot see by looking at each piece of data in isolation. Consider ways to unify everything we know about an individual entity as a complete picture. What you learn is frequently surprising.

- More X is not always better: There is a wishful tendency among those less familiar with the problems of data science to imagine that every problem can be solved with more data, no matter how irrelevant that data happens to be; or that, if we have run out of data, then adding more features to the feature space ought to help; or, if that fails, that adding more categories to our taxonomy should help, and so on. The operative concept is more is always better. And certainly, one is supposed to assume that at least more stuff can never hurt; the solution must be in there somewhere. But the problem is, if you add mostly more noise, the signal gets harder to find, not easier. Careful selection of the right data, the right features, and the right categories is always preferable to indiscriminate addition.

- Compare and contrast: Measuring something in isolation does not tell you very much. Only when you compare the value to some other related thing does it begin to have meaning. If I tell you a certain baseball player hit 50 home runs last season, this will not mean much if you know nothing about the game. But if you know what percentile that puts him in compared to other players, that tells you something, especially if you also take into account plate appearances, difficulty of pitchers faced, and the ball parks he played in. The point is that too often in data science, we are tempted to look too narrowly at only one aspect of a domain in order to get the precise number we are looking for. We also need to look more broadly in order to understand the implications of that value: to know whether it means anything of importance.

- Divide and conquer: When you have a lot of data you are trying to make sense of, the best strategy for doing this is to divide it into smaller and smaller chunks that you can more easily comprehend. But this only works if you divide up the data in a way that you can make sense of when you put it all back together again. For example, one way to divide up data is by letter of the alphabet, but this is unlikely to make any one category much different than any other, and thus the problem has not become any easier within each subcategory. But if I focus on concepts rather than syntax, I stand a much better chance of being enlightened at the end.

- "There's more than one way to…": Being a cat lover, I shy away from completing that statement, but the sentiment is no less true for being illustrated in such an unpleasant way. Once we find a solution or approach, our brains seem to naturally just turn off. We have to avoid this trap and keep looking for other ways to arrive at the result. If we apply these additional ways and get the same answer, we can be far more confident than we were that the answer is correct. If we apply the additional approaches and get a different answer, that opens up whole new areas for analysis that were closed to us before. Either way, we win.

- Use your whole brain (and its visual cortex): Find a way to make the data draw a picture, and you will see something new and important that was hidden before. Of course, the challenge is to draw the picture that illustrates the key elements of importance across the most visible dimensions. Our brains have evolved over time to take in vast amounts of data through the eyes and convert it effortlessly into a reasonably accurate view of what is going on around us. Find a way to put that powerful specialized processor to work on your data problem and you will inevitably be astounded at what you can see.

- Everything is a taxonomy/feature vector/network: At the risk of oversimplifying things a bit, there are really only three basic things you need to know to make sense of data: What the entities are that you care about and how they relate to each other (the taxonomy), how you can describe those entities as features (feature vector), and how you can represent the way those entities interact (network). Every problem involves some subset or combination of these ideas. It really is that simple.

- Time is not a magazine: The data we take to begin our investigation with is usually static, meaning it sits in a file that we have downloaded from somewhere, and we make sure that file does not change over time (we may even back it up to be absolutely sure). This often leads us to forget that change is the only constant in the universe, and over time we will find that our file bears less and less relation to the new reality of now. Find a way to account for time and to use time recorded in data to learn how things evolve.

- All data is local: A corollary to the problem of time is the problem of localization. Most data files we work with are subsets of the larger data universe, and thus we have to generalize what we learn from them to make them applicable to the real universe. That generalization problem is going to be much harder than you realize. Prejudice toward what we know and ignorance of what we do not is the bane of all future predictions. Be humble in the face of your own limited awareness.

- Prepare for surprise: If you are not constantly amazed by what you find in data, you are doing something wrong.

Hopefully this brief introduction gives you some sense of the ideas to keep in mind as you begin to master this discipline. Discovery is always hard and always involves synthesizing different kinds of data and analytics. The crucial step is to make all those moving parts work together constructively to illuminate what lies just beyond the known. The key ingredient is figuring out what to count and how to count it. In the end, everything is just combinatorics all the way down!

I hope this book helps you to solve complex and important problems of this type. More than that, I encourage you to develop your own methods for accelerating discovery and publish them as I have done mine. This problem is too important for one small group of data scientists in one organization to have all the fun. Come join us.

CHAPTER 2

Why Accelerate Discovery?

Scott Spangler and Ying Chen

THERE IS A CRISIS emerging in science due to too much data. On the surface, this sounds like an odd problem for a scientist to have. After all, science is all about data, and the more the better. Scientists crave data; they spend time and resources collecting it. How can there be too much data? After all, why can scientists not simply ignore the data they do not need and keep the data they find useful?

But therein lies the problem. Which data do they need? What data will end up proving useful? Answering this question grows more difficult with increasing data availability. And if data grows exponentially, the problem may reach the point where individual scientists cannot make optimal decisions based on their own limited knowledge of what the data contains. I believe we have reached this situation in nearly all sciences today. We have certainly reached it in some sciences.

So by accelerating discovery, I do not simply mean doing science the way we do it today, only faster; I really mean doing science in a profoundly new way, using data in a new way, and generating hypotheses in a new way. But before getting into all that, I want to present some historical context in order to show why science the way it has always been practiced is becoming less and less viable over time.

To illustrate what I mean, consider the discovery of evolution by Charles Darwin. This is one of the most studied examples of great science in history, and in many ways his example provided the template for all scientific practice for the next 150 years. On the surface, the story is remarkably elegant and straightforward. Darwin travels to the Galapagos Islands, where he discovers a number of new and unique species. When he gets back from his trip, he notices a pattern of species changing over time. From this comes the idea of species "evolution," which he publishes to much acclaim and significant controversy. Of course, what really happened is far more complex and illuminating from the standpoint of how science was, and for the most part is still, actually practiced.

First of all, as inhabitants of the twenty-first century, we may forget how difficult world travel was back in Darwin's day. Darwin's voyage was a survey mission that took him around the world on a sailing ship, the *Beagle*. He made many stops and had many adventures. Darwin left on his trip in 1831 and returned *five years* later, in 1836. During that time, he collected many samples from numerous locations and he took copious notes on everything he did and saw. After he got back to England, he then spent many years collating, organizing, and systematically cataloguing his specimens and notes. In 1839, he published, to much acclaim, a book describing the incidents of this voyage (probably not the one you are thinking of, that one came much later): *Journal and Remarks, Voyage of the Beagle*. Darwin then spent the next 20 years doing research and collecting evidence on plants and animals and their tendency to change over time. But though he was convinced the phenomenon was real, he still did not have a mechanism by which this change occurred.

Then Darwin happened upon *Essay on the Principle of Population* (1798) by Thomas Malthus. It introduced the idea that animals produce more offspring than typically actually survive. This created a "struggle for existence" among competing offspring. This led Darwin directly to the idea of "natural selection." *The Origin of Species* was published in 1859, 28 years after the *Beagle* left on its voyage. And of course, it was many decades later before Darwin's theory would be generally accepted.

There are certain key aspects of this story that I want to highlight as particularly relevant to the question "Why Accelerate Discovery?" The first has to do with the 20 years it took Darwin to collect and analyze the data he felt was necessary to develop and validate his theory. The second is related to the connection that Darwin made between his own work and that of Malthus. I think both of these phenomena are characteristic of the big data issue facing scientists both then and now. And if we think about them carefully in the context of their time and ours, we can see how it becomes imperative that scientists working today use methods and tools that are far more powerful than those of Darwin and his contemporaries.

THE PROBLEM OF SYNTHESIS

When Darwin returned from his 5-year voyage, he had a formidable collection of notes and specimens to organize and catalogue. This step took him many years; longer, in fact, than it took him to collect the data in the first place, but it was crucial to the discovery process. We often think of scientific discovery as a Eureka moment—a bolt from the blue. But in reality, it is much more frequently the result of painstaking labor carried out to collect, organize, and catalogue all the relevant information. In essence, this is a problem of synthesis. Data hardly ever comes in a form that can be readily processed and interpreted. In nearly every case, the genius lies not in the finding and collecting of the data but in the organization scheme that makes the interpretation possible. In a very real sense, all significant scientific discoveries are about overcoming the data-synthesis problem.

Clearly, data synthesis is hard (because otherwise everyone would do it), but what makes it so? It is often not easy to see the effort required if only the result is observed. This is because the most difficult step, the part that requires the real genius, is almost invisible. It is hidden within the structure of the catalogue itself. Let us look at the catalogue of specimens Darwin created.

Darwin's task in specimen organization cataloguing was not just to record the species and physical characteristics of each specimen—it was to find the hidden relationships between them, as illustrated in Figure 2.1. Organizing data into networks of entities and relationships is a recurring theme in science. Taxonomies and ontologies are another manifestation of this. Taxonomies break entities down into classes and subclasses based on some measure of similarity, so that the further down the tree you go, the more alike things are within the same class. Ontologies represent a more general kind of entity network that expresses how entities relate to each other in the world. Creating such networks from raw data is the problem of synthesis. The more data there is, and in particular the more heterogeneous the forms of that data, the more challenging synthesis becomes.

THE PROBLEM OF FORMULATION

Once Darwin had synthesized his data, it became clear to him that species did indeed change over time. But merely to observe this phenomenon was not enough. To complete his theory, he needed a mechanism by which

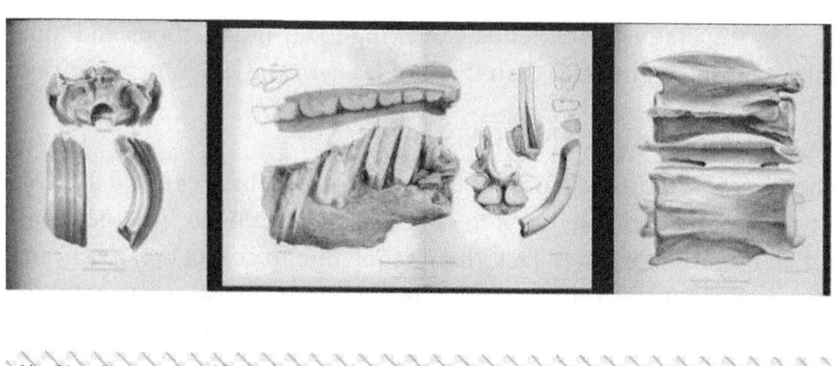

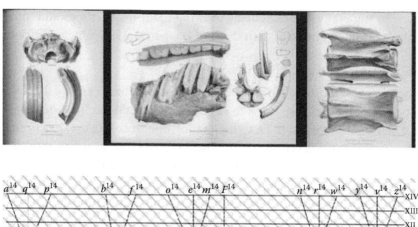

FIGURE 2.1 Illustrations from *The Origin of Species.*

this change takes place. He needed to create a model that could explain how the data points (i.e., the species) connected to each other; otherwise all he would have is a way to organize the data, without having any additional insight into what the data meant. Creating this additional insight that emerges from synthesis is the problem of formulation.

Formulation requires the creation of an equation or algorithm that explains a process or at least simulates or approximates mathematically how that process behaves in the physical world.

From a data-science perspective, formulation requires extracting patterns that may appear across many disparate, heterogeneous data collections. Going beyond synthesis to explanation may require data visualization and sometimes even analogy. It requires pattern matching and being able to draw from a wide array of related data. This is what Darwin was able to do when he drew on the writings of Thomas Malthus to discover the driving mechanism behind species change. Darwin reused an existing formulation, the struggle for existence among competing offspring (i.e., "survival of the fittest"), and applied it to competition among all living things in order to arrive at a formulation of how species evolve.

The process of formulation begins with observation. The scientist observes how entities change and interact over time. She observes which properties of entities tend to occur together and which tend to be independent. Often, data visualization—charts or graphs, for example—is used to summarize large tables of numbers in a way that the human visual cortex can digest and make sense of. The synthesis of data is one of the key steps in discovery—one that often looks obvious in retrospect but, at the beginning of research, is far from being so in most cases.

WHAT WOULD DARWIN DO?

The process of synthesis and formulation used by Darwin and other scientists worked well in the past, but this process is increasingly problematic. To put it bluntly, the amount and variety of data that needs to be synthesized and the complexity of the models that need to be formulated has begun to exceed the capacity of individual human intelligence. To see this, let us compare the entities and relationships described in *The Origin of Species* to the ones that today's biologists need to grapple with.

Today's biologists need to go well beyond the species and physical anatomy of organisms. Today, biology probes life at the molecular level. The number of different proteins that compose the cells in the human organism is over a million. Each of these proteins has different functions in the cell. Individual proteins work in concert with other proteins to create additional functionality. The complexity and richness of all these interactions and functions is awe inspiring. It is also clearly beyond the capability of a single human mind to grasp. And all of this was entirely unknown to Darwin.

To look at this in a different way, the number of scholarly publications available for Darwin to read in his field might have been on the order of around 10,000–100,000 at most. Today, that number would be on the order of fifty million [1].

How do the scientists of today even hope to fathom such complexity and scale of knowledge? There are two strategies that every scientist employs to one degree or another: specialization and consensus. Each scientist chooses an area of specialization that is narrow enough to encompass a field wherein they can be familiar with all the important published literature and findings. Of course, this implies that as time goes on and more and more publications occur, specialization must grow more and more intense. This has the obvious drawback of narrowing the scope of each scientist's knowledge and the application of their research. In addition, each scientist will read only the publications in the most prestigious, high-profile journals. These will represent the best consensus opinion of the most important research in their area. The drawback is that consensus in science is frequently wrong. Also, if the majority of scientists are pursuing the same line of inquiry, the space of possible hypothesis is very inefficiently and incompletely explored.

THE POTENTIAL FOR ACCELERATED DISCOVERY: USING COMPUTERS TO MAP THE KNOWLEDGE SPACE

But all is not lost for the scientists of today, for the very tools that help generate the exponentially increasing amounts of data can also help to synthesize and formulate that data. Due to Moore's Law, scientists have and will most likely continue to have exponentially increasing amounts of computational power available to them. What is needed is a way to harness that computational power to carry out better synthesis and formulation—to help the scientist see the space of possibilities and explore that space much more effectively than they can today. What is needed is a methodology that can be repeatedly employed to apply computation to any scientific domain in such a way as to make the knowledge space comprehensible to the scientist's brain.

The purpose of this book is to present one such methodology and to describe exactly how to carry it out, with specific examples from biology and elsewhere. We have shown this method to be an effective way to synthesize all published literature in a given subject area and to formulate new properties of entities based on everything that we know about those entities from previous results. This leads us to conclude that the methodology is an effective tool for accelerating scientific discovery. Since the methods we use are in no way specific to these examples, we think there is a strong possibility that they may be effective in many other scientific domains as well.

Moreover, regardless of whether our particular methodology is optimal or effective for any particular scientific domain, the fact remains that all scientific disciplines that are pursued by ever-increasing numbers of investigators must ultimately address this fundamental challenge: Eventually, the rate of data publication will exceed the individual human capacity to process it in a timely fashion. Only with the aid of computation can the brain hope to keep pace. The challenges we address here and the method we employ to meet those challenges will continue to be relevant and essential for science for the foreseeable future.

So clearly the need exists and will continue to increase for aiding scientific discovery with computational tools. But some would argue that no such tools exist, or that if they do exist, they are still too rudimentary to really create value on a consistent basis. Computers can do computation and information retrieval, but scientific discovery requires creativity and thinking "outside the box," which is just what computers cannot do. A few years ago, the authors would have been largely in agreement with this viewpoint, but something has changed in the field of computer science that makes us believe that accelerating scientific discovery is no longer a distant dream but is actually well within current capability. Later in this chapter, we will describe these recent developments and preview some of the implications of these emerging capabilities.

WHY ACCELERATE DISCOVERY: THE BUSINESS PERSPECTIVE

Discovery is central and critical to the whole of humanity and to many of the world's most significant challenges. Discovery represents an ability to uncover things that are not previously known. It underpins all innovations (Figure 2.2).

Looking at what we human beings consume—for example, consumer goods such as food, clothing, household items, and energy—we would quickly realize that we need significant innovations across the board. We need to discover new ways to generate and store energy, new water

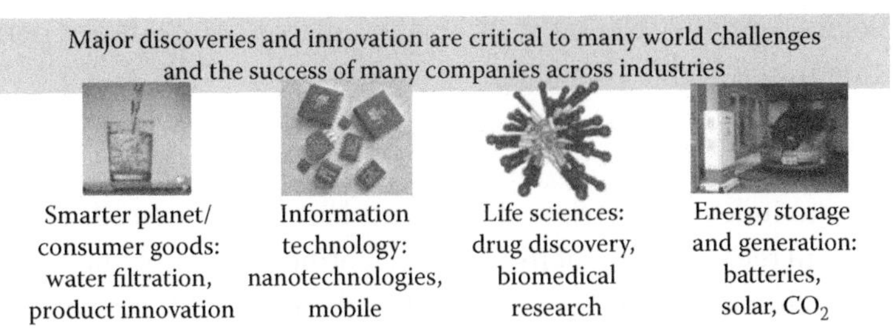

FIGURE 2.2 Example application areas for Accelerated Discovery.

filtration methods, and new product formations for food and other goods so that they are more sustainable for our environments and healthier for human beings. We need these innovations more desperately than ever.

Looking at what we make and build—for example, new computer and mobile devices, infrastructures, and machines—again, the need for discovery and innovation is at the center of all these. We need new kinds of nanotechnologies that can scale human capacity to unimaginable limits, new materials that have all the desired properties that will lower energy consumption while sustaining its intended functions, and new designs that can take a wide variety of factors into consideration.

Looking at ourselves, human beings, our own wellbeing depends heavily on the discovery and innovation in healthcare, life sciences, and a wide range of social services. We need a much better understanding of human biology. We need to discover new drugs and new therapies that can target diseases much more effectively and efficiently.

Yet today, the discovery processes in many industries are slow, manual, expensive, and ad hoc. For example, in drug discovery, it takes on average 10–15 years to develop one drug, and costs hundreds of millions of dollars per drug. The attrition rate of drug development today is over 90%. Similarly, new energy forms, such as the lithium battery, take tens of years to discover. New consumer product formations are mostly done on a trial-and-error basis. There is a need across all industries for a reliable, repeatable process to make discovery more cost-effective.

COMPUTATIONAL TOOLS THAT ENABLE ACCELERATED DISCOVERY

Accelerated Discovery is not just one capability or algorithm but a combination of many complementary approaches and strategies for synthesizing information and formulating hypotheses. The following existing technologies represent the most important enablers of better hypothesis generation in science.

Search

The ability to index and retrieve documents based on the words they contain across all relevant content in a given scientific field is a primary enabler of all the technologies that are involved in Accelerated Discovery. Being able to selectively and rapidly acquire all the relevant content concerning a given subject of interest is the first step in synthesizing the meaning of that content. The easy availability, scalability, and application of search to this problem space have made everything else possible.

Business Intelligence and Data Warehousing

The ability to store, retrieve, and summarize large amounts of structured data (i.e., numeric and categorical data in tables) allows us to deal with all kinds of information in heterogeneous formats. This gives us the critical ability to survey scientific discoveries over time and space or to compare similar treatments on different populations. The ability to aggregate data and then accurately compare different subsets is a technology that we apply over and over again in our approach as we seek to determine the credibility and reliability of each fact and conclusion.

Massive Parallelization

In recent years, Hadoop and MapReduce frameworks [2] have made parallelization approaches much more applicable to real-world computing problems. This gives us the ability to attack hard problems involving large amounts of data in entirely new ways. In short, we can build up a number of simple strategies to mine and annotate data that can, in aggregate, add up to a very sophisticated model of what the data actually means. Massive parallelization also allows us to try out thousands of approaches and combinations in real time before selecting the few candidates that are most likely to succeed based on our models and predictions.

Unstructured Information Mining

Most of the critical information in science is unstructured. In other words, it comes in the form of words, not numbers. Unstructured information mining provides the ability to reliably and accurately convert words into other kinds of structures that computers can more readily deal with. As we will see in this book, this is a key element of the accelerated discovery process. This allows us to go beyond retrieving the right document, to actually discovering hidden relationships between the elements described by those documents.

Natural Language Processing

The ability to recognize entities, relationships or transitions, and features and properties and to attribute them appropriately requires natural language processing. This technology allows us to parse the individual elements of the sentence, identify their part of speech, and determine to what they refer. It can also allow us to discover the intentionality of the author. These natural language processing abilities enable the precise determination of what is known, what is hypothesized, and what is still to be determined through experimentation. It creates the underlying fact-based framework from which our hypotheses can be generated.

Machine Learning

To do Accelerated Discovery in complex domains requires more than just establishing the factual statements in literature. Not all literature is equally trustworthy, and the trustworthiness may differ depending on the scope and context. To acquire the level of sophistication and nuance needed to make these determinations will require more than human programming can adequately provide. It will require learning from mistakes and past examples in order to get better and better over time at deciding which information is credible and which is suspect. Machine learning is the technology that provides this type of capability. In fact, it has proven remarkably adept at tackling even heretofore intractable problems where there is sufficient training data to be had [3]. Machine learning will enable our Accelerated Discovery approach to apply sophisticated judgment at each decision point and to improve that judgment over time.

Collaborative Filtering/Matrix Factorization

Collaborative filtering is a technique made famous by Amazon and Netflix [4], where it is used to accurately identify the best movie or book for a given customer based on the purchase history of that customer and other similar customers (customers who buy similar things). Customer purchases are a special kind of entity-entity network. Other kinds of entity-entity networks are similarly amenable to this kind of link prediction. We can use a generalization of this approach as a way to predict new links in an existing entity-entity network, which can be considered to be a hypothesis of a new connection between entities (or a new property of an entity)that is not currently known but is very likely based on everything we know about the relevant entities.

Modeling and Simulation

In order to reason accurately about the physical world we have to be able to simulate its processes *in silico* and predict what would happen if an experiment were tried or a new property or relationship was actually found to exist. These types of simulations will help reveal potential downstream problems or contradictions that might occur if we were to hypothesize a physically unrealizable condition or some impossible connection between entities. Moreover, modeling and simulation can help determine what the likely impact would be on the physical system as a whole of any new property or relationships being discovered, in order to foresee whether such a discovery would be likely to be uninteresting or quite valuable because it would imply a favorable outcome or have a wide impact in the field.

Service-Oriented Architectures

Clearly, doing Accelerated Discovery requires a large array of heterogeneous software components providing a wide variety of features and functions across multiple platforms. Service-oriented architectures (SOA) provide a uniform communication protocol that allows the components to communicate across the network using complex and evolving data representations. It also allows new implementations and algorithms to be easily swapped in as they become available. SOAs represent an indispensable tool for enabling the large, sophisticated, and distributed systems needed for accelerated discovery applications to emerge from components that can largely be found on the shelf or in open-source libraries.

Ontological Representation Schemes

In addition to being able to extract entities and relationships from unstructured content, we also need powerful ways to represent those entities and their features and connections in a persistent fashion, and in a way that makes it possible to do reasoning over these objects. Existing ontological representation schemes (e.g., OWL [5]) make it possible to store entities in a way that retains all the pertinent contextual information about those entities while still maintaining a degree of homogeneity. This homogeneity makes it possible to design algorithms that can discover or infer new properties based on all known existing patterns. The ability to store such representations in a scalable database and/or index provides the capability of growing the stored version of what is known to the level necessary to comprehend an entire scientific domain.

DeepQA

While question answering is not a central feature of Accelerated Discovery, the two applications share many common components. Both require the computational digestion of large amounts of unstructured content, which then must be used in aggregated to form a conclusion with a likelihood estimate. Both also support their answers with evidence extracted from text sources.

Reasoning under Uncertainty

Machine learning techniques allow us to predict the likelihood that some conclusion or fact is true. Reasoning under uncertainty is how we use this probabilistic knowledge to form new hypotheses or to invalidate or ignore some fact that is highly unlikely. Bayesian inferencing [6] is one example of an existing framework that we can apply to uncertain causal networks in order to do credible deduction of probable end states. This capability is central to telling the difference between a likely outcome and something that is wildly fanciful.

ACCELERATED DISCOVERY FROM A SYSTEM PERSPECTIVE

The previous list of enabling technologies available to support Accelerated Discovery (AD) is necessary to the task, but incomplete. What is needed is a coherent framework in which these technologies can effectively work together to achieve the desired outcome.

To support and enable such continuous data transformations and discovery, we must design our discovery solution carefully. In particular, our discovery solution must *adapt and scale* to a wide range of changing dynamics, including data content, domain knowledge, and human interactions. This is crucial because in all industry domains, domain content and knowledge are constantly changing and expanding. If we do not design our discovery system to cope with such changes, the outcome will be a system that lacks longevity and capability. Most, if not all, of today's discovery solutions can only deal with limited volume and diversity of content and knowledge.

To enable adaptation and scaling, we instituted two system design principles: *agility* and *adaptivity*. Agility means that a discovery system must be able to rapidly generate outputs in the face of changes in data content, knowledge, and human inputs. This is far from a reality in today's discovery systems. For example, a discovery system may be built for one kind of data input formats. When the data input format changes, significant manual intervention may be needed and downstream system components may also need to change accordingly. Such designs make a discovery process extremely lengthy and error prone. We will describe our approach to build agility into the system from the very beginning.

Adaptivity means that a discovery solution must consider "changes in all forms" to be the first-class citizen; for example, changes in individual system components, changes in data content, and changes in knowledge. We envision that various underlying technology components will go through their evolution to become better over time, and the same is true of data content and knowledge bases. A discovery system must have the notion of adaptivity built into it from day one.

To enable agility, we suggest that all major system components be designed with a "core-abstraction plus configurable customization" approach. The core abstraction defines all the major services that the system components intend to support. The configurable customizations allow for changes and adaptations of the core abstractions for specific needs in data-content formats, knowledge repositories, and interactions with other components. For example, a content collection component may have common and core services dealing with the processing of typical unstructured documents. A configurable customization can define the specific fields and format extensions that are needed for those unstructured sources without code change in the core abstraction services.

To enable adaptivity, we defined generalized data input and output formats, called *common data models* (CDMs), and common interfaces around all system components. This allows developers to change the component engine itself without impacting the overall function of the discovery system. It also allows us to adapt to new changes in data sources and knowledge bases by simply mapping them to CDMs without changing the rest of the system.

Figure 2.3 summarizes the key system components of a discovery solution. The boxes are the major system components. We will also provide a summary of the description to each of the following major system components:

Content Curator

Content curator is responsible for managing domain content sources. It includes collecting, cleansing, and making diverse content sources available for downstream processing, end-user queries, and browsing. Typical functions include data ingestion, extraction, transformation, and loading into some content repository. It also includes functions such as indexing and searching.

Domain-pedia

Domain-pedia is responsible for managing domain knowledge. It must ingest, update, and process data knowledge from existing knowledge

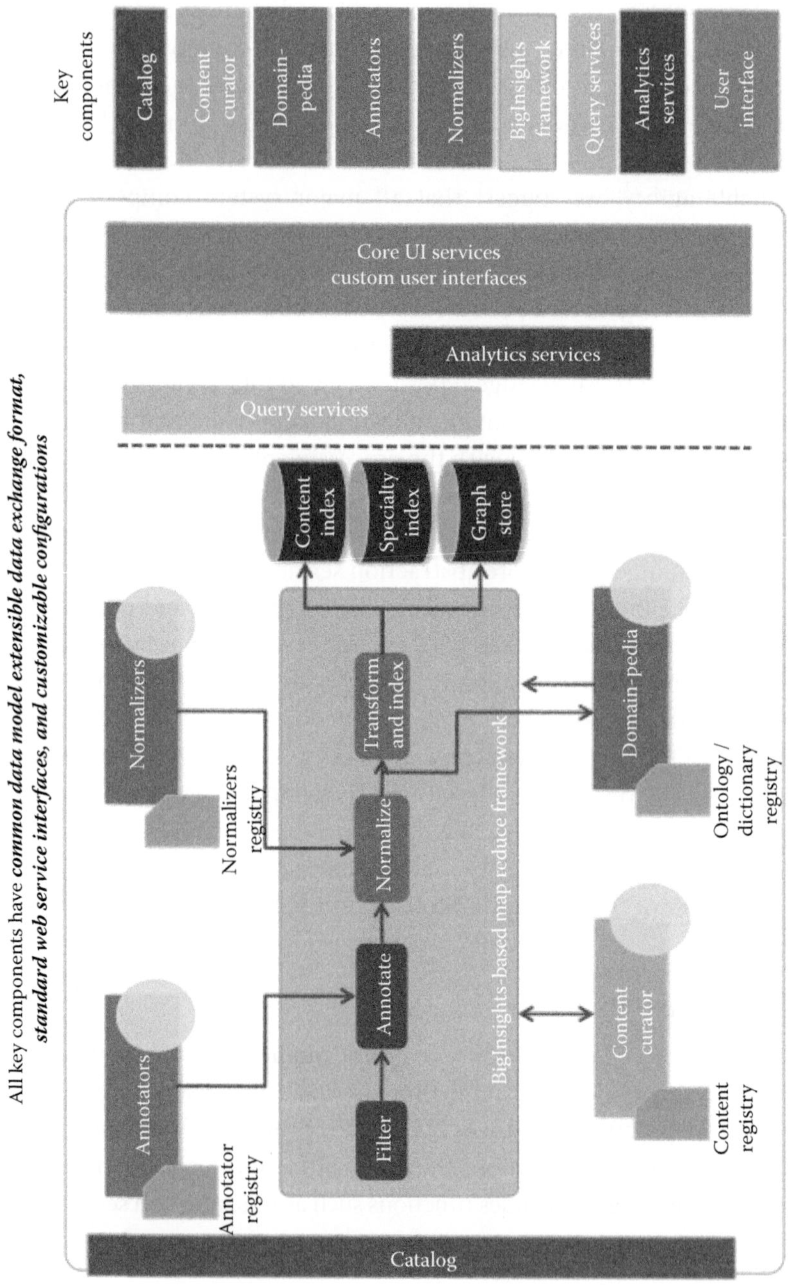

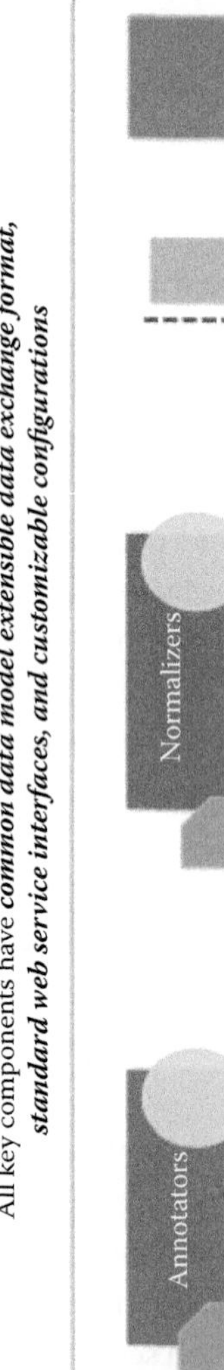

FIGURE 2.3 **(See color insert.)** Functional model.

sources as well as some of the downstream processing, such as the semantic entity extraction process. It can also be a resource for runtime processing and analytics and end-user searching and browsing, similar to what one might do on Wikipedia, such as searching for knowledge around a given protein.

Annotators

Annotators are the engines that pull semantic domain concepts out of unstructured text information, such as chemicals, genes, and proteins, and their relationships.

Normalizers

Normalizers are the engines that organize the vocabularies around various domain concepts into a more consistent form. As the name indicates, they normalize domain concepts into standardized forms, such as unique chemical structures and protein names.

BigInsights Framework

The BigInsights framework is an orchestration engine that manages the interactions between the components described above in a scalable and efficient fashion by mapping runtime content, knowledge, annotation, and normalization processing in a large-scale Hadoop-like infrastructure framework. Such a framework is like the blood vessels of the human being; without it, we only have pieces and parts of the system, rather than a live system.

Query Services

Query services provide consistent data access interfaces for end-user and other system components to query underlying data repositories without knowing what format each data repository might be in.

Analytics Services

Analytics services include runtime algorithms to enable the discovery and construction of more complex knowledge representations. For example, they may produce network representations based on the underlying knowledge repository of a gene-to-gene relationship.

User Interface

The user interactions of a discovery system can be diverse. They can range from basic searches and reporting to more complex visualizations and workflows. Our user interface component is built with a "platform + applications" principle. That is, we developed a suite of common user-interface widgets that can be leveraged by a wide range of use cases. We then design specific applications that are targeted for specific use cases by leveraging the common widgets as much as possible. This way, our discovery system can quickly be adapted to support different use cases without applications having to be rewritten each time.

Catalogue

Finally, the catalogue component manages the system records about all system components and their configurations and metadata about the content sources and knowledge sources. It creates and manages a list of system and data catalogues. System administrators are the typical users of such a component.

Clearly, a discovery system is complex and dynamic. Without the design principles that have been described, a discovery solution can quickly find itself stuck in face of changing content, knowledge, and user-interaction paradigms.

ACCELERATED DISCOVERY FROM A DATA PERSPECTIVE

The process of Accelerated Discovery can essentially be thought of as a data transformation process. Having just described the system for transforming that data, let us look at the process again from a data perspective and see how the data may be changed as we move through the discovery process.

The discovery process is inherently a continuous transformation from raw pieces of data and information to enriched pieces of knowledge and more comprehensive knowledge representations, all the way to brand new discoveries and hypotheses. A discovery solution/platform can therefore be viewed as a system that supports and enables such data transformations and end-user interactions. Figure 2.4 summarizes four major data transformations driven by each of the four discovery process steps. We will now discuss each of these steps of transformation in detail.

Initial Domain Content and Knowledge Collection

The bottom inner circle of Figure 2.4 marks the beginning of the data transformation journey. To enable major discoveries, we must ensure that the system is aware of a vast and diverse set of prior domain knowledge and domain content. Without this step, the downstream analysis and

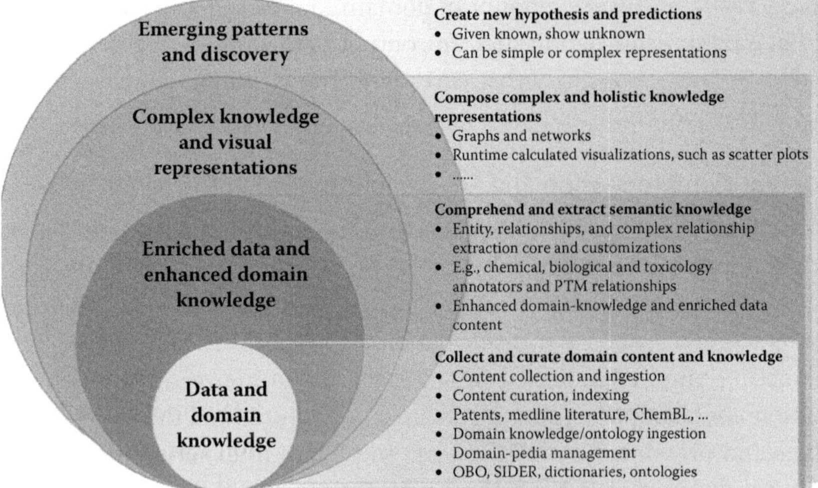
The Discovery Platform—A Data Perspective
The discovery platform is a system that continuously transforms from initial raw data and domain knowledge to brand new discoveries through a series of data transformation steps. Each step along the way will enable services and bring value to our clients and partners
Emerging patterns and discovery
Complex knowledge and visual representations
Enriched data and enhanced domain knowledge
Data and domain knowledge
Create new hypothesis and predictions
• Given known, show unknown
• Can be simple or complex representations
Compose complex and holistic knowledge representations
• Graphs and networks
• Runtime calculated visualizations, such as scatter plots
• ......
Comprehend and extract semantic knowledge
• Entity, relationships, and complex relationship extraction core and customizations
• E.g., chemical, biological and toxicology annotators and PTM relationships
• Enhanced domain-knowledge and enriched data content
Collect and curate domain content and knowledge
• Content collection and ingestion
• Content curation, indexing
• Patents, medline literature, ChemBL, ...
• Domain knowledge/ontology ingestion
• Domain-pedia management
• OBO, SIDER, dictionaries, ontologies

FIGURE 2.4 Data evolution.

discovery will be extremely limited in scope, and wrong conclusions could be drawn. This is often the case with today's bioinformatics tools, which operate on small and narrowly scoped data sets.

We differentiate *domain knowledge* and *domain content* deliberately here since they mean different things. Domain knowledge means prior knowledge that has been captured digitally, such as manually curated domain ontologies, taxonomies, dictionaries, and manually curated structured databases. For example, in drug discovery, such domain knowledge may include ChemBL database [7], OBO ontologies [8], and other dictionaries.

Domain content means raw digital data content that might capture existing domain knowledge but has not been curated systematically to allow a broad set of scientists to gain such knowledge easily. For example, many of the unstructured information sources, such as patents, published conference and journal articles, and internal reports, often contain knowledge known by the individual scientists who wrote the documents. However, if this knowledge has not been made widely and easily accessible, much of it is locked down and unusable. Domain content also includes structured data and semistructured data such as genomic screening information and experiments. Many such sources of raw data also require significant cleansing and processing before they can be made available and accessible.

A discovery solution must be able to collect, cleanse, and make accessible a vast and diverse amount of domain knowledge and content in its initial data transformation step. The output of this initial step is a content and knowledge repository that is ready for downstream analysis, indexing, data exploration, and browsing.

Content Comprehension and Semantic Knowledge Extraction

The second transformation has to do with the ability to derive an enriched set of domain knowledge from the initial content and knowledge collection. Specifically, when it comes to unstructured and semistructured content sources, such a transformation step is critical in capturing and extracting knowledge buried in text, tables, and figures in a systematic fashion; for example, extracting chemical structures and their properties, genes and proteins described in text, and tables of experimental results. Other ways to comprehend the content also include classification and taxonomy generation. Such methods help organize content more meaningfully and allow scientists to examine data with different lenses.

Such a step often requires natural language processing, text mining, and machine learning capabilities. In addition, it also requires systems to coalesce and cross-map different styles of vocabulary into something that is more consistent. For example, one chemical compound may have over 100 different names. Unless such chemical compounds are cross-mapped and normalized in some fashion, there is very little hope that scientists can gain comprehensive knowledge about them, let alone discover new insights.

A well-designed system component that carries out such forms of data comprehension will result in an enriched content and knowledge repository. Such a repository not only unlocks and captures domain knowledge buried in unstructured data, but also cross-maps different domain vocabularies in a more consistent fashion. An analogy of such a knowledge repository is a "domain-pedia." That is, it contains all pieces of knowledge gained via machine curation and gathers them together into a repository that is like Wikipedia but more in-depth and comprehensive for the domain under study.

Complex and High-Level Knowledge Composition and Representation

Building on the repositories created from the previous data transformation steps, the third data transformation step attempts to generate more holistic knowledge representations by composing fragmented pieces of knowledge and data into more holistic and complex views, such as graphs and networks. Such compositions represent known knowledge, but the knowledge becomes much more visible and accessible to scientists than before.

Compared to the previous steps, which focus more on gathering pieces of fragmented content and knowledge in one place and making them more easily accessible, this step focuses more on various ways to compose content and knowledge. Such views and representations allow scientists to have a better chance of gaining new insights and making discoveries.

Such a transformation is facilitated by a combination of techniques, including graph- and network-based algorithms, visualizations, statistics, and machine learning on top of the underlying content and knowledge repositories. This is a step where many different combinations of views and representations may be created, and human-machine interactions via creative visualizations become essential.

New Hypothesis and Discovery Creation

The last data transformation in this process leapfrogs from the forms of data transformation described above into new hypotheses and discoveries. The key to this step lies in *prediction*. Since the previous data transformations are meant to operate on vast and diverse content and knowledge, the input dimensions for this discovery and predictive step can be far more significant than what traditional approaches have to deal with. For example, the feature space of the models can be extremely large. This may require totally new approaches to modeling and prediction.

The discovery output of this step, when validated, can become new knowledge that feeds back once again into the entire data transformation and discovery process. Clearly, these data transformations are not static. They are continuous, self-enhancing, and self-correcting. New content sources and knowledge may be added and incorporated, and obsolete content and knowledge may be cleansed or archived.

Notice also that end users and businesses can take advantage of each step of the data transformations and create business value before the final steps are completed. The initial data collection and curation itself can be of tremendous value as it will have already brought multiple fragmented sources of data together in one place and made content searchable and browsable. One of the most basic uses of a discovery solution is simply to query data sets that have been brought together into a single index.

The second step of the data transformation fills a huge gap that exists today across industries. We now can extract tens of millions of chemical structures from patents and publications in hours or minutes. In the past, such an endeavor would have taken hundreds of chemists manually reading documents months or even years. Scientists can now immediately find all chemical compounds invented in the past.

The third step of the data transformation reveals more comprehensive views of the scientific domain to scientists. Even without machines automatically predicting and discovering new insights, such comprehensive representations will make it much more possible for humans to spot new patterns. The last step makes machine-based discovery visible to the end users.

ACCELERATED DISCOVERY IN THE ORGANIZATION

Many enterprises have begun to realize the need for computationally aided discovery. However, existing IT infrastructure, data-center frameworks, and data-processing paradigms may not be easily reworked to support an end-to-end discovery process. This is because many such infrastructures are built on historical needs and assumptions. The underlying software and hardware are often insufficient to scale and adapt to what is needed by a discovery solution. Because of this, we believe new business models and business processes will be needed to enable discovery systematically.

In particular, with the rapid growth of public content and knowledge repositories, cloud-based infrastructure, and scalable cognitive computing capabilities built on distributed architecture such as Hadoop, it has become more attractive to structure "managed discovery service" business models to enable the rapid adoption of a discovery solution.

A managed discovery service can allow a packaged cloud-compute infrastructure, preloaded relevant public content and knowledge repositories, configured discovery middle-ware software stack, and predefined use cases to be supported. It can also be extended to incorporate additional content and knowledge sources based on customer needs. It can be customized to support use cases that customers desire.

A managed discovery service can be structured in multiple ways to allow different cost-pricing structures to be implemented. For example, a pure public content–driven discovery solution can potentially be made available via a multitenant Software-as-a-Service (SaaS) model to allow cost sharing. When private content and use cases are incorporated, one can structure a hybrid model or single-tenant model, which would incur higher cost but would have higher levels of security and service-level

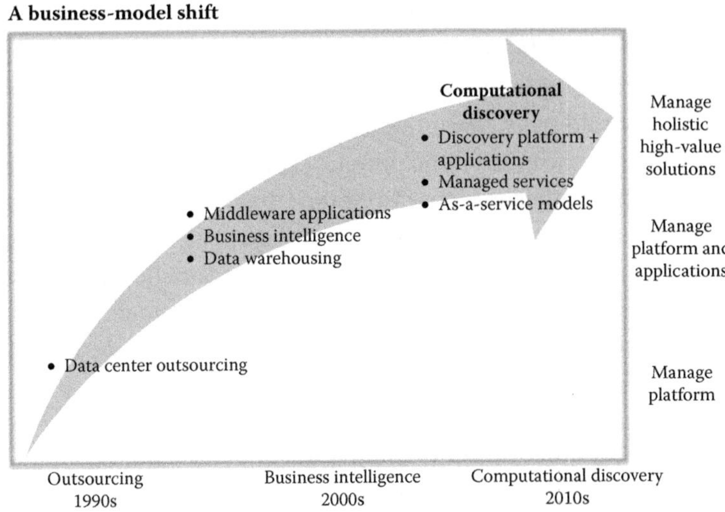

FIGURE 2.5 Business model evolution.

guarantees. When appropriate, even an on-premise model can be structured; for example, if an enterprise has sufficient infrastructure support, the discovery solution vendor can provide a managed discovery service on-premise.

Overall, a managed discovery service model can significantly simplify discovery, enable coherent and smooth data transformations and integration, and accelerate speed-to-value. It also avoids the significant interruption of existing IT and data-center infrastructure. It allows for the leverage of existing investment in the data and IT environment and the gradual transformation from today's environment to the future discovery and cognitive computing based paradigm. Figure 2.5 summarizes such a predicted business-model shift.

CHALLENGE (AND OPPORTUNITY) OF ACCELERATED DISCOVERY

Of course, computer science is not immune to the same information overload that plagues the other sciences. Thus, one of the challenges involved in designing a solution for Accelerated Discovery is that it does involve a complex combination of so many different technologies and approaches. Probably, no single computer scientist exists who is highly proficient in all of the requisite areas. But putting together a team of computer scientists with expertise in all the important areas, along with a corresponding team of experts in the scientific domain, should make it feasible to build a working system. The scientific and technical progress this kind of collaboration could realize would be truly game changing, and not just in the domain of application. It could truly revolutionize science and society.

At IBM, we have witnessed the power of such a multifaceted collaboration before with the Watson Jeopardy Grand Challenge [9]. In this instance, a team of experts from many different computer-science disciplines was formed in order to create a system that could carry out question answering at a level far beyond what most experts in the field deemed possible. The Watson solution combined many of the same technologies we have listed: NLP, search, reasoning under uncertainty, unstructured information mining, massive parallelism, and machine learning, along with game theory, betting strategies, and reasoning approaches for time and geography. In the end, the combination proved far more powerful than even some of the individual creators of the system thought possible. It proved to be better at playing the game show than even the best human champions.

We have been inspired by this example to attempt to achieve the same kind of revolutionary success in the field of scientific discovery. This book will describe in detail exactly how we applied the technologies already listed to the problem of generating hypotheses in this field and will provide some early results in cancer research that this approach has yielded. We will also provide a roadmap for our current and future work in this area, which we feel will eventually revolutionize the way discovery is done.

The reader may wonder why, with the project not yet complete and with only some early promise to show, we would choose to write a book now. Mostly this is because our team is relatively small and the work that lies before us is daunting, even that involved in tackling just one or two domains. Science is vast, and the potential benefit of this kind of approach if applied to many other disciplines is too great to ignore. This book is an open invitation to the scientific community to come join us in this quest. The tools are readily at hand. The task is nontrivial but highly interesting and well worth doing. Let us get down to work.

REFERENCES

1. Jinha, A. E., 2010. 50 million: An estimate of the number of scholarly articles in existence. *Learned Publishing*, *23*(3): 258–263(6).
2. Shvachko, K., et al. 2010. The Hadoop distributed file system. Mass Storage Systems and Technologies (MSST), 2010 IEEE 26th Symposium, IEEE, Washington, DC.

3. Geer, D. 2005. Statistical machine translation gains respect. *Computer, 38*(10): 18–21.
4. Zhou, Y., et al. 2008. Large-scale parallel collaborative filtering for the Netflix prize. In *Algorithmic Aspects in Information and Management* (pp. 337–348). Berlin: Springer.
5. Bechhofer, S. 2009. OWL: Web ontology language. In *Encyclopedia of Database Systems* (pp. 2008–2009). Berlin: Springer.
6. Box, G. E. P., and Tiao, G. C. 2011. *Bayesian Inference in Statistical Analysis* (Vol. 40). Hoboken, NJ: Wiley.
7. Gaulton, A., et al. 2012. ChEMBL: A large-scale bioactivity database for drug discovery. *Nucleic Acids Research, 40*(D1): D1100–D1107.
8. The Open Biological and Biomedical Ontologies. http://obo.sourceforge.net.
9. Ferrucci, D. 2010. Build Watson: An overview of DeepQA for the Jeopardy! challenge. In *Proceedings of the 19th International Conference on Parallel Architectures and Compilation Techniques.* New York: ACM.

CHAPTER 3

Form and Function

> [As a writer] it's a mistake to think you are an activist, championing some movement. That's the path to mental stagnation. The job is just to try to understand what's going on.
>
> DAVID BROOKS
> *The New York Times, 2014*

THE FIRST OBJECTIVE OF Accelerated Discovery (AD) is to represent the known world in a given scientific domain. If this sounds overly ambitious and a bit grandiose, it is meant to. For this is really what sets AD apart from search and data-mining technology. The necessity for taking on this challenge is readily apparent: if you do not understand what is going on in the domain, if you do not relate to the important elements, what hope do you have to further the science? To build on science you must first know the science. Everything follows from this. To generate any new hypothesis, you must first know what has gone on before.

Science is about understanding the universe. Scientists seek to understand two general categories of knowledge about things in the universe: form and function. What is a thing made of, how does it relate to other things, where did it come from, and what does it do? In a sense, all scientific endeavors can be boiled down to these fundamental questions of form and function. As data scientists in the service of domain scientists, we should seek those same answers.

The process of AD, then, readily emerges from these fundamental questions. In science, we are given problems and lots of heterogeneous data.

How can we serve? Our service is to organize that information and relate it directly to the forms and functions of the science. This chapter will briefly explain at a high level how this is done. The next eight chapters will dive into greater detail on form and function. This will be followed by a number of real-life examples of AD that put these principles into practice.

THE PROCESS OF ACCELERATED DISCOVERY

The AD process moves step by step, up through layers of increasing complexity, to build up order from chaos. We begin with the most basic building block of order, the entity. The discovery and organization of domain-specific entities is the most fundamental task of the scientist, because if the entities do not exist, there is no coherent way to think about the domain. Consider the periodic table of the elements in chemistry. Before there was this basic framework on which to reason, progress was slow and sporadic. With the advent of this framework, it became possible to make more rapid progress. Data science is no different. We must build up a systematic entity structure that mirrors the important domain concepts if we are to make any sustained progress (Figure 3.1).

Two problems are usually present in entity detection: (1) what are the entities and (2) how do they appear. In some cases (such as the elements

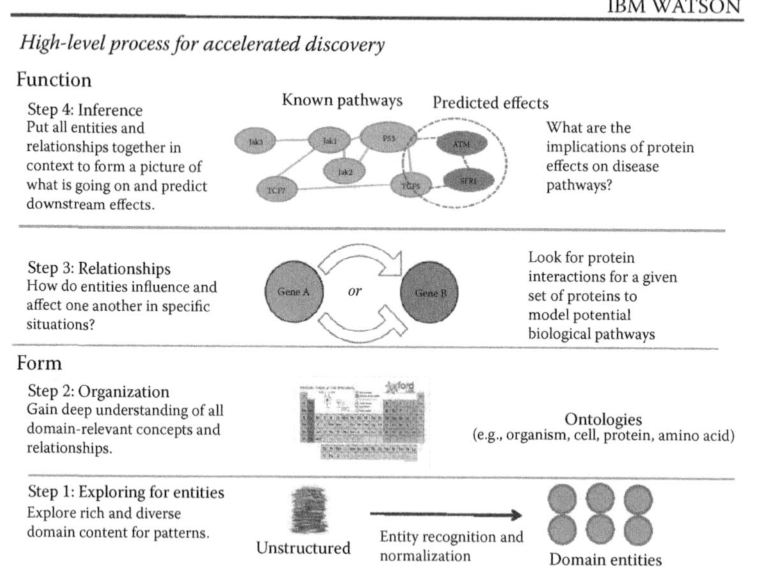

FIGURE 3.1 Process for accelerated discovery.

of the periodic table), the answer to (1) is obvious. In other cases (such as the factors that influence protein viscosity), it is far less so. The answer to (2) is almost never certain at first. Human beings are individualistic creatures who love to express themselves originally. Scientists are no different. So there is rarely any certainty that two different scientists will describe the same thing in the same way. It is for this reason that entity detection and normalization will always remain one of the hardest challenges in data science. But it is a key challenge to address, because entity normalization makes it possible to summarize the results of many disparate sources and kinds of data into a coherent framework. It is also one of the chief ways that data science can further the impact of past scientific research on future scientific discovery.

Chemical entities are a great example of a complex entity type, wherein the process of normalization in order to identify which chemical is being described is of key importance and nontrivial complexity. In Figure 3.2, we show how chemicals can be described both with drawings and text (heterogeneous sources), which then need to be normalized to a canonical form, such as an International Chemical Identifier (InChI) key [1].

From individual entities, we begin to organize. Which entities belong together, which are separate? Can we create a type system that describes how the entities go together? Is there an underlying structural framework

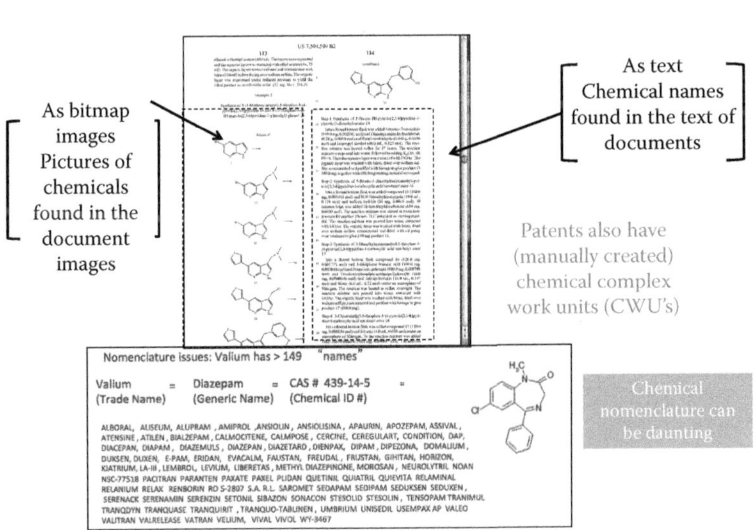

FIGURE 3.2 Chemical entity.

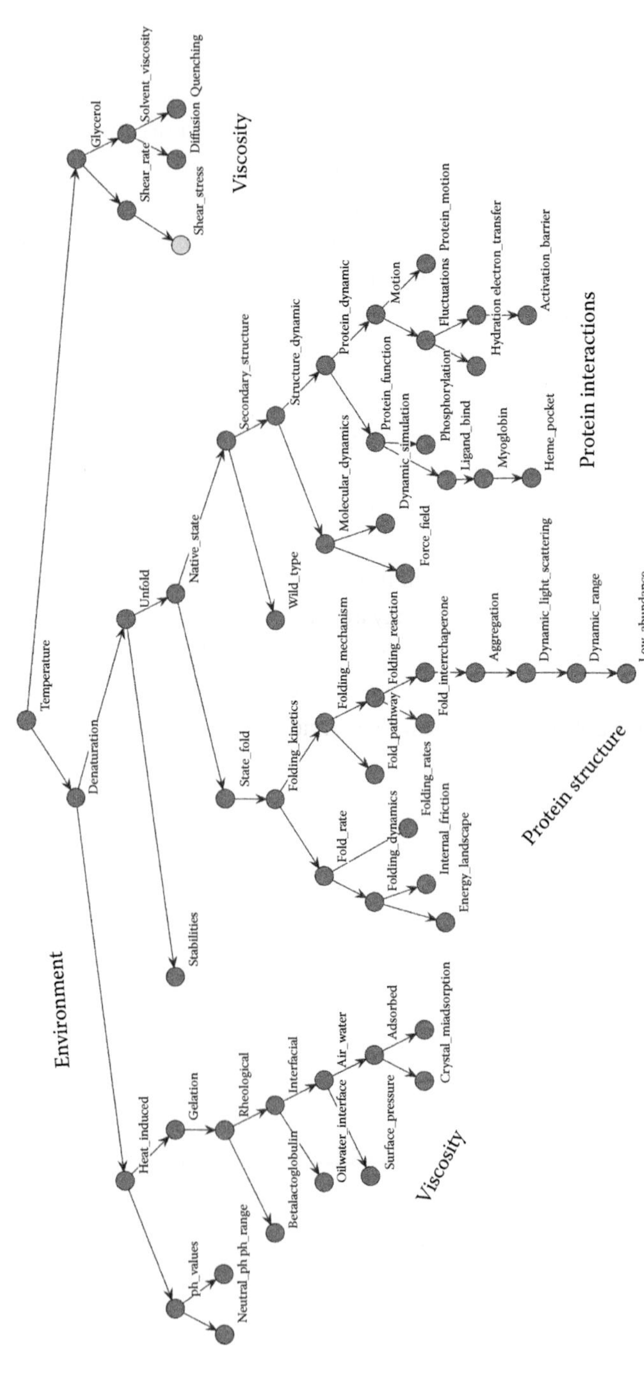

FIGURE 3.3 An ontology.

that describes how one type of entity composes another type? Once again, the organization scheme may be clear cut or it may have to be inferred from what we see in the data, but either way we must make sure that whatever organization scheme we infer is made to line up with physical reality. Domain expertise is a critical element in organizing the entity ontology. Ontologies then enable knowledge at many different levels and across many different but related areas of the domain to come together to create new insights (Figure 3.3).

Up to this point, our process has been all about form. Now we turn to function. We must deal with dynamic events, entities doing things to each other—we must explain how and why things happen.

The next step is the detection of relationships between entities. This is typically a specific event that has been observed to happen in a given context where one (or more) entities act upon another to cause some change or subsequent reaction. As we shall see, the potentially complex nature of this kind of connection will require a much more fine-grained species of text analytics in order to recognize and classify the physical event. Still, as with the entity space, relationships may also be normalized and have types and ontologies. And likewise, our representation must mirror physical reality as much as possible, with the aid of domain expertise (Figure 3.4).

Putting it all together, we create a summary of how, in a given situation, all the relevant entities relate to each other. This summary can be

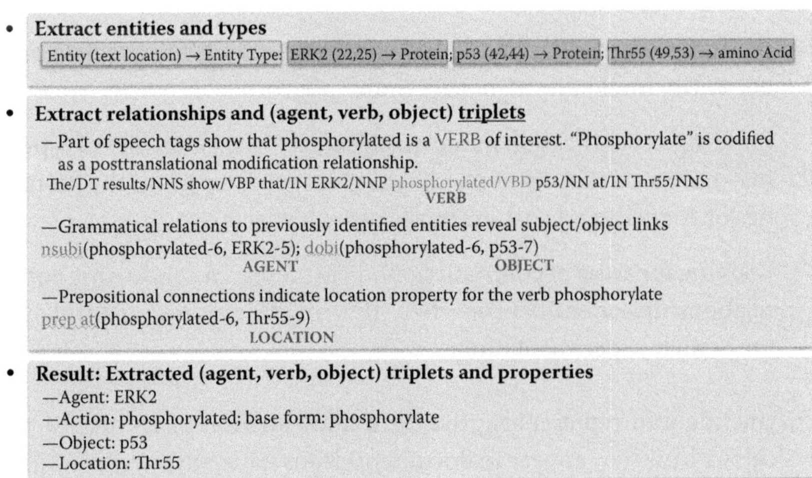

Sentence: "The results show that ERK2 phosphorylated p53 at Thr55."
Extract entities and types
Entity (text location) → Entity Type: ERK2 (22,25) → Protein; p53 (42,44) → Protein; Thr55 (49,53) → amino Acid
Extract relationships and (agent, verb, object) triplets
—Part of speech tags show that phosphorylated is a VERB of interest. "Phosphorylate" is codified as a posttranslational modification relationship.
The/DT results/NNS show/VBP that/IN ERK2/NNP phosphorylated/VBD p53/NN at/IN Thr55/NNS
VERB
—Grammatical relations to previously identified entities reveal subject/object links
nsubj(phosphorylated-6, ERK2-5); dobj(phosphorylated-6, p53-7)
AGENT
OBJECT
—Prepositional connections indicate location property for the verb phosphorylate
prep at(phosphorylated-6, Thr55-9)
LOCATION
Result: Extracted (agent, verb, object) triplets and properties
—Agent: ERK2
—Action: phosphorylated; base form: phosphorylate
—Object: p53
—Location: Thr55

FIGURE 3.4 Relationships.

a table, a map, a network (Figure 3.5), or anything you can think of, so long as it communicates at a macro level the gist of what is going on in the entity space. The challenge here is not to overwhelm the scientist's mind with too much of a good thing. As we get better and better at detecting and representing the entities and relationships that exist in our knowledge corpus, we must also get better at highlighting the interesting ones and filtering out the extraneous stuff. Otherwise we only create a different kind of chaos (Figure 3.5).

But how does the extraction and representation of form and function lead to hypothesis generation, which a key goal of AD? The answer is that the representation provides a way to evaluate and predict new properties of entities and new relationships between entities. The precise means of carrying out such prediction may vary from discipline to discipline, and for the most part it will necessarily lie outside the scope of this book. In the example chapters, we will show a few methods by which this may be accomplished, but this should in no way be considered the full set of what is possible.

Some approaches to hypothesis generation include

1. Inferring properties of an entity based on similar entities, using the documents that contain those entities and the text in those documents as a means of defining similarity.
2. Inferring connections between entities based on relationships already found to exist between other entities in the network.
3. Finding a potential pathway between two entities that predicts how one entity might affect another indirectly.
4. Building a classification model that predicts when an entity of type A may have a certain effect on an entity of type B based on the properties of A and B and past examples of such effects.
5. Looking for areas of contradiction in past research concerning entity relationships or entity properties. This might indicate a fruitful area for further experimentation.

Extracting and representing the form and function of entities in the physical world as they appear in documents leads naturally to new insights and hypotheses about how these entities might interact or behave in novel combinations and new experimental conditions. If done correctly, the

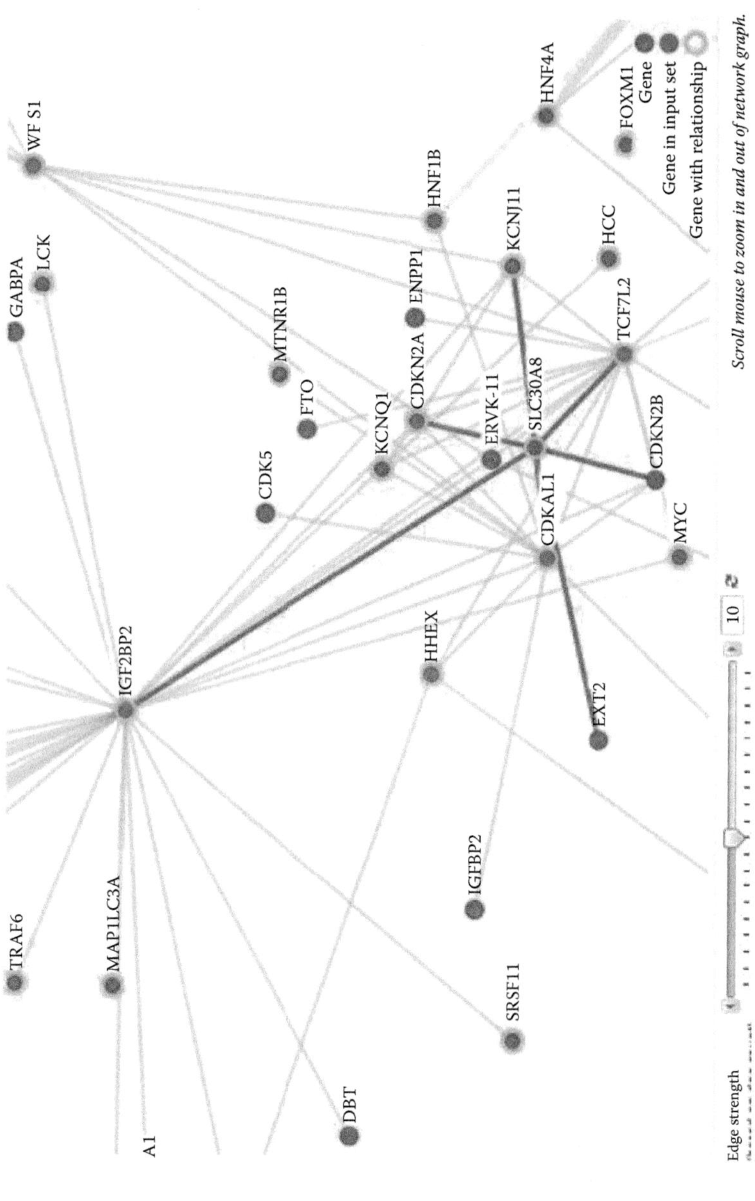

FIGURE 3.5 Summarizing the known via network visualization.

document extractions from past scientific results form a framework on which the next set of experiments can be reliably proposed. In fact, in theory this is how science has always been done. It is only the impossibility of having all past relevant knowledge in a scientific domain reside inside a single mind that makes it necessary, and indeed essential, to realize the knowledge framework of past discoveries in silico.

CONCLUSION

In the next eight chapters, we will describe a method for capturing form and function directly from text documents. I hesitate to even use the word "method" when talking about what we describe here, because it sounds like I am advocating for some one-size-fits-all approach to the analysis of scientific data. Nothing could be further from the case. I simply wish to provide guidance and instruction for those who are interested in, or face challenges around, data and discovery. These are tools in our toolbox that we have applied in many different discovery use cases. As you will see if you read beyond the next eight chapters to the example sections, I apply them in many different ways and in rather ad hoc combinations in order to achieve whatever ends the problem requires. More tools will undoubtedly emerge as time goes on and as we face new challenges. Hopefully this book will at least give you some ideas on how to move forward with your own methods in this space.

REFERENCE

1. Heller, S., McNaught, A., Stein, S., Tchekhovskoi, D., and Pletnev, I. 2013. InChI: The worldwide chemical structure identifier standard. *Journal of Cheminformatics*, 5(1): 7.

CHAPTER 4

Exploring Content to Find Entities

> Exploratory data analysis is detective work…A detective investigating a crime needs both tools and understanding… Equally analysts of data need both tools and understanding. Understanding has different limitations….one needs different sorts of detailed understanding to detect criminals in London slums, in a remote Welsh village, among Parisian aristocrats, in the cattle-raising west, or in the Australian outback…The Scotland Yard detective, however, would be far from useless in the wild west, or in the outback. He has a certain general understanding of conventional detective work that will help him anywhere. In data analysis there are similar general understandings. We can hope to lead you to a few of them. We shall try.
>
> JOHN TUKEY
> *Exploratory Data Analysis*

The process John Tukey describes above refers to structured data analysis, but the thought applies equally well to our more unstructured scenarios. Exploration is the first step in using analytics to comprehend what data means. In this chapter, I will try to define what we mean by exploration in the context of text analytics in general and of Accelerated Discovery in particular. I will then try to provide a general understanding of the practice of exploratory analytics as applied to text and other similar kinds of data. I will then give some specific examples to help clarify how these principles typically work in practice.

This chapter goes into detail on the first step in the process of accelerated discovery: exploring unstructured content to determine the most important entities to extract. The input to this process is a sample of text content that is relevant to the scientific area of interest. The output is a repeatable mechanism for recognizing those entities as they most often occur in the data and identifying which entity occurs in which document.

Note: This chapter covers in an abridged fashion all the relevant concepts documented originally in the book *Mining the Talk* (2007). Those familiar with that work may skip this chapter. Those wishing to know more on the subject would do well to read that work, in addition to John Tukey's book.

SEARCHING FOR RELEVANT CONTENT

The first step in the exploration process is finding content to analyze. Typically we need to compose a query that contains an "or" clause that comprehends a set of concepts that form a unified whole. For example, a drug name and all its synonyms would be such a concept. Another would be genes that all encode protein kinases.

The key is to cast a wide net, but not so wide that there is too much extraneous content—documents that have no relevant information bearing on the scientific issue of interest. In some cases, this will require recasting the net after the initial go around reveals concepts that are inadequately covered in the first query. Or in some cases, the query may need to be filtered to remove extraneous noise from the document population.

HOW MUCH DATA IS ENOUGH? WHAT IS TOO MUCH?

There are a certain number of examples that are required to provide the necessary grist for the entity extraction mill. This is due to the fact that our methods for entity extraction are primarily statistical in nature. With too few examples, statistics will not be of much help in finding good entity terms and categories. Of course this depends partly on what counts as a text example. A single example document should be on the order of a paragraph or an abstract. Ideally the text of each example should have primarily one area of focus or at most a few areas of focus (not ten areas or hundreds). If the documents to be analyzed are longer than this, it is recommended that they be broken up into paragraphs or sentences, depending on the normal length and complexity of each. If the content to be analyzed is shorter than this (e.g., paper titles) then if possible the individual documents should be grouped together in a way that keeps each single example as cohesive as possible (e.g., grouping together titles by the same author).

Given example documents of this length, the number of documents should ideally be roughly between 1000 and 100,000. Quantities much smaller than 1000 will give too little scope for finding interesting categories and entities. They will also give too little variability in learning to recognize all the ways in which each entity will occur in text. Quantities much larger than 100,000 documents will make computation over and survey of the document set difficult while adding little value. In cases where the query would return a much larger set of documents, a random sample should suffice to insure adequate coverage without unduly compromising data completeness.

HOW COMPUTERS READ DOCUMENTS

It goes without saying that computers read documents differently from humans. They do not understand the sentences they read but instead treat the words as mere things to count. But the occurrence of words, the proximity of words, how one words occurrence changes the likelihood that another word will occur—all of these things are a kind of second-order information, invisible to the human reader but apparent to the machine.

Looking across thousands of documents, these metalevel patterns tend to indicate strong domain-specific ontologies. Key entities in the domain will tend to occur over and over again and usually in a homogenous context. The context of their occurrence will become a kind of information signature that the computer can recognize and reveal as "interesting" (i.e., not due simply to random chance). This is how domain-specific ontologies can be identified by unsupervised text mining.

But some supervision is still needed, because computers do not understand the physical underpinnings of the terms they are counting. In the next sections, we will explain in detail how to interweave unsupervised text mining with domain expertise in order to create domain-specific entity taxonomies.

EXTRACTING FEATURES

The extraction of features from text is typically done automatically by software. We cover the details of our preferred method here in order to create a mental model of what the software is doing for you so that it can be correctly interpreted. While much fundamental research and practice has laid the groundwork for this method of feature space generation, there are many different methods and approaches that might achieve a similar result [1].

Words are the first thing we count. For each document, we first remove all punctuation, reduce all characters to lower case, and then treat the example as a bag of words. Next, we use a few simplifying rules to remove some words that are unlikely to be helpful.

1. Remove any words that are numbers or that start with numbers. Typically, numbers make poor features because they tend to be unique or are repeated only infrequently. Features that only occur once are not useful for our purposes, because they do not help us to find similarities between examples.
2. Remove any non-content-bearing words. These are also known as *stopwords.*

The next step is to identify which words are merely different words for the same thing, also known as synonyms. Synonyms can be found with domain dictionaries or automatically generated using stemming algorithms. When you look at the reduced form of a sentence processed in this way, it looks like a fairly compact but intelligible version of the original. It is almost like the message one might have sent by telegraph—back in the days where text messages were expensive and every word was dear. In a sense, this is very much the case. Every word that we choose to turn into a feature is an important decision. We do not keep any words that are superfluous because they would simply add noise that obscure the signal we are trying to detect.

This is one kind of feature—individual words. The bag-of-words representation means they are unordered. We lose the context and keep only the occurrence. To help regain some of that context, we also create phrase features. We define phrases as words that occur sequentially.

We do not choose to create phrases longer than two words by default, because they would only add redundant information. For example, "see spot" and "spot run" occurring together in the same example pretty much implies "see spot run." It is possible to conceive of a counterexample, but such examples are exceedingly rare, especially in short documents, and thus they are not of much concern.

The next step in generating a feature space is pruning based on frequency of occurrence. There are two kinds of features we want to prune—those that occur too frequently and those that occur too infrequently. When words occur too frequently they usually do not help in creating differentiable categories. Consider the extreme case where every example contains a particular word. In this case, knowing that an example has that word cannot help determine the category for that example. Therefore, we eliminate words that occur with high frequency, in practice 70% or more. This threshold is based on experience. Words that occur more frequently are usually features that are poor at defining clusters.

What remains is the threshold for infrequency. Infrequent words are also not good features. Features that occur too infrequently will not help in creating differentiable categories. Take the extreme case where a feature only occurs once. Such a feature can at most help to categorize one example. One example is far too small to make an interesting category.

Choosing a fixed threshold of infrequency to eliminate features is no simple matter. For some time, we tried to find a find a cutoff based on raw count (e.g., two or fewer occurrences of a feature in a data set result in elimination of the feature), or based on frequency (e.g., a feature occurring in less than 1% of the documents gets eliminated). These approaches were problematic, for while they might work for a particular data set, they were suboptimal on larger or smaller data sets. Another approach was needed. Instead of looking for a fixed cutoff, we created a fixed number of features. For the goal of our analysis, this makes perfect sense. We want to create a reasonable number of categories no matter how large our data set. In other words, we do not want the number of categories to grow with more data. Since the number of features should be directly related to the number of categories, generating a sufficient number of features to generate a set number of categories has proved to be a workable approach, no matter how many documents in the collection.

With our feature selection methodology understood, it only remains to find the right number of categories and features. We pick these to suit easy taxonomy editing. The number of categories that fits easily in an analyst's brain and on a single computer screen is around thirty (assuming one category per row and an average brain). Keeping the number of categories around this number allows the analyst to see all the categories at once in tabular form. This also turns out to be about the number of categories that can be readily looked at and evaluated in the space of about an hour. In one sitting, a thirty-category taxonomy can be generated and thoroughly edited and comprehended.

For features, imagine we need one feature to differentiate every category from every other category. Each of the 30 categories then needs 29 different features to uniquely identify it. That leads to 870 total features needed. You could argue that this count should really be 435, since the same feature that differentiates category A from B also differentiates category B from A. However, it is not so clear that we want to define a category purely as a negation of features that define other categories, so we do not rely on this simplification. Of course, not every feature the system comes up with is valuable, so we will double that number to be on the safe side, giving us 1740 features. We round up and conclude with the target at 2000. For domains with especially rich vocabularies and larger entity taxonomies we may up this feature set size to as high as 20,000, but this is not typical. We have yet to encounter a domain where a 20,000-feature set was inadequate for the purpose of unsupervised text clustering.

Editing the Feature Space

The ability to peruse the feature space provides the opportunity to correct problems. Two primary issues are detectable with a visual inspection of the feature in alphabetical order:

1. Features that need to be removed because they are not relevant to the purpose of the analysis
2. Features that need to be combined, because their meaning is identical for the purposes of the analysis

Removing spurious features helps generate better taxonomies by having categories reflect relevant topics to the business. Combining features based on synonyms creates a feature set that does not artificially bifurcate based on syntactic distinctions.

Feature edits can be remembered by capturing them in synonym and stopword lists. Stopwords are lists of words that should not be included in the dictionary. Synonyms are list of words that are identical for purposes of feature space generation. The work of editing the dictionary is valuable for every future analysis in the same domain. Synonym lists can be generated automatically using a process known as stemming. Stemming detects base word forms and the variations based on prefixes and suffixes.

FEATURE SPACES: DOCUMENTS AS VECTORS

Once our feature space is defined, we can begin to think of documents not as a collection of words but as a point in a feature space. The advantage of this representation is that it allows us to compare two different documents for similarity with simple vector multiplication. We can also use this representation to summarize a collection of documents with a single vector by taking the average of all the vectors that make up the collection. We refer to this summarized representation as a *centroid*.

For the purposes of clustering, each example in a collection is converted into a numeric representation. To accomplish this, each unique word is assigned a unique integer, and for each example we count how many times each word occurs. If two documents are considered "similar" to the degree that they have similar word content, all we need is a metric with which to compare documents based on these numbers. For this, we turn to the standard Cartesian coordinate system that most of us are familiar with from our high-school math classes. In this system, points that are described by a vector of numeric values can be plotted, with rows representing points and columns representing dimensions· There are a couple of ways we could mathematically measure the similarity between two such numeric vectors. One approach would be Euclidean distance. This is calculated with the well-known formula

$$d(a,b) = \sqrt{\sum_i (a_i - b_i)^2}$$

However, Euclidean distance can be problematic in this context because a long document may be "far" from a short document by virtue of having more words, even if both documents talk about the same subject. If you think about it, what we really want to measure for the purposes of document similarity is not absolute distance but orientation. If we draw a line between the origin and each of the points we wish to compare, it is the angle between the lines that indicates the relative orientation and therefore the nearness of the two points—or, to be more specific, the cosine of that angle.

Cosine distance is the basic evaluation metric we use in our approach when it comes to comparing two documents, a document and a document category, or two different document categories. The beauty of this approach is that it reduces the complexity of comparing two dissimilar documents down to a single equation that produces one numeric output whose value lies within a fixed range. That is really a very powerful simplification.

But always remember, it is just a number. No matter how many decimal places you accurately calculate, it will not tell you why the documents differ or give you any context concerning whether the difference is truly important. It is only as good as the underlying set of features that describe each document. If the features are irrelevant for the task you are trying to accomplish, then there is not much chance that anything useful will be gained from any distance metric.

Now that we have a powerful way to numerically compare documents, we need a way to describe a document collection. This is necessary in order to compare a single document to a collection so as to determine whether that document belongs to that collection, and if so, how well it fits. To model a document collection, we introduce the concept of a centroid. A centroid is the average of all the document vectors in a collection.

Using feature spaces, centroids, and cosine distance, we have a way to numerically compare document collections to documents. We are ready to begin to understand how document clustering works. A cluster is nothing more than a document collection that has a centroid associated with it. A set of clusters that completely categorizes a set of documents is called a taxonomy. The process of generating a taxonomy from a collection of documents is called clustering.

CLUSTERING

Document clustering has been around for decades, but as it is practised, it typically misses the point when it comes to finding domain-specific ontologies. It turns out that one of the drawbacks of typical approaches such as k-means clustering is that they frequently create categories that are difficult to for human beings to interpret. Cluster-naming approaches attempt to address this issue by adding more and more terms to a name to capture the complex concept that is being modeled by a centroid. Unfortunately, this approach puts the onus on the human interpreter to make sense of what the list of words means and how it relates to the entire set of examples contained in the category.

To address this problem and speed up the taxonomy editing process by starting with a categorization that is easier to comprehend, we developed a strategy for document categorization based on categories centered around selected individual terms in the dictionary. We then employ a single iteration of k-means to the generated categories to refine the membership so that documents that contain more than one of the selected terms can be placed in the category that is best suited to the overall term content of the document. Once the clusters are created, we name them with the single term that was used to create each cluster in the first place, thus avoiding the complex name problem associated with k-means clusters.

Selecting which terms to use for generating categories is critically important. Our approach is to rank all discovered terms in the data set based on a normalized measure of cohesion calculated using the following formula:

$$\text{cohesion}(T,n) = \frac{\sum_{x \in T} \cos(\text{centroid}(T), x)}{|T|^{n}}$$

where

T is the set of documents that contain a given term

centroid (T) is the average vector of all these documents

n is a parameter used to adjust for variance in category size (typically $n = 0.9$)

Terms that score relatively high with this measure tend to be those with a significant number of examples having many words in common. Adjusting the n parameter downward tends to surface more general terms with larger matching sets, while adjusting it upward gives more specific terms.

The algorithm selects enough of the most cohesive terms to get 80%–90% of the data categorized. Terms are selected in cohesive order, skipping those terms in the list that do not add a significant number of additional examples (e.g., more than three) to those already categorized with previous terms. The algorithm halts when at least 80% of the data has been categorized and the uncategorized examples are placed in a "miscellaneous" category. The resulting categories are then refined using a single iteration of k-means (i.e., each document is placed in the category of the nearest centroid as calculated by the term membership just described).

While this approach does not completely eliminate the need for domain concept refinement by an analyst (as described in the next sections), it does make the process much less cumbersome by creating categories that are (for the most part) fairly easy to comprehend immediately.

DOMAIN CONCEPT REFINEMENT

Not all clusters are going to map directly to domain concepts. Even those that seem to map directly will require some refinement on closer inspection. In the concept refinement stage, we try to capture a synonym list or rule that defines precisely what we mean by each domain concept in text.

Once an initial taxonomy has been generated, the next step is to provide tools for rapidly changing the taxonomy to reflect the needs of the application. Keep in mind that our goal here is not to produce a "perfect" taxonomy for every possible purpose. Such a taxonomy may not even exist or at least may require too much effort to obtain. Instead, we want to focus the user's efforts on creating a "natural" taxonomy that is practical for a given application. For such applications, there is no right or wrong change to make. It is important only that the change accurately reflect the domain expert user's point of view about the desired structure. In this situation, the user is always right. The tool's job is to allow the user to make whatever changes may be deemed desirable. In some cases, such changes can be made at the category level, while in others, a more detailed modification of category membership may be required.

Category Level

Category level changes involve modifying the taxonomy at a macro level, without direct reference to individual documents within each category. One such modification is merging. Merging two classes means creating a new category that is the union of two or more previously existing category memberships. A new centroid is created that is the average of the combined examples. The user supplies the new category with an appropriate name.

Deleting a category (or categories) means removing the category and its children from the taxonomy. The user needs to recognize that this may have unintended consequences, since all the examples that formerly belonged to the deleted category must now be placed in a different category at the current level of the taxonomy.

Document Level

While some changes to a taxonomy may be made at the class level, others require a finer degree of control. These are called document level changes and consist of moving or copying selected documents from a source category to a destination category. The most difficult part of this operation from the user's point of view is selecting exactly the right set of documents to move so that the source and destination categories are changed in the manner desired.

One of the most natural and common ways to select a set of documents is with a keyword query. Documents that are found using the keyword query tool should be viewed and selected one at a time or as a group to move or establish a new category.

Another way to select documents to move or copy is to employ a "most/least typical" sorting technique whereby the example documents are displayed in sorted order by cosine distance from the centroid of their category [2]. For example, the documents that are least typical of a given category can be located, selected, and moved out of the category they are in. They may then be placed elsewhere or in a new category.

MODELING APPROACHES

The mixed initiative method of taxonomy development described in the previous section introduces a unique set of problems when trying to model the taxonomy created with an automated classifier. First of all, each level of the taxonomic hierarchy may be created using a different categorization approach (e.g., text clustering vs. keyword queries). But even within a single taxonomy level, some categories may have been created by k-means and left alone, while others will be either created or edited by a human expert, so that a centroid model will no longer apply uniformly across all categories.

But if a centroid-based classifier is not sufficient, then what modeling approach should be used? The necessity for using some kind of multi-classifier approach seems clear, since we cannot predict ahead of time which style of categorization the user will employ to create the taxonomy. A simple solution is therefore to train and test a suite of different classifiers at each level of the taxonomy and choose the most accurate classifier (the one having the optimum combination of precision and recall) at each level.

Classification Approaches

We incorporated the following classifiers into our suite of available classifiers in the eClassifier toolkit:

Centroid

This is the simplest classifier. It classifies each document to the nearest centroid (mean of the category) using a cosine distance metric.

Decision Tree

The most basic decision tree algorithm is the well-known ID3 algorithm [3]. Some classification algorithms benefit from additional reduction in the feature space [4,5]. Terms are selected based on their mutual information with the categories [4,6] and by selecting all terms where the mutual information is above some threshold.

Naïve Bayes

There are two variations of naïve Bayes we typically employ. The first is based on numeric features, the second on binary features. Both use the well-known Bayes decision rule and make the naïve Bayes assumption [4,7,8], and they differ only in how the probability of the document given the class, $P(d|C_k)$, is calculated.

Numeric Features

This method, also known as the multinomial model [4] classification, is based on the number of occurrences of each word in the document

$$P(d|C_k) = \prod_{w_i \in d} P(w_i \mid C_k)$$

where the individual word probabilities are calculated form the training data using Laplace smoothing [4]:

$$P(w_i \mid C_k) = \frac{n_{k,i} + 1}{n_k + |V|}$$

where

n_k is the total number of word positions in documents assigned to class C_k in the training data

$n_{k,i}$ is the number of positions in these documents where w_i occurs
V is the set of all unique words

Binary Features

This method, also known as the multivariate model [4], calculates probabilities based on the presence or absence of words in documents, ignoring their frequency of occurrence:

$$P(d \mid C_k) = \prod_{w_i \in V} [B_i P(w_i \mid C_k) + (1 - B_i)(1 - P(w_i \mid C_k)]$$

where B_i is 1 if w_i occurs in d and 0 otherwise, and the individual word probabilities are calculated as

$$P(w_i \mid C_k) = \frac{1 + \sum_{d \in D} B_i P(C_k \mid d)}{2 + \sum_{d \in D} P(C_k \mid d)}$$

where $P(C_k|d)$is 1 if d is in class C_k and 0 otherwise.

Since this method works best in the case of smaller feature spaces, [4] we use the same method as in the decision tree algorithm to do additional feature selection.

Rule Based

A rule induction classifier [9] is based on a fast decision tree system that takes advantage of the sparsity of text data and a rule-simplification method that converts a decision tree into a logically equivalent rule set. This method also uses a modified entropy function that not only favors splits enhancing the purity of partitions but also, in contrast to the Gini or standard entropy metrics, is close to the classification error curve, which has been found to improve text-classification accuracy.

Statistical

The statistical classifier (or support vector machine) is a version of regularized linear classifier that also provides a probability estimate for each class. It also employs the sparse regularization condition described in [10] to produce a sparse weight vector.

The numerical algorithm is described in [10].

DICTIONARIES AND NORMALIZATION

Existing domain ontologies that provide dictionaries and normalized entities are an invaluable resource for codifying the domain entities, helping to insure that each entity refers to a unique object in the physical world. These can sometimes be used directly as synonym lists in order to generate entity extractors. In other cases, we can use these lists to create a mapping between the domain concepts we find via unstructured techniques and the entities of the domain. Whichever method we use, it is important to be sure that the way entities are actually expressed in the documents is accurately reflected in our dictionaries.

COHESION AND DISTINCTNESS

When faced with a complex problem, figuring out where to begin is often half the battle. We begin the editing process faced with many categories, each of them calling out for our attention with its succinct little name holding out the promise of elegantly simple and meaningful content. Alas, it will turn out that this is not entirely the case. In fact, while some categories are relatively simple and straightforward to interpret, others will wind up being far more complex than the simple name implies. This fact should make us pause before we set out on our journey of understanding.

"But why does this matter at all?" you might reasonably ask. If the analyst is eventually going to look at each of the categories anyway, it would seem that the order in which the categories are studied should make no difference to the difficulty of the task or to the end result. Nevertheless, I can say with complete confidence, based on many years' experience and hundreds (if not thousands) of taxonomy edits performed, that, as a practical matter, order makes a significant difference in both degree of difficulty and quality of end result. The reasons, I think, have to do as much with the way the mind learns as they do with text mining principles. After all, at its root, the taxonomy editing process is really nothing more than a kind of self-taught course in understanding the contents of a collection, with the analyst being the student. If you think about how courses are usually laid out, they seldom begin with the hardest, most complex principle first. Instead, they typically begin with the obvious stuff, and then build on the straightforward concepts to tackle the tougher, thornier issues. That natural progression from simple to complex is a practical approach to taxonomy editing as well; if we can start with the simple categories, then by the time we tackle the complex categories, we will already have a store of knowledge about this domain stored in our brains to draw on. The complex category will be less intimidating halfway through the process than it would have been at the beginning. More importantly, the decisions the analyst makes in dealing with the complex category will be better informed, more accurate, and faster.

So, having established that simplicity is an important measure to use in selecting categories, we can ask how we actually measure it. What makes a category simple? In a word, homogeneity. A category where all the examples look alike is an easy category to understand. A category where all the examples are identical is trivial to understand—all you have to do is read one example and you are done, no matter how many times that example occurs. This is an important point to emphasize: Size is not a reliable measure of complexity. It is true that at the extremes where a category contains just one example or only a handful, it must be simple, but once you get beyond a handful, complexity is not really correlated strongly with size. In fact, as we shall see in our helpdesk example, the biggest category, "password reset," is also one of the simplest.

Cohesion

It turns out that homogeneity is reflected very well by the *cohesion* metric we discussed in the previous chapter. Here is a formal definition of cohesion:

$$\text{cohesion}(T) = \frac{\sum_{x \in T} \cos(\text{centroid}(T), x)}{|T|}$$

where

T is the set of documents in the category
centroid*(T)* is the average vector of all these documents

The cosine distance between document vectors is defined to be

$$\cos(X,Y) = \frac{X \cdot Y}{||X|| \cdot ||Y||}$$

Categories that score relatively high with this measure will tend to be those with a significant number of examples having many words in common. In the extreme case, a category consisting of all the same document would have a cohesion value of 1.0, which is the highest possible value this metric can return.

The centroid, mentioned above, is an important concept we will be coming back to again and again. Think of the centroid as a numeric summary of the category in dictionary space. It is a kind of model for the category that represents what a typical document in the category looks like in vector-space representation. What a useful thing to have; and we will make further use of it in the very next section.

As the category editing process continues, there areas of overlap between categories will naturally arise. As much as possible, we want to make sure the categories are distinct, well-defined entities so that any statistics we measure and conclusions we draw at the end will be equally well defined and meaningful. To this end, it is important to be able to see any relationships between categories and make decisions about any adjustments that should be made to clarify intracategory differences. There are several tools we have come up with to measure and communicate how categories are related.

Distinctness

Distinctness is a measure of differentiation between categories. It is defined to be one minus the cosine distance between the category centroid and the centroid of the nearest neighboring category. Thus, the distinctness of a category that has the same centroid as another category would be $1.0 - 1.0 = 0.0$. The highest possible distinctness value would occur when the centroid of the category was completely different (i.e., contained none of the same features) than every other category. This would produce a value of $1.0 - 0.0 = 1.0$.

As is the case here, the two categories at the top of the list (those with the lowest value) will always have the same distinctness value (since they must be nearest neighbors of each other). Whether or not it makes sense to keep these as separate categories is a decision that needs to be made by the analyst. It all depends on how detailed the categorization needs to be and how valuable the distinction is.

SINGLE AND MULTIMEMBERSHIP TAXONOMIES

One simple yet important taxonomy is based purely on the occurrence of keywords or terms. Often these entity names are known a priori by the domain expert, but in other cases they can be discovered by perusing the dictionary of terms generated during the text clustering process. The number of categories in the keyword name taxonomy is usually equal to the number of keywords + two. The two additional categories are "miscellaneous," for those snippets that do not mention any brand or company (if any); and "ambiguous," for those snippets that mention more than one brand/company names. We found an "ambiguous" class approach is preferable to the multi membership approach for two reasons:

1. The analyst does not have to read the same document again in different categories when perusing the category.
2. The mentions of multiple entities could be a qualitatively different event than the mention of a single entity by itself (e.g., to indicate an interaction, complex, or comparison).

Keyword taxonomies can capture nearly any issue of a priori importance to the domain expert, though the keywords themselves may need to be refined to match how the concepts may appear in the data. The assumption is that the occurrence of such issues is important regardless of its prevalence in the data (since prevalent issues would be found anyway in the text clustering taxonomy).

SUBCLASSING AREAS OF INTEREST

Sometimes, a certain category or small set of categories from a clustering or keyword taxonomy is actually an agglomeration of many different domain entities of interest. In such cases, it may make sense to take all the documents in these related categories and do a clustering on this subset alone. This will allow the tool to find more specific concepts that may have been ignored in the higher-level analysis. This process can be repeated iteratively to whatever level of detail is desired. Eventually, all the entities should be rolled up into an overall taxonomy representing the entire set of entities of a given type, at whatever level they appear. Only if the domain expert agrees that it has a physical analogue should the tree structure generated by clustering and subclustering be retained.

GENERATING NEW QUERIES TO FIND ADDITIONAL RELEVANT CONTENT

As the process proceeds, it will frequently turn out that some areas of the domain are not well covered by the initial document set generated from the first query. Subsequent queries should be designed to gather additional content. This additional content should first be analyzed separately from the original, and then, after it is well understood, the entire corpus can be merged and analyzed together to insure the overall consistency, reproducibility, and completeness of the taxonomy.

VALIDATION

Assessing the overall accuracy of the taxonomy is a very challenging and important task. While there is no single method for doing this in all cases, there are a few important strategies we employ to assure the correctness of our entity extractions:

1. Domain-expert evaluation of sample extractions
2. Domain-expert labeling of test sets for automatic computer grading of results
3. Domain-expert perusal of results via an interactive graphical user interface
4. Delta comparison of entity extractions from one entity extraction run to the next to focus on interesting new extractions or missing old ones.
5. Comparison of results to review articles written in the domain or to well-established domain websites that list the entities that exist

SUMMARY

The overall result of the exploration process is a set of taxonomies that describe the important entities in the domain. These taxonomies will match the content to the physical world, so that we know that all the important concepts contained in the unstructured data are sufficiently catalogued and that all the different variations on how the same physical item is expressed are correctly identified.

Chapter 8, Taxonomies, will go into greater detail on other methods for generating taxonomies that go beyond categories directly inferred from content in order to incorporate domain knowledge and structured data more directly.

REFERENCES

1. Moschitti, A., and Basili, R. 2004. Complex linguistic features for text classification: A comprehensive study. In *Advances in Information Retrieval* (pp. 181–196). Berlin: Springer.
2. Spangler, S., and Kreulen, J. 2002. Interactive methods for taxonomy editing and validation. In *Proceedings of the Eleventh International Conference on Information and Knowledge Management*. New York: ACM.
3. Quinlan, J. R. 1986. Induction of decision trees. *Machine Learning*, *1*(1): 81–106.

4. McCallum, A., and Nigam, K. 1998. A comparison of event models for Naïve Bayes text classification. In *AAAI-98 Workshop on Learning for Text Categorization*, Madison, WI.
5. Duda, R. O., Hart, P. E., and Stork, D. E. 2001. *Pattern Classification*, 2nd edn. Hoboken, NJ: Wiley-Interscience.
6. Cover, T. M., and Thomas, J. A. 1991. *Elements of Information Theory.* Hoboken, NJ: Wiley-Interscience.
7. Manning, C. D., and Schütze, H. 2000. *Foundations of Statistical Natural Language Processing.* Cambridge: MIT Press.
8. Mitchell, T. M. 1997. *Machine Learning.* New York: McGraw-Hill.
9. Johnson, D. E., Oles, F. J., Zhang, T., and Goetz, T., 2002. A decision-tree-based symbolic rule induction system for text categorization. *IBM Systems Journal, 41*(3): 428–437.
10. Zhang, T. 2002. On the dual formulation of regularized linear systems. *Machine Learning, 46*: 91–129

CHAPTER 5

Organization

ONCE WE HAVE OUR entities, the next step is to figure out how they fit together. Like a giant jigsaw puzzle, the entities in a scientific domain each play a role in the physical world, and we need to understand and represent that role in order to gain insight and intelligently reason over the information space. The input into the organization process is a set of entities that exist in the content along with the content and any structured information that corresponds to each entity. The output is an ontology that describes what kind of thing each entity is and how it relates structurally to other entities in the physical world. We will discuss how this output can frequently be used as an enabler for new discoveries.

DOMAIN-SPECIFIC ONTOLOGIES AND DICTIONARIES

Each scientific domain has its own system for defining entities, types, and ontologies. The degree to which these ontologies will be well documented and the consistency with which they are followed over time will vary widely. In some respects, this is only to be expected. Discoveries about nature's structure happen over time, and we cannot expect scientists living and writing in one era will have terminology identical to that of scientists in a different era. Thus, every dictionary you find or are supplied with is sure to have areas of incompleteness if not outright errors and inconsistencies.

One of the best initial sources for such ontologies is the Internet and in particular, at least for type sets of small size, Wikipedia [1]. Open-source entity sets exist for most of the well-established ontologies in science, and more are created every day.

These should be a starting point, but each one will need to be carefully validated and compared to the entities already discovered in the data (using techniques in the previous chapter). In some cases, no preexisting ontology will be found. This will require us to create our own organization scheme. The next section will describe a process for doing this in a new scientific domain.

SIMILARITY TREES

Similarity trees are a way to automatically impose some organization on a set of entities where we do not know how they may be related. We use the feature space gleaned from the literature in the previous section to represent each entity as a centroid. This allows us to calculate a distance matrix that measures the distance between each entity and every other entity in the space. Such matrices are fine for computers to read and calculate properties over but notoriously difficult for a domain expert to interpret in order to get a sense of the data's underlying validity and meaning. Thus, some way must be found to convert the numbers into a meaningful picture of entity–entity relationships.

A network graph is one approach that is often tried [2], but this requires determining when two nodes should be considered connected, when in fact all nodes are connected at some level of similarity threshold. We could pick an arbitrary similarity cutoff and draw lines whenever similarity was greater than the specified limit, but that assigns more meaning to the absolute value of the distance metric employed here than is strictly warranted. Relative distance is the more important concept to convey here.

To design the graph we switch the goal around. What does a maximally communicative graph look like? First of all, it should be minimally connected, in other words containing one less arc than the number of nodes. Secondly, it should be a tree because trees are easy to navigate and communicate information based on distance from the root, which is often helpful. Third, the tree should spread connections out fairly evenly among the nodes to avoid extreme situations where one node is connected to all the others—a very uninteresting graph. This leads us to the conclusion that a binary tree (or at least low n-ary) would be highly advantageous if it could be drawn so as to accurately represent the distance matrix. To create a binary tree, we must choose a meaningful root node. Does any particular entity stand out for this honor? In fact, there is one property unique and important in the text vector space—typicality. There is one entity whose vector is closest to the average of all the vectors.

This will be the root. Now as we move down the tree, we will naturally go toward less typical (more unusual) nodes. This turns out to be a very intuitive concept to grasp visually.

Algorithm 5.1 is used to create an n-ary similarity tree from the set of entities, where each entity is represented as a feature vector. The root of the tree is the "most typical" entity, and typicality decreases with increasing distance from the root, so that the leaves of the tree are the "least typical," that is, unique outliers. The algorithm first computes the "most typical" feature vector as the average of the entities and then calls the closestToFV function to select the entity closest to this typical feature vector as the root of the similarity tree. The algorithm also initializes *candidates* as a singleton set comprising the root node; here candidates are the set of nodes currently in the tree at which to potentially attach new child nodes. The algorithm next uses the closestPair function to find the pair (e,c) such that e belongs to entities, c belongs to candidates, and distance (e,c) is minimized over all such pairs. (Thus e is the closest entity to the current set of candidates and c is the candidate closest to e.) Then e is added to the tree as a child of c. Moreover, e is removed from entities, the set of entities that have not yet been added to the tree, and added to candidates. If adding e as a child to c increases the number of c's children to the limit n, then c is removed from candidates to ensure that its n-ary property will not be violated in the future. The algorithm continues to add elements of entities to the tree in a similar manner, until there are no more entities to add. The functions closestToFV and closestPair use Euclidean distance and break ties randomly.

Algorithm 5.1: Create an n-Ary Similarity Tree from a Set of Entities

```
Input: entities, n
Output: n-ary similarity tree
mostTypicalFV = average(entities)
root = closestTo FV(entities, mostTypical FV)
entities.remove(root)
candidates = {root}
while not entities.isEmpty()
      (e, c) = closestPair(entities, candidates)
      c.addChild(e)
      if c.numChildren() == n then
            candidates.remove(c)
```

end if
candidates.add(e)
entities.remove(e)
end while
Return: root

Figure 5.1 depicts what a typical similarity tree looks like. In this example, we see clearly how concepts that are similar as domain constructs also turn out to be detected as having "close" centroids, which in turn leads to them being adjacent in the tree. Also note how "molecular_dynamic" serves as a good overall theme for the entire tree, which is no accident, since it was chosen as having the "most typical" centroid. On the other hand, entities like "activation barrier" are on the fringes of this taxonomy and therefore are displayed on the leaves of the tree.

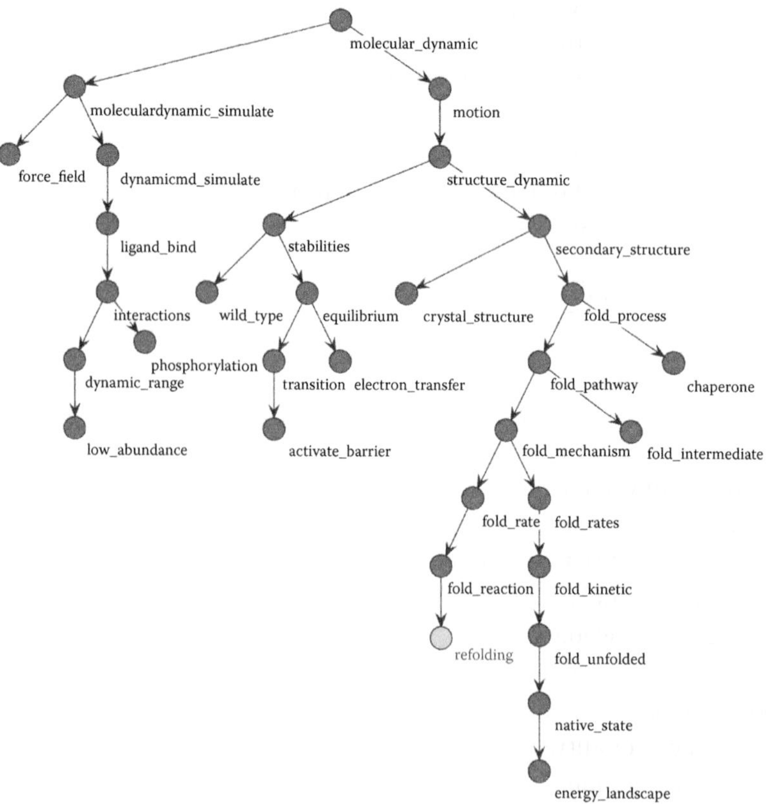

FIGURE 5.1 Similarity tree.

USING SIMILARITY TREES TO INTERACT WITH DOMAIN EXPERTS

Similarity trees help data scientists communicate with domain experts about what entities mean, what context they are used in, what entity types exist, and how the overall pieces of the puzzle fit together. Their fundamental purpose is to bridge the gap between the idealized, simplified representation that exists in textbooks or in the scientist's mind and the messy reality of how things are discussed in a cross section of research articles on a given topic. There will be overlaps, but there is seldom a perfect fit. Where there are incongruities, it is the data scientist's job to decide whether new entities are warranted or whether it would make more sense to either fold these in as special cases of existing entities or remove the altogether from the entity space as not important for the purpose of the analysis.

The other thing similarity trees help with is beginning to think about entity types, that is, which entities go together as a natural group and which belong to dissimilar families. One technique I have found to be effective is to let the expert draw circles on a similarity tree to show natural ways that entities clump together. From this, the data scientist can go back and create an overarching ontology that describes the different entity types and the role that each plays in achieving the analysis objectives. The process can then iterate until a stable ontology is reached.

SCATTER-PLOT VISUALIZATIONS

Similarity trees let us look at entities at a high level. In some instances, it is useful to look at the individual documents that define those entities through their text content. A scatter-plot visualization of the document/entity space is one of the most powerful ways I have found to do this.

The idea is to visually display the vector-space of a bag-of-words document model to the user so that the documents will appear as points in space. The result is that documents containing similar words occur near to each other in the visual display. If the vector-space model were two dimensional, this would be straightforward—we could simply draw the documents as point on an X,Y scatter plot. The difficulty is that the dimensions of the document vector space will be of much higher dimension. In fact, the dimensionality will be the size of the feature space (dictionary), which is typically thousands of terms. Therefore, we need a way to reduce the dimensionality from thousands to two in such a way as to retain most of the relevant information. Our approach uses the CViz method [3], which relies on three category centroids to define the plane of most interest and to project the documents as points on this plane (by finding the intersection with a normal line drawn from point to plane). The selection of which categories to display in addition to the selected category is based on finding the categories with the nearest centroid distance to the selected category. The documents displayed in such a plot are colored according to category membership. The centroid of the category is also displayed. The resultant plot is a valuable way to discover relationships between neighboring concepts in a taxonomy.

Scatter plots treat the feature vector space as an N-dimensional universe, where N is the number of terms in the dictionary. Since it is impossible to draw an N-dimensional universe of points directly, we choose one two-dimensional plane carefully selected from that universe and draw a perpendicular line between any point and that plane. Wherever the point intersects the plane is where we plot the point. This is called a "projection" (similar to the way a movie is projected on to a screen). The key choice we have to make is the position of the plane. If we choose poorly, the projection will be uninteresting and tell us very little about the entities we want to learn about. Choose well, and we will see very clear differentiation between entities. Since three points make a plane, even in high-dimensional space, we only need to select the best three points. The origin (the point where all terms are zero) seems like a good one. The other two points can then naturally be the centroids of two entities we care about. This simple idea can create a very interesting and highly informative plot that describes how the documents define the entities in term dictionary space.

In Figure 5.2, the large dots represent centroids of two different entities. The small dots represent individual documents. The color of each dot represents the entity it belongs to. Some documents mention both entities.

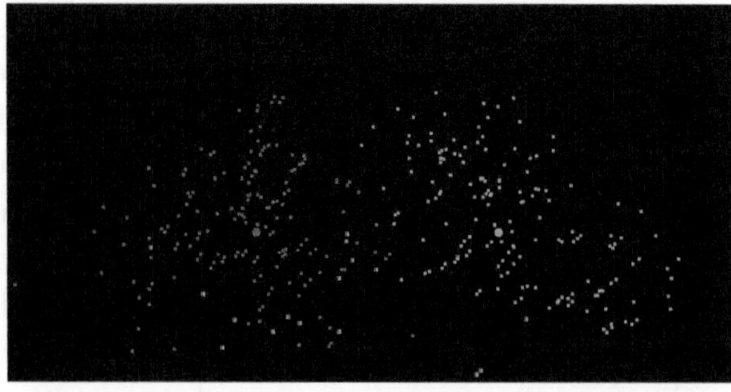

FIGURE 5.2 **(See color insert.)** Scatter plot.

These are shown with two colors (half and half). The origin is not shown, but if a line through the two centroids makes the X axis, the Y axis would run through the origin, perpendicular to the X axis. Documents on the border exactly between the two centroids have content relevant to both entities.

Some things we can infer from looking at scatter-plot visualizations are

1. How well defined is the entity within the documents mentioning it? A tight, cohesive cluster would indicate an entity with little variation in how it is described in literature.

2. How differentiable is the entity from its neighbor? If the document clouds overlap, that could be an indication that these two entities share many characteristics.

3. Are there multiple subtypes of this entity? If we see distinct clumps of documents of the same color, it may mean an entity represents a general concept that can be naturally broken down into smaller concepts.

Visualization through scatter plots is also a good way to dive into the data stream and to be sure the entity means what you think it does. Selecting points that are either near the centroid (typical) or on the fringes (outliers), one can then read the documents behind them and see how the entity is discussed in both ordinary and unusual circumstances.

USING SCATTER PLOTS TO FIND OVERLAPS BETWEEN NEARBY ENTITIES OF DIFFERENT TYPES

In my experience, whenever we see entities of two different types come together in a similarity tree, interesting discoveries are most likely to be found. The subgraph in Figure 5.3, showing antibiotics and anti-inflammatories, illustrates the point.

By coloring elements based on the type of entity, we can quickly note the unusual cases where we have an anti-inflammatory appearing near an antibiotic. As we shall see, this has implications for discovery, in that entities normally classified as one kind of thing when exhibiting properties of another kind of thing have the potential to provide new applications or uses beyond the well-known ones.

Drilling into two particular entities of different types and showing these entities with a scatter-plot visualization provides a rapid means of

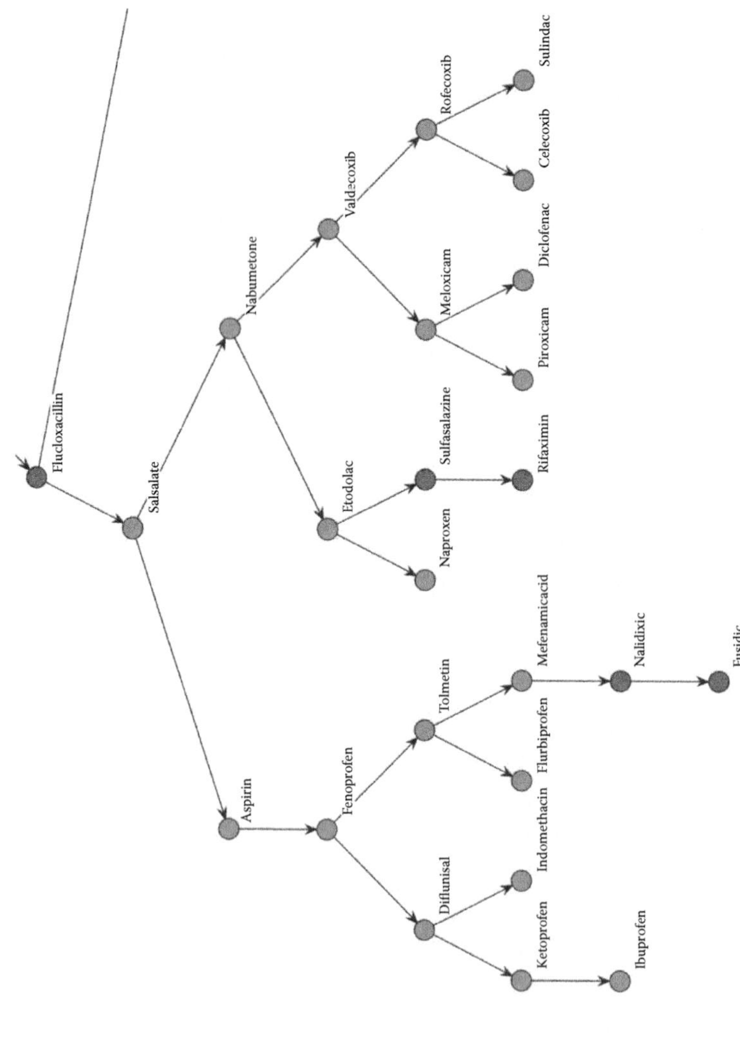

FIGURE 5.3 Adding color to similarity tree.

finding exactly those documents most likely to provide insight into why one entity is also like another entity type. By selecting those documents that appear nearest the other centroid (the centroid of the entity of a different color than the document), one can locate the relevant material much more speedily than with keyword queries.

DISCOVERY THROUGH VISUALIZATION OF TYPE SPACE

As we will see in many examples later on in this book, the visualization of the entity type space provides a powerful tool for discovery. By overlaying on top of the similarity tree something assumed to be known about the entities, we can verify where that knowledge is reflected in the document contents written about those entities and where there may be inconsistencies or further discoveries waiting to happen. Visualizing and exploring entity spaces through similarity trees allows us to combine everything we know in a given information space and see where there may be hidden opportunities for connections or filling in gaps. Visualizations are a way to employ the human cognitive capability that is wired into the visual cortex and use it in the service of scientific discovery. It is a powerful way to marry the best abilities of machine intelligence with the competence and insight of the domain expert.

REFERENCES

1. http://www.wikipedia.org.
2. van Herman, I., Melançon, G., and Marshall, M. S. 2000. Graph visualization and navigation in information visualization: A survey. *IEEE Transactions on Visualization and Computer Graphics*, 6(1): 24–43.
3. Dhillon, I., Modha, D., and Spangler, S. 1998. Visualizing class structures of multi-dimensional data. *Proceedings of 30th Conference on Interface, Computer Science and Statistics*. Berlin: Springer.

CHAPTER 6

Relationships

IN THIS CHAPTER, WE begin to shift gears, moving from form to function. Entities do not just exist in the world—they do things (or have things done to them). Capturing this dynamic as it appears in text and visualizing the result is what we will cover next. We begin by describing how to detect and extract simple relationships.

WHAT DO RELATIONSHIPS LOOK LIKE?

Functional relationships are typically characterized by one entity acting on or influencing another. Thus they grammatically follow a standard pattern: Entity (noun) does something to (verb) another entity (noun). The core of the relationship—the word that identifies its type—is the verb. Our first job in relationship extraction is to identify these verbs and classify them into domain-specific types that are meaningful for our objectives.

Therefore, the same tools that we used for entity detection may wind up being useful for relationship detection as well, namely automatic dictionary generation and text clustering. In this case, we simply focus our attention on terms and clusters that are verbs instead of nouns.

Of course, not everything is this simple. In some cases, relationships will have more than three parts. Also the nature of the relationship may be positive or negative, direct or indirect. All of this must be inferred from other words besides the subject-verb-object triple. But this complexity should be worked up to gradually, step by step. First identify the type of relationships and their various verb forms, then identify the entities that occur around those verbs, and then add the contextual complexity that surrounds the core idea.

HOW CAN WE DETECT RELATIONSHIPS?

Most relationships are bounded by sentences. This is due to the natural structure of noun-verb-object employed in language to describe entities that are acting or being acted on. Therefore in detecting relationships, it makes sense to cluster individual sentences rather than documents. This will naturally cause the verbs in these sentences to take a more prominent role in the clustering and to therefore emerge as major themes.

Focusing especially on sentences containing two entities will often (for obvious reasons) yield the best results. Then there is no substitute for reading lots of sentences until the analyst obtains the gist of what is going on or at least attempts to do so. Domain expert advice is critical here. You may also have the domain expert simply label a set of example sentences in relevant documents with the important relationships identified.

REGULAR EXPRESSION PATTERNS FOR EXTRACTING RELATIONSHIPS

One simple method for automatically extracting relationships, once you have identified the most frequent way the relationships appear in text, is to devise regular expression patterns that match the form in which the relationships typically appear. While this method is not particularly sophisticated, it can be used to produce results that have relatively high precision, allowing the data scientist to create an impressive first approximation to relationship extraction without having to do much work. The advantage to this approach is that it allows you to create some early results and iterate with the domain experts to refine the patterns and better understand the variety of ways relationships occur in text. Here are some examples of regular expressions for relationship detection.

```
EffectiveMalaria:prevent.{0,30}malaria|prevent.{0,30}
plasmodium|effective.{0,100}falicparum|effective.
{0,100}malaria|effective.{0,100}plasmodium|treat.
{0,10}malaria|treat.{0,10}plasmodium|protect.{0,20}
malaria|protect.{0,20}plasmodium|malaria
resolved|efficacious.{0,60}plasmodium|efficacious.
{0,60}malaria
CYCLOSPORININDUCED:cyclosporin.{0,30}induce|csa.{0,5}
induce
```

The .{x,y} syntax indicates how many times the wild card character "." may be repeated. Each of these patterns looks for a verb form next to a noun of particular interest to the objective (malaria in the first instance and cyclosporine in the second). The "|" stands for "or" in regular expression syntax and is used in this example to allow us to list all the ways both the principle noun and the verb might appear in the text.

NATURAL LANGUAGE PARSING

The advantage of regular expressions is their speed, both to write and to execute as a program. In the long run, however, for more complex kinds of relationships with numerous entities that have a high degree of variability, they no longer function well. Instead we need to use an NLP technique called *part of speech tagging* to effectively diagram the sentences of interest and figure out what is acting on what and how.

This method creates the possibility of detecting relationships that are phrased in unusual and unpredictable ways. Thus recall can be greatly enhanced by NLP techniques. NLP can also help to identify the directionality of the relationship, which may prove difficult with pattern matching methods.

Figure 6.1 shows some examples of results generated for protein/protein interactions using NLP parsing. Here, phosphorylation is the verb and proteins are the entity type that serves as both subject (agent) and object.

Sentence: *"The results show that* ***ERK2*** *phosphorylated* ***p53*** *at* ***Thr55.****"*

- **Extract entities and types**
  Entity (text location) → Entity Type: ERK2 (22,25) → Protein; p53 (42,44) → Protein; Thr55 (49,53) → amino Acid
- **Extract relationships and (agent, verb, object) triplets**
  —Part of speech tags show that phosphorylated is a VERB of interest. "Phosphorylate" is codified as a posttranslational modification relationship.
  The/DT results/NNS show/VBP that/IN ERK2/NNP phosphorylated/VBD p53/NN at/IN Thr55/NNS
  VERB
  —Grammatical relations to previously identified entities reveal subject/object links
  nsubi(phosphorylated-6, ERK2-5); dobi(phosphorylated-6, p53-7)
  AGENT OBJECT
  —Prepositional connections indicate location property for the verb phosphorylate
  prep at(phosphorylated-6, Thr55-9)
  LOCATION
- **Result: Extracted (agent, verb, object) triplets and properties**
  —Agent: ERK2
  —Action: phosphorylated; base form: phosphorylate
  —Object: p53
  —Location: Thr55

FIGURE 6.1 Relationship example.

An additional property of the relationships, "location," is also extracted. This combination of entity recognition along with sentence parsing is a powerful technique for understanding sentences at a far deeper level than we could get at with bag-of-words techniques.

Note the importance of recognizing the part of speech to accurately identify the role each entity is playing in the relationship. This is especially helpful when words in different contexts may stand for different entity types. For example, some abbreviations for amino acids may also be confused with abbreviations for genes. The fact that the string occurs as the object of a prepositional phrase helps to determine its role and therefore to make the appropriate connection.

COMPLEX RELATIONSHIPS

Once the basic triples of subject-verb-object are accurately extracted, the data scientist can move on into more sophisticated kinds of relationships that range from involving negation (X is does not or cannot affect Y) to indirection (X has an effect on Y through some intermediary) to teamwork (X and Z together effect Y). One must always weigh the potential benefits of recognizing what is going on at this level of granularity against the time and cost of accurately doing so.

EXAMPLE: P53 PHOSPHORYLATION EVENTS

The protein P53, like all proteins, is a specific chain of amino acid residues. Phosphorylation events are chemical changes that happen to specific amino acids on that chain. We wish to map out all the phosphorylation events that are known to take place on P53 and to discover which agents (other proteins) are involved in those events and where on the P53 chain they are most often documented to be taking place. This requires a very specific type of relationship extraction that not only finds that A → B, where A and B are proteins and "→" is a phosphorylation event, but also where specifically on B the event takes place. Figure 6.2 shows a summary chart providing a summary of all such events found in Medline abstracts using our relationship extraction technology.

Each bar position on the X axis represents the specific amino acid on the P53 protein that is affected. The height of the bar indicates how many Medline abstracts mention that specific event at that location. Clicking on a bar brings up the evidence found for all protein–P53 interactions at that location (Figure 6.3).

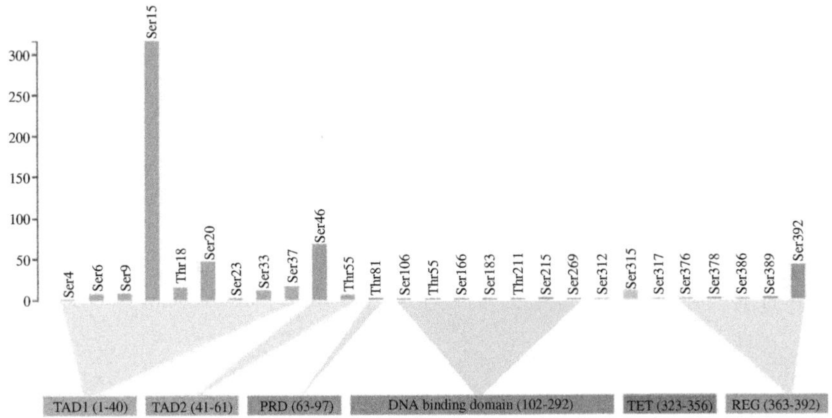

FIGURE 6.2 Relationship summary chart.

Clicking on ATM reveals the evidence found for ATM phosphorylating P53 at Serine-15 (Figures 6.3 and 6.4). We see how proper entity extraction, parsing of sentences, relationship identification, and domain-specific structure and role mapping can be combined to produce a powerful summary of many disparate research articles, precisely identifying the physical process that is unfolding in each one as being the same, even though the description of this process varies substantially from article to article, from a purely text formatting perspective.

PUTTING IT ALL TOGETHER

Figure 6.5 shows how entity detection, relationship detection, and network and confidence scoring come together to create a complete picture of the dynamic interactions in a scientific domain. Clearly this is a complex and multilayered process that requires a sophisticated infrastructure to pull of successfully across a large corpus. The benefits of doing this can be substantial, as we will see in the following example.

EXAMPLE: DRUG/TARGET/DISEASE RELATIONSHIP NETWORKS

Relationships are not always between entities of the same type. In some cases, the entities are heterogeneous. A good example of this is the relationships found between drugs, targets (proteins), and diseases. Typically in pharmacology, drugs affect targets that influence diseases. It is natural then to put all these different types of interactions together to create a picture of what is going on in a drug treatment space or around a given

▾ Agents and Supporting Documents for *TP53* at location *Ser15*

Unknown (276 docs)
ATM (16 docs)
ATR (6 docs)
CHEK1 (2 docs)
BARD1 (2 docs)
NPM1 (2 docs)
MMS (2 docs)
NFKB1 (2 docs)
ACVR1 (1 doc)
UPF1 (1 doc)
SMG1 (1 doc)
UPF2 (1 doc)
MAPK14 (1 doc)
RUNX3 (1 doc)
UVRAG (1 doc)
IFNA1 (1 doc)
DYRK1A (1 doc)
MTX1 (1 doc)
MAPK8 (1 doc)
UBR5 (1 doc)
MAP3K5 (1 doc)
TIMM8A (1 doc)
MBD1 (1 doc)
BRCA1 (1 doc)
IGKV1D-39 (1 doc)
CDKN1A (1 doc)
CDK5 (1 doc)
TIAF1 (1 doc)
EGF (1 doc)

FIGURE 6.3 Support for relationship summary.

target. Figure 6.6 shows all the relationships occurring in the neighborhood around the protein IL7R.

Circles in the graph are proteins, triangles are diseases, and squares are drugs. The links are directional and based on links extracted from individual sentences in Medline abstracts. Figure 6.7 shows some example sentences that contribute to this network.

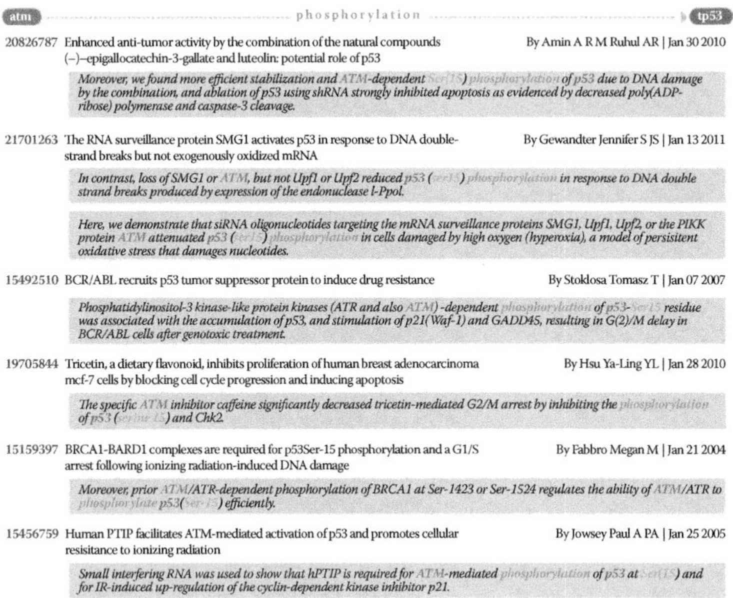

FIGURE 6.4 Evidence for relationship.

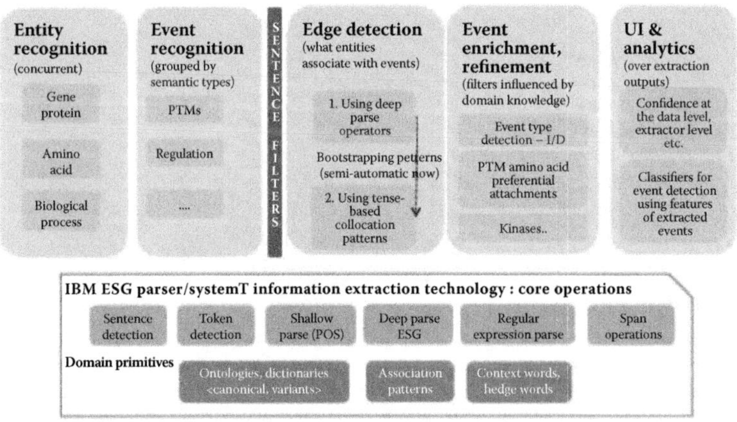

FIGURE 6.5 Process for relationship extraction.

In these examples, the entities and verbs that connect them are accurately identified and grouped so as to clearly illustrate the evidence behind each node and arc in the network. This makes it possible to summarize exactly what influences a drug may have, both intended and unintended, as well as what alternatives might exist for the treatment of a given disease,

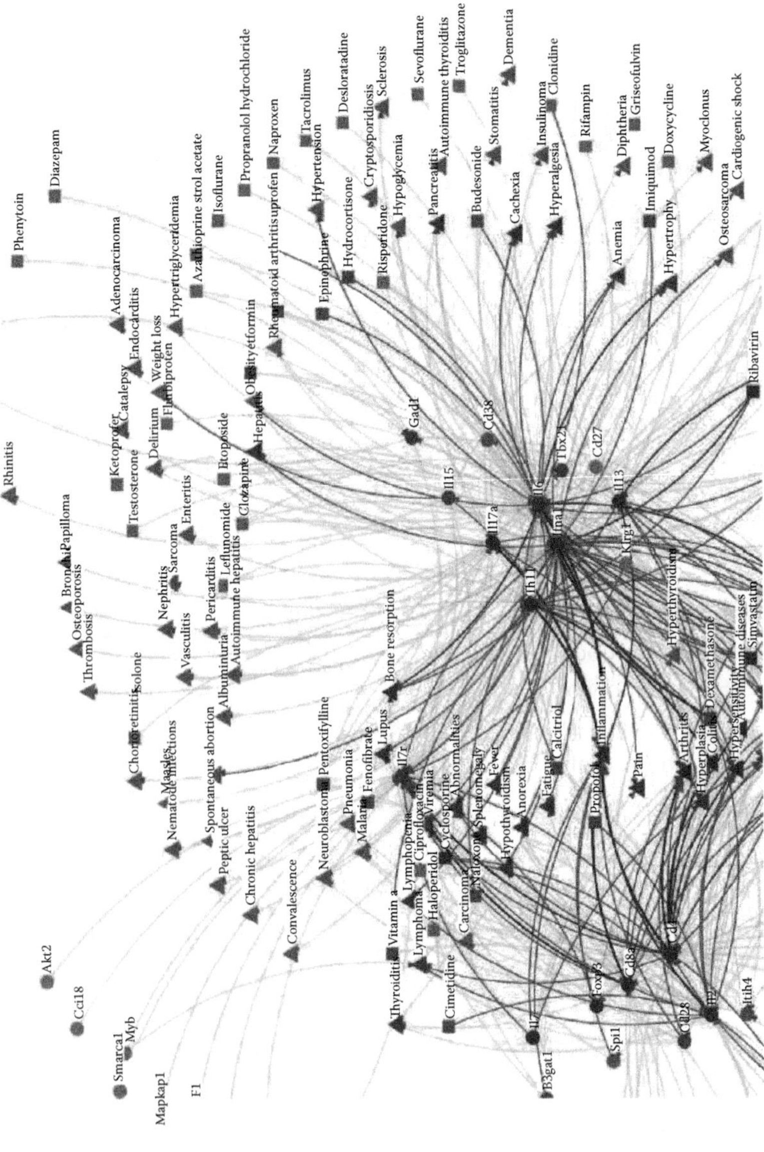

FIGURE 6.6 Complex relationship network.

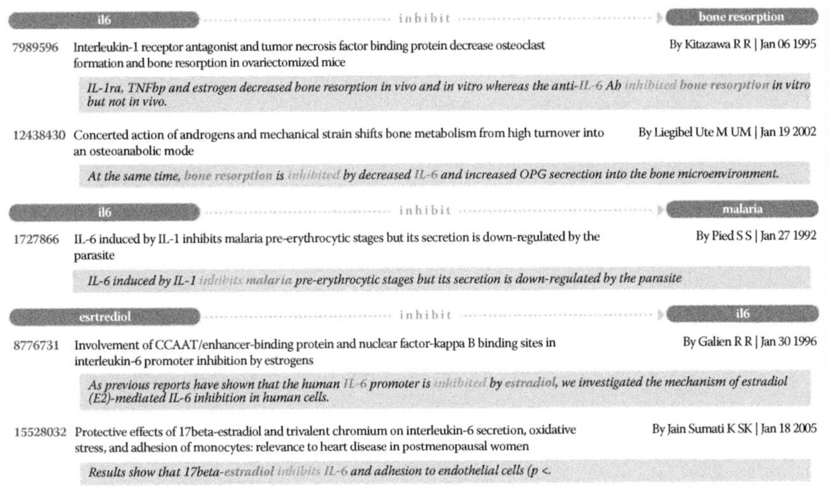

FIGURE 6.7 Supporting evidence for drug-protein-disease network.

while pulling together precise information from many different research articles.

CONCLUSION

Relationship extraction is the centerpiece of the functional analysis of domain-specific documents. It allows us to begin to make progress in understanding how one entity may act on another to change its state, and to see how a chain of events may arise that leads to a potentially unexpected outcome. Entities without relationships are static. Relationships add the dynamics that make our domain representations come alive.

CHAPTER 7

Inference

NOW THAT WE HAVE our entities and relationships, what remains is to put these to use for the purpose of making a new hypothesis or discovery of some kind—deriving a potential fact that does not literally appear in the published text given as input but is derived as a result of taking everything digested into account. Because of the complexity and heterogeneity involved in understanding the physical world as it actually exists, this is usually a daunting problem. Some simplifications and approximations are typically desirable. There are limitless possibilities for how to make use of these approximate models of reality so that we retain the important information and communicate insight. We will describe here a few that have proven useful in our attempts to accelerate discovery. We present these roughly in order of increasing complexity and sophistication.

CO-OCCURRENCE TABLES

Entity-to-entity co-occurrence tables compare different taxonomies (entity types) to discover where an unusually high degree of association might reside. We visualize such relationships via a co-occurrence table (cotable), which shows how the data break down across all the combinations of categories in two different taxonomies.

Assuming no relationship exists that ties one entity to another, we would expect to find around (X * Y) in a cell for a given sentiment and brand, where X is the percentage of times a given entity1 occurs and Y is the percentage of time entity2 occurs. Let us call this expected value E. An exceptional value is something greater than E, indicating an association stronger than we expected. That will be different for every cell in the cotable, since the number of overall occurrences for each entity differs.

Furthermore, we can get a relative significance for different values in the cotable, for example, whether a five occurring in one cell is more interesting than a ten occurring in a different cell, by using the chi-squared test [1]—a statistical test that calculates the likelihood of seeing any particular value in the cell of a cotable. The smaller this probability, the less likely the value, the more interesting it is from a data-mining perspective. When a very low probability value occurs, it suggests that our original assumption about no relationship existing between the taxonomies was incorrect. There actually may be a relationship revealed by the data. However, a correlation does not signify a definitive relationship between categories. It indicates something worth investigating further. We shade the values of the cotable accordingly to show such calculated probabilities. This makes it possible to look at a large number of probability values and immediately spot the most interesting ones. The table can also be interactive, allowing the analyst to sort by a row or column to bring to the top (or left-hand side) the values that are most significant (Figure 7.1).

Cotables can be used to discover a hidden connection between entities of different types, a new kind of relationship, or a new entity property.

Very High Affinity = Moderate Affinity = Low Affinity = No Affinity =

	Count	air_water	oilwater...	interfacial	surface_...	adsorbed	glycerol	diffusion	crystal_...	a
activation_barrier	.1380	2 (1.0)	1 (1.0)	19 (1.0)	0 (1.0)	59 (1.921...	14 (1.0)	94 (0.092...	0 (1.0)	7
dynamic_range	.242	0 (1.0)	0 (1.0)	0 (1.0)	0 (1.0)	1 (1.0)	2 (1.0)	2 (1.0)	0 (1.0)	2
dynamic_simulation	.43	0 (1.0)	0 (1.0)	0 (1.0)	0 (1.0)	0 (1.0)	0 (1.0)	0 (1.0)	0 (1.0)	0
electron_transfer	.291	0 (1.0)	0 (1.0)	13 (2.468...	0 (1.0)	12 (0.003...	6 (1.0)	24 (0.072...	0 (1.0)	4
force_field	162	0 (1.0)	1 (0.3912...	1 (1.0)	0 (1.0)	0 (1.0)	1 (1.0)	6 (1.0)	0 (1.0)	0
ligand_bind	402	0 (1.0)	0 (1.0)	0 (1.0)	0 (1.0)	1 (1.0)	12 (0.283...	15 (1.0)	1 (1.0)	0
low_abundance	34	0 (1.0)	0 (1.0)	0 (1.0)	0 (1.0)	0 (1.0)	0 (1.0)	0 (1.0)	0 (1.0)	0
molecular_dynamics	1553	0 (1.0)	0 (1.0)	23 (1.0)	0 (1.0)	16 (1.0)	11 (1.0)	92 (0.844...	0 (1.0)	1
motion	1207	1 (1.0)	0 (1.0)	24 (0.437...	0 (1.0)	11 (1.0)	52 (1.719...	140 (1.30...	2 (1.0)	2
phosphorylation	.227	0 (1.0)	0 (1.0)	1 (1.0)	0 (1.0)	1 (1.0)	5 (1.0)	3 (1.0)	0 (1.0)	1
protein_function	.281	1 (1.0)	0 (1.0)	7 (0.3092...	0 (1.0)	0 (1.0)	2 (1.0)	11 (1.0)	0 (1.0)	2
protein_motion	.162	0 (1.0)	0 (1.0)	4 (0.4554...	0 (1.0)	2 (1.0)	13 (4.053...	16 (0.026...	0 (1.0)	0
stabilities	128	0 (1.0)	0 (1.0)	3 (0.5805...	0 (1.0)	0 (1.0)	2 (1.0)	10 (0.331...	0 (1.0)	1
structure_dynamic	728	3 (1.0)	0 (1.0)	9 (1.0)	1 (1.0)	5 (1.0)	8 (1.0)	44 (0.785...	0 (1.0)	6
wild_type	190	0 (1.0)	0 (1.0)	0 (1.0)	0 (1.0)	2 (1.0)	6 (0.3710...	12 (0.766...	0 (1.0)	0
Total	11848	90	32	203	52	221	262	689	78	3

Trend Examples View Examples Report OK Filter Enlarged View

FIGURE 7.1 Cotable.

CO-OCCURRENCE NETWORKS

For looking at entities of the same type, co-occurrence networks are often a useful way to discover hidden connections and subgroups of entities that are working together for some purpose. The logic is very simple: If two entities co-occur together in at least N abstracts, they get a link drawn between them. The value of N can be adjusted so as to limit the complexity of the network. Only entities with at least one link will appear in the graph. We can also start with a given set of seed entities and draw all the connecting entities that connect to these with at least one arc (Figure 7.2).

Such a diagram can help to determine how two seemingly unconnected entities may have an indirect connection via another entity with which they each co-occur independently.

RELATIONSHIP SUMMARIZATION GRAPHS

Relationship summarization graphs show a complete picture of how one kind of relationship appears with respect to one entity. Figure 7.3 shows an example of phosphorylation with protein P53.

This graph shows all the different amino-acid locations where we see P53 being phosphorylated by other proteins and how frequently those interactions are recorded in the literature. This makes it possible to understand the nature of P53 phosphorylation and, by drilling into a bar on the chart, to find out exactly which proteins are involved. This could lead to new drug candidates being developed by selecting drugs that can indirectly affect P53 through these intermediate proteins.

HOMOGENEOUS RELATIONSHIP NETWORKS

A homogeneous relationship network is a directed graph in which all the nodes are the same type of entity. A protein interaction network is one example (Figure 7.4).

The purpose of this type of network is to see which proteins are playing a central role in a given biological process or disease pathway. Drilling down allows the user to see exactly what kind(s) of relationship(s) each arc indicates. In contract to the co-occurrence network, each arc has a direction that is derived by parsing individual sentences to determine which protein is acting on the other. This can allow for the discovery of new indirect effects that one protein may have on another.

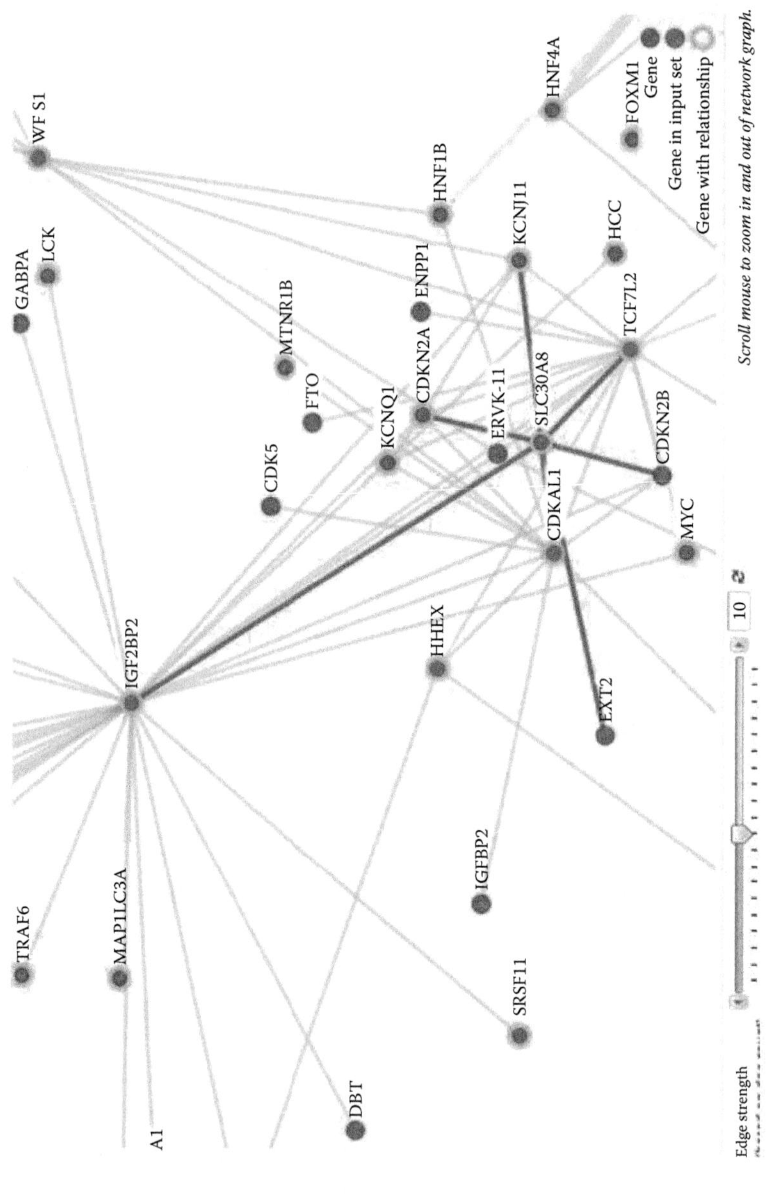

FIGURE 7.2 Co-occurrence network.

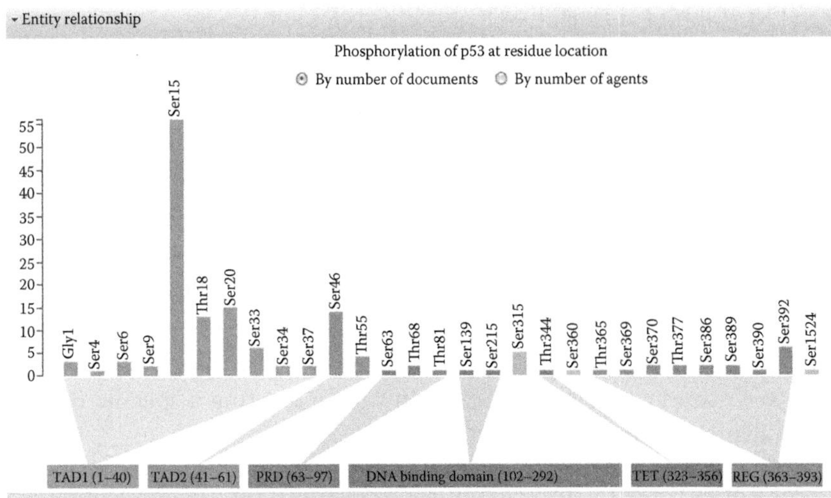

FIGURE 7.3 Relationship summarization.

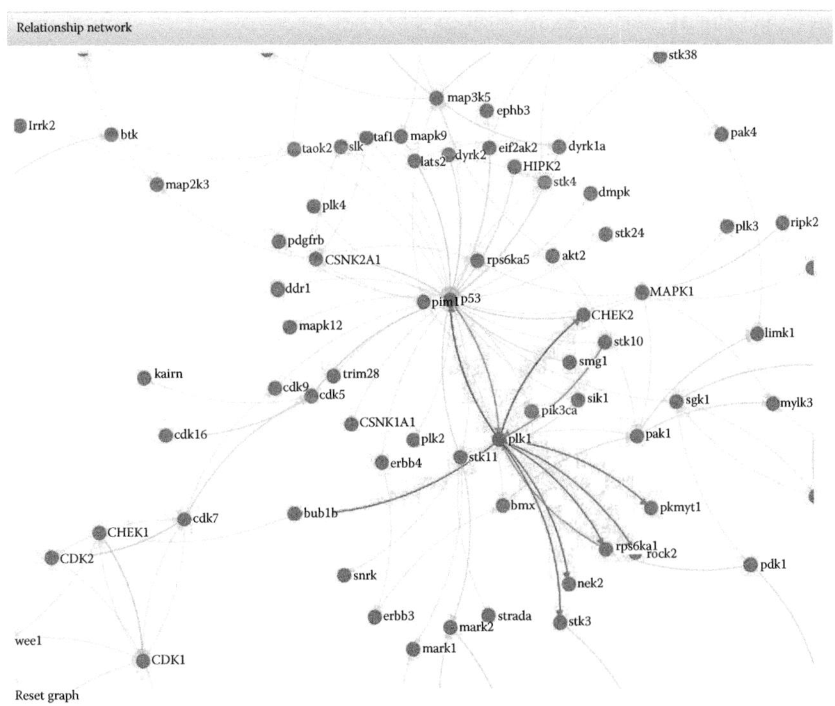

FIGURE 7.4 Relationship network diagram.

HETEROGENEOUS RELATIONSHIP NETWORKS

Heterogeneous relationship networks are similar to homogeneous relationship networks but allow for more than a single type of entity to be displayed. Different icons indicate the type of entity. Because of the complexity of such diagrams, it is important to allow the user to provide additional information to help filter the diagram down to just the most relevant nodes and arcs. One strategy is to start with a handful of entities as input and let the system find the fewest additional nodes that allow these entities to be connected with a minimum spanning tree. Such an approach, which we refer to as "connect the dots," would, for example, allow a drug developer to discovery a potential new pathway for treating a specific disease with a drug that affects a protein target.

NETWORK-BASED REASONING APPROACHES

There are many approaches to reasoning over networks. The chart in Figure 7.5, provides a good summary of these and their applications. We will focus on just a few of them for further description in this book. Ultimately, all of these approaches should be considered when doing inference over entity networks in biology or other sciences.

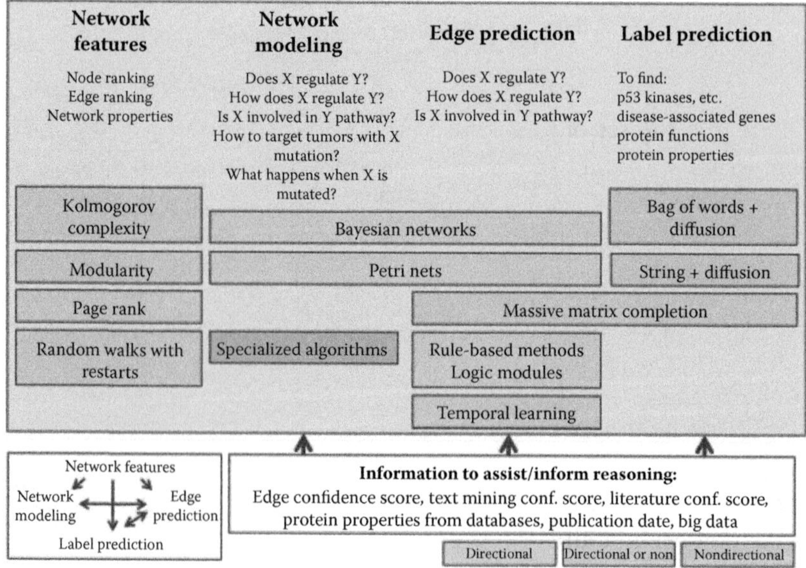

FIGURE 7.5 Approaches to reasoning over networks. (Used with permission of Lichtarge Lab, Baylor College of Medicine.)

GRAPH DIFFUSION

Using the similarity network created between entity centroids with centroid distance as the relative distance between nodes, it is possible to use a graph diffusion technique to infer how properties may be shared among entities not heretofore known to have those properties. Start with a binary vector that labels which nodes in the graph have the property in question. Then use graph diffusion to model how that property would naturally propagate through the graph, given the weights on the edges from Euclidean distance between centroids. This method can be used to create a ranked list of those entities most likely to have the property in question.

One specific form of graph diffusion that we use in our work is called simplified heat diffusion. It is formulated as follows: Given that we have a set of known entities that are considered to have the properties we like, we can use a simple heat-diffusion strategy to give a numeric ranking score to all the other entities. The strategy works as follows: Assume all the known *good* entities start with a heat value of 1.0, and every other entity starts with a heat value of 0.0. Now assume that at the next time step, each entity receives heat from its neighbors at a rate commensurate with the weighted connection in the graph.

$$\text{Heat}(x) = \sum \cos \text{distance}(x, y)^{M}$$

where y is the set of nodes with heat value 1.0. M is an exponent that represents the loss of heat over time as it passes through the connection. It prevents far-away nodes from overwhelming the signal induced by the near nodes. To find the right value of M, we may experiment with training/test sets until we find the best exponent that creates results that rank the good organisms highest.

MATRIX FACTORIZATION

Represent the entities as a nonnegative matrix of values where entity nodes are the rows and columns, and links between nodes are represented with a positive value. Matrix factorization [2] can then predict which additional links that are not already known to exist are most likely to exist in the graph. This is similar to the problem of finding the best movie for each individual based on movies rented by other individuals with similar tastes to you (Figure 7.6).

| IBM Research

Massive-scale matrix completion

- Application: predict important correspondences between items

	Avatar (2.24)	The matrix (1.92)	Up (1.18)
Alice (1.98)	? (4.4)	4 (3.8)	2 (2.3)
Bob (1.21)	3 (2.7)	2 (2.3)	? (1.4)
Charlie (2.30)	5 (5.2)	? (4.4)	3 (2.7)

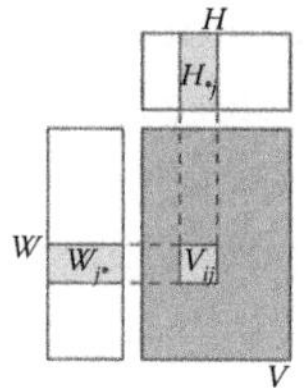

- Model:
  - $L_{ij}(W_{i*}, H_{*j})$: loss at (i, j)
  - Includes prediction error, regularization, auxiliary information, ...
  - Constraints (e.g., non-negativity)
- Find best model: $\min_{W,H} \sum_{(i,j)\in Z} L_{ij}(\mathbf{W}_{i*}, \mathbf{H}_{*j})$

FIGURE 7.6 Matrix completion.

We can use these kinds of matrix calculations to find the most likely missing links from a large graph and suggest them as new hypotheses that will likely be found true, either by a more thorough perusal of the existing literature or by doing a new experiment to validate the hypothesis.

Another possible use for such matrix-generated linkages is to provide a confidence value for existing links between entities. Links that are very unusual or would not have been predicted by the matrix factorization if they were not already there are somewhat suspect and might be flagged, especially if the evidence for them is also weak.

CONCLUSION

The examples in this chapter serve as illustrations of how we can use visualization, statistics, and other analytic models to take all the different kinds of information we have extracted and create a meaningful, interactive picture of what is going on in selected corners of the information space. Such an analysis can greatly accelerate the scientist's ability to understand the state of the art in a given domain and make informed decisions about how to move forward with future experiments or applications in the field.

REFERENCES

1. Greenwood, P. E., and Nikulin, M. S. 1996. *A Guide to Chi-Square Testing.* New York: Wiley.
2. Lee, D. D., and Seung, H. S. 2001. Algorithms for non-negative matrix factorization. *Advances in Neural Information Processing Systems.* Cambridge, MA: MIT Press.

CHAPTER 8

Taxonomies

BEGINNING WITH THIS CHAPTER and continuing for the next three chapters, we will go a little deeper into the methodologies used to implement the process we have just described. I think of this set of chapters as the toolkit, or, in other words, the bag of tricks I have up my sleeve whenever I am faced with a new discovery problem.

This chapter deals with taxonomies, which in my mind have long been the first and most important tool for understanding large amounts of unstructured content. We talked about how to create taxonomies to some degree already in the "Exploration" chapter. This chapter deals with them in more depth, and especially with their application to furthering understanding and making inferences in science.

TAXONOMY GENERATION METHODS

Our goal is to extract insights about a scientific domain from a large corpus of unstructured data. To understand a large corpus of data, human beings often leverage different taxonomies. A taxonomy is a structure that groups similar elements of the unstructured information together in a "natural" way and categorizes the large document set. Deriving insights from unstructured data can therefore be reduced to the problem of creating groups of similar pieces of data together, that is, multiple taxonomies, in a way that adds value.

In Accelerated Discovery, as in most text mining, the key problem is to define and generate the kind of taxonomies that will help us better understand the relevant scientific entities. Through much trial and error and working with real clients, we found the following four taxonomies, each with its own specific generation techniques, to be the most effective at deriving useful knowledge from unstructured information.

1. Text cluster–based taxonomies
2. Time-based taxonomies
3. Keyword taxonomies
4. Numerical value taxonomies

No single taxonomy or the method of generating it alone is sufficient for every situation, but the combination of these methods together creates a powerful template for gaining insights from unstructured data in a robust and repeatable fashion.

SNIPPETS

Before describing the taxonomy generation algorithms, it is important to clarify the content on which these taxonomies are built. Text snippetization is an important technique for analyzing text content. There may be diverse topics in one document, even though only a few sentences might be relevant to the analysis subject. To more precisely analyze the text in the context of scientific objectives, we generate snippets from documents. A snippet is a small text segment around a specified keyword. The text segment can be defined by sentence boundaries or by the number of words. For example, the snippet may cover the sentence before and after the word "protein." In general, snippets are built around the keywords representing a focused topic such as "protein folding" or a set of organism or gene names.

TEXT CLUSTERING

When the user has no preconceived idea about what entities the document collection might contain, text clustering is effective to create an initial breakdown of the documents into clusters, by grouping together documents that have similar word content. To facilitate this process, we represent the documents in a vector-space model. We represent each document as a vector of weighted frequencies of the document features (words and phrases). We use the *txn* weighting scheme, which emphasizes words with high frequency in a document and normalizes each document vector to have unit Euclidean norm.

The words and phrases that make up the document feature space are determined firstly by counting which words occur most frequently (in the most documents) in the text. A standard *stopword* list is used to eliminate words such as "and," "but," and "the" [1]. The top N words are retained in the first pass, where the value of N may vary depending on the length of the documents, the number of documents, and the number of categories to be created. Typically N = 2000 is sufficient for 10,000 short documents of about 200 words to be divided into thirty categories. A second pass counts the frequency of the two-word phrases that occur using these words. Two words are consecutive and have no intervening non-stopwords. We then prune the overall list to keep only the N most frequent words and phrases. This becomes the feature space of the document corpus. Finally, we index the documents by their feature occurrences (i.e., word counts). The user may edit this feature space as desired to improve clustering performance, such as adding words and phrases the user deems important. Stemming is incorporated to create a default synonym table that the user may edit.

Our clustering algorithm is unique in that it specifically addresses the cluster labeling/naming problem [2]. Standard clustering approaches, such as k-means [3] clustering, frequently create categories with names that are difficult for a human being to interpret. To address this problem, we developed a document categorization strategy based on categories centered on selected individual terms in the dictionary. We then employ a single iteration of k-means to the generated categories in order to refine the membership, so that documents that contain more than one of the selected terms can be placed in the category that is best suited to the overall term content of the document. Note that the alternative strategy of putting such documents in more than one category (i.e., multiple membership) is less desirable because it increases the average size of each category and defeats the purpose of summarization via the divide-and-conquer strategy inherent in a document clustering. Once the clusters are created, we name them with the single term that was used to create each cluster in the first place, thus avoiding the complex name problem described above.

Selecting which terms to use for generating categories is critical. Our approach is to rank all discovered terms in the data set based on a normalized measure of cohesion calculated using the following formula:

$$\text{cohension}(T,n) = \frac{\sum_{x \in T} \cos(\text{centroid}(T), x)}{|T|^n}$$

where T is the set of documents that contain a given term, centroid(T) is the average vector of all these documents, and n is a parameter used to adjust for variance in category size (typically $n=0.9$). The cosine distance between document vectors is defined to be

$$\cos(X,Y)=\frac{X\cdot Y}{||X||\cdot||Y||}$$

Terms that score relatively high with this measure tend to be those with a significant number of examples having many common words. Adjusting n downward tends to surface more general terms with larger matching sets, while adjusting it upward gives more specific terms.

The algorithm selects enough of the most cohesive terms to get 80%–90% of the data categorized. Terms are selected in cohesive order, skipping those terms in the list that do not add a significant number (e.g., >3) of additional examples to those already categorized with previous terms. The algorithm halts when at least 80% of the data has been categorized and the uncategorized examples are placed in a "miscellaneous" category. The resulting categories are then refined using a single iteration of k-means (i.e., each document is placed in the category of the nearest centroid as calculated by the term membership just described). Such a text clustering-based taxonomy represents a "table of contents" of the data around a particular area of interest. It allows the analyst to understand the full spectrum of key words or phrases used most commonly used by scientists when describing their domain.

TIME-BASED TAXONOMIES

Time-based taxonomies use the document creation date to classify data into "chronologically contiguous" categories. Journal publications, conference papers, and patents are usually each labeled with a date. When chronologically sorted, these dates divide the snippets for a given topic into chronologically contiguous categories. Many methods can be used to generate time-based taxonomies. They can be applied in different situations and for different purposes. We describe a few methods that we have found useful here.

Partitions Based on the Calendar

Partitions based on the calendar use the artificial demarcations that occur for day, week, month, and year. The appropriate granularity of the partition depends on the span of data being analyzed. Typically between 10 and 30 categories are sufficient, so for a year's worth of data you would partition by month, while for a month's worth of data you might partition by day. Calendar-based partitions are most useful for drawing trends, because the data are easily digestible. The disadvantage is that interesting events may span multiple categories and that the data may tend to "clump" (be heavily skewed) into one or more categories.

Partitions Based on Sample Size

To eliminate data clumping, one strategy is to force equal size categories. A specific number of categories is targeted independent of data (usually ten categories is a good number for analysis). We then sort the data chronologically and split it up into ten equal size categories, each having data that are relatively coincident in time. Sample size–based partitions are most useful for accurately spotting emerging (or declining) topics over time. The disadvantage is that each category may span a different sized time period, making the visualization of results confusing.

Partitions on Known Events

In some situations, particular events that happened in time are established and easily identified, such as discovery of a new organism or property, historical survey articles, or a particular important conference or publication. In this case the data naturally partition themselves into three primary categories: before, during, and after the event. Such an approach guarantees that the time-based partition is related to something important in the data stream. It is also easy to visualize and understand because there are only three classes. However, it may be difficult to isolate the event in time with a high degree of accuracy. This approach is also useless if no particular event occurs or is known to have occurred in the time interval under consideration.

KEYWORD TAXONOMIES

One simple yet important taxonomy is based purely on the occurrence of keywords or terms. One example of such a taxonomy is related organisms or proteins. Often these entity names are known a priori by the analyst, but in other cases they can be discovered by perusing the dictionary of terms generated during the text clustering process. The number of categories in the entity-name taxonomy is usually equal to the number of keywords + 2. The two additional categories are "miscellaneous," for those snippets that do not mention any entity (if any), and "ambiguous," for those snippets that mention more than one entity name. We found an "ambiguous" class approach is sometimes preferable to the multimembership approach for two reasons:

1. Analyst does not have to read the same snippets again in different categories when perusing the category.
2. The mentions of multiple entities could be a qualitatively different event than the mention of a single entity by itself (e.g., to indicate a protein complex).

In addition to physical entities of interest, like organism or proteins, keyword taxonomies can capture nearly any other issue of a priori importance to the scientist, though the keywords themselves may need to be refined to match how the concepts may appear in the data. The assumption is that the occurrence of such issues is important regardless of its prevalence in the data.

Lists of keywords in a scientific domain frequently come from well known, public ontologies—for example, the list of all genes provided by the Human Genome Organisation (HUGO) [4] or of proteins by the Universal Protein Resource (UniProt) [5]. These lists are frequently just the starting point, however. Further refinement must be done to capture all the variations by which these dictionary terms may occur in text.

Regular Expression Patterns

Regular expression patterns are another way to recognize and extract keyword entities.

> A **regular expression** (abbreviated as **regexp** or **regex**, with plural forms **regexps**, **regexes**, or **regexen**) is a string that describes or matches a set of strings, according to certain syntax rules. Regular expressions are used by many text editors and utilities to search and manipulate bodies of text based on certain patterns. Many programming languages support regular expressions for string manipulation. For example, Perl and Tcl have a powerful regular expression engine built directly into their syntax. The set of

> utilities (including the editor sed and the filter grep) provided by Unix distributions were the first to popularize the concept of regular expressions. [6]

What regular expressions provide for us is the ability to represent nearly any kind of text sequence that can be represented as a dictionary of string patterns. We can use regular expressions to create features by employing domain-specific dictionaries when the features space is first created. An example of such a regular expression dictionary is shown below.

```
DateString=\d/\d\d/\d\d
PriceString=\$\d+\.\d\d
PlanetString=Mercury|Venus|Earth|Mars|Jupiter|Saturn|
Uranus|Neptune
IBM=IBM|International Business Machines|big blue
```

The first line creates a feature called DateString whenever it sees something like 9/27/06 anywhere in the text of an example (/d=any digit). The second line creates the term PriceString whenever it sees something like $23.05. The third line creates the term PlanetString whenever one of the names of the planets appears in the text. And the last line creates the term IBM whenever any of the identified names for the company are used.

NUMERICAL VALUE TAXONOMIES

Not all relevant information exists in text. We also need to combine unstructured information with more structured kinds of data. Some kinds of structured information are categorical in nature. An example would be the disease listed for a given patient record. For this type of information, we can consume it much the way we do unstructured text. We only need to be sure to treat the full disease name, given as a categorical value, as if it were a single word in the document. This will allow it to get the correct value in our feature vector.

Numerical values present a harder problem. They are not simply present or absent but consist of a kind and a number that need to be dealt with in such a way that the magnitude of the number is accounted for. We describe here a general approach to converting numeric values into a taxonomy that can be merged with other kinds of information in the domain documents.

Turning Numbers into X-Tiles

Assume we have a single number assigned to each patient, for example, the patient's body temperature given in degrees centigrade. To convert this number into a categorical value in a useful way, we sort the values from low to high and then partition these values into X-tiles; for example, into quintiles if we want five categorical values. The number of tiles we create depends on what is appropriate for each situation. Consult with the domain expert, but also look at actual sample data to be sure the categories make some sense in terms of intracategory similarity and intercategory difference. If numerical values are often repeated, you may need to adjust the category break points to ensure that there is always a distinct difference between values for each category. This is more important than having categories of exactly equal size (as measured by number of examples).

Categories can be named by the numerical range they represent in the data. The name of the measurement itself can then be appended to this range, and this combination can then be a single "word" in the data for the example, which can then be easily combined with document words and other category values. These can then be used to generate taxonomies of any number of categories or in combination to do clustering based on multiple numeric value inputs.

EMPLOYING TAXONOMIES

After useful taxonomies are created, the analyst must understand what the categories in the taxonomy actually contain. Next we look for correlations between categories in different taxonomies. In addition, the dictionary is also compared to the categories and any unusually high correlations between terms and categories are noted.

Understanding Categories

Our primary representation of each category is the centroid. The distance metric that is employed to compare documents to each other and to the category centroids is the cosine similarity metric [3]. During the category editing phase, we do not rigidly require each document to belong to the category of its nearest centroid, nor do we strictly require every document to belong to only one category.

Feature Bar Charts

Summarization can help the user understand what a category contains without having to read through all documents in a category. Summarization techniques that extract text from the individual documents [7] are ineffective in practice for the purpose of summarizing an entire document category, especially when the theme of that category is diverse. Instead, we employ a feature bar chart to help explain what a category contains. This chart has an entry for every dictionary term (feature) that occurs in any document of the category. Each entry consists of two bars: a red bar to indicate what percentage of the documents in the category contain the feature, and a blue bar to indicate how frequently the feature occurs in the background population of documents from which the category was drawn. The bars are sorted in decreasing order of the difference between blue and red, such that the most important features of a category are shown at the beginning of the chart. This method quickly summarizes the important features of a category with their relative importance indicated by the size of the bars.

Sorting of Examples

Reading random samples in the category may lead to a skewed understanding of the category content, especially if the sample is small compared to the category size (which is often the case in practice). To further help users to understand the category content, we sort documents based on the "most typical" first or "least typical" first criteria. In vector-space terms, we essentially sort in order of distance from category centroid (i.e., the most typical is closest to centroid, the least typical is furthest from centroid). Such a technique has two advantages: Reading documents in most typical order can help the user quickly understand what the category is generally about without having to read all documents in the category, while reading the least typical documents can help the user understand the scope of the category and whether there is conceptual purity.

Category/Category Co-Occurrence

Category-to-category co-occurrence compares different taxonomies in order to discover where an unusually high degree of association might reside. One way to visualize such relationships is via a co-occurrence table (cotable), which shows how the data break down across all the combinations of categories in two different taxonomies.

Assuming no relationship exists that ties a particular sentiment to a particular brand, we would expect to find around (X*Y) in a cell for a given sentiment and brand, where X is the percentage of times a given sentiment occurs and Y is the percentage of times the brand occurs. Let us call this expected value E. An exceptional value is something greater than E, indicating an association stronger than we expected. That will be different for every cell in the cotable, since the number of snippets for each sentiment and brand differs.

Furthermore, we can get a relative significance for different values in the cotable, such as distinguishing whether a five occurring in one cell is more interesting than a ten occurring in a different cell, by using the chi-squared test [8]—a statistical test that calculates the likelihood of seeing any particular value in the cell of a cotable. The smaller this probability, the less likely the value, the more interesting it is from a data-mining perspective. When a very low probability value occurs, it suggests that our original assumption about no relationship existing between the taxonomies was incorrect. There actually may be a relationship revealed by the data. However, a correlation does not signify a definitive relationship between categories. It indicates something worth investigating further. We shade the values of the cotable accordingly to show such calculated probabilities. This is much easier to read than many small decimal floating point values.

Dictionary/Category Co-Occurrence

Another type of co-occurrence analysis compares a taxonomy of snippets to the dictionary of words created during text clustering. While such an analysis is not necessarily interesting for the text clustering taxonomy itself, for the other three taxonomies the results can be very enlightening. Such a cotable contains the columns of taxonomy categories and the rows of dictionary terms, sorted in alphabetical order. By sorting for significance against one of the taxonomy classes (highlighted cells) we can answer the following kinds of questions:

1. What issues are emerging as important relatively recently in the data (time vs. dictionary)?
2. What issues are associated with a particular organism or protein (keyword vs. dictionary)?
3. What issues are driving a particular measured value for an entity (numeric values)?

Dictionary-based co-occurrence analysis is one of the most powerful ways to discover insights you do not already know. Text clustering may also reveal significantly large topics and themes driving opinion on the web, but it may miss smaller, less prevalent issues that arise only for a particular brand or in a small window of time. Dictionary co-occurrence fills in such a gap.

REFERENCES

1. Spangler, S., and Kreulen, J. 2002. *Interactive Methods for Taxonomy Editing and Validation*. New York: ACM CIKM.
2. Spangler, W. S., et al. 2006. Machines in the conversation: Detecting themes and trends in information communication streams. *IBM Systems Journal, 45*(4): 785–799.
3. Agrawal, R. 1999. Data mining: Crossing the chasm. Keynote at the 5th ACM SIGKDD International Conference on Knowledge Discovery and Data Mining, San Diego, CA.
4. Povey, S., et al. 2001. The HUGO gene nomenclature committee (HGNC). *Human Genetics, 109*(6): 678–680.
5. UniProt Consortium. 2008. The universal protein resource (UniProt). *Nucleic Acids Research, 36*(Suppl 1): D190–D195.
6. http://en.wikipedia.org/wiki/Regular_expression.
7. Jing, H., Barzilay, R., McKeown, K., and Elhadad, M. 1998. Summarization evaluation methods experiments and analysis. In *AAAI Intelligent Text Summarization Workshop* (pp. 60–68), Stanford, CA.
8. Press, W., et al. 1992. *Numerical Recipes in C* (2nd edn, pp. 620–623). New York: Cambridge University Press.

CHAPTER 9

Orthogonal Comparison

THE CATEGORIES GENERATED VIA taxonomies lead directly to connections through the use of orthogonal comparison. These connections are often evidence of some fundamental relationship that often enables significant insights about the organization contained within the information space. A high degree of co-occurrence is the first symptom of a connection. Co-occurrence means that two different categories or entities occur together. To find the best connections, a proper statistical analysis should be employed, that is, one that does not simply look at the size of a particular co-occurrence but also takes the context of that co-occurrence into account. Assuming no relationship exists that ties together two particular categories from different taxonomies, we would expect to find around $(A \times B)$ occurrences of A and B together, where A is the percentage of times one category occurs and B is the percentage of times the other occurs. Let us call this expected value E. An exceptional value means that $A \times B > E$, indicating an association that is stronger than we expected. The value of E will usually will be different for every combination of categories, since the size of each category may be different.

Furthermore, we can get a relative significance for different co-occurrence values by using, for example, a chi-squared test to calculate the likelihood of seeing any particular value co-occurrence between two independent variables. The smaller this probability, the more interesting it is from a data-mining perspective. When a very low probability value occurs, it suggests that our original assumption that there was no relationship existing between the categories was incorrect. There actually may be a relationship revealed by the data. However, a significant co-occurrence does not signify a definitive relationship between categories. It indicates something worth investigating further.

In addition to category–category co-occurrence relationships, category–feature relationships can also be explored. Feature-based co-occurrence analysis is one of the most powerful ways to discover insights you do not already know. While taxonomies reveal significantly large topics and themes present in the data, they may miss smaller, less prevalent issues that arise only for a particular data segment or in a small window of time. Feature-based co-occurrence fills in the gap.

AFFINITY

A co-occurrence table provides a way to compare two different taxonomies, entity by entity, to observe any interesting relationships that might be present between entities of different taxonomies. More frequent that expected levels of co-occurrence are a signal that somehow the two entities, heretofore assumed to be independent, are in fact connected through some phenomenon or shared intrinsic characteristic. We call such a characteristic an "affinity" between entities. Affinities are assumed to be potentially interesting but not necessarily causal or even important until the evidence shows otherwise.

There are three basic kinds of affinity that we have observed to take place when we measure levels of co-occurrence between orthogonal entities. Each has its own special meaning that is distinct, and so typically we visualize this distinction using a color or shading of the cells in a 2×2 table.

1. High affinity: High affinity means a probability of zero (0.0F) using a Chi-squared test. Zero-probability events (i.e., those where $p < 1.0 \times 10^{-99}$) are typically due to some kind of domain tautology, as in whenever X occurs Y must also occur. An example would be "water" having a high affinity with "oxygen" and "hydrogen" since its molecular formula is H_2O. This does not mean that we will always see water co-occurring with oxygen and hydrogen in every single document, but rather that the co-occurrence is not surprising to a domain expert and is due to some structural configuration in the domain that brings these two elements together on a regular basis. High-affinity relationships are typically "trivial" from the domain expert's point of view, though they may be quite revealing to the data scientist and helpful in structuring the overall domain ontology.

2. Moderate affinity: Moderate affinity means a statistically significant *p* value greater than zero. Typically this means less than 0.001 or at least less than 0.01, depending on the overall size of the cotable (larger cotables demand a higher standard of proof, because they have so many chances to find accidental or coincidental relationships). This level of affinity is the most interesting, because it typically designates a relationship between X and Y wherein whenever X occurs, Y is more likely to occur than usual but is not always determined to do so. This suggests that X may influence Y (or vice versa), which could indicate a causal connection (direct or indirect) or some kind of shared precedent in the causal chain (if X and Y denote events of some kind); or, if X and Y are physical entities, there is the possibility that they interact in some way or have something else in common in terms of physical structure. An example would be a protein connected to a disease. The mutation of the protein may be a critical element of the disease itself, or the protein may be merely be secondarily associated with the disease manifestation. Domain experts are sometimes well aware of these connections and sometimes not. When they are not, it is best to validate the connection by observing some typical examples of documents that contain both entities.

3. Low affinity: Low affinity indicates a *p* value less than 0.5 but greater than the significance level. In this case, the value of the co-occurrence should be greater than we would expect by random chance but less than enough to be sure that chance was not the reason. Low-affinity scores should be evaluated based on the support. It may simply be that there is not enough data for both X and Y to provide a meaningful measure of their potential connectedness. On the other hand, if there is sufficient data present, it may indicate that a weak relationship might still exist between the two entities, for example, there may be not a direct cause but an indirect influence between X and Y. Again, the evidence of examples should be investigated before coming to any conclusion.

COTABLE DIMENSIONS

Setting up a proper co-occurrence table requires thinking carefully about what entities should appear in the rows and columns. First of all, it is important to organize each dimension around a coherent taxonomy.

What this means in practice is that all the rows should be entities of the same kind, all the columns should be entities of the same kind, and the rows should all be different kinds from the columns. This last criterion is somewhat optional. You can create a cotable where the rows and columns are the same, but the relationships found there will usually be less interesting, often having more to do with inherent similarity of structure or role than with some new discovery of value.

But even more important than having rows and columns as different entity types, those types should be "orthogonal" to each other. By that I mean that there should be no overlap, either inherent or implied, between entities of one type and another. A good example of two different taxonomies that are not orthogonal would be "cities" and "states." While the states are all different from the cities, they are definitely overlapping in structure, since each city would naturally co-occur with one and only one state (the state in which it is found). You can easily imagine what an uninteresting cotable a city–state combination would produce. It would merely tell you what you could already discover more easily from an atlas or Wikipedia.

A good example of orthogonal dimensions is "organism" and "environment." While it is true that some specialized organisms live in only one place, it is generally the case that organisms are found in many different locations, and these discoveries are themselves interesting. So each time we find a connection between a specific environment and a particular species, we have the potential to discover interesting knowledge.

COTABLE LAYOUT AND SORTING

The most natural way to present a cotable is with the shortest list of entities across the top (column header) and the longer list down the left-hand side (row header). The value in each cell should be the number of times the row and column occur. A total row and total column should also be included to indicate the frequency of each entity on its own. A total for the entire table (basically a count of all the unique documents that could potentially contain any of the entities, without double counting) should also be provided somewhere (Figure 9.1).

In addition to the number of documents in each cell, it also helps to provide some indication of the probability and the relation to the expected value, or at least whether the combination of row and column has high, medium, or low affinity (or no affinity) based on the definitions provided

Very High Affinity = Moderate Affinity = Low Affinity = No Affinit

	Size	alkane	alkene	aromatic
Thermincola carboxydiphila	1	0 (1.0)	0 (1.0)	0 (1.0)
Thermincola ferriacetica	2	0 (1.0)	0 (1.0)	0 (1.0)
Thermoprotei NO	1	0 (1.0)	0 (1.0)	0 (1.0)
Thermus aquaticus	529	0 (1.0)	0 (1.0)	7 (1.0)
Thioalcalovibrio denitricans	1	0 (1.0)	0 (1.0)	0 (1.0)
Treponema isoptericolens	1	0 (1.0)	0 (1.0)	0 (1.0)
Trichodesmium erythraeum	32	0 (1.0)	0 (1.0)	0 (1.0)
Triticum aestivum	937	1 (1.0)	0 (1.0)	4 (1.0)
Trojanella thessalonices	1	0 (1.0)	0 (1.0)	0 (1.0)
Variovorax paradoxus	72	1 (0.578...	0 (1.0)	6 (0.004...
Variovorax parodoxus	1	0 (1.0)	0 (1.0)	0 (1.0)
Veillonella alcalescens	78	0 (1.0)	0 (1.0)	0 (1.0)
Vibrio alginolyticus	890	0 (1.0)	0 (1.0)	0 (1.0)
Vibrio cholerae	977	0 (1.0)	0 (1.0)	1 (1.0)
Vibrio hepatarius	3	0 (1.0)	0 (1.0)	0 (1.0)
Vibrio sputorum	4	0 (1.0)	0 (1.0)	0 (1.0)
Wolinella succinogenes	191	0 (1.0)	0 (1.0)	2 (1.0)
Xanthobacter autotrophicus	193	55 (0.0)	5 (1.317...	0 (1.0)
Xanthomonas axonopodis	284	0 (1.0)	0 (1.0)	0 (1.0)
Xanthomonas campestris	999	1 (1.0)	0 (1.0)	7 (1.0)
Zoogloea ramigera	65	0 (1.0)	0 (1.0)	1 (1.0)
Zoogloea resiniphila	8	0 (1.0)	0 (1.0)	0 (1.0)
Zymomonas mobilamp	1	0 (1.0)	0 (1.0)	0 (1.0)
Zymomonas mobilis	647	0 (1.0)	2 (0.225...	10 (1.0)
Total	55548	447	75	1567

FIGURE 9.1 A typical cotable showing entity sizes on the left and bottom and an overall total in the lower left.

previously. This can be done through shading or a second value provided in parenthesis inside the cell.

Since the number of rows in a cotable (and even the number of columns) can be quite long—in fact longer than the display screen—it makes sense to provide a sorting utility that will bring to the top for any column (or to the left for any row) those elements that are most highly associated with the selected entity. This association can be measured in two different ways (and both kinds of sorting should be enabled): by overall co-occurrence count (the first number in the cell), or by Chi-squared probability (the number in parenthesis or the number used to determine affinity).

FEATURE-BASED COTABLES

An alternative to using taxonomies as the basic ingredient for cotables is to use a feature space, or dictionary, as the long dimension (rows). Such dictionaries can be entirely data driven, domain driven, or some combination of both. Data-driven dictionaries provide an opportunity to discover which terms are most closely associated with each entity in a taxonomy. Such correlations are frequently helpful in finding new synonyms for an entity or discovering additional entities or relationships that an entity may be involved in. Domain dictionaries allow the data scientist to explore how a particular vocabulary generated from a domain-relevant source may fit with the current domain ontology as represented by the entities in the columns (Figure 9.2).

The term in the feature space can include regular expression patterns, which are defined to be combinations of many different characteristics or entity behaviors. Thus, they can even help uncover or verify domain-specific rules that govern an entity's interactions with its environment or predict qualities an entity might be expected to possess that are not literally known.

Very High Affinity = Moderate Affinity = Low Affinity = No Affinity =

	Count	alkane	alkene	aromatic	benzene	bitumen
ability	4415	58 (7.965...	19 (2.546...	198 (3.42...	76 (3.647...	0 (1.0)
able	3410	66 (2.373...	7 (0.2487...	207 (2.76...	70 (2.012...	0 (1.0)
absence	2424	18 (1.0)	5 (0.3286...	76 (0.339...	24 (1.0)	0 (1.0)
absent	655	7 (0.4468...	0 (1.0)	10 (1.0)	6 (1.0)	1 (1.5936...
absorption	879	5 (1.0)	2 (0.4514...	19 (1.0)	6 (1.0)	0 (1.0)
abundance	666	7 (0.4740...	1 (0.9147...	22 (0.449...	6 (1.0)	0 (1.0)
abundant	720	9 (0.1782...	1 (0.9772...	22 (0.701...	5 (1.0)	1 (1.1321...
acceptor	944	2 (1.0)	1 (1.0)	67 (1.204...	24 (4.717...	0 (1.0)
acceptors	508	0 (1.0)	0 (1.0)	34 (1.190...	9 (0.1039...	0 (1.0)
account	665	10 (0.042...	0 (1.0)	16 (1.0)	3 (1.0)	0 (1.0)
accumulated	960	18 (1.809...	11 (7.712...	49 (1.632...	18 (0.010...	0 (1.0)
accumulation	1696	15 (0.708...	2 (1.0)	47 (1.0)	15 (1.0)	0 (1.0)
acetate	1785	14 (1.0)	3 (0.6991...	88 (4.496...	22 (0.421...	0 (1.0)
acetic	378	2 (1.0)	0 (1.0)	16 (0.096...	3 (1.0)	0 (1.0)
acetobutylicum	746	0 (1.0)	0 (1.0)	8 (1.0)	2 (1.0)	0 (1.0)
acetogenesis	36	0 (1.0)	0 (1.0)	0 (1.0)	0 (1.0)	0 (1.0)
acetyl	760	2 (1.0)	0 (1.0)	29 (0.095...	9 (0.6981...	0 (1.0)
acetyl_coa	345	0 (1.0)	0 (1.0)	23 (1.507...	4 (0.8299...	0 (1.0)
achieved	1305	13 (0.433...	2 (0.8559...	34 (1.0)	17 (0.348...	0 (1.0)
achromobacter	603	8 (0.1491...	0 (1.0)	15 (1.0)	8 (0.4893...	0 (1.0)
achromobacter_xylosoxidans	424	4 (0.7483...	0 (1.0)	10 (1.0)	6 (0.4480...	0 (1.0)
acid	11574	117 (0.00...	19 (0.337...	516 (5.98...	160 (5.15...	0 (1.0)
acid_residues	789	7 (0.7939...	1 (1.0)	38 (6.515...	11 (0.327...	0 (1.0)
acid_sequence	1861	29 (2.145...	1 (1.0)	94 (3.416...	29 (0.025...	0 (1.0)
acid_sequences	775	5 (1.0)	1 (1.0)	43 (3.872...	21 (4.174...	0 (1.0)
acidic	566	5 (0.8332...	1 (0.7861...	17 (0.792...	4 (1.0)	0 (1.0)
acidocaldarius	511	0 (1.0)	0 (1.0)	8 (1.0)	1 (1.0)	0 (1.0)
acids	4152	88 (6.347...	11 (0.017...	245 (1.22...	62 (0.002...	0 (1.0)
acinetobacter	2547	52 (8.499...	1 (1.0)	65 (1.0)	6 (1.0)	0 (1.0)
acinetobacter_calcoaceticus	1300	28 (3.600...	0 (1.0)	38 (0.822...	4 (1.0)	0 (1.0)
acquired	829	3 (1.0)	0 (1.0)	11 (1.0)	5 (1.0)	0 (1.0)
act	677	5 (1.0)	0 (1.0)	24 (0.252...	8 (0.7194...	0 (1.0)
action	1261	7 (1.0)	0 (1.0)	29 (1.0)	15 (0.602...	0 (1.0)
activate	1616	11 (1.0)	5 (0.0526...	72 (5.640...	25 (0.042...	0 (1.0)
activation	1552	14 (0.663...	4 (0.1817...	57 (0.039...	21 (0.221...	0 (1.0)
activator	433	3 (1.0)	2 (0.0629...	13 (0.819...	8 (0.0976...	0 (1.0)
active	5631	70 (1.026...	16 (0.001...	167 (0.48...	44 (1.0)	1 (0.0617...
active_site	1358	36 (1.259...	8 (3.9540...	61 (1.663...	15 (0.819...	0 (1.0)
activities	3723	30 (0.993...	8 (0.1694...	124 (0.05...	63 (5.301...	0 (1.0)
activity	13969	133 (0.02...	19 (0.970...	421 (0.11...	167 (0.03...	0 (1.0)
acute	821	0 (1.0)	0 (1.0)	1 (1.0)	3 (1.0)	0 (1.0)
acyl	537	9 (0.0231...	2 (0.1321...	21 (0.125...	2 (1.0)	0 (1.0)
adaptation	663	13 (8.027...	0 (1.0)	19 (0.944...	6 (1.0)	0 (1.0)

FIGURE 9.2 Dictionary-based cotable.

COTABLE APPLICATIONS

Cotables can be used during all phases of the Accelerated Discovery process. In exploration and organization, cotables help to refine the definitions of the entities and discover or confirm the underlying structure of the entity hierarchies. In relationship extraction, cotables can often identify where relationships exist and help to refine the definitions or patterns that identify them. Finally, in inference, cotables represent a potential means for discovering the key characteristics that define why a certain type of entity has a certain property or lacks it.

Cotables are a uniquely useful tool for figuring out the inner workings of a scientific domain by using statistics to uncover the hidden connections that exist between disparate elements.

EXAMPLE: MICROBES AND THEIR PROPERTIES

In this example, we want to get a picture of what environments different microbes tend to be found in. Some microbes are more ubiquitous than others, and so we would like to focus on microbes that are very specific to each environment of interest. This means we want to see a significant level of co-occurrence between the microbe and the environment, not just a high level of co-occurrence. Figure 9.3 presents an example cotable showing this kind of result.

Microbes are shown on the left-hand side, and various environments are listed across the top. Where we see red highlighting indicates a very high significant level of co-occurrence. In such cases, the microbe in question almost certainly lives exclusively in that type of environment. We can also use significance sorting to find all microbes that seem to be related to a given environment (Figure 9.4).

The number in parenthesis is the chi-squared probability of the level of co-occurrence between organism and "wastewater" occurring by random chance. It should be noted that some the co-occurrence levels (e.g., values of one or two) are much too small for an accurate Chi-squared probability to be calculated. We provide the numbers anyway, not as absolute probability scores but as a relative measure of potential interest in the combination. It is up to the domain expert to determine whether such a small sample size is still of interest. In many cases, we have found that scientists are interested in rare occurrences because they reveal something that was not yet common knowledge.

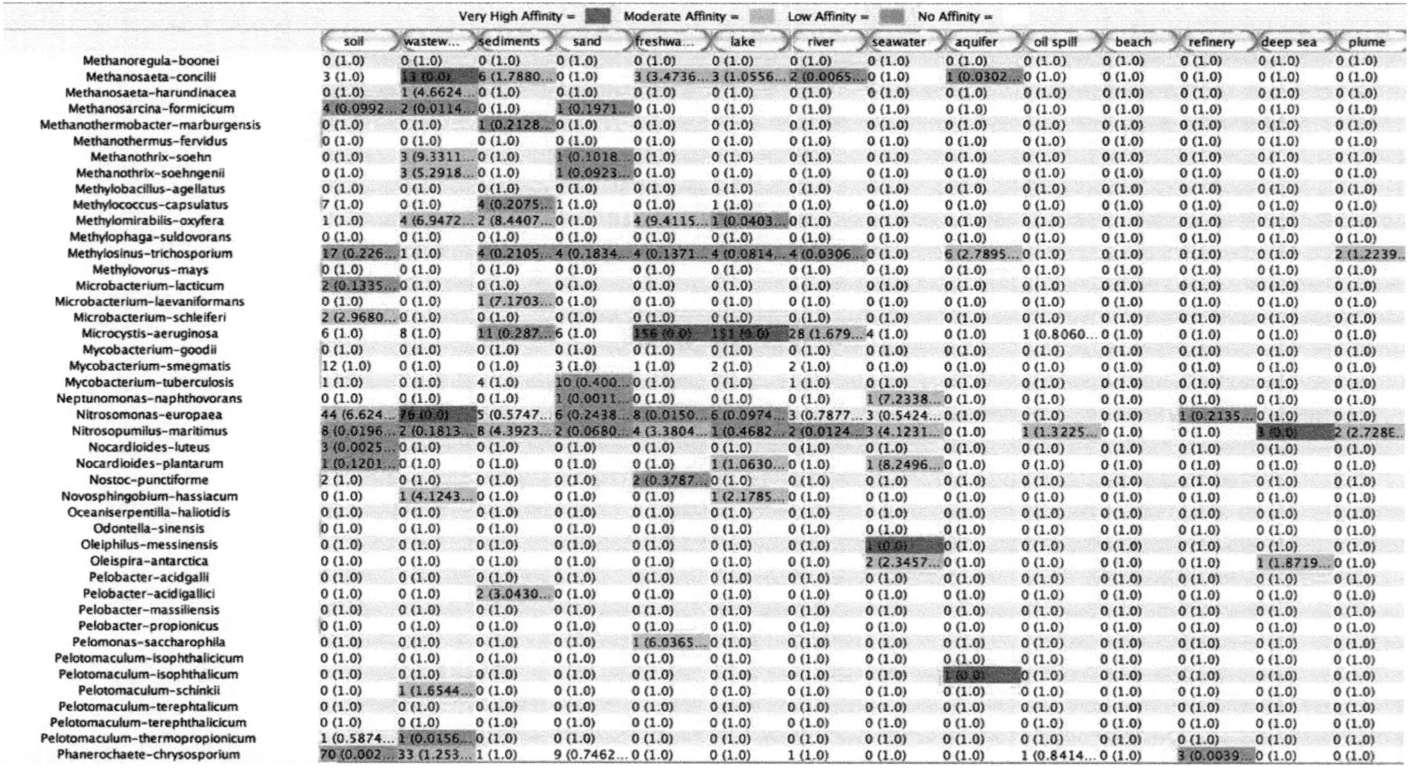

Very High Affinity = Moderate Affinity = Low Affinity = No Affinity =

	soil	wastew...	sediments	sand	freshwa...	lake	river	seawater	aquifer	oil spill	beach	refinery	deep sea	plume
Methanoregula-boonei	0 (1.0)	0 (1.0)	0 (1.0)	0 (1.0)	0 (1.0)	0 (1.0)	0 (1.0)	0 (1.0)	0 (1.0)	0 (1.0)	0 (1.0)	0 (1.0)	0 (1.0)	0 (1.0)
Methanosaeta-concilii	3 (1.0)	13 (0.0)	6 (1.7880...	0 (1.0)	3 (3.4736...	3 (1.0556...	2 (0.0065...	0 (1.0)	1 (0.0302...	0 (1.0)	0 (1.0)	0 (1.0)	0 (1.0)	0 (1.0)
Methanosaeta-harundinacea	0 (1.0)	1 (4.6624...	0 (1.0)	0 (1.0)	0 (1.0)	0 (1.0)	0 (1.0)	0 (1.0)	0 (1.0)	0 (1.0)	0 (1.0)	0 (1.0)	0 (1.0)	0 (1.0)
Methanosarcina-formicicum	4 (0.0992...	2 (0.0114...	0 (1.0)	1 (0.1971...	0 (1.0)	0 (1.0)	0 (1.0)	0 (1.0)	0 (1.0)	0 (1.0)	0 (1.0)	0 (1.0)	0 (1.0)	0 (1.0)
Methanothermobacter-marburgensis	0 (1.0)	0 (1.0)	1 (0.2128...	0 (1.0)	0 (1.0)	0 (1.0)	0 (1.0)	0 (1.0)	0 (1.0)	0 (1.0)	0 (1.0)	0 (1.0)	0 (1.0)	0 (1.0)
Methanothermus-fervidus	0 (1.0)	0 (1.0)	0 (1.0)	0 (1.0)	0 (1.0)	0 (1.0)	0 (1.0)	0 (1.0)	0 (1.0)	0 (1.0)	0 (1.0)	0 (1.0)	0 (1.0)	0 (1.0)
Methanothrix-soehn	0 (1.0)	3 (9.3311...	0 (1.0)	1 (0.1018...	0 (1.0)	0 (1.0)	0 (1.0)	0 (1.0)	0 (1.0)	0 (1.0)	0 (1.0)	0 (1.0)	0 (1.0)	0 (1.0)
Methanothrix-soehngenii	0 (1.0)	3 (5.2918...	0 (1.0)	1 (0.0923...	0 (1.0)	0 (1.0)	0 (1.0)	0 (1.0)	0 (1.0)	0 (1.0)	0 (1.0)	0 (1.0)	0 (1.0)	0 (1.0)
Methylobacillus-agellatus	0 (1.0)	0 (1.0)	0 (1.0)	0 (1.0)	0 (1.0)	0 (1.0)	0 (1.0)	0 (1.0)	0 (1.0)	0 (1.0)	0 (1.0)	0 (1.0)	0 (1.0)	0 (1.0)
Methylococcus-capsulatus	7 (1.0)	0 (1.0)	4 (0.2075...	1 (1.0)	0 (1.0)	1 (1.0)	0 (1.0)	0 (1.0)	0 (1.0)	0 (1.0)	0 (1.0)	0 (1.0)	0 (1.0)	0 (1.0)
Methylomirabilis-oxyfera	1 (1.0)	4 (6.9472...	2 (8.4407...	0 (1.0)	4 (9.4115...	1 (0.0403...	0 (1.0)	0 (1.0)	0 (1.0)	0 (1.0)	0 (1.0)	0 (1.0)	0 (1.0)	0 (1.0)
Methylophaga-suldovorans	0 (1.0)	0 (1.0)	0 (1.0)	0 (1.0)	0 (1.0)	0 (1.0)	0 (1.0)	0 (1.0)	0 (1.0)	0 (1.0)	0 (1.0)	0 (1.0)	0 (1.0)	0 (1.0)
Methylosinus-trichosporium	17 (0.226...	1 (1.0)	4 (0.2105...	4 (0.1834...	4 (0.1371...	4 (0.0814...	4 (0.0306...	0 (1.0)	6 (2.7895...	0 (1.0)	0 (1.0)	0 (1.0)	0 (1.0)	2 (1.2239..
Methylovorus-mays	0 (1.0)	0 (1.0)	0 (1.0)	0 (1.0)	0 (1.0)	0 (1.0)	0 (1.0)	0 (1.0)	0 (1.0)	0 (1.0)	0 (1.0)	0 (1.0)	0 (1.0)	0 (1.0)
Microbacterium-lacticum	2 (0.1335...	0 (1.0)	0 (1.0)	0 (1.0)	0 (1.0)	0 (1.0)	0 (1.0)	0 (1.0)	0 (1.0)	0 (1.0)	0 (1.0)	0 (1.0)	0 (1.0)	0 (1.0)
Microbacterium-laevaniformans	0 (1.0)	0 (1.0)	1 (7.1703...	0 (1.0)	0 (1.0)	0 (1.0)	0 (1.0)	0 (1.0)	0 (1.0)	0 (1.0)	0 (1.0)	0 (1.0)	0 (1.0)	0 (1.0)
Microbacterium-schleiferi	2 (2.9680...	0 (1.0)	0 (1.0)	0 (1.0)	0 (1.0)	0 (1.0)	0 (1.0)	0 (1.0)	0 (1.0)	0 (1.0)	0 (1.0)	0 (1.0)	0 (1.0)	0 (1.0)
Microcystis-aeruginosa	6 (1.0)	8 (1.0)	11 (0.287...	6 (1.0)	156 (0.0)	151 (0.0)	28 (1.679...	4 (1.0)	0 (1.0)	1 (0.8060...	0 (1.0)	0 (1.0)	0 (1.0)	0 (1.0)
Mycobacterium-goodii	0 (1.0)	0 (1.0)	0 (1.0)	0 (1.0)	0 (1.0)	0 (1.0)	0 (1.0)	0 (1.0)	0 (1.0)	0 (1.0)	0 (1.0)	0 (1.0)	0 (1.0)	0 (1.0)
Mycobacterium-smegmatis	12 (1.0)	0 (1.0)	0 (1.0)	3 (1.0)	1 (1.0)	2 (1.0)	2 (1.0)	0 (1.0)	0 (1.0)	0 (1.0)	0 (1.0)	0 (1.0)	0 (1.0)	0 (1.0)
Mycobacterium-tuberculosis	1 (1.0)	0 (1.0)	4 (1.0)	10 (0.400...	0 (1.0)	0 (1.0)	1 (1.0)	0 (1.0)	0 (1.0)	0 (1.0)	0 (1.0)	0 (1.0)	0 (1.0)	0 (1.0)
Neptunomonas-naphthovorans	0 (1.0)	0 (1.0)	0 (1.0)	1 (0.0011...	0 (1.0)	0 (1.0)	0 (1.0)	1 (7.2338...	0 (1.0)	0 (1.0)	0 (1.0)	0 (1.0)	0 (1.0)	0 (1.0)
Nitrosomonas-europaea	44 (6.624...	76 (0.0)	5 (0.5747...	6 (0.2438...	8 (0.0150...	6 (0.0974...	3 (0.7877...	3 (0.5424...	0 (1.0)	0 (1.0)	0 (1.0)	1 (0.2135...	0 (1.0)	0 (1.0)
Nitrosopumilus-maritimus	8 (0.0196...	2 (0.1813...	8 (4.3923...	2 (0.0680...	4 (3.3804...	1 (0.4682...	2 (0.0124...	3 (4.1231...	0 (1.0)	1 (1.3225...	0 (1.0)	0 (1.0)	3 (0.0)	2 (2.728E..
Nocardioides-luteus	3 (0.0025...	0 (1.0)	0 (1.0)	0 (1.0)	0 (1.0)	0 (1.0)	0 (1.0)	0 (1.0)	0 (1.0)	0 (1.0)	0 (1.0)	0 (1.0)	0 (1.0)	0 (1.0)
Nocardioides-plantarum	1 (0.1201...	0 (1.0)	0 (1.0)	0 (1.0)	0 (1.0)	1 (1.0630...	0 (1.0)	1 (8.2496...	0 (1.0)	0 (1.0)	0 (1.0)	0 (1.0)	0 (1.0)	0 (1.0)
Nostoc-punctiforme	2 (1.0)	0 (1.0)	0 (1.0)	0 (1.0)	2 (0.3787...	0 (1.0)	0 (1.0)	0 (1.0)	0 (1.0)	0 (1.0)	0 (1.0)	0 (1.0)	0 (1.0)	0 (1.0)
Novosphingobium-hassiacum	0 (1.0)	1 (4.1243...	0 (1.0)	0 (1.0)	0 (1.0)	1 (2.1785...	0 (1.0)	0 (1.0)	0 (1.0)	0 (1.0)	0 (1.0)	0 (1.0)	0 (1.0)	0 (1.0)
Oceaniserpentilla-haliotidis	0 (1.0)	0 (1.0)	0 (1.0)	0 (1.0)	0 (1.0)	0 (1.0)	0 (1.0)	0 (1.0)	0 (1.0)	0 (1.0)	0 (1.0)	0 (1.0)	0 (1.0)	0 (1.0)
Odontella-sinensis	0 (1.0)	0 (1.0)	0 (1.0)	0 (1.0)	0 (1.0)	0 (1.0)	0 (1.0)	0 (1.0)	0 (1.0)	0 (1.0)	0 (1.0)	0 (1.0)	0 (1.0)	0 (1.0)
Oleiphilus-messinensis	0 (1.0)	0 (1.0)	0 (1.0)	0 (1.0)	0 (1.0)	0 (1.0)	0 (1.0)	1 (0.0)	0 (1.0)	0 (1.0)	0 (1.0)	0 (1.0)	0 (1.0)	0 (1.0)
Oleispira-antarctica	0 (1.0)	0 (1.0)	0 (1.0)	0 (1.0)	0 (1.0)	0 (1.0)	0 (1.0)	2 (2.3457...	0 (1.0)	0 (1.0)	0 (1.0)	0 (1.0)	1 (1.8719...	0 (1.0)
Pelobacter-acidgalli	0 (1.0)	0 (1.0)	0 (1.0)	0 (1.0)	0 (1.0)	0 (1.0)	0 (1.0)	0 (1.0)	0 (1.0)	0 (1.0)	0 (1.0)	0 (1.0)	0 (1.0)	0 (1.0)
Pelobacter-acidigallici	0 (1.0)	0 (1.0)	2 (3.0430...	0 (1.0)	0 (1.0)	0 (1.0)	0 (1.0)	0 (1.0)	0 (1.0)	0 (1.0)	0 (1.0)	0 (1.0)	0 (1.0)	0 (1.0)
Pelobacter-massiliensis	0 (1.0)	0 (1.0)	0 (1.0)	0 (1.0)	0 (1.0)	0 (1.0)	0 (1.0)	0 (1.0)	0 (1.0)	0 (1.0)	0 (1.0)	0 (1.0)	0 (1.0)	0 (1.0)
Pelobacter-propionicus	0 (1.0)	0 (1.0)	0 (1.0)	0 (1.0)	0 (1.0)	0 (1.0)	0 (1.0)	0 (1.0)	0 (1.0)	0 (1.0)	0 (1.0)	0 (1.0)	0 (1.0)	0 (1.0)
Pelomonas-saccharophila	0 (1.0)	0 (1.0)	0 (1.0)	0 (1.0)	1 (6.0365...	0 (1.0)	0 (1.0)	0 (1.0)	0 (1.0)	0 (1.0)	0 (1.0)	0 (1.0)	0 (1.0)	0 (1.0)
Pelotomaculum-isophthalicicum	0 (1.0)	0 (1.0)	0 (1.0)	0 (1.0)	0 (1.0)	0 (1.0)	0 (1.0)	0 (1.0)	0 (1.0)	0 (1.0)	0 (1.0)	0 (1.0)	0 (1.0)	0 (1.0)
Pelotomaculum-isophthalicum	0 (1.0)	0 (1.0)	0 (1.0)	0 (1.0)	0 (1.0)	0 (1.0)	0 (1.0)	0 (1.0)	1 (0.0)	0 (1.0)	0 (1.0)	0 (1.0)	0 (1.0)	0 (1.0)
Pelotomaculum-schinkii	0 (1.0)	1 (1.6544...	0 (1.0)	0 (1.0)	0 (1.0)	0 (1.0)	0 (1.0)	0 (1.0)	0 (1.0)	0 (1.0)	0 (1.0)	0 (1.0)	0 (1.0)	0 (1.0)
Pelotomaculum-terephtalicum	0 (1.0)	0 (1.0)	0 (1.0)	0 (1.0)	0 (1.0)	0 (1.0)	0 (1.0)	0 (1.0)	0 (1.0)	0 (1.0)	0 (1.0)	0 (1.0)	0 (1.0)	0 (1.0)
Pelotomaculum-terephthalicicum	0 (1.0)	0 (1.0)	0 (1.0)	0 (1.0)	0 (1.0)	0 (1.0)	0 (1.0)	0 (1.0)	0 (1.0)	0 (1.0)	0 (1.0)	0 (1.0)	0 (1.0)	0 (1.0)
Pelotomaculum-thermopropionicum	1 (0.5874...	1 (0.0156...	0 (1.0)	0 (1.0)	0 (1.0)	0 (1.0)	0 (1.0)	0 (1.0)	0 (1.0)	0 (1.0)	0 (1.0)	0 (1.0)	0 (1.0)	0 (1.0)
Phanerochaete-chrysosporium	70 (0.002...	33 (1.253...	1 (1.0)	9 (0.7462...	0 (1.0)	0 (1.0)	1 (1.0)	0 (1.0)	0 (1.0)	1 (0.8414...	0 (1.0)	3 (0.0039...	0 (1.0)	0 (1.0)

FIGURE 9.3 Microbe cotable.

		Very High Af
	Count	wastewater
Nitrosomonas-europaea	466	76 (0.0)
Methanosaeta-concilii	66	13 (0.0)
Comamonas-denitrificans	15	5 (2.5659651E-33)
Desulfobacca-acetoxidans	6	3 (8.552713E-31)
Desulfovibrio-aminophilus	8	3 (3.491309E-23)
Malikia-granosa	1	1 (1.6544915E-21)
Pelotomaculum-schinkii	1	1 (1.6544915E-21)
Sporotomaculum-syntrophicum	1	1 (1.6544915E-21)
Desulfobulbus-rhabdoformis	4	2 (4.5099692E-21)
Desulfobulbus-rhabdoform	5	2 (5.3539232E-17)
Comamonas-testosteroni	278	16 (5.907885E-14)
Comamonas-testos	279	16 (6.8661026E-14)
Candidatus-Methylomirabilis	25	4 (6.947225E-13)
Methylomirabilis-oxyfera	25	4 (6.947225E-13)
Phanerochaete-chrysosporium	1003	33 (1.2538449E-11)
Acidovorax-defluvii	2	1 (2.722778E-11)
Cryptanaerobacter-phenolicus	2	1 (2.722778E-11)
Desulfoglaeba-alkanexedens	2	1 (2.722778E-11)
Desulfotomaculum-alkaliphilum	2	1 (2.722778E-11)
Magnospira-bakii	2	1 (2.722778E-11)
Marinobacter-excellens	2	1 (2.722778E-11)
Zoogloea-resiniphila	8	2 (7.3800126E-11)
Pseudomonas-plecoglossicida	32	4 (5.06225E-10)
Brachymonas-petroleovorans	3	1 (7.532539E-8)
Desulfobulbus-elongatus	3	1 (7.532539E-8)
Desulfovibrio-carbinolicus	3	1 (7.532539E-8)
Sporotomaculum-hydroxybenzoicum	3	1 (7.532539E-8)
Methanoculleus-bourgensis	12	2 (2.0299647E-7)
Pseudomonas-stutzeri	819	24 (3.204133E-7)
Methanothrix-soehngenii	27	3 (5.2918165E-7)
Photobacterium-phosphoreum	292	12 (6.287656E-7)
Methanothrix-soehn	28	3 (9.331157E-7)
Novosphingobium-hassiacum	4	1 (4.1243434E-6)
Syntrophobacter-wolinii	15	2 (4.953409E-6)
Alcaligenes-faecalis	549	17 (5.3509953E-6)
Pseudomonas-mendocina	215	9 (1.186089E-5)
Rubrivivax-gelatinosus	83	5 (1.4785157E-5)
Hydrogenophaga-taeniospiralis	5	1 (4.6624165E-5)
Methanosaeta-harundinacea	5	1 (4.6624165E-5)
Zoogloea-ramigera	66	4 (9.9912446E-5)
Methanobrevibacter-arboriphilus	21	2 (1.9738718E-4)
Deltaproteobacteria-bssA	6	1 (2.3848195E-4)
Rhodopseudomonas-palustris	477	13 (5.512615E-4)
Pseudomonas-putida	999	22 (6.333846E-4)

FIGURE 9.4 Significance sorting.

ORTHOGONAL FILTERING

The philosophical underpinnings of orthogonal filtering come from the "Distributed reasoning systems" or "Combination of experts approach in artificial intelligence" [1]. The idea is that any single model is likely to be unreliable but that multiple and independently generated models used in concert can be far more reliable than any individual models.

The insight of orthogonal filtering is to combine two independent models, for example viscosity and protein structure, and look for what lies in the intersection. The concepts are considered to be "independent" or "orthogonal" if they are not expected to occur together often.

The orthogonal filtering approach should retain relatively high recall if the component models used begin with high recall, while greatly increasing precision. In the formulas in the following list, we use "biologics" to represent one model that describes the biological entities of interests and "physics" to represent a second model that captures the physical properties that users want to detect, track, and be alerted to, that is, the filter model. Those two models form the two orthogonal dimensions to be joined by the orthogonal filtering method.

Let

N = population of snippets to draw from

B = a subset of N containing those articles that match biologics

H = a subset of N containing those articles that match physical properties

Br = relevant subset of B

Hr = relevant subset of H

t = the target population of on topic articles

BH = the subset of N containing those articles that match both brand and hotword models.

BHr = relevant subset of BH

$$\text{Recall(B)} = \text{Br/t} \tag{9.1}$$

$$\text{Recall(H)} = \text{Hr/t} \tag{9.2}$$

$$\text{Precision(B)} = \text{Br/B} \tag{9.3}$$

$$\text{Precision(H)} = \text{Hr/H} \tag{9.4}$$

Assuming the independence of brand and hotword models, that is, the "orthogonality of the models," the expected value of BH would be

$$\text{BH} = (\text{B/N}) * (\text{H/N}) * \text{N} = \text{B} * \text{H/N} \tag{9.5}$$

$$\text{Recall(BH)} = \text{BHr/t} \tag{9.6}$$

Another way to think of recall(BH) is as the reduction of recall(B) by the amount of recall(H):

$$\begin{aligned}\text{Recall(BH)} &= \text{Recall(B)} * \text{Recall(H)} \\ &= (\text{Br/t}) * (\text{Hr/t}) \\ &= \text{Br} * \text{Hr}/(\text{t} * \text{t})\end{aligned} \tag{9.7}$$

Combining Equation 9.6 with Equation 9.7 yields:

$$\text{BHr/t} = \text{Br} * \text{Hr}/(\text{t} * \text{t}) \tag{9.8}$$

which becomes

$$\text{BHr} = \text{Br} * \text{Hr/t} \tag{9.9}$$

$$\text{Precision(BH)} = \text{BHr/BH} \tag{9.10}$$

Combining Equations 9.9 and 9.5 with Equation 9.10 produces

$$\text{Precision(BH)} = \text{Br} * \text{Hr} * \text{N}/(\text{t} * \text{B} * \text{H}) \tag{9.11}$$

Note that in the special case where t=B*H/N (the expected value),

$$\text{Precision} = \text{Br} * \text{Hr/t} * \text{t} = \text{Recall}$$

As an example of the power of this approach to increase precision without causing serious degradation in recall, suppose B and H queries both have 90% recall, but only 10% precision. Let N=10,000, B=1000, H=1000, Br=90, Hr=90, and t=100. The combination of these queries produces the following values:

$$\text{Recall(BH)} = 90 * 90\,/\,(100 * 100) = 8100\,/\,10{,}000 = 81\%$$

$$\begin{aligned}\text{Precision(BH)} &= 90 * 90 * 10{,}000/(100 * 1000 * 1000) \\ &= 81{,}000{,}000/100{,}000{,}000 = 81\%\end{aligned}$$

Thus, for a decrease of only 9% in recall (missed data that is relevant) we get a 71% increase in precision (quality of results). This dramatic increase in precision allows us to take very simple models that would normally be too inexact to work effectively and turn them into precision instruments that provide nearly exactly the data we want.

Note that the key to this method lies in the selection of *orthogonal* models. That is, typically, one model does not co-occur with another with higher than expected frequency given an independence assumption, such as brands versus hot issues. When the models are orthogonal, the expected value of BH will be relatively small as indicated by Formula 9.5, since only a subset of B and H is expected to fall into the intersection.

On the other hand, if the two models are not orthogonal—that is, if they represent concepts that might be alike—the expected value of BH will be larger. In the extreme case, when two models completely overlap—that is, they represent the same kinds of concepts, such as viscosity and rheology—the expected value of BH = B = H. This will normally be significantly larger than B*H/N. When combining this expected value to compute precision measure for Precision(BH) = Br*Hr/(t*B), this value is likely to be much smaller than that was produced by selecting two orthogonal dimensions as shown in Formula 9.12, that is, Br*Hr*N/(t*B*H).

Clearly, orthogonal filtering dramatically reduces the size of the resulting article set with only a small loss of recall. Nonorthogonal modeling of the core models and filtering models would not significantly enhance precision. Note that orthogonal filtering is also applicable to general search-based technologies. That is, if one were to find particular documents, the most effective search terms would be those that use keywords that are more or less orthogonal. A one-dimensional multistep drill-down-based search approach often produces much more noise and is more time consuming. We will see an example of how orthogonal filtering can be used to enhance the process of accelerated discovery in the example chapter on protein viscosity.

CONCLUSION

Comparing orthogonals is a useful way to explore the domain-entity concept space at all stages of accelerated discovery. Even before the entity space is completely understood, it may be useful to look at such comparisons to get a feel for where the entities may be missing, redundant, or misplaced. Once the entities are solidified, cotables become a valuable means of discovering entity affinities, which may lead to more precise relationships in time. This is the first step in designing relationship annotators that capture precisely how the two connected things are actually interacting. Finally, we can use orthogonal comparison in the later stages of discovery to locate sets of similar entities that share properties, even when those properties are not precisely well understood.

REFERENCE

1. Rich, E. and Knight, K. 1991. *Artificial Intelligence* (2nd edn, pp. 433–444). New York: McGraw-Hill.

CHAPTER 10

Visualizing the Data Plane

ONE OF THE PRINCIPLES of Accelerated Discovery is that we can gain insight by concentrating everything we know about an entity into a single comprehensive representation. This representation, in its simplest form, is a vector of feature values, where the features represent all the different kinds of things we can know about an entity (its properties, its environment, what it is related to, what it interacts with, etc.). The dimensionality of such a feature vector naturally tends to be extremely high. It is not unusual to see feature vectors with tens of thousands, hundreds of thousands, or even millions of distinct values.

But simply creating a vector is not much use if we cannot visualize and interpret its meaning. So the process of visualizing the data plane of entities is a key technology that deserves a more substantial, detailed description of how it can be accomplished. This chapter describes our process for illuminating entity vectors via graphical visualizations.

ENTITY SIMILARITY NETWORKS

Entities are objects with feature values that can be thought of as vectors in N-space, where N is the number of features. Similarity between any two entities can be calculated as a distance between the two entity vectors. A similarity network can be drawn between a set of entities based on connecting two entities that are relatively near to each other in N-space. Binary relative neighborhood trees are a special type of entity-relationship network, designed to be useful in visualizing the entity space. They have the intuitively simple property that the more typical entities occur at the top of the tree and the more unusual entities occur at the leaf nodes. By limiting the number of links to n + 1 per node (one parent, n children), we create a regularized flat tree structure that is much easier to visualize and navigate at both a course and a fine level by domain experts.

The ability to summarize and visualize a complex ontology is a well-known and long-studied problem. The current best approach to solving this problem is based on creating entity similarity networks. But these networks, as they become larger, become nearly impossible for the domain expert to comprehend due to the complexity of the possible interconnections. The assumption is that the best connection to draw between entities is always the mathematically optimal one (e.g., the shortest distance between two points is a straight line). Unfortunately, this mathematically optimal diagram may present no regularized structures that make the network visually graspable for the purposes of human comprehension. Instead we propose generating a regularized n-ary (e.g., binary) tree of entities that is approximately the same in terms of creating short paths between similar entities, but has properties that make it far more intuitive to grasp visually at both the broad and detailed level. The overall intuition is to start with "typical" entities at the root of the tree and work down toward "odd" entities at the leaves. This mimics the way human experts ordinarily classify information manually, which is to start with the most ordinary, general common cases and then work toward more and more unusual, atypical, and specific cases in a diagnostic hierarchy.

Previous solutions to this problem either use an arbitrary similarity cutoff to determine when to connect entities or create some form of relative neighborhood graph. None of these approaches make any use of the position in network as an indicator of generality. They also typically become harder to understand the larger they grow.

The process of building an entity tree begins with finding the root node. This is selected to be the entity that is "most typical" in the feature space of all entities. At each subsequent step in the tree generation process, we select a node that is "nearest" to any node in the tree that does not already have its full complement of children. For example, if the tree to be generated is a binary tree, then the next node to be added can only be a child of a node that does not already have two children. This process of adding next-best entities to the tree continues until entities are placed in the tree.

We first describe each entity as a vector in the feature space. Each vector describes the entity in terms of the features that occur whenever that entity is present. The more frequent the entity co-occurrence, the larger the feature value. We also create an average feature vector, A, which represents the average of all features across all entities.

To begin building the tree we first select a root node. The entity that is most typical, taken to be the one whose feature vector is closest to the average, A, is chosen as the root. To find the next node in the tree we look to see which node is closest to the root node among all the other nodes. This node then becomes a child of the root node. The next node of the three (the third node) could either be a child of the root node or a child of the other node already in the tree. We compare distances and choose the node that is closest to either of the two nodes already in the tree and add it as a child of the node to which it is closest.

At this point, let us imagine that the root node has two children. The next node we choose to add to the tree cannot be added to the root node if the tree is binary (because each node is allowed only two children). Therefore the fourth node in the tree (in this case) can only be added to one of the two existing child nodes. Again, the node that is closest to one of these two nodes is chosen.

This process continues until all the nodes are added somewhere in the tree. Figure 10.1 shows an example of such a tree, based on microorganisms and the text that mentions them in research abstracts.

USING COLOR TO SPOT POTENTIAL NEW HYPOTHESES

If we add another, independent, layer of information to the similarity tree, it can become a powerful way to visualize how one particular property distributes across an entity type. For example, the diagram containing microbes in Figure 10.2 has been colored to indicate which microbes are anaerobic (not needing oxygen) and which are aerobic (needing oxygen).

We can see clearly first of all that the property is well differentiated across the microbes in the tree. The anaerobics (in green) tend to clump together with other anaerobics. One question we might want to explore is which aerobic microbes might have some properties of anaerobics. This would lead us to focus on an area of the tree that had a mixture of colors, like the one in Figure 10.3. The microbes indicated in red near the green microbes are likely candidates to share some anaerobic properties.

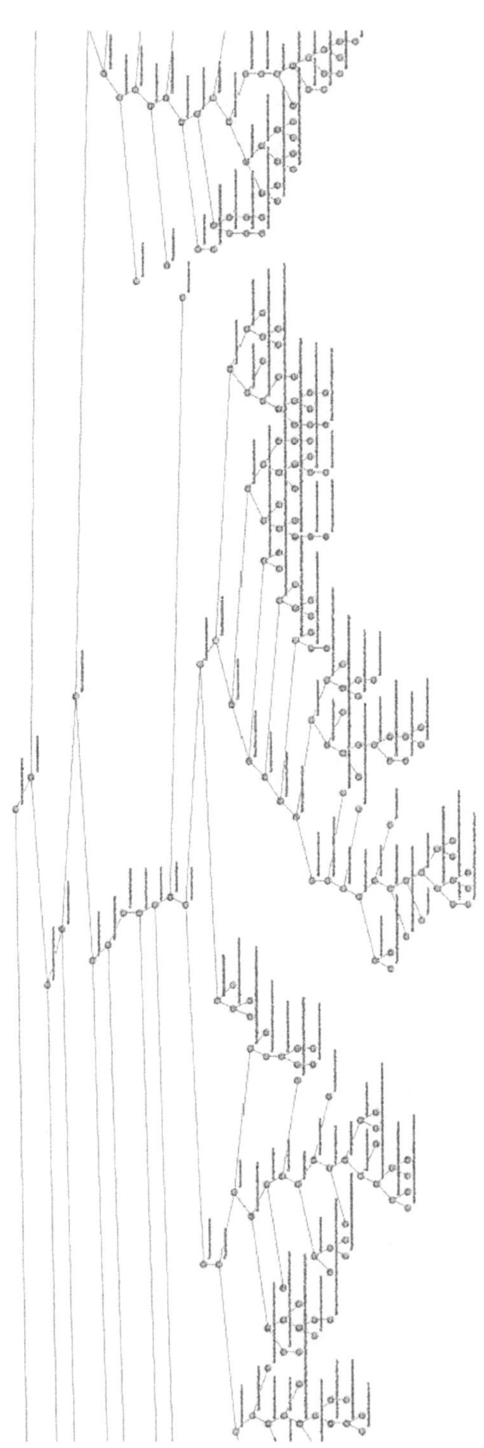

FIGURE 10.1 Entity similarity network.

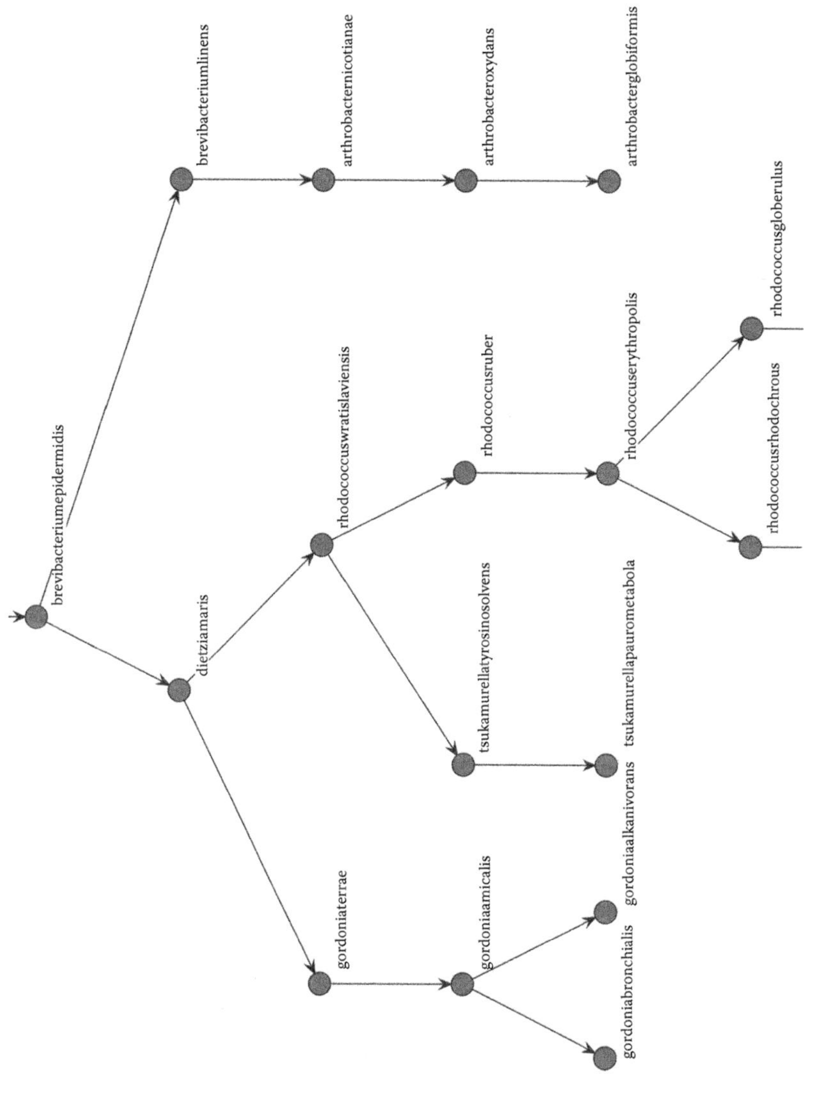

FIGURE 10.2 **(See color insert.)** Forming hypothesis using color.

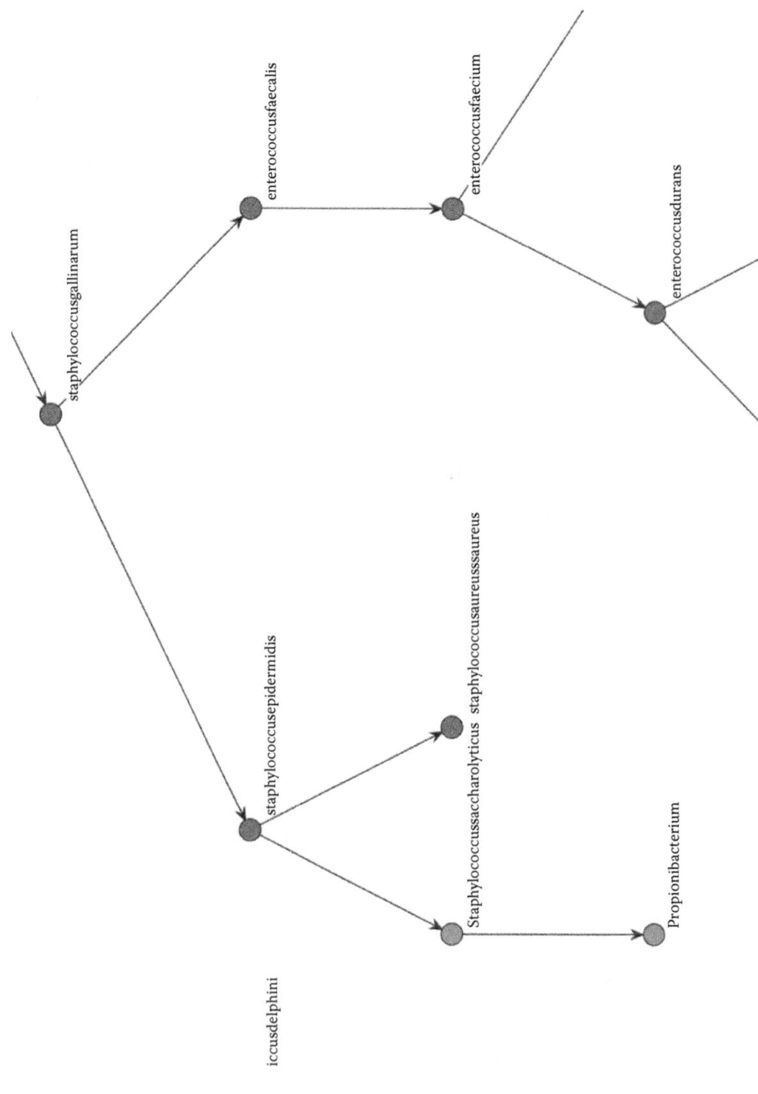

FIGURE 10.3 **(See color insert.)** Detailed view of mixed color.

VISUALIZATION OF CENTROIDS

Entity similarity networks give a sense of how many different nodes are related to each other. If we zoom in to look at a smaller number of entities, we can add more context around the entity definition itself, allowing us not only to see more closely the entity neighborhood, but also to understand better how the individual documents that compose the entity feature vector are arranged. A centroid is really just an average, and any average value runs the risk of oversimplifying the complex landscape of component values that make it up. For example, there may be significant outliers that skew the average or subclusters of documents that make up an alternative subspecies of an entity that is not yet well understood. Visualization of centroids will help uncover such detail.

Given that documents can be represented as vectors embedded in high-dimensional Euclidean space R^d and that proximity in R^d implies similarity, models of the underlying data may be constructed where each document is treated as a vector in a multidimensional feature space. Each of these vectors may also be given a class label.

Our main aim is to visually understand the spatial relationships between various classes in order to answer questions such as

How well separated are different classes?

What classes are similar or dissimilar to each other?

Are the classes linearly separable?

How coherent or well formed is a given class?

Answers to these questions can enable the data scientist to infer interclass relationships that may not be part of the given classification and additionally to gauge the quality of the classification and the quality of the feature space.

Discovery of interesting class relationships in such a visual examination can help in the design of better classifiers. To this end, we describe the use of carefully chosen two-dimensional projections to display the data.

Projecting high-dimensional data to lower dimensions has been done for some time in data visualization and other applications, for example in principal components analysis.

Our class-preserving projections are tailored to expose the class structure of multidimensional data and are most closely related to the projections of classical linear discriminant analysis.

Our main tool for visualizing multidimensional data will be linear projections onto two-dimensional planes, where the loss of information can be mitigated by the careful choice of these planes. We want to choose those planes that best preserve interclass distances.

One way to maintain good separation of the projected classes is to maximize the distance between the projected means. Where three centroids are involved, this may be achieved by choosing vectors that select as the X axis, two of the centroids to be visualized, and as the Y axis, a normal line to a third centroid to be visualized. If more than three centroids are involved, then we may either choose three at random and, using motion graphics, rotate among different choices of the three centroids; or we may use principle component analysis on the centroids themselves and choose the first two principle components as the X and Y axes.

In Figure 10.4, we see centroids as large dots for three different microbes, where the documents (Medline abstracts) that make up the centroid are

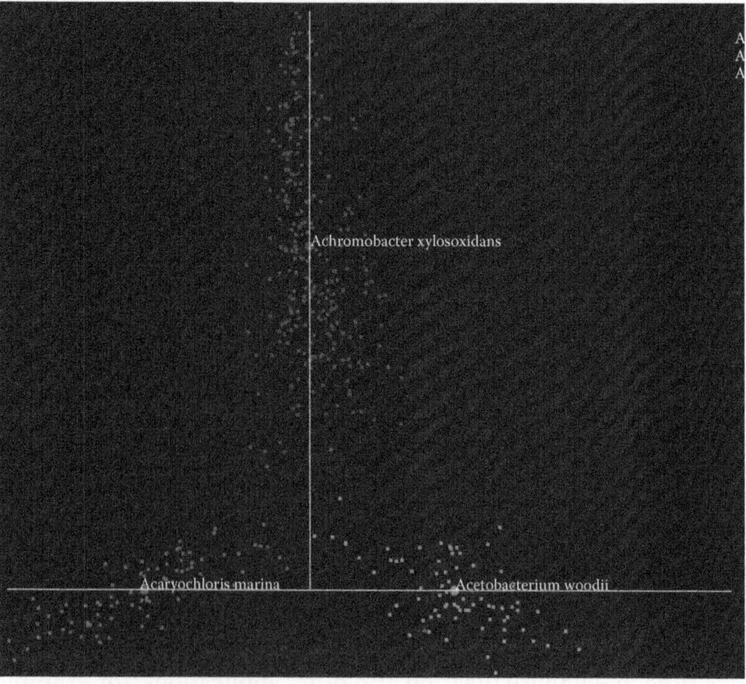

FIGURE 10.4 **(See color insert.)** Scatter plot.

small dots of the same color. The X and Y axes are shown going through the centroids. This maximizes the information communicated about centroid (microbe) characterization with respect to documents.

Though this plot only contains two dimensions, we have chosen these dimensions in such a way that the information relating documents to centroids is mostly preserved. The centroids define the plane, so we actually view them exactly as they are in high-dimensional space. The documents probably do not lay right on the plane of the three centroids, but we draw a normal line to indicate on the plane where it intersects. This is the closest possible approximation to the relevance of the document to each of the three centroids.

What can we learn from such a visualization? Quite a bit. At a high level, we get a sense of how cohesive or diffuse the documents written about each entity are. We also see where there may be overlaps or bleed between documents that discuss different organisms. These overlaps might be indications of potential connections between different organisms or at least some shared properties. What is more, we can spot outliers that may indicate mistakes made by our entity annotator, or at least unusual content that might be instructive. Finally, we can spot potential subclusters of data that might indicate a means or need to subclass an entity that we thought was homogeneous into separate distinct organisms or structures.

EXAMPLE: THREE MICROBES

We create a scatter plot that visualizes the three microbes we saw earlier in this chapter (Figure 10.5). What we notice immediately is the two aerobic microbes are much more alike than the anaerobic one. This would tend to show that there is little overlap between the properties of these organisms after all. If we wished to dive deeper, we could select a few of the documents located closest to the borders between two clusters, since these documents are likely to have the most shared properties. Here is such a document.

Example 10.1

Example 1 (#30871): 2394188 Cloning and sequencing of hemolysin gene from clinical Aeromonas hydrophila. Aerolysin is one of the important virulence factors for Aeromonas hydrophila infection. To understand the characteristics of the aerolysin gene in clinical A. hydrophila, a genomic library was constructed by using pUC19

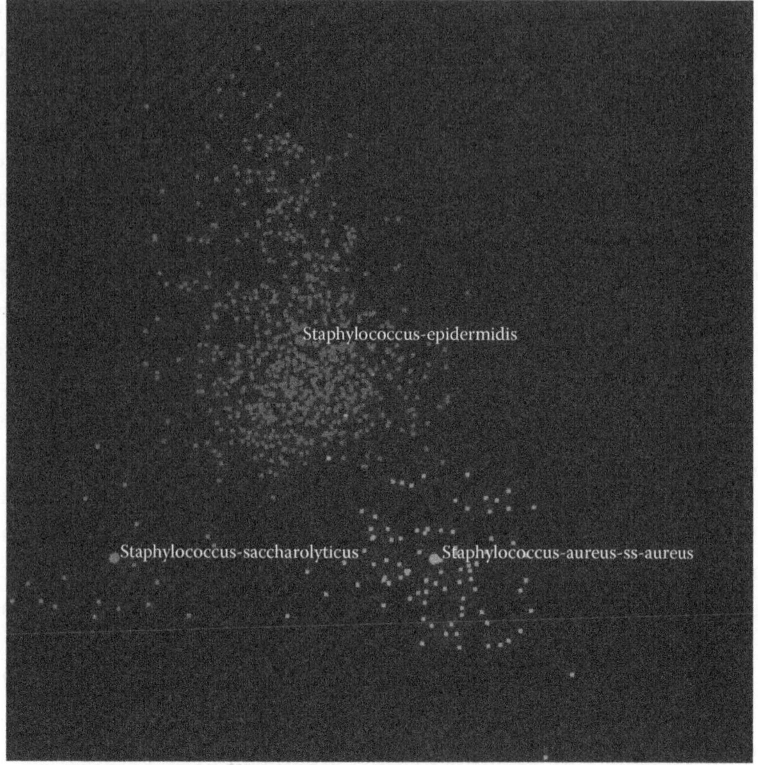

FIGURE 10.5 Microbe scatter plot.

as cloning vector. The positive clone containing the aerolysin gene was selected by the colony hybridization method, using the aerolysin probe (an 48 mer oligonucleotide) of aquatic A. hydrophila. Four positive out of 1,200 transformants were obtained from the primarily screened genomic library, and were further identified for specific binding capability by the dot blot hybridization method. One of three positive clones, designated as pAH–1, was further analyzed by the restriction mapping technique. For further sequencing the aerolysin gene nucleotides, the 3.0 kb fragment of A. hydrophila isolated from pAH–1 was cloned into pBluescriptll, pKS+, resulting in plasmid pKAH–1. Subclones of pKAH–1 were constructed and determined for the presence of 48 mer aerolysin gene sequence by dot blot hybridization method. These (subclones pKS+SS and pSK+SS) were selected for nucleotide sequencing by single-stranded dideoxy sequencing method. The nucleotide sequence similarity coefficient

> between clinical and aquatic strains of A. hydrophila was 76%; whereas between clinical strains of A. hydrophila and A. sobria was 71%. Since the length of the A. hydrophila DNA fragment cloned into pAH–1 is 3.0 kb, a larger size than the aerolysin gene of aquatic A. hydrophila (1.45 kb) and, also, includes 3′ region of aerolysin gene in aquatic A. hydrophila, the indication is that the clone, pKAH–1, contains an entire aerolysin gene of A. hydrophila. The similarity between a small region (containing 8 amino acids) of the aerolysin in the clinical A. hydrophila and the alpha toxin of Staphylococcus aureus suggests that there is functional significance in this region [1].

This discusses a precise function of *Staphylococcus aureus* that may prove useful in understanding its properties vis-à-vis other anaerobic microbes.

CONCLUSION

The tools presented in this chapter provide an overview of how entities described by unstructured documents in high-dimensional feature spaces can be visualized to help the scientist better understand the hidden connections between them. Through such visualizations, it is possible to quickly spot the interesting areas of overlap that present new opportunities for experiment and exploitation via new applications. This is often the first step in hypothesis generation. In the next chapter, we will see how this step can be built on using networks.

REFERENCE

1. Liou, J.J., et al. 1990. [Cloning and sequencing of hemolysin gene from clinical *Aeromonas hydrophila*]. *Zhonghua Minguo wei sheng wu ji mian yi xue za zhi* [*Chinese Journal of Microbiology and Immunology*] 23.2:134–146.

CHAPTER 11

Networks

THROUGHOUT MY CAREER AS a data scientist, I have always been dubious about the utility of network diagrams for the understanding of unstructured data. The problem has always been that, while it is very easy to draw nodes connected by arcs and display them in a stunning visualization on a computer screen, it is very often unclear what real insight is gained from the exercise. The fact that a picture looks compelling does not in fact make it useful. The reason for this is often that the nodes and arcs have not been sufficiently thought through so that what is being connected in the graph has some relevance to a scientific problem. But even if the nodes are the important scientific entities and the edges represent some significant connection between them, the mere fact of putting the nodes and edges onto a screen as a graph is often not useful in and of itself.

But lately I have begun to revise my opinion about the utility of networks as a useful tool for understanding what is going on. What has changed my opinion is the necessity of grappling with the interconnected nature of biology and seeing the insight that can come from "connecting the dots." Consider the following simple example:

$$\frac{\begin{array}{l} A \rightarrow B \\ B \rightarrow C \quad \text{implies} \end{array}}{A \rightarrow C}$$

This sort of logic can be a powerful tool for discovery. So it makes sense to have a tool that presents those hidden connections visually across disparate document sources. This is something computers can readily find that humans may miss, and conversely computers may find many such relationships without knowing which ones are interesting, so the network diagram becomes the best way for computer and human expert to communicate and collaborate to find a new and interesting discovery.

PROTEIN NETWORKS

Proteins are the building blocks of cells. They are large molecules that have complex geometries, and their chemical and physical structure determines their behavior. Proteins can be modified by other proteins, causing them to change their behavior. Cellular function is determined by these protein–protein interactions. When cells malfunction (e.g., due to disease) the protein–protein interactions go awry. The complex interactions of proteins in the cell are only partly understood. There are thousands of proteins in each cell, and they interact in millions of ways. This is the protein interactome, and it serves as an illustrative example of how visual computer-generated networks can help us understand what is actually going on and to form new hypotheses.

Note: The following example is for illustration purposes only; it was not done in collaboration with a trained biologist and therefore its conclusions should not be mistaken for a medically effective treatment.

Frequently, with more and more genetic sequencing being done, biologists will discover that some genes are expressed for certain diseases. This would tend to indicate the possible involvement of the protein coded by that gene in the disease process. Furthermore, if we had on hand a compound that could directly or indirectly affect that protein, we would be possibly able to use that compound as a treatment for the disease. The following example starts with such a gene–disease association and then uses networks to visually connect the dots and find both a mechanism explaining the association as well as a potential drug treatment.

MULTIPLE SCLEROSIS AND IL7R

In 2007, an article published in *Nature* disclosed an association between the IL7R gene and multiple sclerosis (Figure 11.1). To investigate the mechanism behind this association, we first begin by drawing the connections that have been discovered in all medical literature around IL7R. This network is shown in Figure 11.2.

Interleukin 7 receptor α chain (*IL7R*) shows allelic and functional association with multiple sclerosis

Simon G Gregory[1,9], Silke Schmidt[1,9], Puneet Seth[2], Jorge R Oksenberg[3], John Hart[1], Angela Prokop[1], Stacy J Caillier[3], Maria Ban[4], An Goris[5], Lisa F Barcellos[6], Robin Lincoln[3], Jacob L McCauley[7], Stephen J Sawcer[4], D A S Compston[4], Benedicte Dubois[5], Stephen L Hauser[3], Mariano A Garcia-Blanco[2], Margaret A Pericak-Vance[8] & Jonathan L Haines[7], for the Multiple Sclerosis Genetics Group

Multiple sclerosis is a demyelinating neurodegenerative disease with a strong genetic component. Previous genetic risk studies have failed to identify consistently linked regions or genes outside of the major histocompatibility complex on chromosome 6p. We describe allelic association of a polymorphism in the gene encoding the interleukin 7 receptor α chain (*IL7R*) as a significant risk factor for multiple sclerosis in four independent family-based or case-control data sets (overall $P = 2.9 \times 10^{-7}$). Further, the likely causal SNP, rs6897932, located within the alternatively spliced exon 6 of *IL7R*, has a functional effect on gene expression. The SNP influences the amount of soluble and membrane-bound isoforms of the protein by putatively disrupting an exonic splicing silencer.

FIGURE 11.1 IL7R and MS.

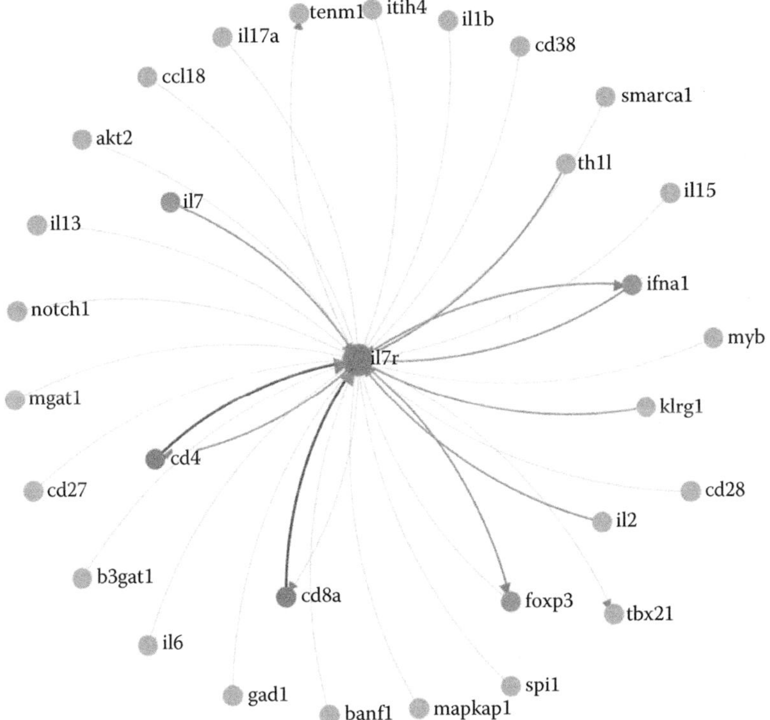

FIGURE 11.2 IL7R relationships.

Each node in this network represents a single gene/protein (for our purposes, we assume that each gene encodes one protein and the name of the gene/protein entity is the name of the gene). The directed arcs in the network (A→B) indicate a sentence was found in Medline abstracts that indicated a causal effect that protein A has on protein B. The thicker the

Il7r ····· **Regualtion positive** ····· cd8a

19350559 Progressive CD127 down-regulation correlates with increased apoptosis of CD8 T cells during chronic HIV-1 infection By Zhang Shu-Ye SY | Jan 09 2009

*These data indicate that **CD127** loss might impair IL-7 signaling and **increase CD8** T-cell apoptosis during HIV-1 infection.*

Il7r ····· **Regualtion negative** ····· cd4

19380817 IL-7 receptor expression provides the potential for long-term survival of both CD62Lhigh central memory T cells and Th1 effector cells during Leishmania major infection By Colpitts Sara L SL | Jan 15 2009

*Finally, blockade of **IL7R** signaling **decreased** the number of T-bet(+)**CD4**(+) T cells, reduced IFN-gamma production, and inhibited delayed-type hypersensitivity responses in immune mice challenged with L.*

FIGURE 11.3 Evidence.

line, the more evidence is associated with the connection. In Figure 11.3, we see examples of such evidence for two of the arcs. Note that CD127 is a synonym for IL7R.

Next we look for any possible connection to multiple sclerosis. We use "autoimmune disease" as a more general stand-in for MS here in order to pull in any research that might prove relevant (Figure 11.4).

While we see no direct connection between IL7R and autoimmune diseases, we do see several potential indirect associations. One of the most promising ones goes through CD4. We already saw evidence of IL7R impacting (regulating negative) CD4+T cells. Now there is some evidence that these same cells might be the cause of autoimmune diseases such as MS (Figure 11.5).

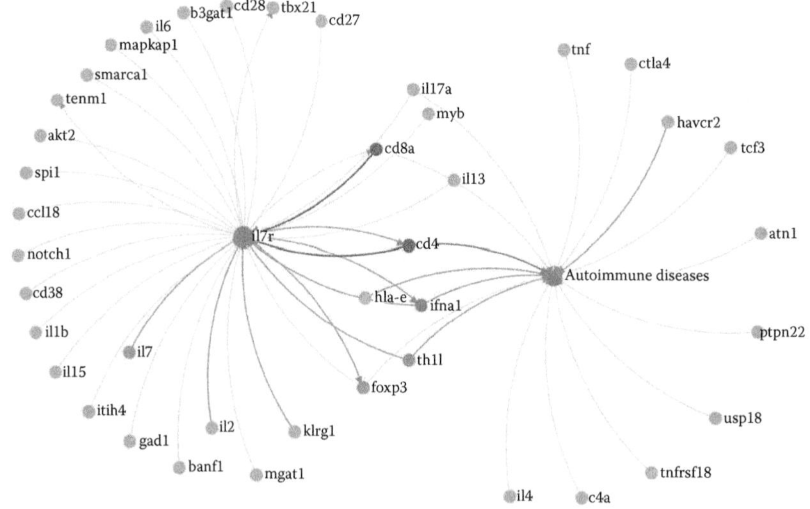

FIGURE 11.4 IL7R and autoimmune diseases.

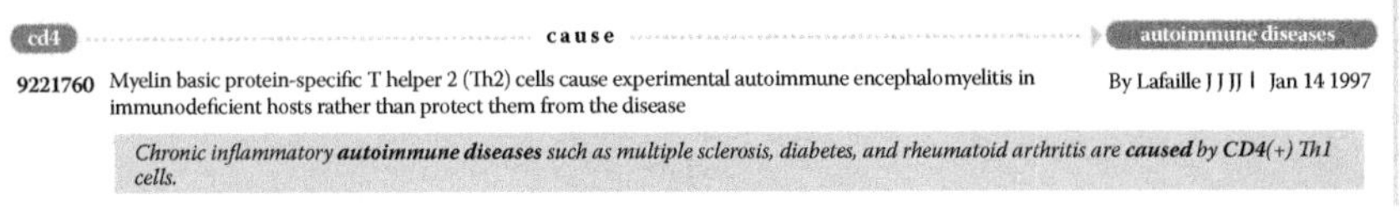
cd4 cause autoimmune diseases

9221760 Myelin basic protein-specific T helper 2 (Th2) cells cause experimental autoimmune encephalomyelitis in immunodeficient hosts rather than protect them from the disease — By Lafaille J J JJ | Jan 14 1997

*Chronic inflammatory **autoimmune diseases** such as multiple sclerosis, diabetes, and rheumatoid arthritis are **caused** by CD4(+) Th1 cells.*

FIGURE 11.5 Evidence.

The next step is to go backward from IL7R and look for a potential drug that might be able to affect that protein. Adding drugs to our network uncovers an interesting connection through the notch1 protein (Figure 11.6).

Three different drugs affect notch1, which in turn regulates IL7R. The evidence for these interactions is show in Figure 11.7.

So now we have at least potential leads in the form of chemical compounds that might indirectly affect IL7R, which in turn indirectly affects autoimmune diseases. It would now be interesting to take one of these drugs and see if there is any concrete evidence that it has an effect on autoimmune diseases. We did this search, and below we reproduce the title and abstract of an article in Medline that published a finding on just such an association in rats (Figure 11.8).

Clearly, computer-generated networks based on entities and relationships extracted from text have potential utility in uncovering new associations between chemical compounds and diseases. This kind of

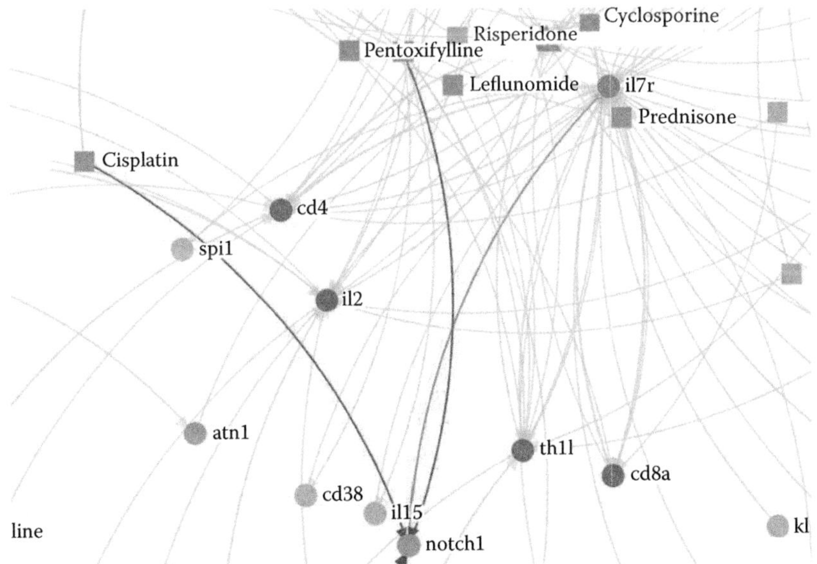

FIGURE 11.6 Notch1 and drugs that affect it.

FIGURE 11.7 Evidence.

network-based reasoning approach should generalize readily to other domains and applications.

EXAMPLE: NEW DRUGS FOR OBESITY

Genetic population studies have found that some variants of the FTO gene appear to be correlated with obesity in humans [1]. We would like to determine a mechanism and also discover a potential treatment that might affect FTO. Using network analysis we begin by looking for things that might influence FTO in cells. What we find is shown in Figure 11.9.

Leptin seems to be a hormone that affects FTO. The evidence for the linkage is shown in Figure 11.10.

Now we expand the network to look for drugs that might affect leptin (Figure 11.11). This is a fairly large list, so to focus our efforts on the drugs that are most certain to be effective, we focus on those relationships that have at least two different sources of evidence. This creates the simplified network shown in Figure 11.12).

When we select Olanzapine, we see the details shown in Figure 11.13. So there seems to be an impact of olanzapine on leptin, though it is not clear in which direction. Another drug, fenofibrate, also seems promising (Figure 11.14).

Title	**Valproic acid ameliorates inflammation in experimental autoimmune encephalomyelitis rats**
Authors	Zhang Z ; Zhang Z-Y ; Wu Y ; Schluesener H J; Institute of Immunology, Third Military Medical University of PLA, Gaotanyan Main Street 30, Chongoing 400038, People's Republic of China. zhangzhiren@yahoo.com
Journal	Neuroscience. 2012-09-27: 221():140-50.
Abstract	Valproic acid (VPA) is a short-chain branched fatty acid with anti-inflammatory, neuro-protective and axon remodeling effects. Here we have studied effects of VPA in gpMBP(68-84)-induced experimental autoimmune encephalomyelitis (EAE). Both preventive (from Day 0 to Day 18) and therapeutic (from Day 7 to Day 18 or from Day 9 to Day 19) VPA (500 mg/kg, intra-gastric) administration to EAE rats once daily greatly reduced the severity and duration of EAE, and suppressed mRNA levels of interferon-γ (IFN-γ), tumor necrosis factor-α (TNF-α), interleukin-1β (IL-1β) and IL-17, matrix metalloprotienase 9 (MMP9), inducible nitric oxide synthase (INOS) and transcription factor T-bet but increased levels of IL-4 mRNA in EAE spinal cords. Furthermore, preventive VPA treatment greatly attenuated accumulation of macrophages amd lymphocytes in EAE spinal cords. VPA treatment altered the cytokine milieu of lymph nodes, modulating the Th profile from Th1 and Th17 to a profile of Th2 and regualtory T cells. In addition, in vitro study showed that VPA inhibited non-specific lymphocyte profileration in a dose-dependent manner. In summary, our data demonstrated that VPA could suppress systemic and local inflammation to improve outcome of EAE, suggesting that VPA might be a candidate for treatment of multiple sclerosis.
Chemicals (1)	Structure: 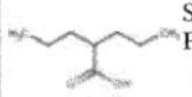 Chemical name: valproic acid SMILE: CCCC(CCC)C(O)=O Found by ChEMBL See ChEMBL assays & targets References: Articles: 20749 Patents: 22967 total, 3675 in claims
PMID	22800566

FIGURE 11.8 Abstract showing connection between drug and disease.

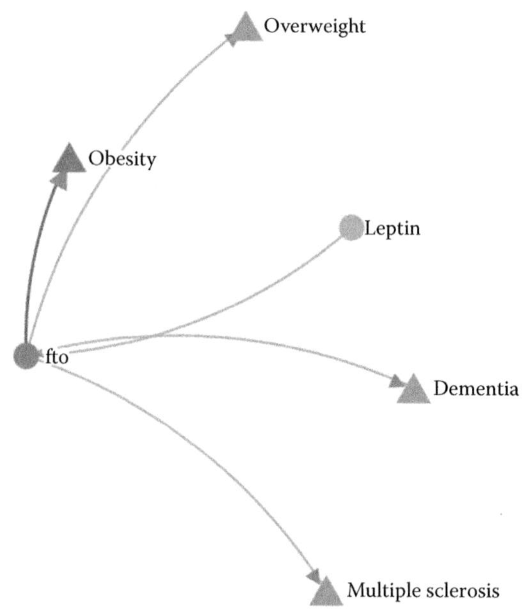

FIGURE 11.9 FTO network.

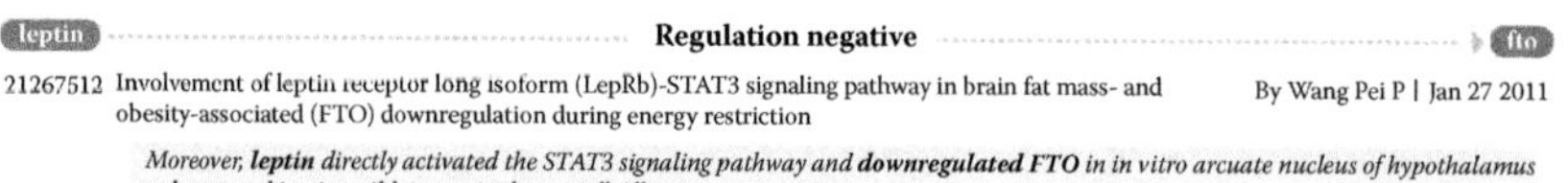

leptin
Regulation negative
fto
21267512 Involvement of leptin receptor long isoform (LepRb)-STAT3 signaling pathway in brain fat mass- and obesity-associated (FTO) downregulation during energy restriction
By Wang Pei P | Jan 27 2011
Moreover, leptin directly activated the STAT3 signaling pathway and downregulated FTO in in vitro arcuate nucleus of hypothalamus cultures and in vivo wild-type mice but not db/db mice.

FIGURE 11.10 Evidence.

Searching in Medline for fenofibrate and obesity yields the article shown in Figure 11.15. So the connection indeed appears to be valid.

CONCLUSION

The use of networks allows us to combine entities and relationships extracted from many different sources into a complete picture that is difficult to obtain by searching and reading one paper at a time. This kind of visualization and reasoning is a key ingredient to be employed in the later phases of Accelerated Discovery.

REFERENCE

1. Frayling, T. M., et al. 2007. A common variant in the FTO gene is associated with body mass index and predisposes to childhood and adult obesity. *Science*, 316(5826): 889–894.

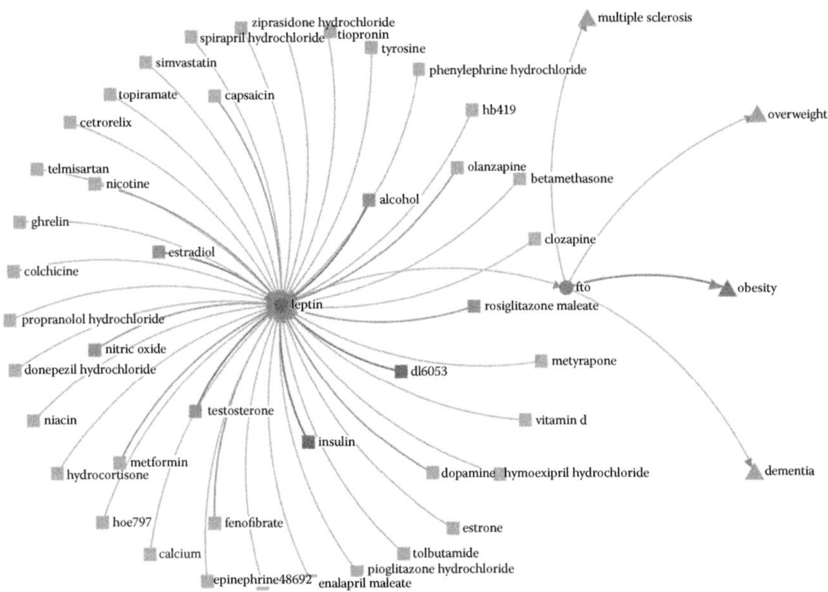

FIGURE 11.11 Drugs that affect leptin.

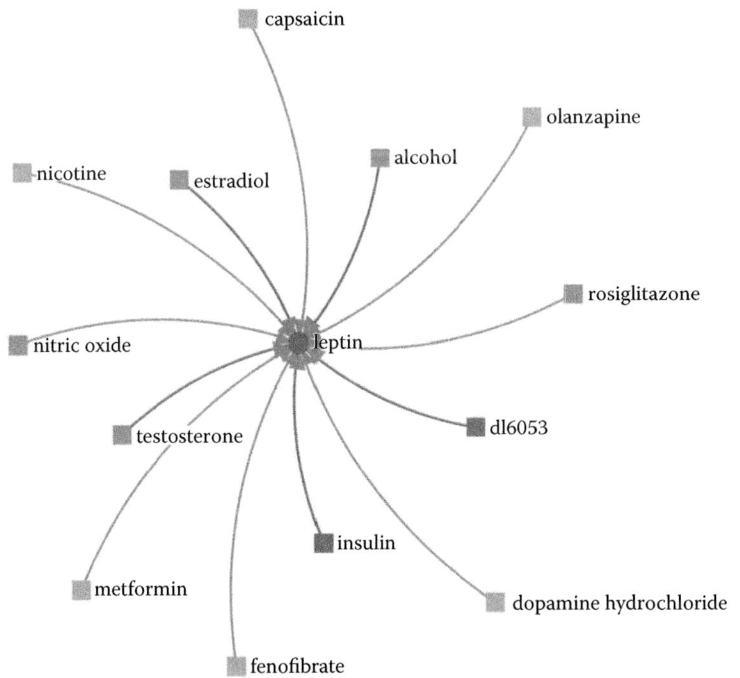

FIGURE 11.12 Drugs with strong support.

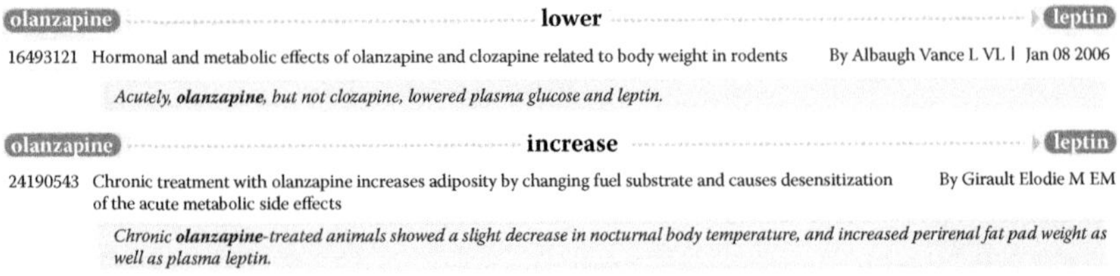

olanzapine ········ **lower** ········ leptin

16493121 Hormonal and metabolic effects of olanzapine and clozapine related to body weight in rodents By Albaugh Vance L VL | Jan 08 2006

*Acutely, **olanzapine**, but not clozapine, lowered plasma glucose and leptin.*

olanzapine ········ **increase** ········ leptin

24190543 Chronic treatment with olanzapine increases adiposity by changing fuel substrate and causes desensitization of the acute metabolic side effects By Girault Elodie M EM

*Chronic **olanzapine**-treated animals showed a slight decrease in nocturnal body temperature, and increased perirenal fat pad weight as well as plasma leptin.*

FIGURE 11.13 Evidence.

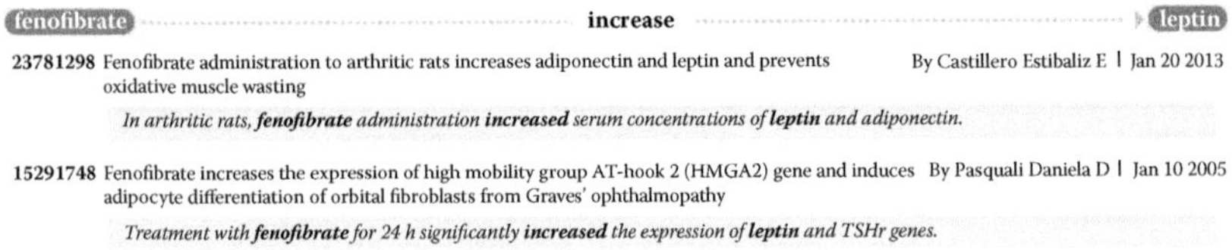

fenofibrate ········ **increase** ········ leptin

23781298 Fenofibrate administration to arthritic rats increases adiponectin and leptin and prevents oxidative muscle wasting By Castillero Estibaliz E | Jan 20 2013

*In arthritic rats, **fenofibrate** administration **increased** serum concentrations of **leptin** and adiponectin.*

15291748 Fenofibrate increases the expression of high mobility group AT-hook 2 (HMGA2) gene and induces adipocyte differentiation of orbital fibroblasts from Graves' ophthalmopathy By Pasquali Daniela D | Jan 10 2005

*Treatment with **fenofibrate** for 24 h significantly **increased** the expression of **leptin** and TSHr genes.*

FIGURE 11.14 Evidence for fenofibrate.

15131765: Fenofibrate prevents obesity and hypertriglyceridemia in low-density lipoprotein receptor-null mice

Highlight entities

Abstract:
Our previous study demonstrated that fenofibrate improves both lipid metabolism and obesity, in part through hepatic peroxisome proliferator-activated receptor alpha (PPARalpha) activation, in female ovariectomized, but not in sham-operated, low-density lipoprotein receptor-null (LDLR-null) mice. The aim of this study was to determine whether fenofibrate prevents obesity and hypertriglyceridemia in male LDLR-null mice. Mice fed a high-fat diet for 8 weeks exhibited increases in body and white adipose tissue (WAT) weights and developed severe hypertriglyceridemia compared with mice fed a low-fat control diet. However, these effects were effectively prevented by fenofibrate. Mice given a fenofibrate-supplemented high-fat diet showed significantly reduced body weight, WAT weight, and serum triglycerides versus high-fat diet-fed animals. Triton WR1339 study showed that fenofibrate-induced reduction in circulating triglycerides was due to the decreased secretion of triglycerides from the liver. Moreover, the administration of fenofibrate not only resulted in liver hypertrophy and reduction in hepatic lipid accumulation, but also regulated the transcriptional expression of PPARalpha target genes, such as hepatic acyl-coenzyme A (CoA) oxidase and apolipoprotein C-III (apoC-III). Therefore, our results suggest that alterations in hepatic PPARalpha action by fenofibrate seem to suppress diet-induced obesity and severe hypertriglyceridemia caused by LDLR deficiency in male mice.

Journal: Metabolism: clinical and experimental

Published: 2004-07-08

Authors: Jeong Sunhyo S Department of Life Sciences, Mokwon University, Taejon, Korea. , Kim Mina M , Han Miyoung M , Lee Hyunghee H , Ahn Jiwon J , Kim Moonza M , Song Yang-Heon YH , Shin Chuog C , Nam Ki-Hoan KH , Kim Tae Woo TW , Oh Goo Taeg GT , Yoon Michung M

FIGURE 11.15 Abstract showing fenofibrate and obesity link.

CHAPTER 12

Examples and Problems

THE NEXT SET OF chapters deals with specific applications of the Accelerated Discovery technology during actual customer engagements or demonstrations. We begin with a set of problems that are illustrative of the basic principles but are also fairly simple for the reader to work through on their own in order to come up with a result in a short period of time. Then we move on to the more sophisticated examples of solutions that required many weeks to complete. All of these problems and examples apply the same methodology, but you will notice that each of them is unique in some way. This illustrates an important point I want to make about the process. The methodology I have described is meant to be applied flexibly and to adapt to the circumstances of each individual problem area. Not every problem involves all the elements of the process, and it is not necessary to put all the basic elements in place before beginning to apply the more advanced ones. I think the examples and problems I have chosen for this book illustrate this idea well.

PROBLEM CATALOGUE

1. Antibiotics: This example has two parts. The first part deals with comparing two different types of drug entities in order to look for interesting overlaps in properties. The second part deals with SOS proteins in the *E. coli* bacteria that help confer drug resistance. Both parts use visualizing the data plane as a tool for discovering new properties in the domain.

2. Orphan diseases: Here we use cotables and entity relationships to find existing drugs that may be relevant to diseases that are not heavily researched.

EXAMPLE CATALOGUE

1. Target selection: The problem is to find the best target protein to focus on in developing a new treatment for a disease. This example provides a nice overview of all four phases of the method.

2. Alternative indications: The purpose here is to find new diseases that may be treated with an existing protein antibody. This is example is unique for its use of gene expression information as well as Medline publications as its primary data sources. It shows how the techniques of entity extraction and taxonomy development using feature spaces can apply across many different kinds of information.

3. Side effect: This example deals with understanding the full range of side effects exhibited by a drug. The focus of this example is on accurately defining the entities and relationships.

4. Protein viscosity: In order to design a protein antibody that can be delivered, viscosity must be taken into account. This example looks at how to organize an entity space, starting from scratch.

5. Anaerobic microbes: How do we determine the best microbes for biodegrading oil spills? It turns out that orthogonal comparison is a very effective way to accomplish this.

6. Drug repurposing: The fastest way to get to market with a new treatment is to repurpose an existing drug. Doing this requires a network analysis of protein-protein interactions.

7. Adverse events: This example deals with how to predict and ameliorate unwanted effects of new compounds.

8. P53 kinases: Early on in our Accelerated Discovery work with Baylor College of Medicine, we made an extraordinary discovery using our techniques. This example tells that story.

As you read through these examples, keep in mind how each one leverages the Accelerated Discovery process to help the scientist do her job more effectively, in less time, and with a wider vision than was possible before. Though all of the examples are related to biology, the nonbiologist reader is encouraged to extrapolate how these techniques might apply equally well in their scientific field.

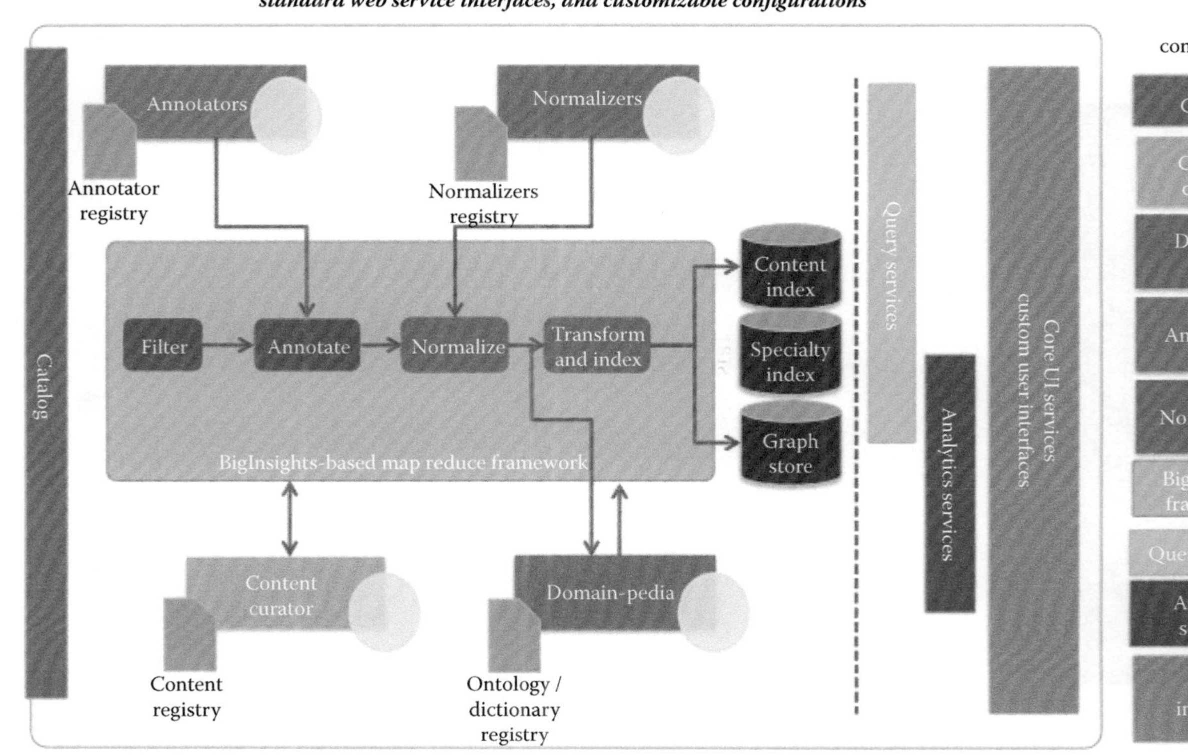

FIGURE 2.3 Functional model.

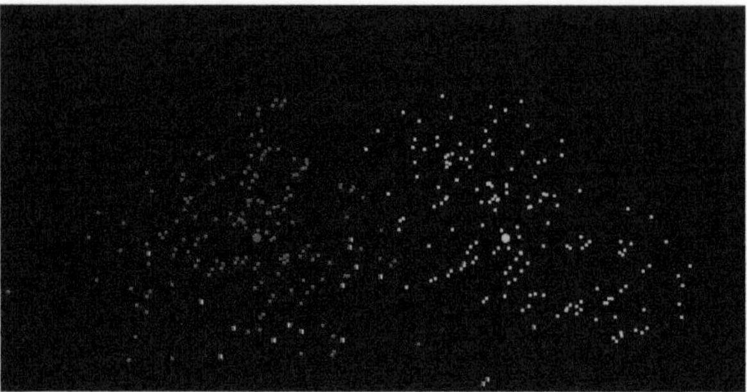

FIGURE 5.2 Scatter plot.

brevibacteriumepidermidis
dietziamaris
brevibacteriumlinens
gordoniaterrae
rhodococcuswratislaviensis
arthrobacternicotian
gordoniaamicalis
tsukamurellatyrosinosolvens
rhodococcusruber
arthrobacteroxydans
gordoniabronchialis
gordoniaalkanivorans
tsukamurellapaurometabola
rhodococcuserythropolis
arthrobacterglobifor
rhodococcusrhodochrous
rhodococcusgloberulus

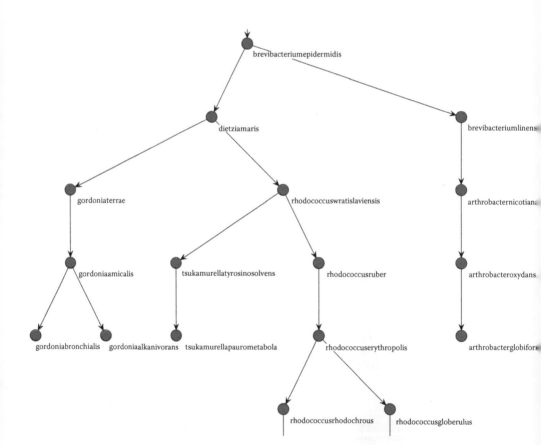

FIGURE 10.2 Forming hypothesis using color.

ccusdelphini
staphylococcusgallinarum
staphylococcusepidermidis
enterococcusfaecalis
Staphylococcussaccharolyticus
staphylococcusaureusssaureus
enterococcusfaecium
Propionibacterium
enterococcusdurans

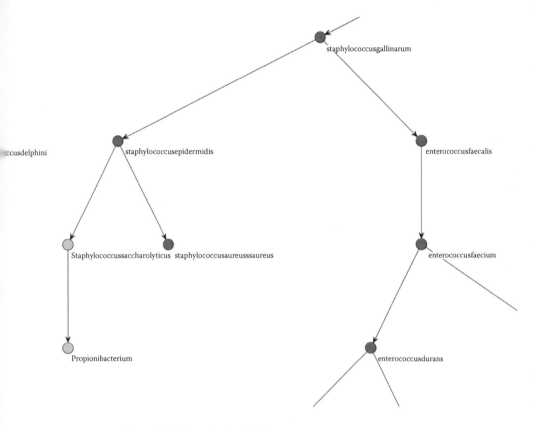

FIGURE 10.3 Detailed view of mixed color.

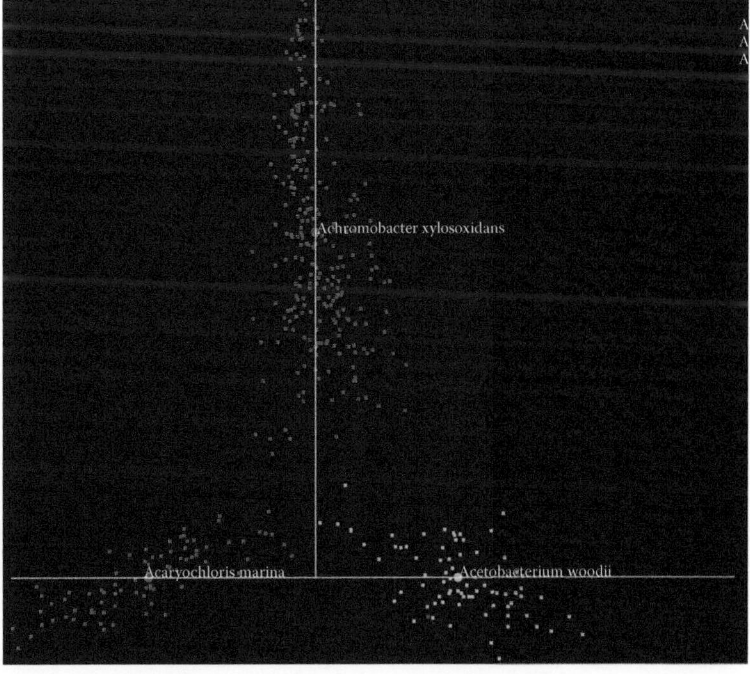

FIGURE 10.4 Scatter plot.

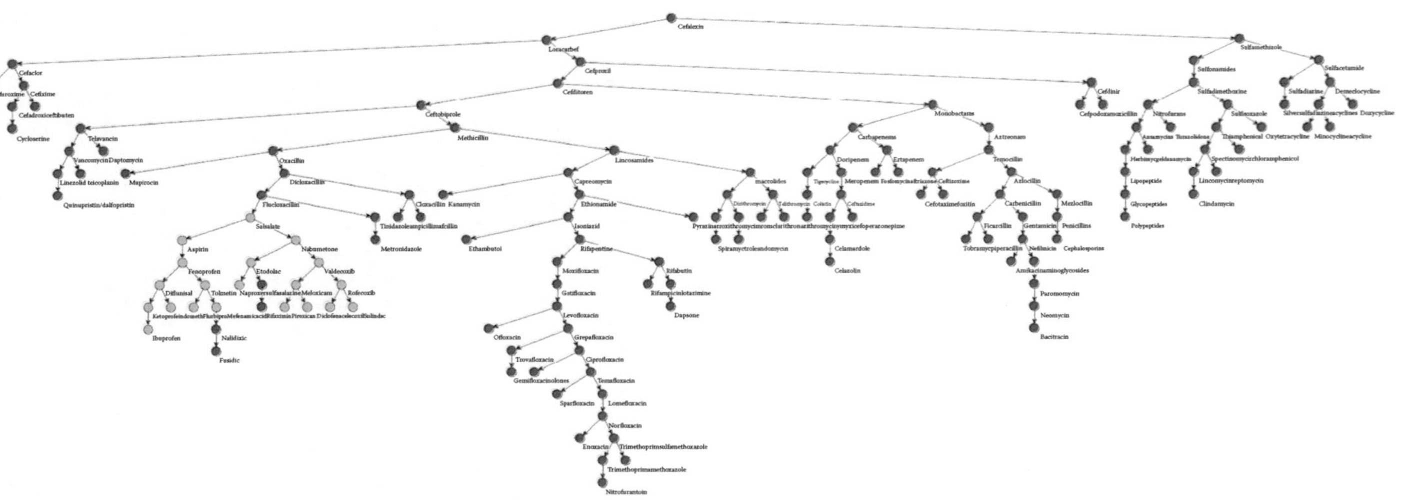

FIGURE 13.1 Anitbiotics and anti-inflammatories.

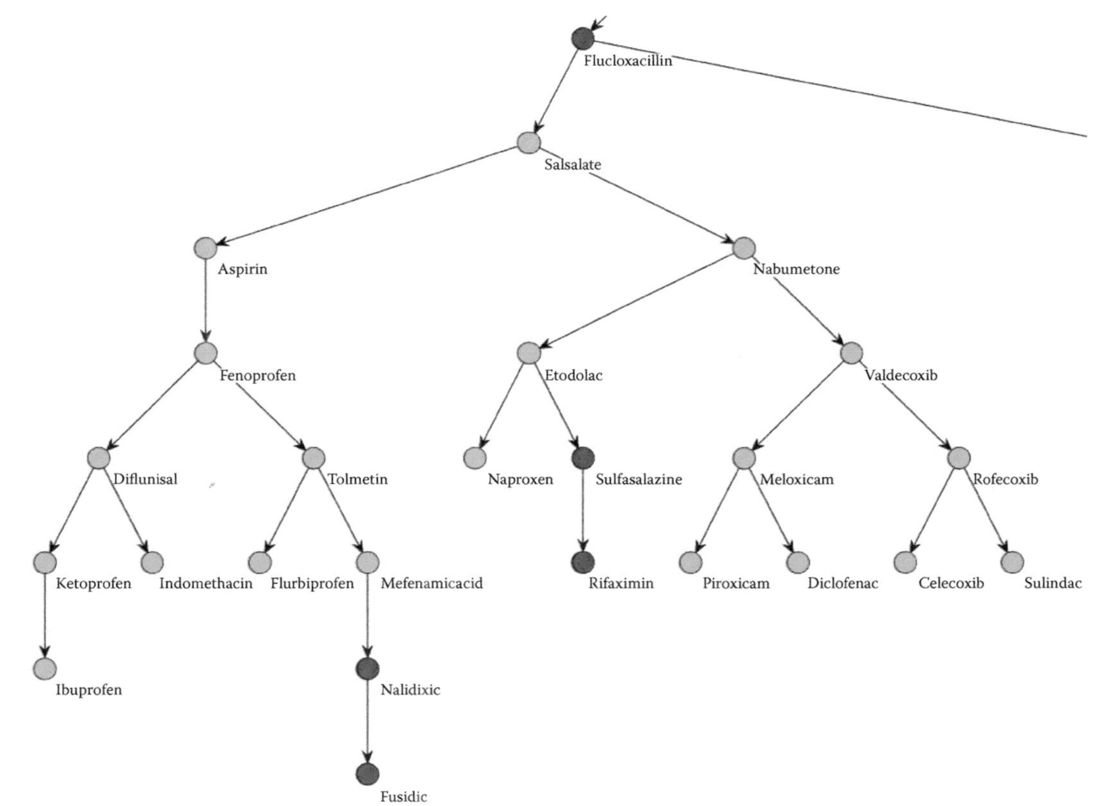

FIGURE 13.2 Detailed view of overlap area.

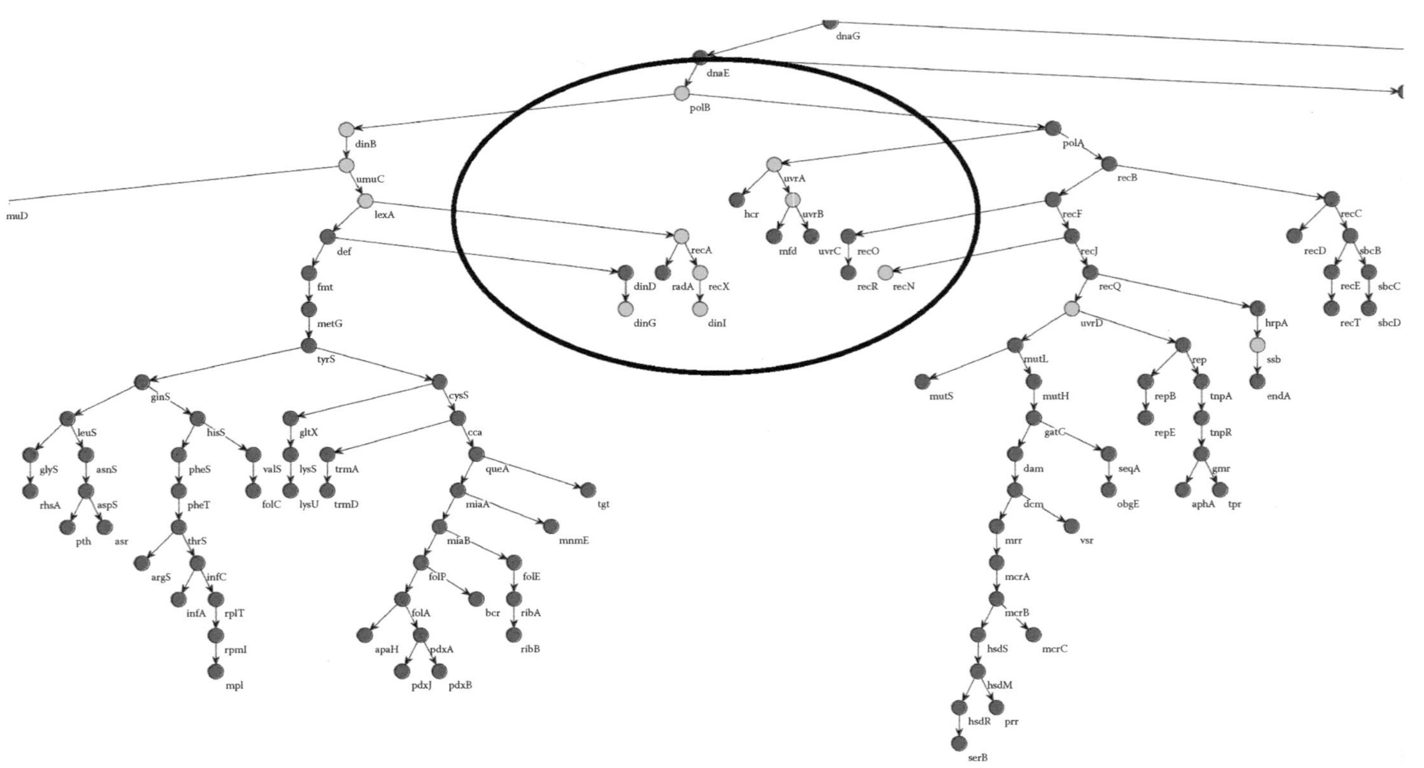

FIGURE 13.4 *E. Coli* proteins.

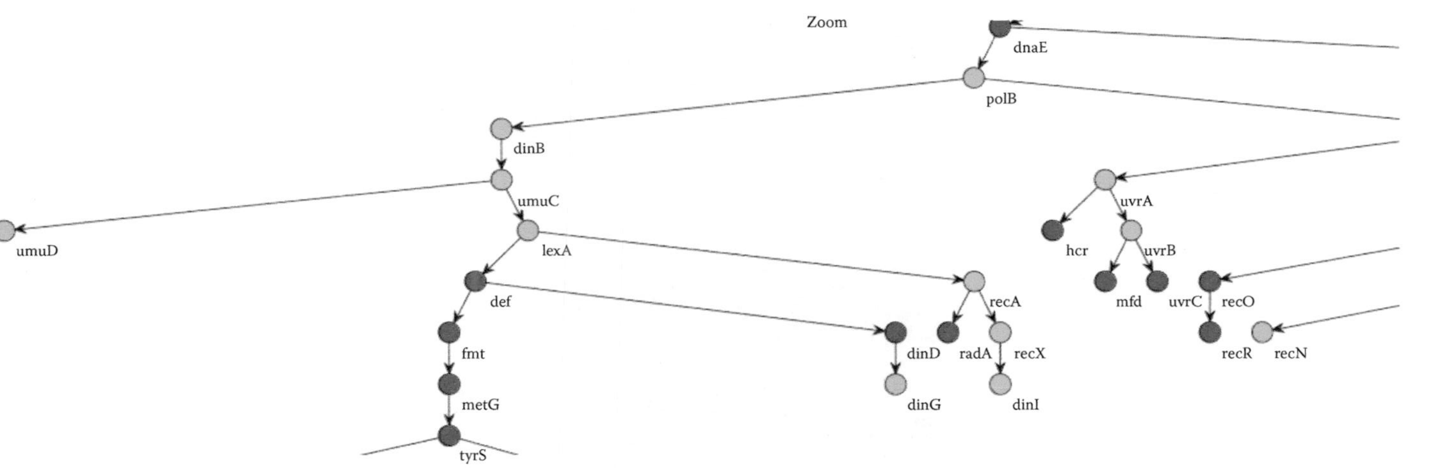

FIGURE 13.5 Area of overlap.

FIGURE 13.6 radA and recA.

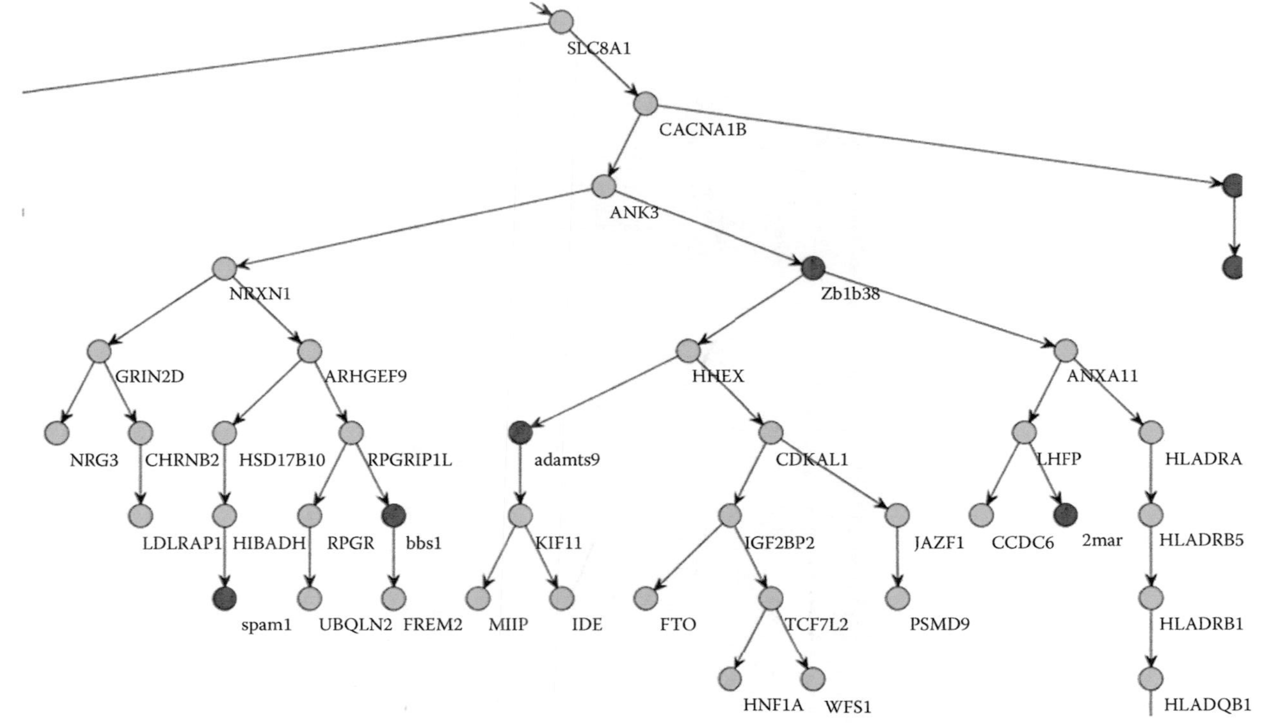

FIGURE 15.2 Area of high concentration of T2D genes.

FIGURE 16.3 Patients with moderate and severe COPD.

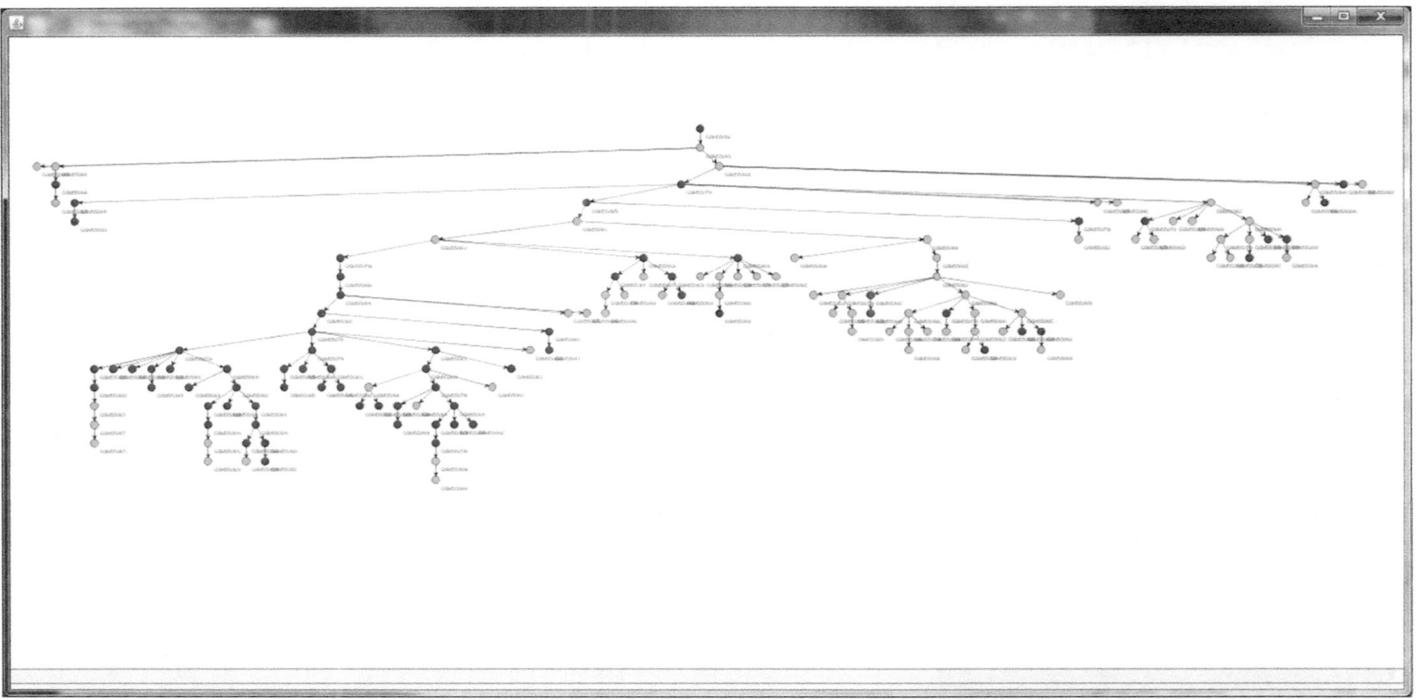

FIGURE 16.4 Patient similarity tree, colored by severity of COPD.

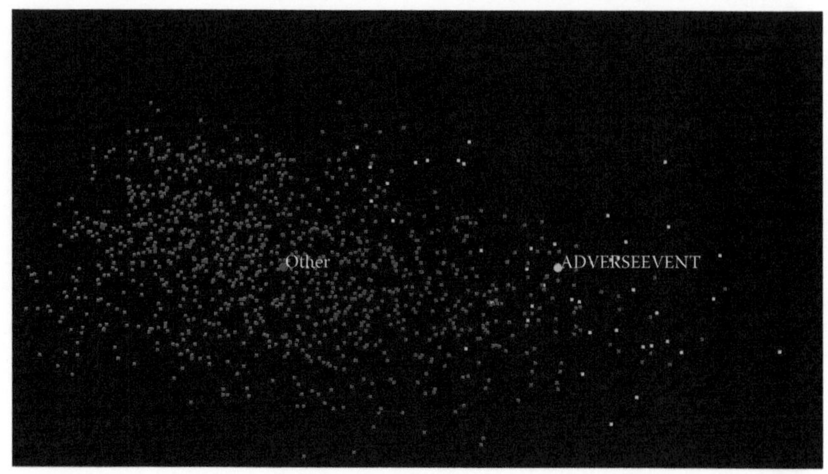

FIGURE 17.3 Cyclosporin abstracts, tagged and not tagged in MESH.

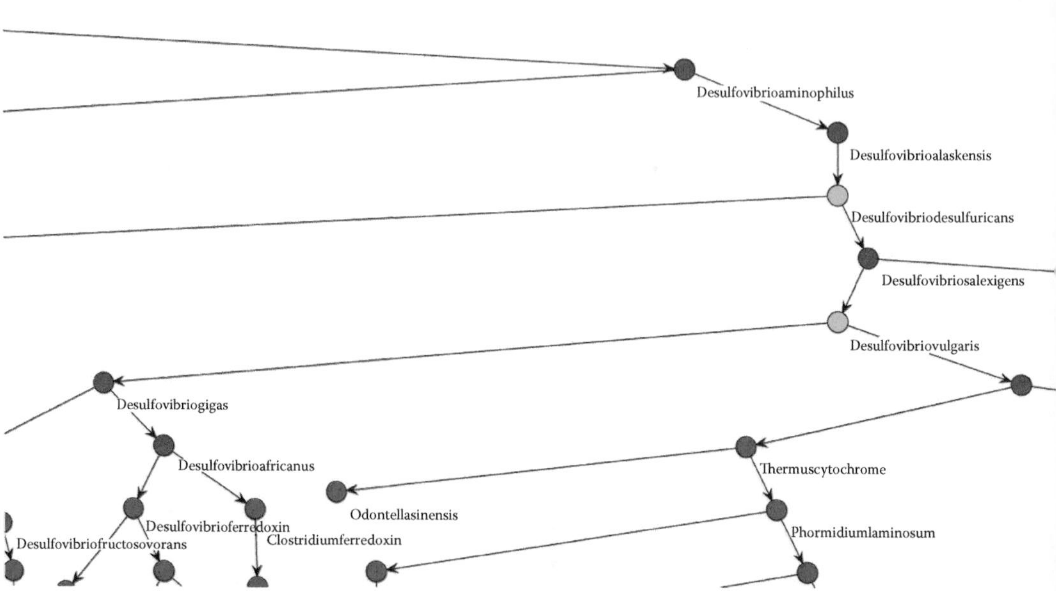

FIGURE 19.6 Blow up views of interesting areas in relative neighborhood graph of organisms.

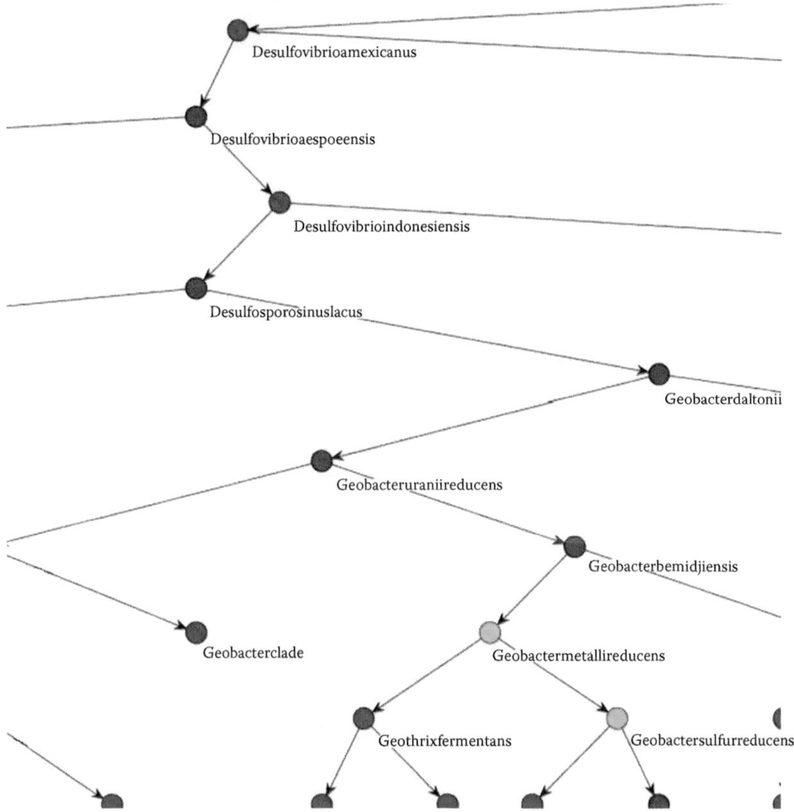

FIGURE 19.6 (Continued)

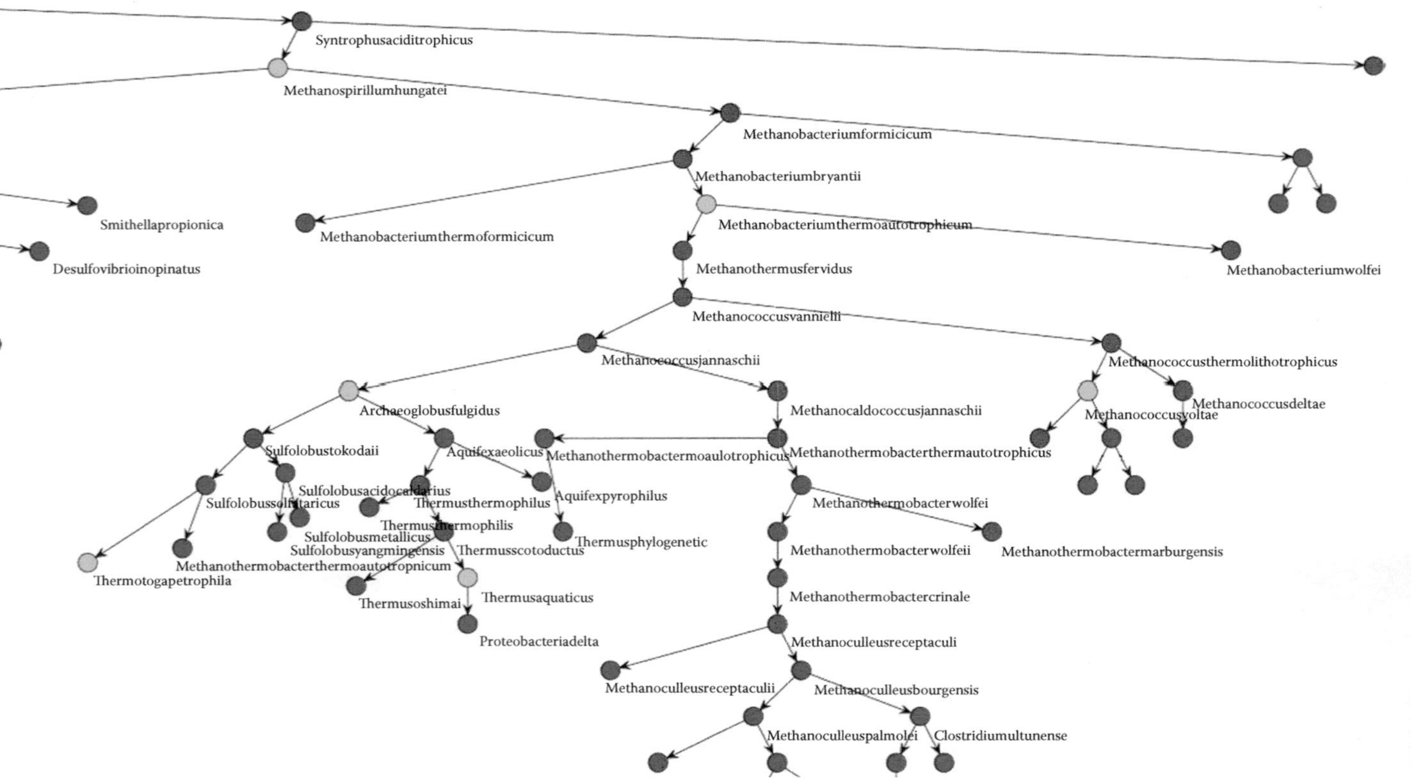

FIGURE 19.6 (Continued)

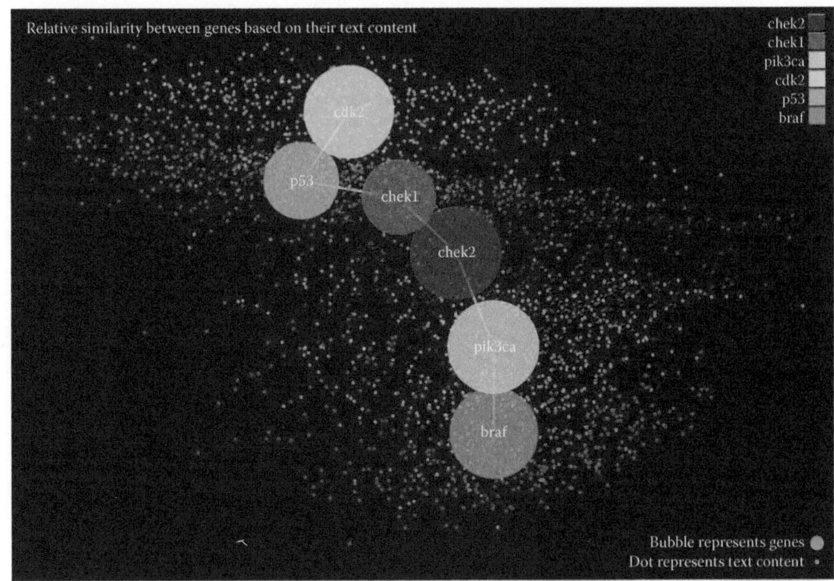

FIGURE 22.1 Gene network based on content centroids.

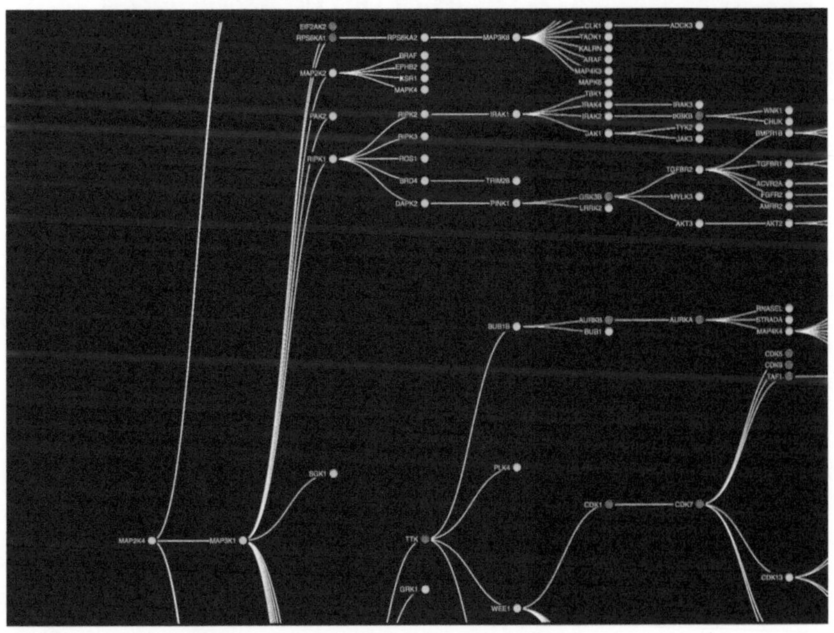

FIGURE 22.2 Kinase similarity network.

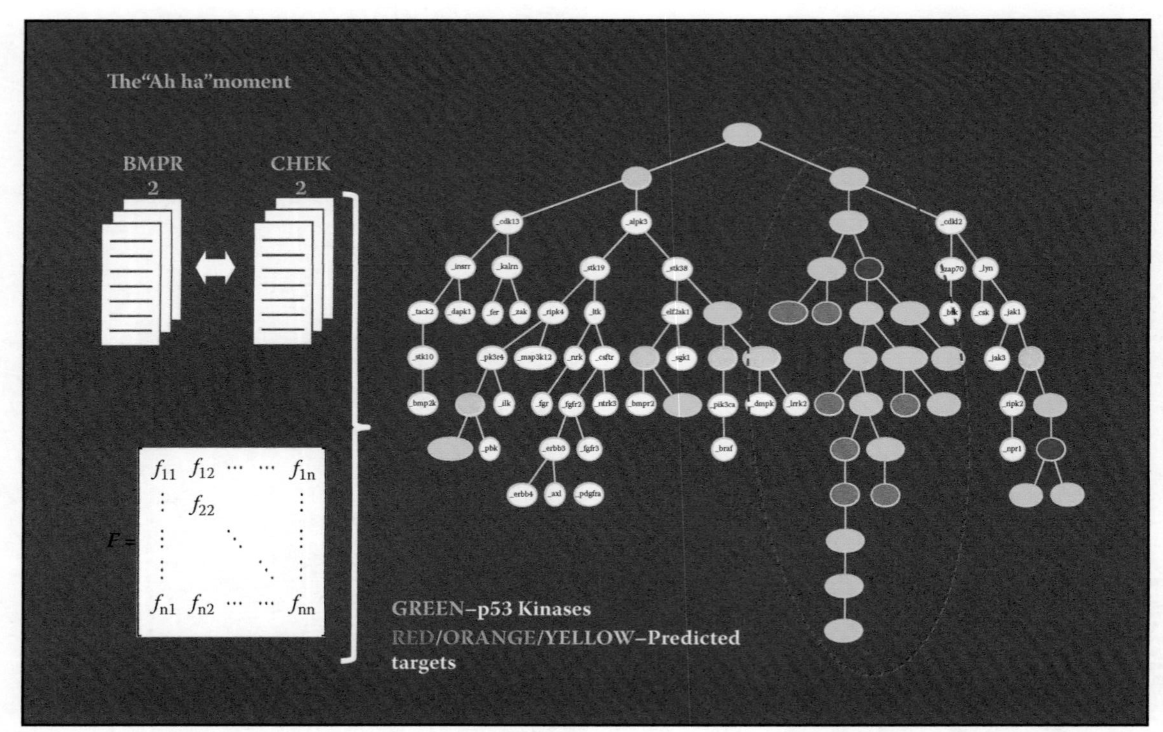

FIGURE 22.3 P53 kinases clump together.

CHAPTER 13

Problem: Discovery of Novel Properties of Known Entities

A COMMON PROBLEM THAT FACES scientists in the early stages of research is finding the best starting place. As individuals, we all of necessity have a very local frame of reference when it comes to knowledge. But this area of greatest familiarity to ourselves is actually the space least likely to divulge a novel discovery, since by its very nature it is ground we have already thoroughly trod. How do we look beyond the well known to the greener pastures of unfamiliarity?

This is exactly where simple search technologies are found most wanting. How do we search for what we do not know? What we need is not a navigator of the knowledge system but a map—something that will let us see the unexplored country.

ANTIBIOTICS AND ANTI-INFLAMMATORIES

Both antibiotic drugs and anti-inflammatory drugs deal with the human immune system, but in very different ways. Antibiotics target the invading pathogen, while anti-inflammatory drugs seek to counter an overactive immune response. Nevertheless, this tenuous connection has led some drug companies to wonder if there might be certain antibiotics that could work as anti-inflammatories (or vice versa).

Which antibiotics are most likely to work as anti-inflammatories?

Hint: First determine the entities and then determine how to collect sufficient data to understand what we know about those entities.

What data source and entities will provide the necessary content and framework to reason about possible hidden properties?

For this purpose, Medline abstracts will do nicely because they have very relevant and comprehensive material on both kinds of drugs. Next, we need an entity space to help us retrieve, organize, and visualize the relevant content. This is a list of approved drugs for inflammation as well as a list of known antibiotics. Fortunately, such lists are readily available on Wikipedia. These are not comprehensive but will serve for the purposes of illustration.

Next, we create a set of queries that return abstracts relating to each of these drugs. We limit ourselves to 100 abstracts for each drug; adding more does not really improve the result. The abstracts are then analyzed to extract the most frequently occurring words and phrases (bigrams). This dictionary is then used to create a vector space for the documents (each document represented as a bag of words). We can then create a centroid for each drug based on the abstracts that mention that drug.

How can we compare the different entities to each other to find potential entities that sit on the boundary between antibiotic and anti-inflammatory?

Hint: A similarity network will help visualize which drugs are similar to each other.

Now we measure the cosine distance between each centroid and every other centroid. This distance matrix is the basis for our similarity tree. We select as our root node the centroid that is closest to the average for all the centroids, considering this to be the most typical drug. Then we add nodes to the tree in a greedy fashion, first finding the drug most similar to the root, then the drug most similar to those two drugs, and so on. We limit each node to two children in order to improve the overall readability of the graph and to prevent situations wherein most nodes simply hang from the same parent. Next we color the nodes of the graph based on whether each drug is an antibiotic (red) or an anti-inflammatory (green) (Figure 13.1).

Notice how the anti-inflammatory drugs all clump together in one area of the tree. This is a remarkably clean differentiation, given that the algorithm knows nothing about drug type. What this implies is that the abstracts that talk about anti-inflammatory drugs all do so using a similar set of words

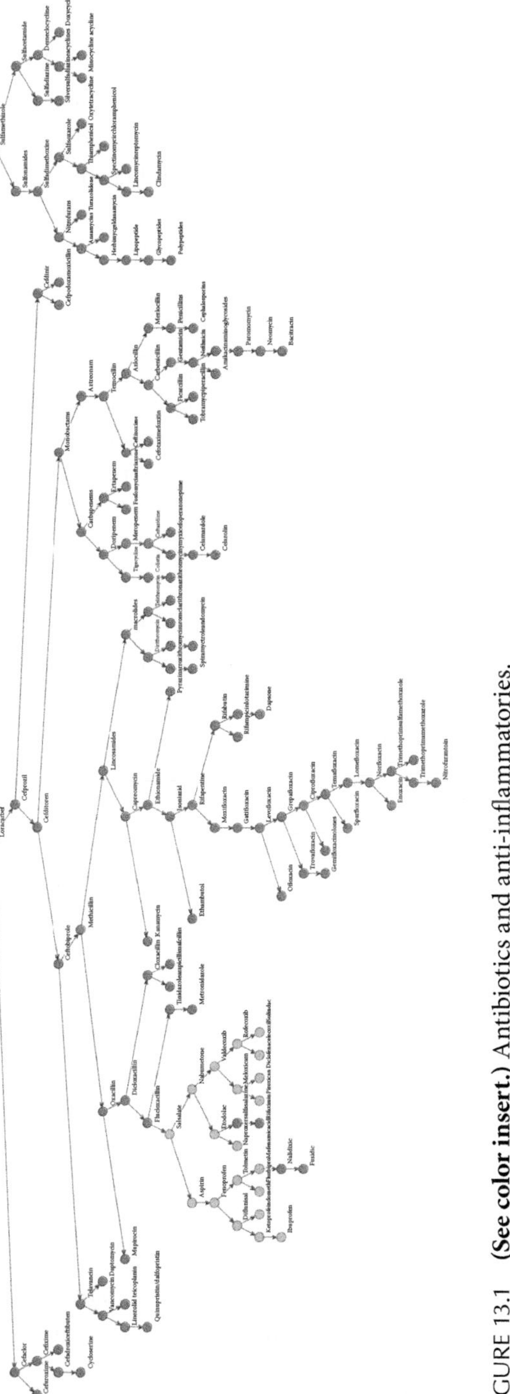

FIGURE 13.1 **(See color insert.)** Antibiotics and anti-inflammatories.

and phrases. This is not really that surprising, but what is remarkable is that very few other drugs seem to share that property. We can then focus our attention precisely on those few drugs that are anti-inflammatory but also seem to be related to some known antibiotics. We can see that four antibiotics are mixed in among the anti-inflammatories. Zooming into that branch of the tree shows the information presented in Figure 13.2.

This gives us a few good candidates to choose from in terms of antibiotics that might have anti-inflammatory properties.

How do we further validate our hypothesis?

Hint: Visualize the document space and find the documents that sit on the border between entities of different types.

Now we need to use the scatter-plot technology described earlier to zoom in further. In particular, we want to learn whether or not there is much overlap between the articles describing a particular anti-inflammatory drug and a particular antibiotic. If so, this could provide the lead we are looking for. A new hypothesis could be formed that suggests that the anti-inflammatory drug in question is somehow showing properties that we associate with antibiotics. Zooming in further, we can look at how the individual documents are laid out between two of the drugs, sulfasalazine and etodolac (Figure 13.3).

This plot, showing the vector-space distances between documents and centroids, shows clearly that there is very little actual overlap between the two drugs in terms of how they are talked about in Medline abstracts. Still, we can choose a few documents in the sulfasalazine cloud that are closest to the etodolac centroid. This reveals the following abstract:

> Thirty-two patients had had a prior resection of Crohn's disease. According to an adaptive design, patients were treated with sulfasalazine if able to take oral drugs; with steroids if unable to take, or unresponsive to, sulfasalazine; and with added azathioprine if unresponsive to sulfasalazine and steroids and unsuitable for surgery....Significant improvement occurred in all categories of patients. [1]

So given this evidence, it seems that sulfasalazine would be a promising antibiotic to try in the case of inflammatory diseases, such as Crohn's disease.

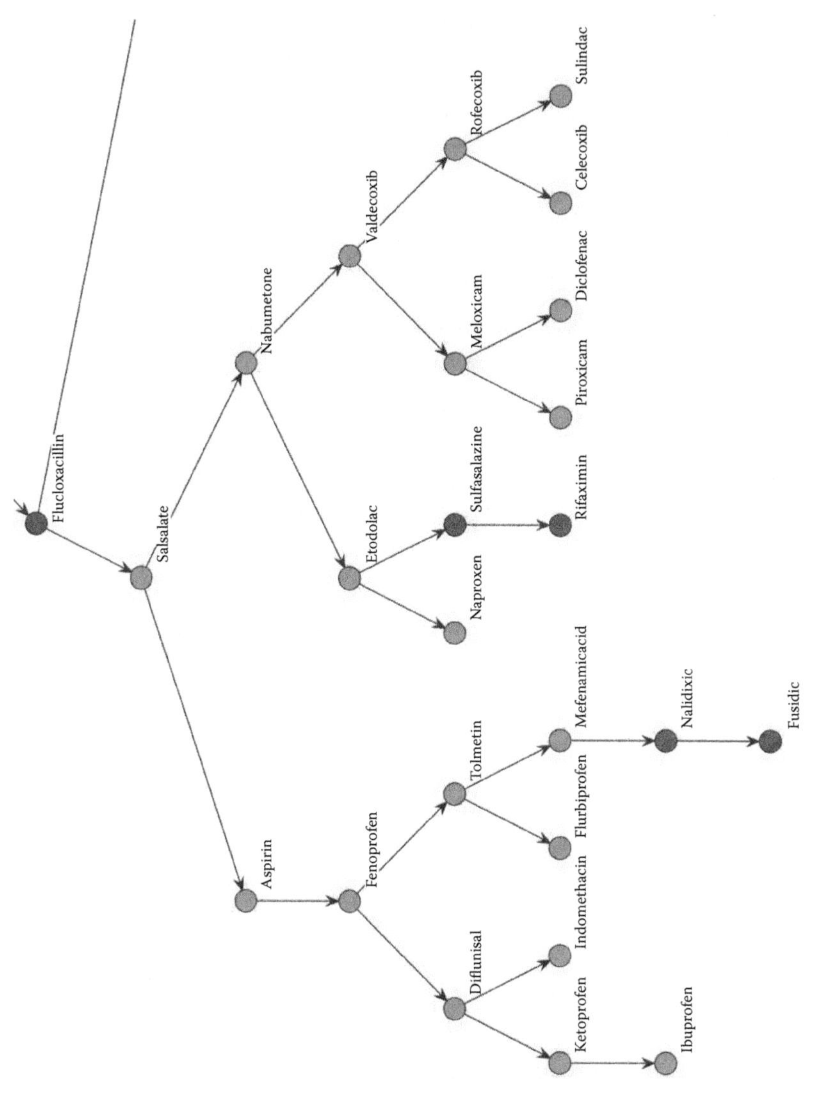

FIGURE 13.2 **(See color insert.)** Detailed view of overlap area.

FIGURE 13.3 Etodolac and sulfasalazine.

SOS PATHWAY FOR *ESCHERICHIA COLI*

Bacteria mutate very quickly, and this is how they develop immunity over time to antibiotics. Recently, some research has pointed to the possibility that one particular set of proteins, those in the SOS pathway, are most responsible for this ability to develop drug resistance. This opens up a new path for research to find ways to prevent these proteins from performing this function as well as they do in order to slow the evolution of drug-resistant bacteria.

How can we find additional proteins potentially relevant to SOS pathway function?

Hint: Think of the *Escherichia coli* proteins as the entity space.

Given a list of proteins for *E. coli*, we create a set of queries that downloads the Medline abstracts that mention these proteins along with *E. coli*. This then creates a vector space based on frequently occurring words and phrases that in turn leads to centroids representing the proteins. A most typical protein is found and the entire *E. coli* protein space is then graphed as a similarity tree. The SOS pathway proteins are then colored green and the other proteins are red (Figure 13.4).

Notice how the SOS pathway proteins are clumping together in the similarity tree. The SOS pathway is a feature that appears to be reflected well in the text that is written about these proteins.

The circled area is the section of the tree where the SOS pathway proteins ended up. A blow up view of this area is shown in Figure 13.5.

Fortunately, we see some promising leads here that will be useful in generating a new hypothesis. There are clearly some additional proteins that appear to be related to the SOS pathway proteins.

Next, we look at the detailed scatter-plot view of two of these proteins, one that is known to be in the SOS pathway, and another that is not. If we

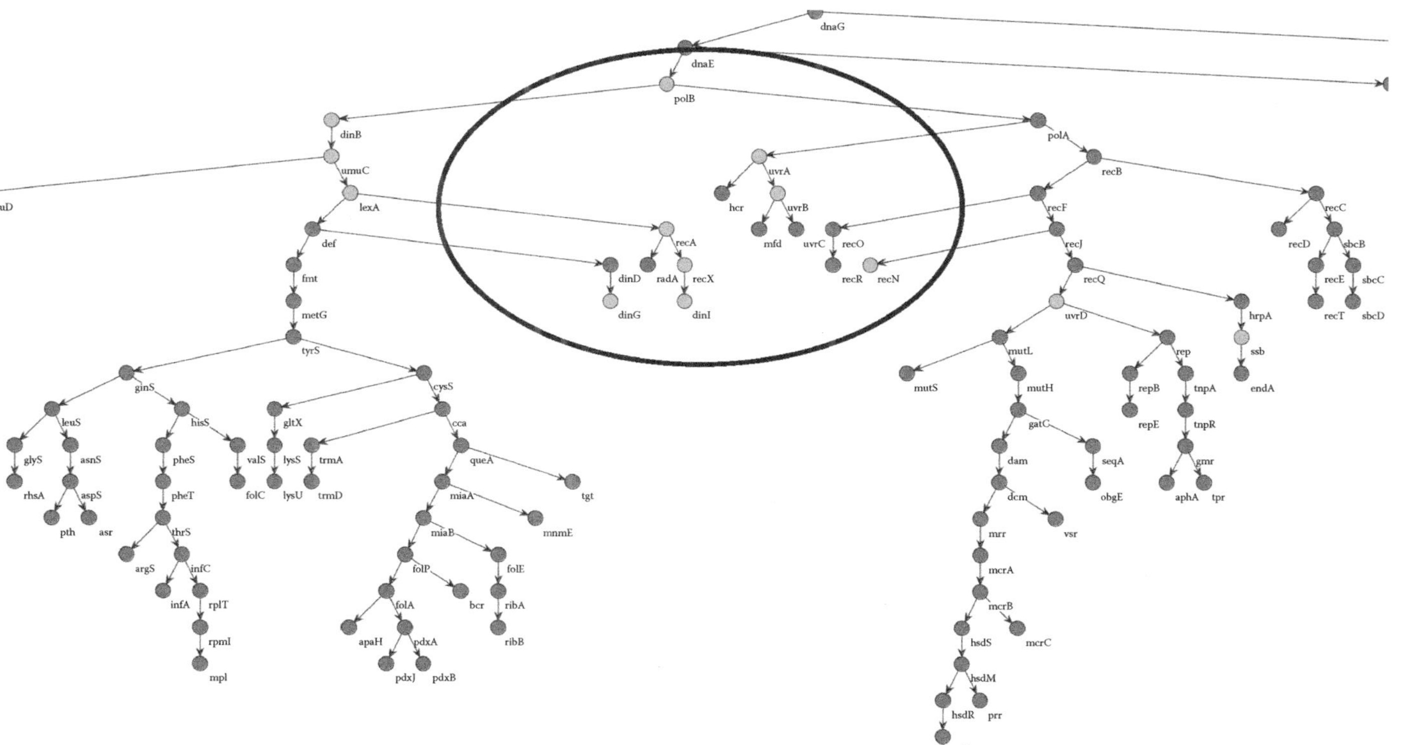

FIGURE 13.4 **(See color insert.)** *E. coli* proteins.

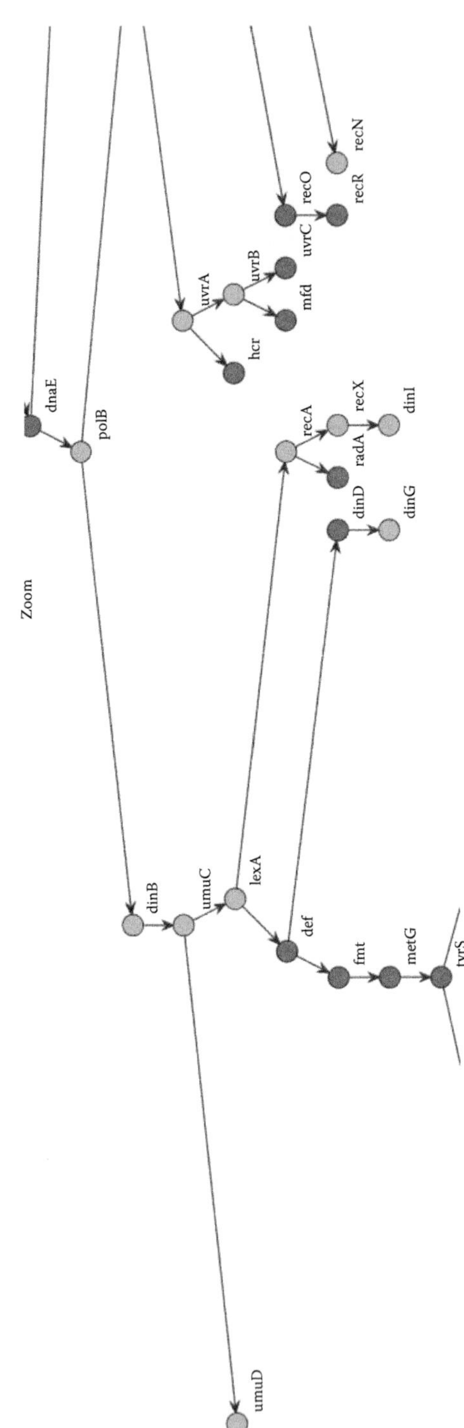

FIGURE 13.5 **(See color insert.)** Area of overlap.

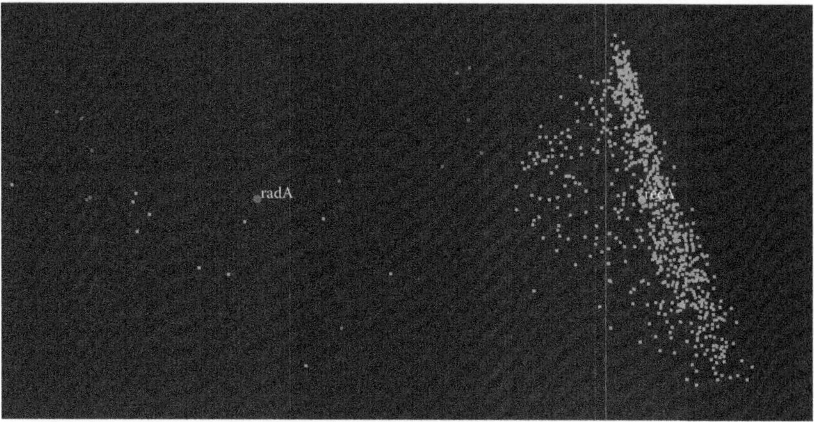

FIGURE 13.6 **(See color insert.)** radA and recA.

look at details for recA and radA in the document feature vector space, we see the scatter plot shown in Figure 13.6.

Clearly, radA and recA have many overlapping concepts and abstracts. Here is one title from one article mentioning both radA and recA that is most telling in this context.

> 3526390 Quantitation of the involvement of the recA, recB, recC, recF, recJ, recN, lexA, radA, radB, uvrD, and umuC genes in the repair of X-ray-induced DNA double-strand breaks in Escherichia coli [2]

So even though radA was not in our original list of SOS pathway genes, it does appear to be involved in the repair of DNA damage, which is the function of that pathway.

CONCLUSIONS

Both of these examples show the value of mapping out an entity space defined using documents that contain those entities in order to suggest which entities might have properties attributable to other similar entities. The key elements of this method of Accelerated Discovery is either two sets of entities (as in the example concerning the antibiotics vs. anti-inflammatories) or a small set of entities within a larger set (as in the example concerning the *E.coli* SOS pathway). Note that in each case, the entities involved were all of the same general type (drugs in the first case and proteins in the second). The hypothesis is that one or more of the elements in one set share some attributes with elements of the other set. Similarity trees based on text feature spaces help to visualize the best candidates for this kind of discovery, pointing the researcher in a promising direction but leaving them the freedom to direct the search as they see fit.

REFERENCES

1. Goldstein, F., Thornton, J. J., and Abramson, J. 1976. Anti-inflammatory drug treatment in Crohn's disease. *The American Journal of Gastroenterology*, *66*(3): 251–258.
2. Sargentini, N. J., and Smith, K. C. 1986. Quantitation of the involvement of the recA, recB, recC, recF, recJ, recN, lexA, radA, radB, uvrD, and umuC genes in the repair of x-ray-induced DNA double-strand breaks in *Escherichia coli*. *Radiation Research*, *107*(1): 58–72.

CHAPTER 14

Problem: Finding New Treatments for Orphan Diseases from Existing Drugs

MALARIA IS A PARASITE that affects red blood cells and the liver, where red blood cells are created. Malaria is a treatable disease, but over time the malaria parasite mutates in such a way that the standard treatments become less effective. New treatments are needed, but investment in malaria research is limited because the disease is most prevalent in poorer countries that cannot pay much for advanced drugs. This is why malaria is sometimes referred to as an "orphan disease," a term given to diseases that are not heavily researched, though their effect on human suffering is still significant.

One way to find new drugs for malaria without much investment in research is to look among the already approved drugs for other uses to see which of these, alone or in combination, might also prove to be effective against malaria. How might we quickly identify such drugs?

Hint: Over the years, malaria has been much studied and observed. Over 60,000 articles reference malaria in Medline abstracts. If we could comb through these and summarize all the findings and observations relating to malaria and known drugs, we could potentially discover a number of obscure associations that might turn out to be significant.

What data sources and entities will provide the necessary content?

We begin by obtaining a list of approved drugs and intersecting that list with the Medline abstracts on malaria. This process produces a set of over 200 approved drugs that are mentioned with malaria, only a handful of which are actually known established treatments for that disease.

To dig deeper, we need to find something more than co-occurrence in abstracts to determine relevance. How might we do this?

Hint: Think about detecting a more precise relationship between drug and disease.

One way to detect a complex pattern is to create a rule that captures the general syntax of what we are looking for, one that we can easily apply to large amounts of text. Here we want to capture the idea of drug effectiveness on a certain disease, so we create an "effectiveness" annotator.

To determine how effectiveness is expressed in Medline abstracts, we observe many sentences that contain a drug name of a known antimalarial along with a synonym for malaria and look to see what kinds of expressions are prevalent. Here is one such example:

> Amodiaquine has several advantages over sulfadoxine-pyrimethamine combination and may be considered to be an effective drug in an endemic zone with a moderate level of chloroquine resistance.

The drug name along with the word "effective" is a good indication that the article argues that the drug can be used to treat malaria. Further investigation revealed that the following patterns were generally most often seen in this regard.

IC50:IC50

An IC50 test is "a measure of the effectiveness of a substance in inhibiting a specific biological or biochemical function" [1]. It measures how much of a substance is needed to inhibit the function by half. Seeing this in the same abstract as a drug and malaria is a strong indication that some effect of the drug on malaria has been observed.

```
EffectiveMalaria:prevent.{0,30}malaria|prevent.{0,30}
plasmodium|effective.{0,100}falicparum|effective.
{0,100}malaria|effective.{0,100}plasmodium|treat.
{0,10}malaria|treat.{0,10}plasmodium|protect.{0,20}
malaria|protect.{0,20}plasmodium|malaria
```

```
resolved|efficacious.{0,60}plasmodium|efficacious.
{0,60}malaria
```

This pattern attempts to recognize when the word effective (or its synonyms) is used in combination with malaria or its synonyms.

```
ActiveAgainstMalaria:active.{0,30}plasmodium|active.
{0,30}malaria|active.{0,30}faliparum|susceptib.{0,30}
falciparum|susceptib.{0,30}malaria|susceptib.{0,30}
plasmodium|antimalarial effect|potential benefit.
{0,30}malaria
```

This pattern attempts to find a slightly less strong indication that shows some possible association between a drug and malaria.

```
NoEffectMalaria:no.{0,10}effec.{0,60}malaria|no.{0,10}
effec.{0,60}plasmodium|not.{0,10} effec.{0,60}
malaria|not.{0,10} effec.{0,60}plasmodium|ineffective.
{0,60}malaria|ineffective.{0,60}plasmodium|ineffective.
{0,60}falciparum
```

This pattern indicates no effect of the drug on malaria. This contrary evidence can be used to eliminate some drugs that may otherwise look promising.

Now that we have a useful set of patterns, how do we find the most likely antimalarial drugs?

If we apply these patterns to the set of drugs that occur with malaria, the best candidates based on all Medline articles become much more readily apparent (Figure 14.1).

The drug list has been sorted based on a chi-squared test to determine relevance to the EffectiveMalaria pattern. The drugs beginning with a capital letter are those well known to treat malaria. The interesting finding is that those drugs, such as azithromycin or dapsone, were not considered by the customer to be known already as established malaria treatment options. We can also combine the three effectiveness categories to get an even more straightforward list (Figure 14.2).

Using probabilities to sort these drugs rather than simple frequency helps to prevent overly favoring drugs that simply occur frequently in Medline. We can also break this down by type of malaria (Figure 14.3).

The results of this analysis were published in an article about IBM and GSK in the *New York Times* [2].

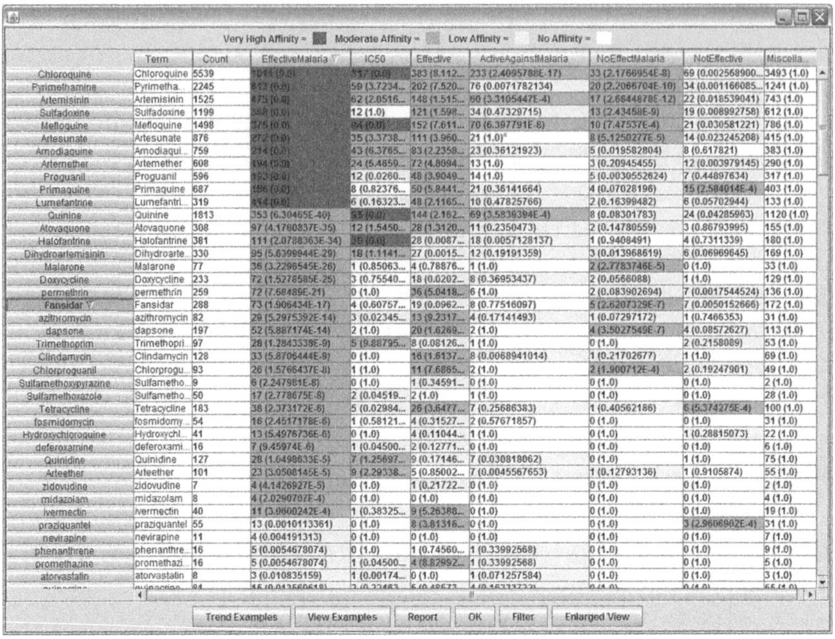

Very High Affinity = ■ Moderate Affinity = ■ Low Affinity = ■ No Affinity = □

	Term	Count	EffectiveMalaria	IC50	Effective	ActiveAgainstMalaria	NoEffectMalaria	NotEffective	Miscella...
Chloroquine	Chloroquine	5539	1041 (0.0)	317 (0.0)	383 (8.112...	233 (2.4095788E-17)	33 (2.1760954E-8)	69 (0.002568900...	3493 (1.0)
Pyrimethamine	Pyrimetha...	2245	813 (0.0)	59 (3.7234...	202 (7.520...	76 (0.0071782134)	20 (2.2066704E-10)	34 (0.001166085...	1241 (1.0)
Artemisinin	Artemisinin	1525	475 (0.0)	62 (2.0516...	148 (1.515...	60 (3.3105447E-4)	17 (2.6844878E-12)	22 (0.018539041)	743 (1.0)
Sulfadoxine	Sulfadoxine	1199	358 (0.0)	12 (1.0)	121 (1.598...	34 (0.47329715)	13 (2.43458E-9)	19 (0.008992758)	612 (1.0)
Mefloquine	Mefloquine	1498	375 (0.0)	64 (0.0)	152 (7.611...	70 (6.397791E-8)	10 (7.47537E-4)	21 (0.030581221)	786 (1.0)
Artesunate	Artesunate	876	272 (0.0)	35 (3.3738...	111 (3.960...	21 (1.0)	8 (5.1250277E-5)	14 (0.023245208)	415 (1.0)
Amodiaquine	Amodiaqui...	759	214 (0.0)	43 (6.3765...	83 (2.2358...	23 (0.36121923)	5 (0.019582804)	8 (0.617821)	383 (1.0)
Artemether	Artemether	608	194 (0.0)	24 (5.4659...	72 (4.8094...	13 (1.0)	3 (0.20945455)	12 (0.003979145)	290 (1.0)
Proguanil	Proguanil	596	193 (0.0)	12 (0.0260...	48 (3.9049...	14 (1.0)	5 (0.0030552624)	7 (0.44897634)	317 (1.0)
Primaquine	Primaquine	687	186 (0.0)	8 (0.82376...	50 (5.8441...	21 (0.36141664)	4 (0.07028196)	15 (2.584014E-4)	403 (1.0)
Lumefantrine	Lumefantri...	319	154 (0.0)	6 (0.16323...	48 (2.1165...	10 (0.47825766)	2 (0.16399482)	6 (0.05702944)	133 (1.0)
Quinine	Quinine	1813	353 (6.30465E-40)	55 (0.0)	144 (2.162...	69 (3.5839394E-4)	8 (0.08301783)	24 (0.04285963)	1120 (1.0)
Atovaquone	Atovaquone	308	97 (4.1760837E-35)	12 (1.5450...	28 (1.3120...	11 (0.2350473)	2 (0.14780559)	3 (0.86793995)	155 (1.0)
Halofantrine	Halofantrine	381	111 (2.0788363E-34)	35 (0.0)	28 (0.0087...	18 (0.0057128137)	1 (0.9408491)	4 (0.7311339)	180 (1.0)
Dihydroartemisinin	Dihydroarte...	330	95 (5.6399944E-29)	18 (1.1141...	27 (0.0015...	12 (0.19191359)	3 (0.013968619)	6 (0.06969645)	169 (1.0)
Malarone	Malarone	77	36 (3.2296545E-26)	1 (0.85063...	4 (0.78876...	1 (1.0)	2 (2.7783746E-5)	0 (1.0)	33 (1.0)
Doxycycline	Doxycycline	233	72 (1.5278585E-25)	3 (0.75540...	18 (0.0202...	8 (0.36953437)	2 (0.0566088)	1 (1.0)	129 (1.0)
permethrin	permethrin	259	72 (7.68489E-21)	0 (1.0)	36 (5.0418...	6 (1.0)	2 (0.083902694)	7 (0.0017544524)	136 (1.0)
Fansidar	Fansidar	288	73 (1.906434E-17)	4 (0.60757...	19 (0.0962...	8 (0.77516097)	5 (2.6207329E-7)	7 (0.0050152666)	172 (1.0)
azithromycin	azithromycin	82	29 (5.2975392E-14)	3 (0.02345...	13 (9.2317...	4 (0.17141493)	1 (0.07297172)	1 (0.7466353)	31 (1.0)
dapsone	dapsone	197	52 (5.887174E-14)	2 (1.0)	20 (1.6269...	2 (1.0)	4 (3.5027549E-7)	4 (0.08572627)	113 (1.0)
Trimethoprim	Trimethopri...	97	28 (1.2843339E-9)	5 (9.88795...	8 (0.08126...	1 (1.0)	0 (1.0)	2 (0.2158089)	53 (1.0)
Clindamycin	Clindamycin	128	33 (5.8706444E-9)	0 (1.0)	16 (1.6137...	8 (0.0068941014)	1 (0.21702677)	1 (1.0)	69 (1.0)
Chlorproguanil	Chlorprogu...	93	26 (1.5766437E-8)	1 (1.0)	11 (7.6865...	2 (1.0)	2 (1.900712E-4)	2 (0.19247901)	49 (1.0)
Sulfamethoxypyrazine	Sulfametho...	9	6 (2.247981E-8)	0 (1.0)	1 (0.34591...	0 (1.0)	0 (1.0)	0 (1.0)	2 (1.0)
Sulfamethoxazole	Sulfametho...	50	17 (2.778675E-8)	2 (0.04519...	2 (1.0)	1 (1.0)	0 (1.0)	0 (1.0)	28 (1.0)
Tetracycline	Tetracycline	183	38 (2.373172E-6)	5 (0.02984...	26 (3.6477...	7 (0.25686383)	1 (0.40562186)	6 (5.374275E-4)	100 (1.0)
fosmidomycin	fosmidomy...	54	16 (2.4517178E-6)	1 (0.58121...	4 (0.31527...	2 (0.57671857)	0 (1.0)	0 (1.0)	31 (1.0)
Hydroxychloroquine	Hydroxychl...	41	13 (5.4976736E-6)	0 (1.0)	4 (0.11044...	1 (1.0)	0 (1.0)	1 (0.28815073)	22 (1.0)
deferoxamine	deferoxami...	16	7 (9.45974E-6)	1 (0.04500...	2 (0.12771...	0 (1.0)	0 (1.0)	0 (1.0)	6 (1.0)
Quinidine	Quinidine	127	28 (1.0498633E-5)	7 (1.25697...	9 (0.17146...	7 (0.030818062)	0 (1.0)	1 (1.0)	75 (1.0)
Arteether	Arteether	101	23 (3.0508145E-5)	9 (2.29338...	5 (0.85002...	7 (0.0045567653)	1 (0.12793136)	1 (0.9105874)	55 (1.0)
zidovudine	zidovudine	7	4 (4.1426927E-5)	0 (1.0)	1 (0.21722...	0 (1.0)	0 (1.0)	0 (1.0)	2 (1.0)
midazolam	midazolam	8	4 (2.0290707E-4)	0 (1.0)	0 (1.0)	0 (1.0)	0 (1.0)	0 (1.0)	4 (1.0)
ivermectin	ivermectin	40	11 (3.0600242E-4)	1 (0.38325...	9 (5.26388...	0 (1.0)	0 (1.0)	0 (1.0)	19 (1.0)
praziquantel	praziquantel	55	13 (0.0010113361)	0 (1.0)	8 (3.81316...	0 (1.0)	0 (1.0)	3 (2.9606902E-4)	31 (1.0)
nevirapine	nevirapine	11	4 (0.004191313)	0 (1.0)	0 (1.0)	0 (1.0)	0 (1.0)	0 (1.0)	7 (1.0)
phenanthrene	phenanthre...	16	5 (0.0054678074)	0 (1.0)	1 (0.74560...	1 (0.33992568)	0 (1.0)	0 (1.0)	9 (1.0)
promethazine	promethazi...	16	5 (0.0054678074)	1 (0.04500...	4 (8.82992...	1 (0.33992568)	0 (1.0)	0 (1.0)	5 (1.0)
atorvastatin	atorvastatin	8	3 (0.010835159)	1 (0.00174...	0 (1.0)	1 (0.071257584)	0 (1.0)	0 (1.0)	3 (1.0)

Trend Examples | View Examples | Report | OK | Filter | Enlarged View

FIGURE 14.1 Drugs and effectiveness cotable.

ANALYSIS 14.1

John Baldoni, senior vice president for technology and science at GlaxoSmithKline, got in touch with IBM shortly after watching Watson's "Jeopardy" triumph. He was struck that Watson frequently had the right answer, he said, "but what really impressed me was that it so quickly sifted out so many wrong answers."

That is a huge challenge in drug discovery, which amounts to making a high-stakes bet, over years of testing, on the success of a chemical compound. The failure rate is high. Improving the odds, Mr. Baldoni said, could have a huge payoff economically and medically.

Glaxo and IBM researchers put Watson through a test run. They fed it all the literature on malaria, known anti-malarial drugs and other chemical compounds. Watson correctly identified known anti-malarial drugs, and suggested 15 other compounds as potential drugs to combat malaria. The two companies are now discussing other projects.

"It doesn't just answer questions, it encourages you to think more widely," said Catherine E. Peishoff, vice president for computational and structural chemistry at Glaxo. "It essentially says, 'Look over here, think about this.' That's one of the exciting things about this technology."

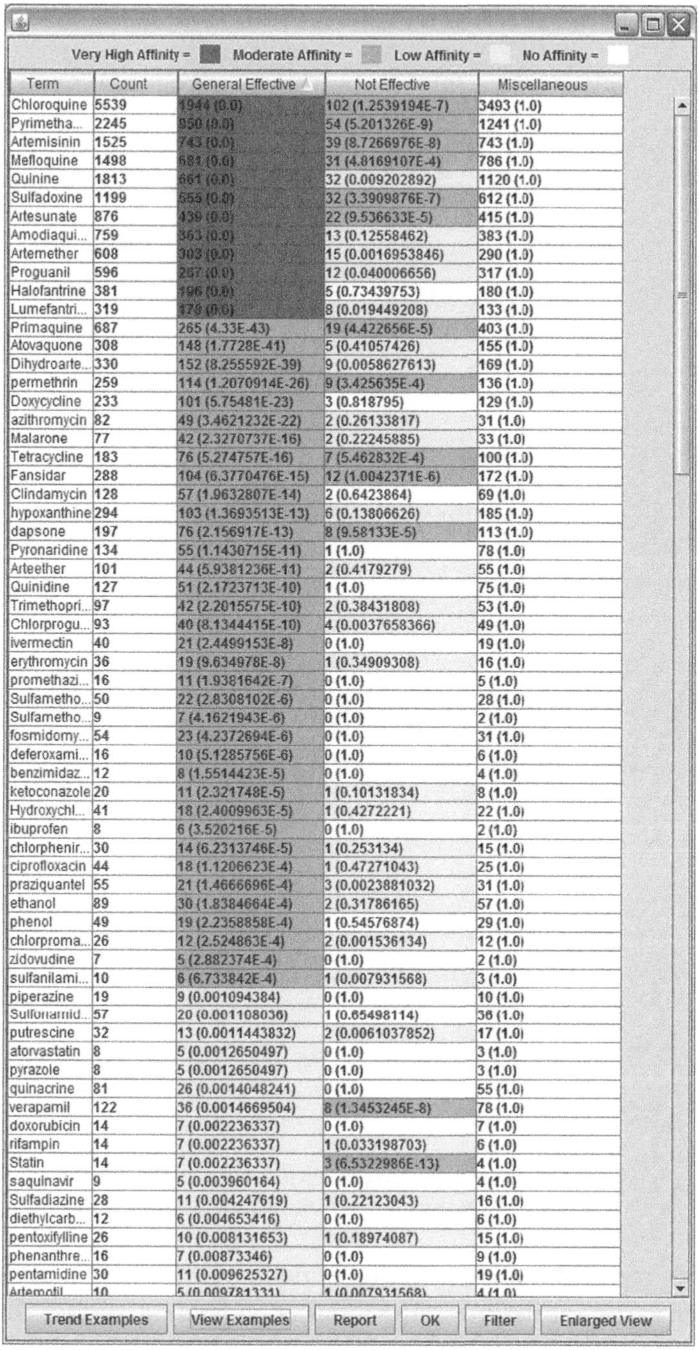

Term	Count	General Effective	Not Effective	Miscellaneous
Chloroquine	5539	1944 (0.0)	102 (1.2539194E-7)	3493 (1.0)
Pyrimetha...	2245	950 (0.0)	54 (5.201326E-9)	1241 (1.0)
Artemisinin	1525	743 (0.0)	39 (8.7266976E-8)	743 (1.0)
Mefloquine	1498	681 (0.0)	31 (4.8169107E-4)	786 (1.0)
Quinine	1813	661 (0.0)	32 (0.009202892)	1120 (1.0)
Sulfadoxine	1199	555 (0.0)	32 (3.3909876E-7)	612 (1.0)
Artesunate	876	439 (0.0)	22 (9.536633E-5)	415 (1.0)
Amodiaqui...	759	363 (0.0)	13 (0.12558462)	383 (1.0)
Artemether	608	303 (0.0)	15 (0.0016953846)	290 (1.0)
Proguanil	596	267 (0.0)	12 (0.040006656)	317 (1.0)
Halofantrine	381	196 (0.0)	5 (0.73439753)	180 (1.0)
Lumefantri...	319	179 (0.0)	8 (0.019449208)	133 (1.0)
Primaquine	687	265 (4.33E-43)	19 (4.422656E-5)	403 (1.0)
Atovaquone	308	148 (1.7728E-41)	5 (0.41057426)	155 (1.0)
Dihydroarte...	330	152 (8.255592E-39)	9 (0.0058627613)	169 (1.0)
permethrin	259	114 (1.2070914E-26)	9 (3.425635E-4)	136 (1.0)
Doxycycline	233	101 (5.75481E-23)	3 (0.818795)	129 (1.0)
azithromycin	82	49 (3.4621232E-22)	2 (0.26133817)	31 (1.0)
Malarone	77	42 (2.3270737E-16)	2 (0.22245885)	33 (1.0)
Tetracycline	183	76 (5.274757E-16)	7 (5.462832E-4)	100 (1.0)
Fansidar	288	104 (6.3770476E-15)	12 (1.0042371E-6)	172 (1.0)
Clindamycin	128	57 (1.9632807E-14)	2 (0.6423864)	69 (1.0)
hypoxanthine	294	103 (1.3693513E-13)	6 (0.13806626)	185 (1.0)
dapsone	197	76 (2.156917E-13)	8 (9.58133E-5)	113 (1.0)
Pyronaridine	134	55 (1.1430715E-11)	1 (1.0)	78 (1.0)
Arteether	101	44 (5.9381236E-11)	2 (0.4179279)	55 (1.0)
Quinidine	127	51 (2.1723713E-10)	1 (1.0)	75 (1.0)
Trimethopri...	97	42 (2.2015575E-10)	2 (0.38431808)	53 (1.0)
Chlorprogu...	93	40 (8.1344415E-10)	4 (0.0037658366)	49 (1.0)
ivermectin	40	21 (2.4499153E-8)	0 (1.0)	19 (1.0)
erythromycin	36	19 (9.634978E-8)	1 (0.34909308)	16 (1.0)
promethazi...	16	11 (1.9381642E-7)	0 (1.0)	5 (1.0)
Sulfametho...	50	22 (2.8308102E-6)	0 (1.0)	28 (1.0)
Sulfametho...	9	7 (4.1621943E-6)	0 (1.0)	2 (1.0)
fosmidomy...	54	23 (4.2372694E-6)	0 (1.0)	31 (1.0)
deferoxami...	16	10 (5.1285756E-6)	0 (1.0)	6 (1.0)
benzimidaz...	12	8 (1.5514423E-5)	0 (1.0)	4 (1.0)
ketoconazole	20	11 (2.321748E-5)	1 (0.10131834)	8 (1.0)
Hydroxychl...	41	18 (2.4009963E-5)	1 (0.4272221)	22 (1.0)
ibuprofen	8	6 (3.520216E-5)	0 (1.0)	2 (1.0)
chlorphenir...	30	14 (6.2313746E-5)	1 (0.253134)	15 (1.0)
ciprofloxacin	44	18 (1.1206623E-4)	1 (0.47271043)	25 (1.0)
praziquantel	55	21 (1.4666696E-4)	3 (0.0023881032)	31 (1.0)
ethanol	89	30 (1.8384664E-4)	2 (0.31786165)	57 (1.0)
phenol	49	19 (2.2358858E-4)	1 (0.54576874)	29 (1.0)
chlorproma...	26	12 (2.524863E-4)	2 (0.001536134)	12 (1.0)
zidovudine	7	5 (2.882374E-4)	0 (1.0)	2 (1.0)
sulfanilami...	10	6 (6.733842E-4)	1 (0.007931568)	3 (1.0)
piperazine	19	9 (0.001094384)	0 (1.0)	10 (1.0)
Sulfonamid...	57	20 (0.001108036)	1 (0.65498114)	36 (1.0)
putrescine	32	13 (0.0011443832)	2 (0.0061037852)	17 (1.0)
atorvastatin	8	5 (0.0012650497)	0 (1.0)	3 (1.0)
pyrazole	8	5 (0.0012650497)	0 (1.0)	3 (1.0)
quinacrine	81	26 (0.0014048241)	0 (1.0)	55 (1.0)
verapamil	122	36 (0.0014669504)	8 (1.3453245E-8)	78 (1.0)
doxorubicin	14	7 (0.002236337)	0 (1.0)	7 (1.0)
rifampin	14	7 (0.002236337)	1 (0.033198703)	6 (1.0)
Statin	14	7 (0.002236337)	3 (6.5322986E-13)	4 (1.0)
saquinavir	9	5 (0.003960164)	0 (1.0)	4 (1.0)
Sulfadiazine	28	11 (0.004247619)	1 (0.22123043)	16 (1.0)
diethylcarb...	12	6 (0.004653416)	0 (1.0)	6 (1.0)
pentoxifylline	26	10 (0.008131653)	1 (0.18974087)	15 (1.0)
phenanthre...	16	7 (0.00873346)	0 (1.0)	9 (1.0)
pentamidine	30	11 (0.009625327)	0 (1.0)	19 (1.0)
Artemotil...	10	5 (0.009781331)	1 (0.007931568)	4 (1.0)

FIGURE 14.2 Drugs sorted by general effectiveness against malaria.

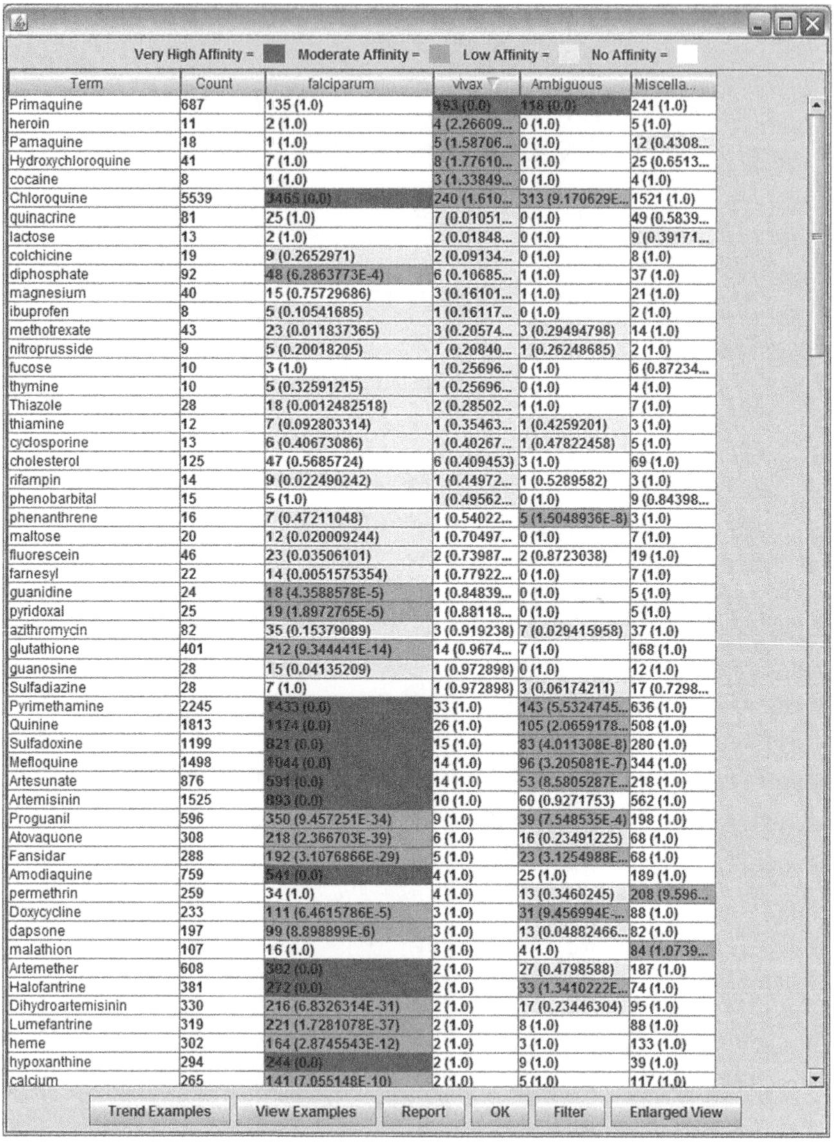

Very High Affinity = ■ Moderate Affinity = ■ Low Affinity = ■ No Affinity = □

Term	Count	falciparum	vivax	Ambiguous	Miscella...
Primaquine	687	135 (1.0)	193 (0.0)	118 (0.0)	241 (1.0)
heroin	11	2 (1.0)	4 (2.26609...	0 (1.0)	5 (1.0)
Pamaquine	18	1 (1.0)	5 (1.58706...	0 (1.0)	12 (0.4308...
Hydroxychloroquine	41	7 (1.0)	8 (1.77610...	1 (1.0)	25 (0.6513...
cocaine	8	1 (1.0)	3 (1.33849...	0 (1.0)	4 (1.0)
Chloroquine	5539	3465 (0.0)	240 (1.610...	313 (9.170629E...	1521 (1.0)
quinacrine	81	25 (1.0)	7 (0.01051...	0 (1.0)	49 (0.5839...
lactose	13	2 (1.0)	2 (0.01848...	0 (1.0)	9 (0.39171...
colchicine	19	9 (0.2652971)	2 (0.09134...	0 (1.0)	8 (1.0)
diphosphate	92	48 (6.2863773E-4)	6 (0.10685...	1 (1.0)	37 (1.0)
magnesium	40	15 (0.75729686)	3 (0.16101...	1 (1.0)	21 (1.0)
ibuprofen	8	5 (0.10541685)	1 (0.16117...	0 (1.0)	2 (1.0)
methotrexate	43	23 (0.011837365)	3 (0.20574...	3 (0.29494798)	14 (1.0)
nitroprusside	9	5 (0.20018205)	1 (0.20840...	1 (0.26248685)	2 (1.0)
fucose	10	3 (1.0)	1 (0.25696...	0 (1.0)	6 (0.87234...
thymine	10	5 (0.32591215)	1 (0.25696...	0 (1.0)	4 (1.0)
Thiazole	28	18 (0.0012482518)	2 (0.28502...	1 (1.0)	7 (1.0)
thiamine	12	7 (0.092803314)	1 (0.35463...	1 (0.4259201)	3 (1.0)
cyclosporine	13	6 (0.40673086)	1 (0.40267...	1 (0.47822458)	5 (1.0)
cholesterol	125	47 (0.5685724)	6 (0.409453)	3 (1.0)	69 (1.0)
rifampin	14	9 (0.022490242)	1 (0.44972...	1 (0.5289582)	3 (1.0)
phenobarbital	15	5 (1.0)	1 (0.49562...	0 (1.0)	9 (0.84398...
phenanthrene	16	7 (0.47211048)	1 (0.54022...	5 (1.5048936E-8)	3 (1.0)
maltose	20	12 (0.020009244)	1 (0.70497...	0 (1.0)	7 (1.0)
fluorescein	46	23 (0.03506101)	2 (0.73987...	2 (0.8723038)	19 (1.0)
farnesyl	22	14 (0.0051575354)	1 (0.77922...	0 (1.0)	7 (1.0)
guanidine	24	18 (4.3588578E-5)	1 (0.84839...	0 (1.0)	5 (1.0)
pyridoxal	25	19 (1.8972765E-5)	1 (0.88118...	0 (1.0)	5 (1.0)
azithromycin	82	35 (0.15379089)	3 (0.919238)	7 (0.029415958)	37 (1.0)
glutathione	401	212 (9.344441E-14)	14 (0.9674...	7 (1.0)	168 (1.0)
guanosine	28	15 (0.04135209)	1 (0.972898)	0 (1.0)	12 (1.0)
Sulfadiazine	28	7 (1.0)	1 (0.972898)	3 (0.06174211)	17 (0.7298...
Pyrimethamine	2245	1433 (0.0)	33 (1.0)	143 (5.5324745...	636 (1.0)
Quinine	1813	1174 (0.0)	26 (1.0)	105 (2.0659178...	508 (1.0)
Sulfadoxine	1199	821 (0.0)	15 (1.0)	83 (4.011308E-8)	280 (1.0)
Mefloquine	1498	1044 (0.0)	14 (1.0)	96 (3.205081E-7)	344 (1.0)
Artesunate	876	591 (0.0)	14 (1.0)	53 (8.5805287E...	218 (1.0)
Artemisinin	1525	893 (0.0)	10 (1.0)	60 (0.9271753)	562 (1.0)
Proguanil	596	350 (9.457251E-34)	9 (1.0)	39 (7.548535E-4)	198 (1.0)
Atovaquone	308	218 (2.366703E-39)	6 (1.0)	16 (0.23491225)	68 (1.0)
Fansidar	288	192 (3.1076866E-29)	5 (1.0)	23 (3.1254988E...	68 (1.0)
Amodiaquine	759	541 (0.0)	4 (1.0)	25 (1.0)	189 (1.0)
permethrin	259	34 (1.0)	4 (1.0)	13 (0.3460245)	208 (9.596...
Doxycycline	233	111 (6.4615786E-5)	3 (1.0)	31 (9.456994E-...	88 (1.0)
dapsone	197	99 (8.898899E-6)	3 (1.0)	13 (0.04882466...	82 (1.0)
malathion	107	16 (1.0)	3 (1.0)	4 (1.0)	84 (1.0739...
Artemether	608	382 (0.0)	2 (1.0)	27 (0.4798588)	187 (1.0)
Halofantrine	381	272 (0.0)	2 (1.0)	33 (1.3410222E...	74 (1.0)
Dihydroartemisinin	330	216 (6.8326314E-31)	2 (1.0)	17 (0.23446304)	95 (1.0)
Lumefantrine	319	221 (1.7281078E-37)	2 (1.0)	8 (1.0)	88 (1.0)
heme	302	164 (2.8745543E-12)	2 (1.0)	3 (1.0)	133 (1.0)
hypoxanthine	294	244 (0.0)	2 (1.0)	9 (1.0)	39 (1.0)
calcium	265	141 (7.055148E-10)	2 (1.0)	5 (1.0)	117 (1.0)

Trend Examples | View Examples | Report | OK | Filter | Enlarged View

FIGURE 14.3 Drugs vs. species of malaria.

We can repeat this analysis for other orphan diseases such as chagas, leishmania, and tuberculosis. The result of combining all four diseases into a cotable against known drugs is shown in Figure 14.4.

The results of this analysis show the effectiveness of using entities (drugs and diseases) in combination with defined relationship patterns

Very High Affinity = Moderate Affinity = Low Affinity =

Term	Count	Malaria	Chagas	Leishma...	Tubercu...
isoniazid	4479	2 (1.0)	0 (1.0)	3 (1.0)	833 (0.0)
chloroquine	4417	794 (0.0)	3 (1.0)	2 (1.0)	2 (1.0)
pyrimethamine	1960	520 (0.0)	3 (1.0)	3 (1.0)	2 (1.0)
ethambutol	1757	0 (1.0)	0 (1.0)	1 (1.0)	271 (0.0)
rifampin	1555	1 (1.0)	0 (1.0)	2 (1.0)	267 (0.0)
quinine	1518	286 (0.0)	0 (1.0)	1 (1.0)	1 (1.0)
streptomycin	1507	1 (1.0)	0 (1.0)	1 (1.0)	216 (0.0)
pyrazinamide	1487	0 (1.0)	0 (1.0)	1 (1.0)	305 (0.0)
mefloquine	1241	306 (0.0)	0 (1.0)	1 (1.0)	0 (1.0)
sulfadoxine	1029	332 (0.0)	0 (1.0)	0 (1.0)	0 (1.0)
glutathione	734	24 (0.923...	16 (3.510...	12 (0.001...	10 (1.0)
calcium	669	7 (1.0)	5 (0.5121...	5 (0.8540...	12 (1.0)
amodiaquine	582	172 (0.0)	0 (1.0)	0 (1.0)	0 (1.0)
primaquine	572	155 (0.0)	4 (0.6517...	1 (1.0)	0 (1.0)
pentamidine	498	1 (1.0)	23 (4.330...	51 (0.0)	4 (1.0)
proguanil	424	138 (0.0)	0 (1.0)	0 (1.0)	0 (1.0)
trypanothione	401	1 (1.0)	18 (4.072...	12 (2.320...	0 (1.0)
glycerol	375	2 (1.0)	6 (0.0067...	1 (1.0)	6 (1.0)
cholesterol	367	6 (1.0)	1 (1.0)	13 (3.627...	10 (1.0)
heme	346	9 (1.0)	0 (1.0)	1 (1.0)	6 (1.0)
hypoxanthine	343	8 (1.0)	10 (4.594...	2 (1.0)	0 (1.0)
ofloxacin	338	0 (1.0)	1 (1.0)	0 (1.0)	51 (2.218...
ciprofloxacin	315	3 (1.0)	0 (1.0)	1 (1.0)	37 (5.658...
halofantrine	309	82 (0.0)	1 (1.0)	0 (1.0)	0 (1.0)
urea	308	7 (1.0)	3 (0.3279...	9 (2.0898...	3 (1.0)
nadh	289	2 (1.0)	3 (0.2740...	0 (1.0)	10 (0.712...
infliximab	270	0 (1.0)	0 (1.0)	0 (1.0)	17 (0.002...
methotrexate	267	4 (1.0)	1 (1.0)	1 (1.0)	4 (1.0)
atovaquone	253	75 (0.0)	0 (1.0)	1 (1.0)	0 (1.0)
tetracycline	243	29 (1.102...	0 (1.0)	1 (1.0)	3 (1.0)
heparin	236	2 (1.0)	0 (1.0)	0 (1.0)	9 (0.5174...
kanamycin	234	1 (1.0)	0 (1.0)	0 (1.0)	23 (2.368...
doxycycline	232	63 (0.0)	0 (1.0)	3 (0.2652...	1 (1.0)
glycine	224	4 (1.0)	1 (1.0)	0 (1.0)	4 (1.0)
spermidine	217	6 (1.0)	7 (1.3373...	3 (0.2161...	0 (1.0)
potassium	216	1 (1.0)	2 (0.4690...	10 (2.404...	10 (0.189...
diminazene	210	0 (1.0)	14 (1.484...	1 (1.0)	0 (1.0)
rifabutin	208	1 (1.0)	0 (1.0)	0 (1.0)	46 (0.0)
glucosamine	204	2 (1.0)	0 (1.0)	3 (0.1765...	1 (1.0)
dapsone	204	41 (1.0E-...	0 (1.0)	0 (1.0)	4 (1.0)
ethionamide	200	0 (1.0)	0 (1.0)	0 (1.0)	31 (2.994...
trimethoprim	199	23 (2.235...	3 (0.0724...	1 (1.0)	12 (0.016...
ketoconazole	199	0 (1.0)	14 (1.429...	19 (0.0)	4 (1.0)
prednisolone	197	1 (1.0)	1 (1.0)	0 (1.0)	13 (0.004...
fructose	195	0 (1.0)	1 (1.0)	0 (1.0)	0 (1.0)
ethanol	194	4 (1.0)	2 (0.3775...	3 (0.1483...	4 (1.0)
uridine	193	3 (1.0)	4 (0.0047...	0 (1.0)	1 (1.0)
suramin	190	0 (1.0)	18 (0.0)	2 (0.5438...	0 (1.0)
guanine	190	1 (1.0)	5 (1.2567...	3 (0.1375...	1 (1.0)

FIGURE 14.4 Malaria, chagas, tuberculosis, and *Leishmania*.

(effectiveness) in order to accurately identify and summarize all the relevant information about drugs that might be effective for treating a disease. Such background knowledge is critical to ensure the researchers do not waste time reinventing the wheel during discovery. In order to get the maximum value from research, we need to devote it to those areas that provide the most value, and retrospective studies such as these help to ensure that research effort is directed in the most effective way.

REFERENCES

1. http://en.wikipedia.org/wiki/IC50.
2. Lohr, S. 2013. And now, from I.B.M., Chef Watson. *The New York Times*, February 27. http://www.nytimes.com/2013/02/28/technology/ibm-exploring-new-feats-for-watson.html.

CHAPTER 15

Example: Target Selection Based on Protein Network Analysis

One of the most critical early decisions in the drug discovery process is the correct target to go after with a molecule. Typically, the target will be a particular protein on a cell type involved in the disease. The difficulty is in determining which target protein to choose.

Gene expression information taken from large population studies of people who have a given disease can be somewhat helpful in determining a set of candidate proteins. Yet seldom do such statistical studies reveal a single genetic culprit. Instead, gene studies often find hundreds of genes to be significantly expressed for a given disease. So the problem boils down to which one (or few) of these proteins corresponding to these genes do we target.

Here is where the process of Accelerated Discovery based on mining abstracts from literature can be a powerful tool.

TYPE 2 DIABETES PROTEIN ANALYSIS

In this example, we focus on genes known through population studies to be related to type 2 diabetes (T2D). The first step is to draw a similarity

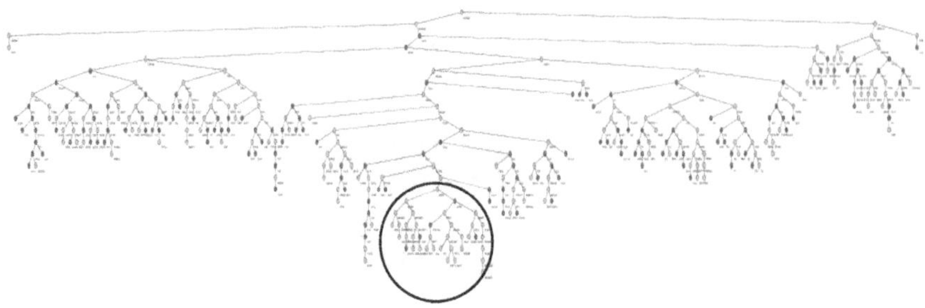

FIGURE 15.1 T2D genes.

graph of those genes along with a set of arbitrarily chosen non-T2D associated genes (Figure 15.1).

Note that in a graph containing hundreds of genes, one particular subgraph looks especially dense with T2D nodes. If we zoom into this subgraph, we see the picture shown in Figure 15.2.

We theorize that this set of genes must have some function in common to be so clustered together based on text content written about them. But in order to go further, we need to discover the nature of that commonality. One tool we can use is pathway information that is co-occurring in Medline with these specific genes. Using a dictionary of pathways, we discovered an interesting association between ten of these genes and one particular pathway, type 1 diabetes mellitus (Figure 15.3).

The fact that all of these genes co-occur significantly with a diabetes-related pathway makes them an excellent subset to focus on. To go further, we need to understand the precise mechanism involved—how the proteins corresponding to these genes are physically interacting. One way to visualize such interactions is to draw a co-occurrence network of proteins. In such a network, two proteins are connected by a line if they occur together in at least a certain number of abstracts. Figure 15.4 shows what such a network looks like if we focus on these ten genes, plus any additional genes that co-occur frequently with them.

Some of these genes are from our original set of ten. The other genes were introduced to the graph based on frequent co-occurrence in Medline (at least ten abstracts). The result is the discovery of a new gene, SLC30A8, which is highly connected to those genes that are expressed in T2D patients. Even though this gene is not one of those expressed, it may turn out to play an important role in the disease by either activating or inhibiting one of the expressed proteins during some process that influences diabetes.

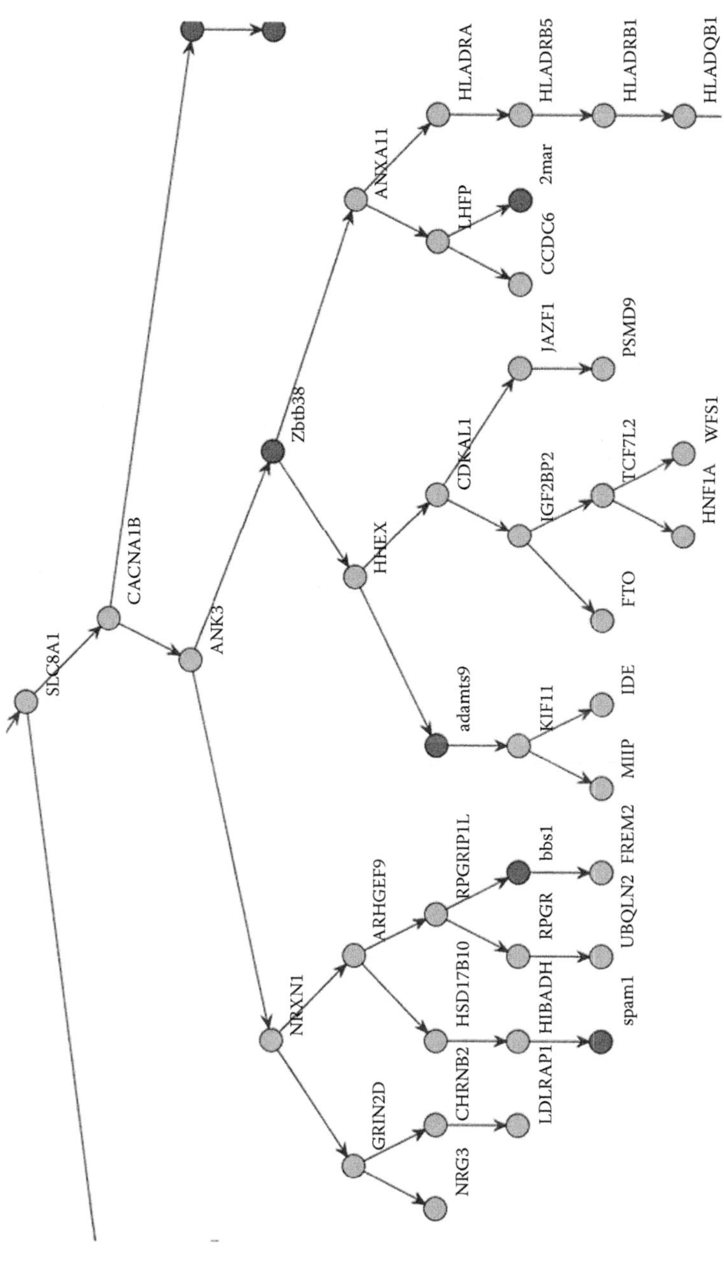

FIGURE 15.2 **(See color insert.)** Area of high concentration of T2D genes.

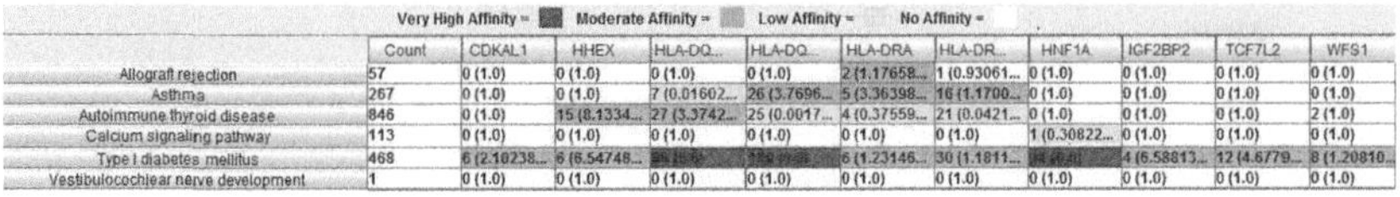

Very High Affinity = ■ Moderate Affinity = ■ Low Affinity = ■ No Affinity = □

	Count	CDKAL1	HHEX	HLA-DQ...	HLA-DQ...	HLA-DRA	HLA-DR...	HNF1A	IGF2BP2	TCF7L2	WFS1
Allograft rejection	57	0 (1.0)	0 (1.0)	0 (1.0)	0 (1.0)	2 (1.17658...	1 (0.93061...	0 (1.0)	0 (1.0)	0 (1.0)	0 (1.0)
Asthma	267	0 (1.0)	0 (1.0)	7 (0.01602...	26 (3.7696...	5 (3.36398...	16 (1.1700...	0 (1.0)	0 (1.0)	0 (1.0)	0 (1.0)
Autoimmune thyroid disease	846	0 (1.0)	15 (8.1334...	27 (3.3742...	25 (0.0017...	4 (0.37559...	21 (0.0421...	0 (1.0)	0 (1.0)	0 (1.0)	2 (1.0)
Calcium signaling pathway	113	0 (1.0)	0 (1.0)	0 (1.0)	0 (1.0)	0 (1.0)	0 (1.0)	1 (0.30822...	0 (1.0)	0 (1.0)	0 (1.0)
Type I diabetes mellitus	468	6 (2.10238...	6 (6.54748...	[illegible]	[illegible]	6 (1.23146...	30 (1.1811...	[illegible]	4 (6.58813...	12 (4.6779...	8 (1.20810...
Vestibulocochlear nerve development	1	0 (1.0)	0 (1.0)	0 (1.0)	0 (1.0)	0 (1.0)	0 (1.0)	0 (1.0)	0 (1.0)	0 (1.0)	0 (1.0)

FIGURE 15.3 Connection of genes to pathway.

To understand that process more deeply, we draw a more detailed, directional network that is based on a sentence-by-sentence analysis of protein–protein relationships, looking for the precise way in which one protein is influencing another (Figure 15.5).

The keywords shown in the figure are indicators of a relationship that we use to identify the precise kind and direction of the interaction. Figure 15.6 shows a network drawn using this type of information on these proteins.

The directional network shown comes from sentences mined from Medline abstracts mentioning these particular genes. Zooming in on the relationships involving interferon-gamma (IFNG) reveals an article that discusses this gene in relation to glucose metabolism—a very relevant biological function for T2D. Thus, IFNG would appear to be a good potential target for further study when designing a drug for T2D.

While this methodology is far from mature, it does point the way toward a systematic process for better understanding the precise relationships between proteins involved in disease, so that drug developers can make the best possible choice of target protein to go after in order to have the most likely probability of creating an effective molecule. As more and more information is published regarding the effects and interactions of proteins, this kind of analysis will grow more and more indispensable to accelerating drug discovery and reducing the cost involved in poor target selection.

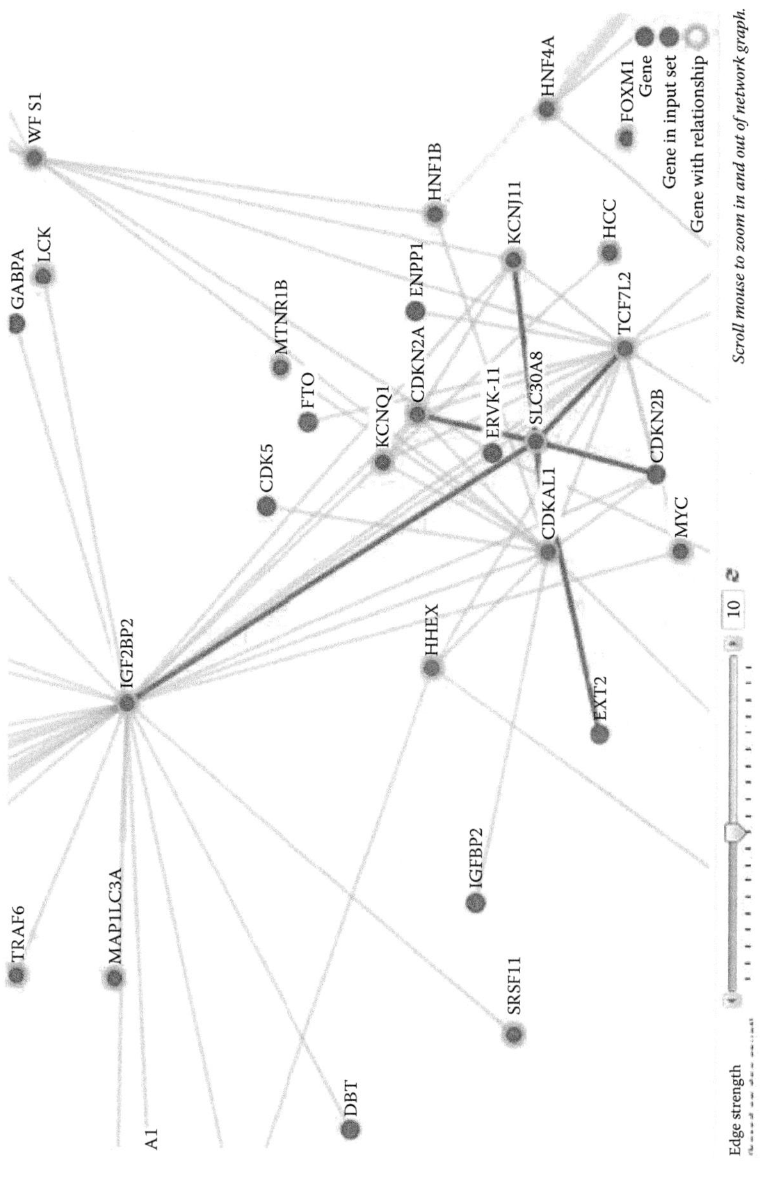

FIGURE 15.4 Gene co-occurrence network.

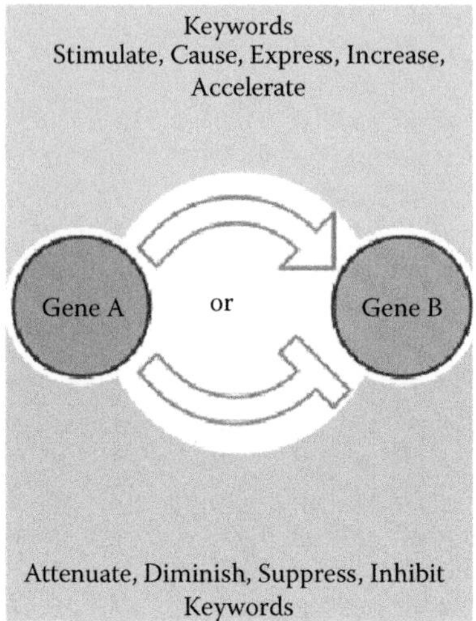

FIGURE 15.5 Gene networks.

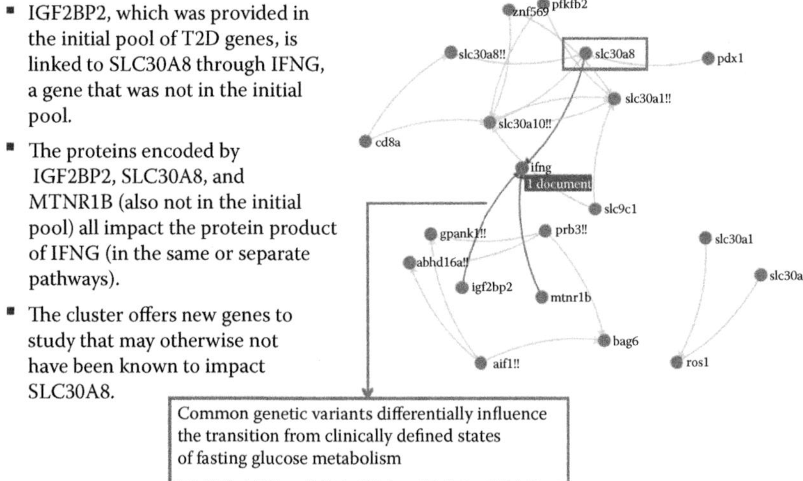

FIGURE 15.6 Protein–protein interactions for T2D.

CHAPTER 16

Example: Gene Expression Analysis for Alternative Indications

Scott Spangler, Ignacio Terrizzano, and Jeffrey Kreulen

PROTEIN ANTIBODIES TARGET THE inhibition of a particular protein in a cancer cell. Drug companies may create an antibody for one type of cancer based on the tendency of that type of cancer cell to express a particular gene. For example, HER-2 is a gene expressed in many breast cancers. Monoclonal antibody trastuzumab is effective against certain types of breast cancer cells that express that gene.

When a drug company has an antibody that is effective against a particular protein for one type of cancer, they will also want to know of any additional cancers to which that antibody might apply. This is referred to as an alternative indication for that drug. We can use our Accelerated Discovery analytical methods to help drug companies find these alternative indications from publicly available data sources.

NCBI GEO DATA

The National Center for Biotechnical Information (NCBI) Gene Expression Omnibus (GEO) data repository [1] was set up by the National Institute of Health as an "international public repository that archives and freely distributes microarray, next-generation sequencing, and other forms of high-throughput functional genomics data submitted by the research community." It contains gene expression data sets for thousands of tumors and other diseases. This information is cross-referenced to Medline publications, so that the context of the tumors under study can be obtained.

Our approach to using gene expression information in conjunction with text information about the indication (i.e., disease or tumor) is to create "documents" for each patient that describe the patient's condition along with the genes that patient's tumor expressed. These documents will contain not just text but all forms of information we have extracted or can derive that relate to that patient.

NCBI GEO data comes in the form of large tables containing floating point gene expression values for every gene for every patient in the study. The number of rows in the table represents the number of "probes" that are measured by the genetic sequencing apparatus. The number of columns is the number of different tumor samples that are sequenced in the study. Each probe corresponds to one or more genes, and sometimes more than one probe points to the same gene.

We convert NCBI GEO data into a format that can be represented as a document using the process described in Figure 16.1.

We first look at all the data for each probe across the patient population in each study. Sorting the expression values from high to low, we look at absolute difference between the third maximum and third minimum in the set (in order to avoid problems with outliers). The 1000 most differentially expressed probes then become our feature space. We do this to ensure that we focus on the probes that are most differentially expressed, ignoring those that have only small differences across the patient population. These are most likely to be noise variables. Our approach can deal with a small amount of noise, but too many noise variables will cause false correlations to be accidentally detected.

For these probes, we then look for the largest gap when the expression values are sorted in increasing order. This is an unusual step, requiring some explanation. The underlying model we are assuming for the gene expression values is a bimodal distribution with two peaks (Figure 16.2).

Ideally, in those cases where the gene in question is highly associated with a disease, for a given study we would see the patients showing one phenotype represented by one of these bumps, while the second phenotype would be the other bump. Note that it is most typical for these studies to have exactly two phenotypes. In cases where there are more, we would

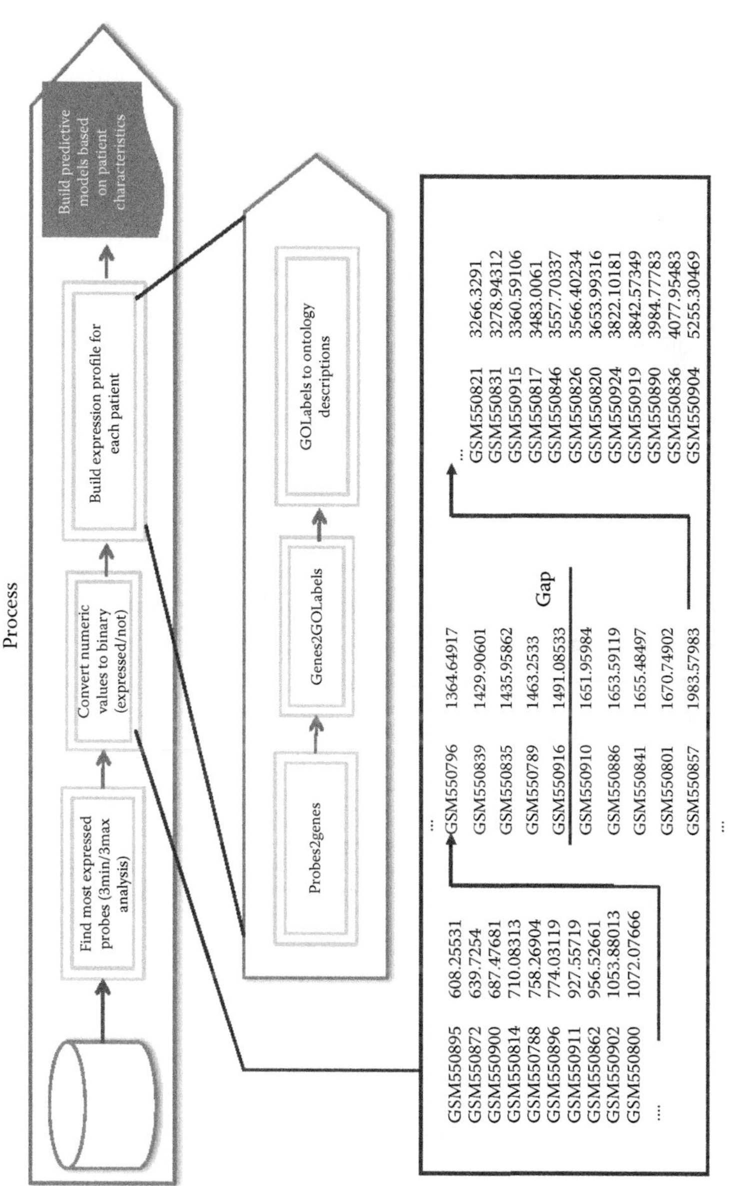

FIGURE 16.1 Process for analyzing gene expression data.

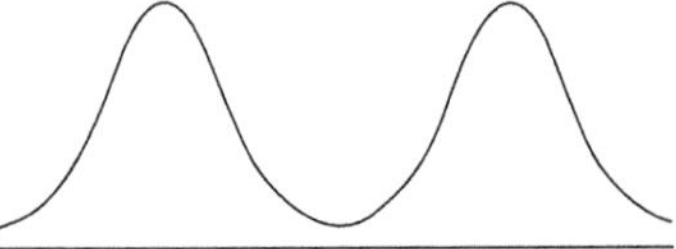

FIGURE 16.2 Bimodal distribution.

expect to see more bumps, but in such cases we still want to find the deepest valley between bumps to serve our purposes.

The valley between the bumps is where we want to divide the population in terms of "expressed" or "not expressed" gene labels. What we notice is that in this area between the bumps, the expression values will tend to be thinly populated along the x axis (which is the gene expression value). Therefore, we choose to divide the data set at the place where we see the largest space (gap) between data points. This will intuitively be the place where we can best distinguish phenotypes based on gene expression values. One phenotype is higher than this gap, and the other is lower.

In other words, every value above this gap is assumed to be "expressed" and every value below is assumed to be not expressed. The probe is then converted to one or more genes (based on the gene sequencing platform used) and the genes are also labeled according to their gene ontology (GO) descriptions [2]. This gives us a rich set of features from which to choose when we describe each patient's genetic profile.

Here is an example of what this feature space produces for one particular set of genetic expression values extracted from patients taking part in a study of chronic obstructive pulmonary disease (COPD). Each patient's sputum was sequenced and the top 1000 genes were used as the features for that patient's description. Each patient was also labeled as having moderate or severe COPD. A scatter plot showing the genetic information for the entire patient pool is shown in Figure 16.3.

Clearly, this method reveals a strong genetic correlation between moderate and severe COPD. We can also view patients as individual entities and compare the genetic similarity of their sputum cells with each other as a similarity tree (Figure 16.4).

The color indicates severity of the disease (red is the severe form). Again, we see the severity is clumping together, indicating that genetic expression plays a role in severity.

We can use this kind of information as a way to find alternative indications. For this purpose, we build a new document index that treats each patient's information as a document, combining the gene expression

FIGURE 16.3 **(See color insert.)** Patients with moderate and severe COPD.

values we created from NCBI GEO data using the top 1000 genes per study and finding the largest gap in the patient population for that study. We add to these patient documents diseases extracted from Medline abstracts that correspond to each study, along with the text of the abstracts. So in effect, we have three different kinds of entities in each patient document: genes expressed, diseases studied, and the text of the study. This allows us to see, for a given gene, the types of patients that are expressing that gene and what indications they have. Figure 16.5 shows an example for IGF2.

The numbers in this table provide key information for the scientist to use in determining the significance of each disease finding. First, the diseases are sorted by frequency (the total number of patients who have that gene expressed). This ensures we focus first on diseases where we have the most data. Frequency by itself is not enough to indicate a correlation between gene and disease. For example, some diseases are just more frequently studied than others. Leukemia is a great example in the table above. There are 25,780 total leukemia patients in the NCBI GEO data set. Hepatitis, however, has only been studied 3340 times. So even though the number of times we see the gene expressed with each disease is nearly identical, we find it much more likely that hepatitis is causally linked with expression of IGF2. The other is most likely mere coincidence.

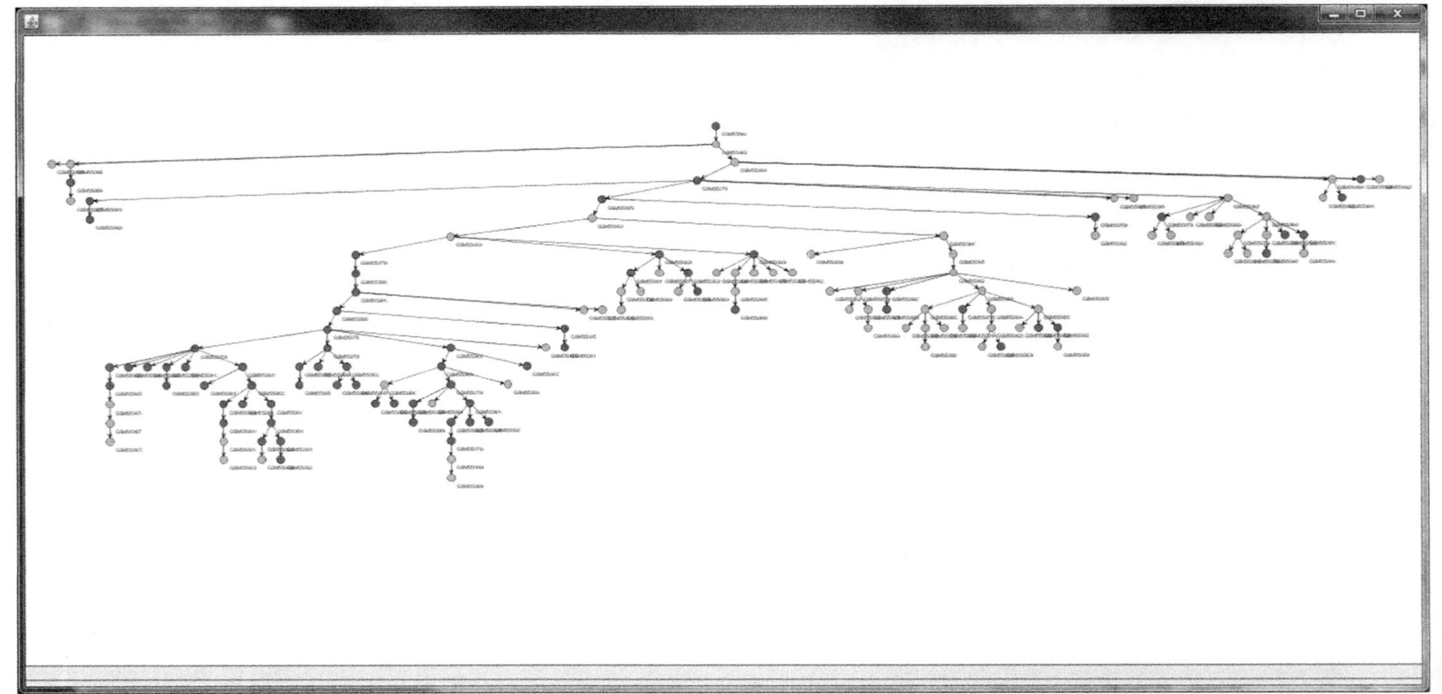

FIGURE 16.4 **(See color insert.)** Patient similarity tree, colored by severity of COPD.

The highlighting in Figure 16.5 indicates which disease gene combinations are significant given the overall occurrence of the gene and the disease in the patient population in all of NCBI GEO, using a chi-squared test and ensuring that the actual value is greater than the expected value. Clearly we find the known correlation to breast cancer cells, but there is a further correlation to patients with colorectal cancer and ovarian cancer. This points to two potential new indications for an IGF2 antibody.

We can also go the other way and look at a particular disease to find what genes are most often expressed. Figure 16.6 shows the example of glioblastoma.

High affinity Low affinity

Disease	# of Patients		% of Patients	Expected value
	Gene & disease	Disease	Gene / disease	
NEOPLASMS	15972	158031	10.11	11861.51
CARCINOMA	3991	31663	12.6	2376.57
BREAST NEOPLASMS	3842	41214	9.32	3093.45
NEOPLASM METASTASIS	2134	18194	11.73	1365.61
CARCINOGENESIS	2130	20253	10.52	1520.15
ADENOCARCINOMA	2082	12032	17.3	903.1
COLORECTAL NEOPLASMS	1805	7940	22.73	595.96
INFLAMMATION	1793	30592	5.86	2296.18
LUNG NEOPLASMS	1781	14926	11.93	1120.32
CARCINOMA, HEPATOCELLULAR	1240	6352	19.52	476.77
WOUNDS AND INJURIES	1079	17133	6.3	1285.97
COLONIC NEOPLASMS	999	4073	24.53	305.71
OVARIAN NEOPLASMS	975	4822	20.22	361.93
HEPATITIS	928	3340	27.78	250.69
LEUKEMIA	927	25780	3.6	1935.0
OBESITY	921	13374	6.89	1003.83
SARCOMA	877	3384	25.92	254.0
STOMACH NEOPLASMS	745	2475	30.1	185.77
CARCINOMA, SQUAMOUS CELL	714	6156	11.6	462.06
FIBROSIS	645	10937	5.9	820.91
CHROMOSOMAL INSTABILITY	605	3082	19.63	231.33
CARCINOMA, NON-SMALL-CELL LUNG	572	4861	11.77	364.86
SMALL CELL LUNG CARCINOMA	533	5240	10.17	393.3
HEPATITIS B	491	4070	45.89	80.31
ADENOMA	455	2397	18.98	179.91
HEPATITIS C	454	2263	20.06	169.86
LIPOSARCOMA	452	1247	36.25	93.6

FIGURE 16.5 IGF2-related diseases.

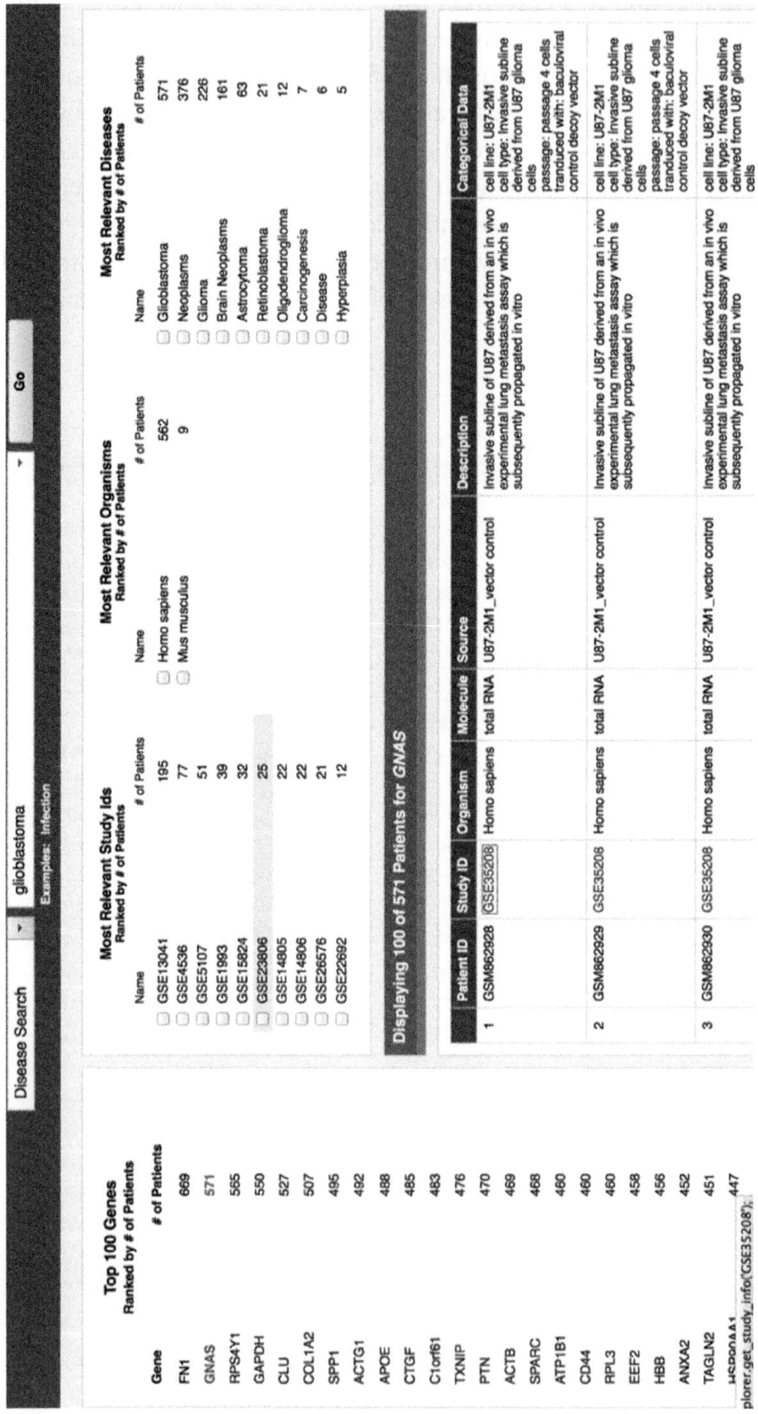

Disease Search | glioblastoma | Go

Examples: Infection

Top 100 Genes
Ranked by # of Patients

Gene	# of Patients
FN1	669
GNAS	571
RPS4Y1	565
GAPDH	550
CLU	527
COL1A2	507
SPP1	495
ACTG1	492
APOE	488
CTGF	485
C1orf61	483
TXNIP	476
PTN	470
ACTB	469
SPARC	468
ATP1B1	460
CD44	460
RPL3	460
EEF2	458
HBB	456
ANXA2	452
TAGLN2	451
HSP90AA1	447

plorer.get_study_info('GSE35208');

Most Relevant Study Ids
Ranked by # of Patients

Name	# of Patients
GSE13041	195
GSE4536	77
GSE5107	51
GSE1993	39
GSE15824	32
GSE23806	25
GSE14805	22
GSE14806	22
GSE26576	21
GSE22692	12

Most Relevant Organisms
Ranked by # of Patients

Name	# of Patients
Homo sapiens	562
Mus musculus	9

Most Relevant Diseases
Ranked by # of Patients

Name	# of Patients
Glioblastoma	571
Neoplasms	376
Glioma	226
Brain Neoplasms	161
Astrocytoma	63
Retinoblastoma	21
Oligodendroglioma	12
Carcinogenesis	7
Disease	6
Hyperplasia	5

Displaying 100 of 571 Patients for *GNAS*

	Patient ID	Study ID	Organism	Molecule	Source	Description	Categorical Data
1	GSM862928	GSE35208	Homo sapiens	total RNA	U87-2M1_vector control	Invasive subline of U87 derived from an in vivo experimental lung metastasis assay which is subsequently propagated in vitro	cell line: U87-2M1 cell type: Invasive subline derived from U87 glioma cells passage: passage 4 cells tranduced with: baculoviral control decoy vector
2	GSM862929	GSE35208	Homo sapiens	total RNA	U87-2M1_vector control	Invasive subline of U87 derived from an in vivo experimental lung metastasis assay which is subsequently propagated in vitro	cell line: U87-2M1 cell type: Invasive subline derived from U87 glioma cells passage: passage 4 cells tranduced with: baculoviral control decoy vector
3	GSM862930	GSE35208	Homo sapiens	total RNA	U87-2M1_vector control	Invasive subline of U87 derived from an in vivo experimental lung metastasis assay which is subsequently propagated in vitro	cell line: U87-2M1 cell type: Invasive subline derived from U87 glioma cells

FIGURE 16.6 Glioblastoma-related genes and studies that support that finding.

3441 Patients found for *diseases:(glioblastoma)* out of 339297

Top 100 Genes
Ranked by # of patients
High affinity Low affinity

Gene	# of Patients		% of Patients	Expected value
	Gene & disease	Gene	Disease/gene	
GAPDH	1055	117220	0.9 %	1188.79
CD44	962	69193	1.39 %	701.72
ATP1B1	941	63331	1.49 %	642.27
RPS4Y1	935	62860	1.49 %	637.5
FN1	927	73274	1.27 %	743.11
COL1A2	914	59443	1.54 %	602.84
GNAS	905	88434	1.02 %	896.86
H3F3AP4	888	52569	1.69 %	533.13
IGFBP5	879	51177	1.72 %	519.01
ACTG1	869	84377	1.03 %	855.71
ACTB	859	113375	0.76 %	1149.8
SPARC	849	63144	1.34 %	640.38
RPL13	846	85099	0.99 %	863.04
HSP90AA1	844	88406	0.95 %	896.57
H3F3A	817	74228	1.1 %	752.79

FIGURE 16.7 Genes correlated with glioblastoma.

This finding may give us a lead on the proteins for which we should be developing new antibodies (Figure 16.7).

CONCLUSION

The combination of heterogeneous information sources can be realized through proper entity definition. By carefully converting the numeric values of gene expression data sets into categorical features, we can create a data set that is equivalent to text data and in turn combine it with text features obtained from other connected sources. This allows us to use all the analytical tools and techniques we have in our toolkit for Accelerated Discovery on a much wider array of data. This in turn gives us the power to use statistics and search capability to gain insights that are hidden from view when looking at one study at a time.

REFERENCES

1. NCBI (National Center for Biotechnology Information). 2014. Gene Expression Omnibus (GEO) overview. NCBI. http://www.ncbi.nlm.nih.gov/geo/info/overview.html.
2. Gene Ontology Consortium. 2004. The Gene Ontology (GO) database and informatics resource. *Nucleic Acids Research*, *32*(suppl 1): D258–D261.

CHAPTER 17

Example: Side Effects

Drugs are designed and engineered to treat disease or the symptoms of disease. But the molecules that we ingest as drugs frequently do more than one thing. Some of these additional things are side effects. When engineering a new drug, it helps to be aware of what side effects are taking place for those related drugs currently on the market or in clinical trials. This knowledge can help the drug designer avoid chemical signatures or off-target effects that may cause problems when the drug is administered to a large patient population.

We begin with a search against Medline to find abstracts containing references to our molecule. If none are found, then it makes sense to look at chemically similar molecules. In this example, we see that cyclosporine is chemically similar to the molecule that is our drug.

Notice that to implement this kind of searching requires that we know what a chemical structure is and how it appears in text. We must use name-to-structure software to convert text names for chemicals into a normalized chemical representation (known as a SMILE string or InChI key. These representations then allow us to compare molecules to see which ones appearing in Medline are identical or structurally similar to the target molecule (Figure 17.1).

We then select one particular year to focus on, 2012, so as to keep the size of the data set manageable for the purposes of deeper exploration. Next, we would like to have some actual side effects to look at as models to which to compare all the articles. We can have a domain expert label a few of these for us, or we can in fact use medical subject headings (MESH)

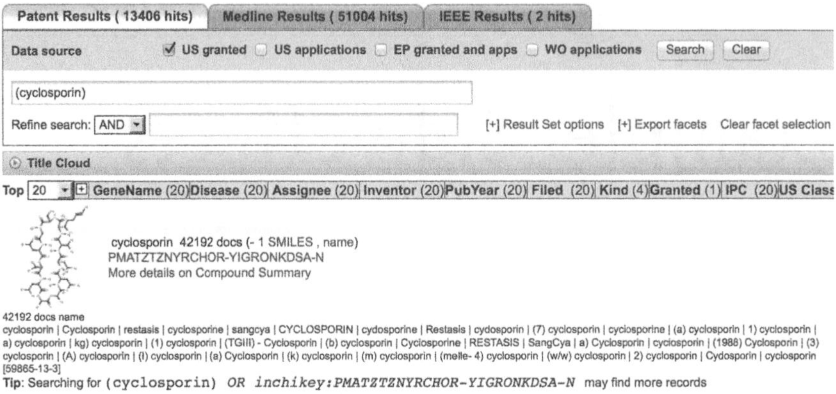

FIGURE 17.1 Chemical search.

tags, which label side effects for this drug. There are 41 such events labeled in MESH for cyclosporine in 2012 (Figure 17.2).

Now we would like to visualize the document space of side effects in the context of all documents about cyclosporine. This is accomplished by use of a scatter-plot visualization technique that focuses on a bag-of-words vector space for each document and projects the document vector points onto a plane derived from a triangle whose vertices are the centroids of the two clusters and the origin. Figure 17.3 shows what such a plot looks like for cyclosporin side effects versus other cyclosporine articles.

What this reveals about side effects for cyclosporine is twofold. First, the events form a natural cluster in text vector space. This means that the

FIGURE 17.2 MESH-tagged abstracts for cyclosporine adverse events in 2012.

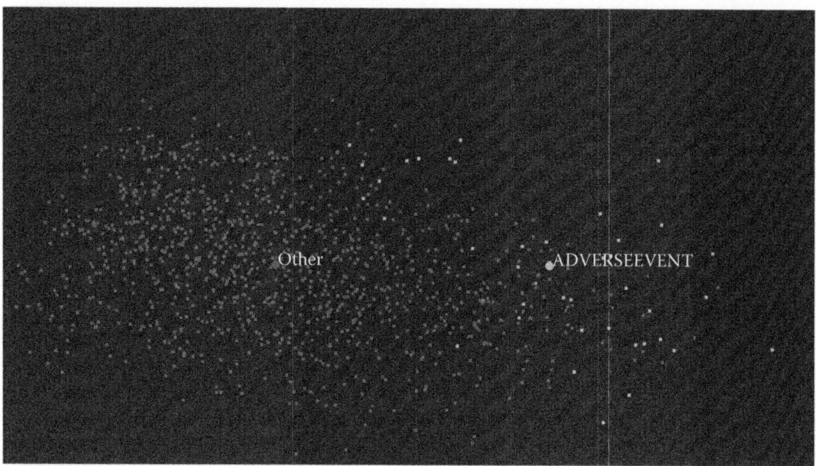

FIGURE 17.3 **(See color insert.)** Cyclosporine abstracts, tagged and not tagged in MESH.

content of these articles is at least somewhat regular and identifiable as being adverse-event related. Secondly, the side effects are somewhat distinct from the other articles. This means we can probably use these examples to easily find additional content for cyclosporine that is adverse-event related.

Next, we do a text clustering to see what concepts emerge from the cyclosporine articles and how those concepts might be related to side effects. The summary table of this text clustering is shown in Figure 17.4.

Clearly we can see that many of the clusters automatically generated have a strong correlation with side effects. Also, the fact that most of the side effects are concentrated in just a handful of clusters is encouraging. This should allow us to discover just a few important concepts that are critical to identifying these events in articles.

Using these clusters, we investigate each of the 41 side effects in turn to discover what particular side effect or indication is described. We start with a list of published side effects from the drug label database and then add to these the additional side effects we observe in the ground truth. This creates the list in Table 17.1, which we apply to the cyclosporine documents to get counts of occurrence in 2012 for each side effect.

This shows 450 articles that mention cyclosporine and an side effect. This is most likely far too many, since many of these mentions of side effects may have nothing to do with cyclosporine. The mention may simply be coincidental. To get more precision, we need to add another level

Class Name	Size	Cohesion	Distinctness	% matching ADVERSEEVENT
nephrotoxicity	13 (1.20%)	53.68%	32.19%	46.15%
aplastic_anemia	18 (1.67%)	57.23%	44.80%	22.22%
csa_induced	42 (3.89%)	62.86%	15.63%	14.29%
patients_treated	16 (1.48%)	54.31%	21.03%	12.50%
acute_rejection	39 (3.61%)	52.49%	23.82%	10.26%
years	21 (1.95%)	41.16%	43.29%	9.52%
control_group	23 (2.13%)	56.43%	23.47%	8.70%
cyclosporine_csa	35 (3.24%)	48.32%	17.09%	8.57%
follow	14 (1.30%)	43.92%	35.89%	7.14%
kidney_transplant	30 (2.78%)	49.89%	23.82%	6.67%
cyclosporin_csa	18 (1.67%)	43.03%	28.70%	5.56%
ulcerative_colitis	19 (1.76%)	54.56%	44.76%	5.26%
versus host_disease	19 (1.76%)	54.40%	19.15%	5.26%
psoriasis	21 (1.95%)	57.07%	42.63%	4.76%
csa_treatment	21 (1.95%)	52.05%	21.23%	4.76%
age	23 (2.13%)	46.41%	21.56%	4.35%
effects_csa	24 (2.22%)	59.05%	15.63%	4.17%
csa_group	28 (2.59%)	59.37%	23.47%	3.57%
transplantation	29 (2.69%)	39.58%	34.78%	3.45%
gvhd_prophylaxis	18 (1.67%)	66.73%	19.15%	0.00%
belatacept	15 (1.39%)	63.74%	34.52%	0.00%
activate cells_nfat	17 (1.58%)	62.92%	27.11%	0.00%
pore mptp_open	21 (1.95%)	60.62%	36.05%	0.00%
hepatitis virus_hcv	28 (2.59%)	58.63%	60.15%	0.00%
membrane_potential	23 (2.13%)	57.33%	17.00%	0.00%
dry_eye	22 (2.04%)	56.62%	52.27%	0.00%
infliximab	14 (1.30%)	52.61%	29.11%	0.00%
mitochondrial permeability_tr...	27 (2.50%)	51.53%	17.00%	0.00%
patients_receive	25 (2.32%)	51.02%	21.03%	0.00%
nuclear_factor	21 (1.95%)	50.80%	27.11%	0.00%
hematopoietic_stem	15 (1.39%)	50.70%	30.55%	0.00%
renal_transplant	31 (2.87%)	49.56%	27.67%	0.00%
cell_line	22 (2.04%)	50.18%	35.92%	0.00%
gp	21 (1.95%)	49.23%	46.39%	0.00%
nephrotic_syndrome	25 (2.32%)	48.87%	41.63%	0.00%
transplant_recipient	21 (1.95%)	47.74%	27.97%	0.00%
refractory	17 (1.58%)	47.52%	25.32%	0.00%
methotrexate	23 (2.13%)	46.80%	29.11%	0.00%
signaling	34 (3.15%)	46.09%	34.25%	0.00%
graft	20 (1.85%)	42.01%	32.99%	0.00%
therapy	30 (2.78%)	42.16%	25.32%	0.00%
expression	28 (2.59%)	39.57%	34.41%	0.00%

FIGURE 17.4 Text clustering of cyclosporine abstracts.

of detail to the picture. This is the relationship that connects drug to side effect (Figure 17.5).

```
CYCLOSPORININDUCED|cyclosporin.{0,30}induce|csa.{0,5}
induce|cyclosporin.{0,10}withdraw|
csa.{0,10}withdraw|withdraw.{0,10}
cyclosporin|withdraw.{0,10}csa
INCREASEDRISK|increase.{0,30}risk
SIDEEFFECT|side effect|adverse|complication|acute
effect|drug eruption
```

We create a set of patterns based on observing particular sentences that contain cyclosporine and any side effects in the ground truth set of known side effects. These detailed patterns, covering most of the ground truth set, provide a kind of connection between drug and adverse event. They help to provide the connecting context that improves precision with very little sacrifice of recall. When we combine this pattern detection with the side effects found earlier, we can see a marked improvement in our ability to hone in on side effects (Figure 17.6).

TABLE 17.1 Side Effects of the Drug

Class Name	Class Size	Percentage
Toxicity	124	10.31
Hepatitis	62	5.15
Nephrotoxicity	44	3.66
Nephropathy	38	3.16
Edema	24	2.00
Hypertension	19	1.58
Renal issues	16	1.33
Thrombocytopenia	13	1.08
Skin cancer	12	1.00
Rash	10	0.83
Gingival hyperplasia	10	0.83
Encephalopathy	8	0.67
Diarrhea	8	0.67
Metabolic syndrome	8	0.67
Headache	5	0.42
Myalgia	5	0.42
Pancreatitis	5	0.42
Hyperlipidemia	5	0.42
Anaemia	4	0.33
Hyperuricemia	4	0.33
Thrombotic thrombocytopenic purpura	3	0.25
Myopathy	3	0.25
Hepatotoxicity	3	0.25
Leucopenia	2	0.17
Hypomagnesemia	2	0.17
Hepatotoxicity	2	0.17
Hepertrichosis	1	0.08
Nausea	1	0.08
Gynecomastia	1	0.08
Jaundice	1	0.08
Hirsutism	1	0.08
Peripheral neuropathy	1	0.08
Pyrexia	1	0.08
Fatigue	1	0.08
Thrombotic microangiopathy	1	0.08
Bone loss	1	0.08
Bronchiolitis obliterans syndrome	1	0.08
Total	450.0	37.41

Class name	Class size	Other	ADVERSEEVENT
CYCLOSPORININDUCED	75	65	10
INCREASEDRISK	31	27	4
SIDEEFFECT	339	316	23
Total	1079	1038	41

FIGURE 17.5 Adverse event patterns.

This co-occurrence table shows the three patterns and the side effects intersected. The total number of unique articles (removing duplicates) turns out to be just 217. Figure 17.7 shows some examples of the articles that combine the three characteristics (cyclosporine + side effect + relationship pattern).

Very High Affinity = Moderate Affinity = Low Affinity = No Affinity =

Term	Count	SIDEEFFECT	CYCLOSPORININDUCED	INCREASEDRISK	ADVERSEEVENT
toxicity	124	87 (1.8232878E...	32 (7.0666903E-19)	1 (1.0)	0 (1.0)
hepatitis	62	21 (0.12793069)	4 (1.0)	3 (0.2806984)	0 (1.0)
nephrotoxicity	44	20 (0.00216058...	22 (6.510365E-31)	2 (0.43655893)	0 (1.0)
nephropathy	38	8 (1.0)	9 (2.9392975E-5)	1 (1.0)	0 (1.0)
edema	24	11 (0.022214474)	1 (1.0)	0 (1.0)	0 (1.0)
hypertension	19	7 (0.26076812)	3 (0.12016786)	0 (1.0)	0 (1.0)
renal issues	16	4 (1.0)	8 (6.0277065E-12)	0 (1.0)	0 (1.0)
thrombocytopenia	13	4 (0.67208266)	0 (1.0)	0 (1.0)	0 (1.0)
skin cancer	12	0 (1.0)	3 (0.012402789)	7 (4.2018262E-33)	0 (1.0)
rash	10	6 (0.012535613)	0 (1.0)	0 (1.0)	0 (1.0)
gingival hyperplasia	10	3 (0.7529262)	1 (0.69289285)	0 (1.0)	1 (0.002627462)
diarrhea	8	2 (1.0)	1 (0.5262601)	1 (0.08497791)	0 (1.0)
metabolic syndrome	8	2 (1.0)	2 (0.04156885)	3 (9.892553E-10)	1 (6.061595E-4)
encephalopathy	8	3 (0.442058)	0 (1.0)	0 (1.0)	1 (6.061595E-4)
headache	5	2 (0.46224812)	0 (1.0)	0 (1.0)	0 (1.0)
myalgia	5	1 (1.0)	0 (1.0)	0 (1.0)	0 (1.0)
hyperlipidemia	5	4 (0.0053119133)	1 (0.24386157)	0 (1.0)	0 (1.0)
pancreatitis	5	0 (1.0)	1 (0.24386157)	0 (1.0)	0 (1.0)
hyperuricemia	4	2 (0.26445016)	0 (1.0)	0 (1.0)	0 (1.0)
anaemia	4	3 (0.023654794)	1 (0.15035845)	0 (1.0)	0 (1.0)
hepatotoxicity	3	3 (0.0031644527)	0 (1.0)	0 (1.0)	0 (1.0)
myopathy	3	1 (0.76097053)	0 (1.0)	0 (1.0)	0 (1.0)
thrombotic thrombocytopenic purpura	3	0 (1.0)	1 (0.069235705)	0 (1.0)	0 (1.0)
hepatotoxicity	2	2 (0.01601372)	0 (1.0)	0 (1.0)	0 (1.0)
leucopenia	2	0 (1.0)	0 (1.0)	0 (1.0)	0 (1.0)
hypomagnesemia	2	1 (0.4304909)	0 (1.0)	0 (1.0)	1 (4.1898746E-1
bronchiolitis obliterans syndrome	1	1 (0.08868995)	0 (1.0)	0 (1.0)	0 (1.0)
fatigue	1	1 (0.08868995)	0 (1.0)	0 (1.0)	0 (1.0)
gynecomastia	1	1 (0.08868995)	0 (1.0)	0 (1.0)	0 (1.0)
hirsutism	1	1 (0.08868995)	0 (1.0)	0 (1.0)	0 (1.0)
jaundice	1	1 (0.08868995)	0 (1.0)	0 (1.0)	0 (1.0)
nausea	1	1 (0.08868995)	0 (1.0)	0 (1.0)	0 (1.0)
pyrexia	1	1 (0.08868995)	0 (1.0)	0 (1.0)	0 (1.0)
peripheral neuropathy	1	0 (1.0)	0 (1.0)	0 (1.0)	0 (1.0)
thrombotic microangiopathy	1	0 (1.0)	0 (1.0)	0 (1.0)	0 (1.0)
bone loss	1	0 (1.0)	1 (2.2694835E-4)	0 (1.0)	0 (1.0)
hypertrichosis	1	0 (1.0)	1 (2.2694835E-4)	0 (1.0)	0 (1.0)
Total	1079	277	74	29	10

FIGURE 17.6 Cotable of adverse events and patterns.

nephrotoxicity-CYCLOSPORININDUCED

Number	Text Description
1	22696872 New insights on the anti-inflammatory effect of some Egyptian plants against renal dysfunction induced by cyclosporine This study was undertaken to investigate the anti-inflammatory role of fennel, carob, doum and mixture of them in improving the renal dysfunction induced in rats by the cyclosporine. Sixty female albino rats were divided into six groups: healthy control rats, cyclosporine injected rats (positive control), other groups were injected by cyclosporine for 7 days and then diet was supplemented with either fennel, doum, carob or mixture of them. After 45 days of supplementation, rats were scarified. Serum and urinary samples were obtained for different biochemical analysis. The analysis included the determination of creatinine levels in serum and urinary samples, serum ammonia, transforming growth factor-beta1 (TGF-beta1) and tumor necrosis factor-alpha (TNF-alpha), urinary N-acetyl-beta D-glucosaminidase (NAG), beta2 microglobulin as well as calculating the creatinine clearance. Also, an histopathological examination for the kidney tissue was performed. The present study showed that cyclosporine induced the nephrotoxicity as appeared by elevation of serum and urinary levels of creatinine, urinary level of beta2 microglobulin, serum levels of ammonia, TGF-beta1 and TNF-alpha and the NAG level while decreased the creatinine clearance. Addition of fennel, carob, doum or mixture of them significantly improved the kidney functions. Moreover, anti-inflammatory status of animals injected with cyclosporine and supplemented with fennel, carob, doum and mixture of them, showed a significant amelioration in the kidney functions as compared to animals injected with the cyclosporine only. Histopathological investigation of kidney tissue of rat treated with the cyclosporine showed a moderate degree of renal damages. While, groups fed on fennel, carob, doum or mixture of them showed a great improvement in the kidney morphological structure. Diet supplementation with fennel, carob, doum have a promising anti-inflammatory influence on attenuating the complications associated with the renal dysfunction. TYPE:main
2	22564819 Mapping cyclosporine-induced changes in protein secretion by renal cells using stable isotope labeling with amino acids in cell culture (SILAC) Nephrotoxicity is an adverse event that strongly limits the use of the immunosuppressant cyclosporine in solid organ transplantation and the precise molecular mechanisms underlying this toxicity remain unclear. MS-based proteomic analysis of the secretome of HEK-293 renal cells exposed to cyclosporine was performed to identify changes in protein secretion, as a first step to discover potential biomarkers of such nephrotoxicity. To detect and quantify the perturbed proteins in the culture medium we used SILAC and nano-scale liquid chromatography followed by MALDI-TOF/TOF mass spectrometry. Among 106 proteins identified, 80 were quantified in both forward/reverse SILAC experiments and quantitative proteomic analysis revealed altered levels of expression for 24 secreted proteins. These included the down-regulation of a number of extracellular matrix/cell adhesion components, and the up-regulation of secreted cyclophilins A and B, macrophage inhibition factor and phosphatidylethanolamine-binding protein 1. These changes in protein secretion were not prevented by co-incubation with the antioxidant N-acetylcysteine, suggesting that they were not triggered by cyclosporine-induced oxidative stress. The results from the present study provide important new knowledge to gain insights into the molecular mechanisms of cyclosporine-related toxicity. Some of the proteins identified here should be tested as potential biomarkers of cyclosporine nephrotoxicity in subsequent clinical studies. COPYRIGHT:Copyright � 2012 Elsevier B.V. All rights reserved. TYPE:main
3	22745070 Protective effect of schisandrin B against cyclosporine A-induced nephrotoxicity in vitro and in vivo Schisandrin B (Sch B) is an active ingredient of the fruit of Schisandra chinensis. It has many therapeutic effects arising from its tonic, sedative, antitussive and antiaging activities and is also used in the treatment of viral and chemical hepatitis. The aim of this study was to investigate the protective effects of Sch B on cyclosporine A (CsA)-induced nephrotoxicity in mice and HK-2 cells (a human proximal tubular epithelial cell line). After gavage with Sch B (20 mg/kg) or olive oil (vehicle), mice received CsA (30 mg/kg) by subcutaneous injection once daily for four weeks. Renal function, histopathology, and tissue glutathione (GSH) and malondialdehyde (MDA) levels were evaluated after the last treatment. The effects of Sch B on CsA-induced oxidative damage in HK-2 cells were investigated by measuring cell viability, the release of lactate dehydrogenase (LDH), the level of reactive oxygen species (ROS), and the cellular GSH and ATP concentrations. Cellular apoptosis was assessed by flow cytometry. Treatment with Sch B in CsA-treated mice significantly suppressed the elevation of blood urea nitrogen (BUN) and serum creatinine levels and attenuated the histopathological changes. Additionally, Sch B also decreased renal MDA levels and increased GSH levels in CsA-treated mice. Using an in vitro model, Sch B (2.5, 5 and 10 ?M) significantly increased the cell viability and reduced LDH release and apoptosis induced by CsA (10 ?M) in HK-2 cells. Furthermore, Sch B increased the intracellular GSH and ATP levels and attenuated CsA-induced ROS generation. In conclusion, Sch B appears to protect against CsA-induced nephrotoxicity by decreasing oxidative stress and cell death. TYPE:main
4	22155090 A pharmacologically-based array to identify targets of cyclosporine A-induced toxicity in cultured renal proximal tubule cells Mechanisms of cyclosporine A (CsA)-induced nephrotoxicity were generally thought to be hemodynamic in origin; however, there is now accumulating evidence of a direct tubular effect. Although genomic and proteomic experiments by our group and others provided overall information on genes and proteins up- or down-regulated by CsA in proximal tubule cells (PTC), a comprehensive view of events occurring after CsA exposure remains to be described. For this purpose, we applied a pharmacologic approach based on the use of known activities of a large panel of potentially protective compounds and evaluated their efficacy in preventing CsA toxicity in cultured mouse PTC. Our results show that compounds that blocked protein synthesis and apoptosis, together with the CK2 inhibitor DMAT and the PI3K inhibitor apigenin, were the most efficient in preventing CsA toxicity. We also identified GSK3, MMPs and PKC pathways as potential targets to prevent CsA damage. Additionally, heparinase-I and MAPK inhibitors afforded partial but significant protection. Interestingly, antioxidants and calcium metabolism-related compounds were unable to ameliorate CsA-induced cytotoxicity. Subsequent experiments allowed us to clarify the hierarchical relationship of targeted pathways after CsA treatment, with ER stress identified as an early effector of CsA toxicity, which leads to ROS generation, phenotypical changes and cell death. In summary, this work presents a novel experimental approach to characterizing cellular responses to cytotoxics while pointing to new targets to prevent CsA-induced toxicity in proximal tubule cells. COPYRIGHT:Copyright � 2011 Elsevier Inc. All rights reserved. TYPE:main

FIGURE 17.7 Example abstracts containing target concepts.

We can imagine going from this fairly easily to a sentence-based annotator that recognizes this kind of triple in any text present in a research article or internal report.

We see in this example how the discovery of the appropriate domain-specific ontologies can make identification and summarization of the information space far more practical and accurate than search alone. This kind of summarization is key to enabling Accelerated Discovery, because it allows the domain expert to get a complete picture of the historical record without having to read all the articles published on the subject of interest.

CHAPTER 18

Example: Protein Viscosity Analysis Using Medline Abstracts

PROTEINS ARE AMAZING MOLECULES. They are made up of sequences of amino acids, and their properties are defined not only by the order and composition of the amino acid chain but also by the shape that chain makes in three-dimensional space. This configuration is sometimes referred to as "protein folding" and it affects what the protein can do and how it interacts with other proteins.

Proteins make up all the cells in our body, and their amino acid sequences are determined by our DNA. There are over 30,000 different proteins in our cells, and each kind has specific roles to play; for example, TP53 is one protein whose role in the cell is to respond to stress. When activated, it may turn the cell off (a.k.a. apoptosis or "cell death"), which can actually be a good thing if the cell is damaged or degraded. Other proteins are produced by cells in order to perform important functions. One such protein is called an "antibody." An antibody is a protein that binds to other proteins in order to "deactivate" them. Antibodies are the immune systems way of fighting disease. Our immune system actually designs specific proteins for specific diseases in order to kill them off by targeting the proteins of those disease organisms.

It turns out that antibodies are also a means by which drug companies can create and deliver medicine to those who suffer from diseases that their own immune systems cannot fight effectively. Rituximab (Rituxan®) is an example of such an antibody that is used to treat non-Hodgkin lymphomas. It targets the protein CD20, a human protein that is expressed primarily on B-cells, which are the ones affected in this type of cancer. By binding to CD20, rituximab effectively kills those cells, both healthy and cancerous cells, with the hope that only the healthy cells will be replaced and the cancer will be destroyed.

In order to deliver antibodies as a drug, they typically need to be injected. To do this, the protein needs to be suspended in a saline solution. The solution has to have a certain minimum concentration (density) of protein or else it takes too much of it to comfortably inject at one time. But when proteins are put closer together, they start to rub more against each other, and these interactions will affect the solution viscosity. If the viscosity becomes too high, the solution becomes too hard to inject. It turns out that many proteins that would make great antibodies in theory get rejected because of this simple problem—poor viscosity prevents them from being injected as a drug. So one way to make better protein antibodies, or to make them faster, would be to predict their viscosity properties ahead of time and make modifications that would improve those properties. As of this writing, no one knows precisely how to do this.

DISCOVERY OF ONTOLOGIES

Our challenge is to mine the medical literature to find potential clues that might help us to design proteins with better viscosity more quickly. To do this, we must first understand the literature space. Unsupervised clustering of text documents is our best tool for beginning to map out a space when we do not have an initial idea of what concepts, entities, and relationships are important. We begin by doing a query against Medline abstracts to find abstracts that mention viscosity (and its synonyms) along with protein antibody (and its synonyms). This creates a set of around 1500 articles to work with. Now, we do text clustering to create an initial taxonomy across those abstracts. This gives us a set of concepts to begin seeding the discussion with our domain experts. But a list is a somewhat uninspiring representation. To make it more visually interesting and to stimulate the discussion, we organize the concepts into a binary tree structure with a root node that represents the central concept of our query and leaf nodes that represent the more atypical entities. We then give the tree to our domain experts and ask them to tell us what they think. Do these concepts capture the important elements of the protein viscosity domain or not? And what might be missing? Figure 18.1 shows what that feedback looks like.

The domain expert provided the circles on top of a text-mining-generated result over the Medline abstracts. In subsequent discussions with the domain expert, it became clear that one area of this diagram was particularly relevant to how protein structure might determine viscosity. This is the area in the upper circle in Figure 18.1. So we now create a new text clustering based on just the abstracts contained in the articles from the blue circled clusters. This generates another taxonomy shown in Figure 18.2.

The domain expert finds many areas of interest in this diagram and circles those that seem to be especially interesting. Having exhausted what we can do with this small data set, we now attempt to expand outside the bounds of viscosity-related articles to focus primarily on protein structure and interaction—the areas that the expert found most appealing from our initial taxonomies. A new query generated over 10,000 abstracts, a subset of which is used to generate the taxonomy shown in Figure 18.3.

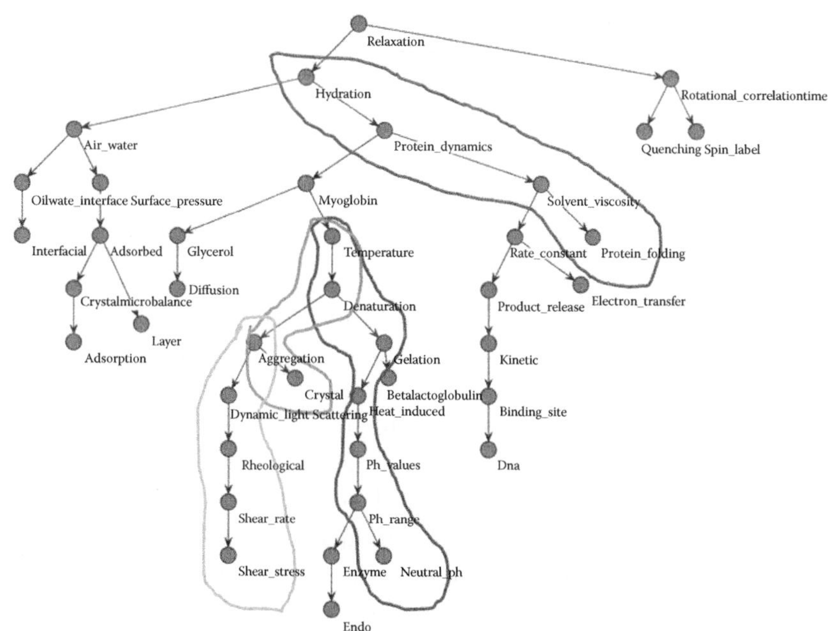

FIGURE 18.1 Domain expert annotation of concept ontology.

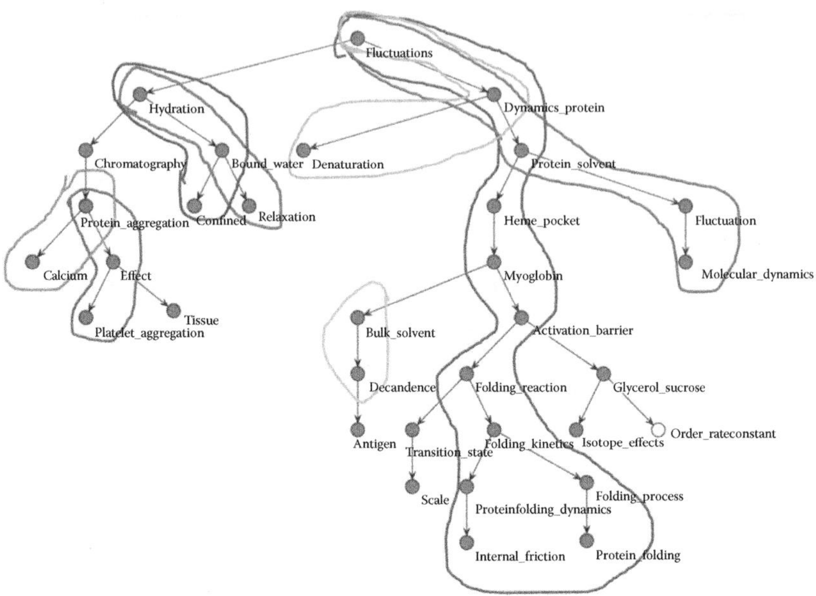

FIGURE 18.2 Further refinement of ontology.

The domain expert's circles this time focus on two areas that look especially promising: The lower circled areas make up the protein structure area and the upper circle is the protein dynamics space. Drilling deeper into these areas with another clustering on those documents alone yields this (Figure 18.4).

Roughly speaking, the left-hand side represents dynamics and the right hand side structure. The picture is now fairly comprehensive. Putting this altogether, along with some concepts we found in the initial analysis that are also important, the complete picture emerges (Figure 18.5).

In addition to our protein structure and protein interaction taxonomies from before, two new taxonomies seem to emerge: one that speaks to the environmental conditions that tend to influence viscosity and the second having to do with viscosity measurement and characterization. The complete ontology of this domain can then be listed as shown in Figure 18.6.

One can quibble that glycerol might belong in yet another taxonomy having to do with other chemicals that influence viscosity, or that folding dynamics should also be a part of protein interactions, but it is not the point to have the perfect domain representation at this early stage. Rather, it is to see that the domain concepts do tend to organize themselves in a way that is reflected in the text vector space, which computers can readily

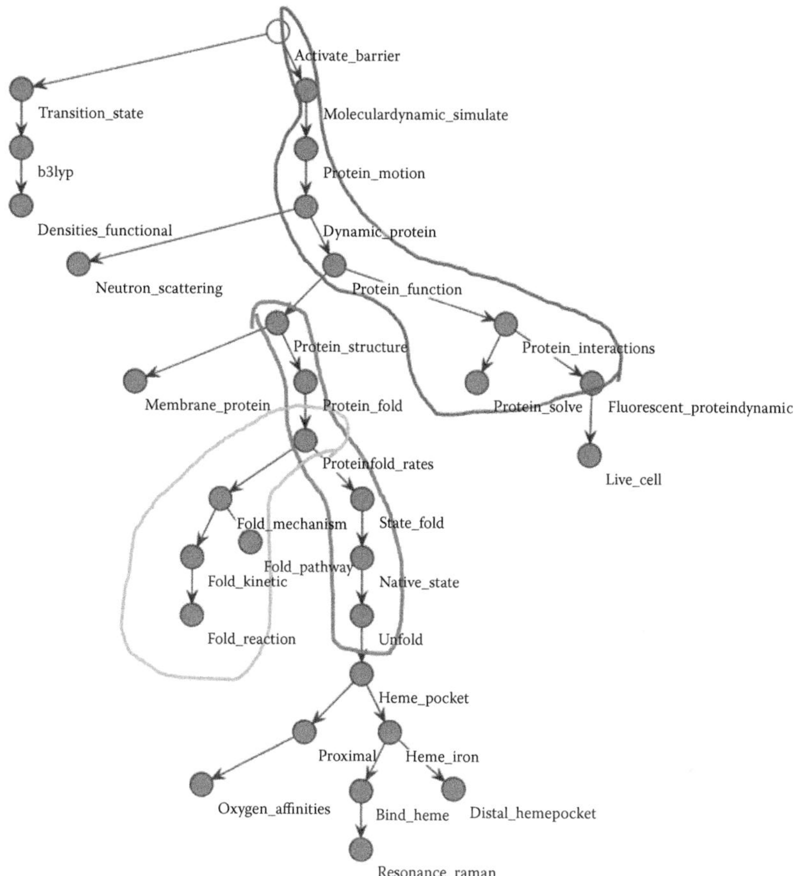

FIGURE 18.3 Protein dynamics ontology.

calculate and reason over (as we see by the fact that each of these taxonomies is localized in the concept clustering tree).

We have now created a coherent plan for thinking about this domain from several different perspectives. Multiple taxonomies are especially important in understanding complex scientific texts. Frequently, it will turn out that important relationships emerge between entities of different types. This brings us to the concept of "orthogonal filtering."

USING ORTHOGONAL FILTERING TO DISCOVER IMPORTANT RELATIONSHIPS

Getting back to our protein viscosity problem, we can use the orthogonal filtering approach to focus on sentences in Medline abstracts that combine terms from two different taxonomies. There are

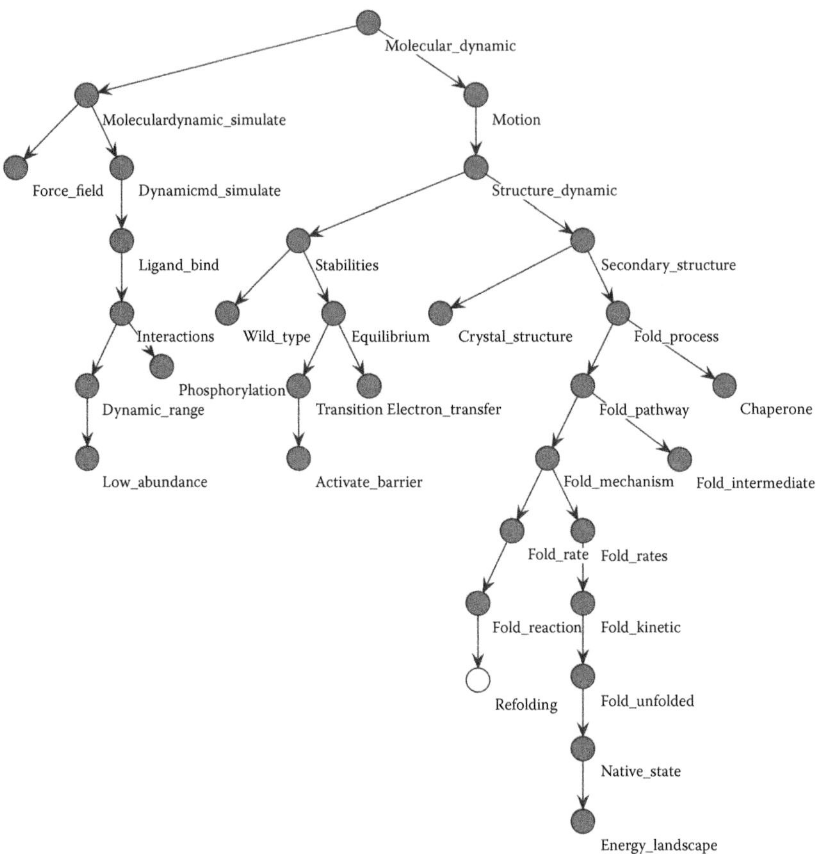

FIGURE 18.4 Dynamics and structure.

$$\binom{4}{2} = 6$$

ways to combine the different taxonomies in pairs. We will look at each of these in turn to see what emerges (Figure 18.7).

Here a co-occurrence table is helpful in order to see the space of intersections between entities of two independent taxonomies. For example, one such table for viscosity and interaction is shown in Figure 18.8.

The total counts on the left-hand side and the bottom row indicate the number of abstracts for each individual query, shown in the row and column headers. The numbers in each cell represent the number of abstracts found to contain both queries and the calculated probability of finding

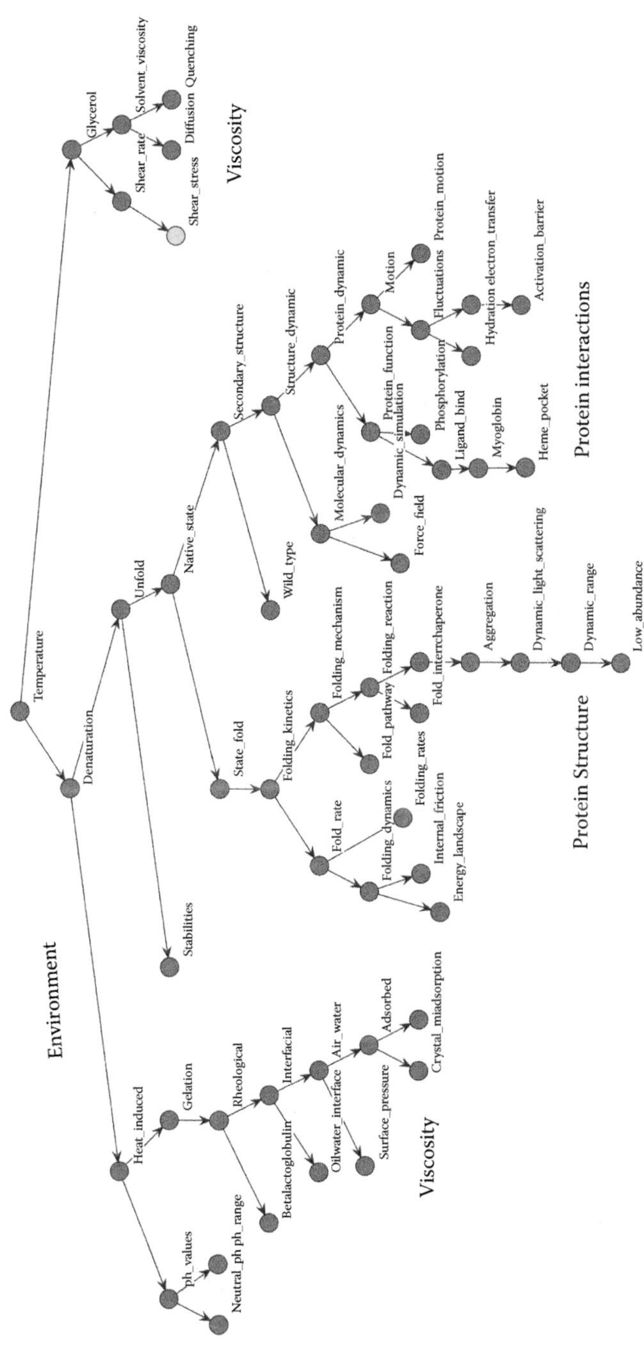

FIGURE 18.5 Overall protein ontology.

Viscosity terms	Environmental terms	Protein structure	Protein interaction
Air_water	Temperature	Fluctuations	Activation_barrier
Oilwater_interface	Denaturation	Protein_dynamics	Dynamic_simulation
Interfacial	Gelation	Heme_pocket	Protein_motion
Surface_pressure	Betalactoglobulin	Myoglobin	Protein_function
Adsorbed	Heat_induced	Folding_reaction	Molecular_dynamics
Glycerol	Ph_values	Folding_kinetics	Force_field
Diffusion	Ph_range	Folding_dynamics	Ligand_bind
Crystalmicrobalance	Neutral_ph	Internal_friction	Phosphorylation
Adsoprtion	Hydration	Folding_mechanism	Dynamic_range
Aggregation	Solvent_viscosity	Folding_rates	Low_abundance
Dynamic lightscattering	Quenching	State_fold	Motion
Rheological		Native_state	Structure_dynamic
Shear_rate		Unfold	Stabilities
Shear_stress		Fold_pathway	Wild_type
		Chaperone	Electron_transfer
		Fold_intermediate	
		Fold_rate	
		Energy_landscape	
		Secondary_structure	

FIGURE 18.6 Complete ontology of protein viscosity concepts.

such a value using a chi-squared test for independence. Colors are used to draw the eye toward interesting interactions (low probability values) that might be more than mere coincidence.

So for example, focusing on the intersection of "glycerol" and "motion" reveals this sentence:

> Increasing the level of *glycerol* increases the *motion* of the protein and changes the protein conformation. [1]

So there is indeed a direct physical relationship between these two terms from orthogonal taxonomies, which is revealed by their relatively frequent co-occurrence in Medline abstracts (Figure 18.9).

Here focusing on "temperature" and "folding dynamics" reveals this sentence:

Combining two (or more) independent ontologies that are both relevant yields abstracts that are likely to be most important and relevant.

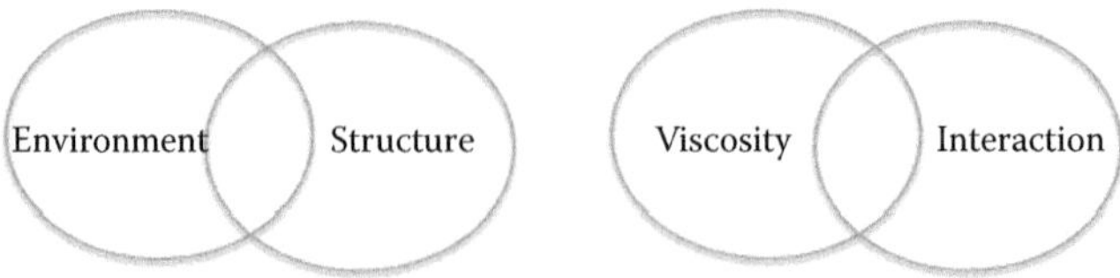

This also provides a way to focus attention on the elements of the abstract that are most relevant.

FIGURE 18.7 Orthogonal filtering using two ontologies.

Very High Affinity = Moderate Affinity = Low Affinity = No Affinity =

	Count	air_water	oilwater_interface	interfacial	surface_pressure	adsorbed	glycerol	diffusion	crystal_microbalance	adsorption	aggregation	rheological	shear_rate
stabilities	128	0 (1.0)	0 (1.0)	3 (0.5805...	0 (1.0)	0 (1.0)	2 (1.0)	10 (0.331...	0 (1.0)	1 (1.0)	14 (3.26222...	2 (1.0)	0 (1.0)
motion	1207	1 (1.0)	0 (1.0)	24 (0.437...	0 (1.0)	11 (1.0)	52 (1.719...	140 (1.30...	2 (1.0)	2 (1.0)	16 (1.0)	6 (1.0)	2 (1.0)
structure_dynamic	728	3 (1.0)	0 (1.0)	9 (1.0)	1 (1.0)	5 (1.0)	8 (1.0)	44 (0.785...	0 (1.0)	6 (1.0)	14 (1.0)	1 (1.0)	0 (1.0)
ligand_bind	402	0 (1.0)	0 (1.0)	0 (1.0)	0 (1.0)	1 (1.0)	12 (0.283...	15 (1.0)	1 (1.0)	0 (1.0)	3 (1.0)	0 (1.0)	0 (1.0)
protein_function	281	1 (1.0)	0 (1.0)	7 (0.3092...	0 (1.0)	0 (1.0)	2 (1.0)	11 (1.0)	0 (1.0)	2 (1.0)	7 (1.0)	1 (1.0)	0 (1.0)
electron_transfer	291	0 (1.0)	0 (1.0)	13 (2.468...	0 (1.0)	12 (0.003...	6 (1.0)	24 (0.072...	0 (1.0)	4 (1.0)	5 (1.0)	0 (1.0)	0 (1.0)
phosphorylation	227	0 (1.0)	0 (1.0)	1 (1.0)	0 (1.0)	1 (1.0)	5 (1.0)	3 (1.0)	0 (1.0)	1 (1.0)	10 (0.68056...	0 (1.0)	0 (1.0)
dynamic_simulation	43	0 (1.0)	0 (1.0)	0 (1.0)	0 (1.0)	0 (1.0)	0 (1.0)	0 (1.0)	0 (1.0)	0 (1.0)	2 (0.7937888)	0 (1.0)	0 (1.0)
force_field	162	0 (1.0)	1 (0.39125293)	1 (1.0)	0 (1.0)	0 (1.0)	1 (1.0)	6 (1.0)	0 (1.0)	0 (1.0)	0 (1.0)	0 (1.0)	0 (1.0)
low_abundance	34	0 (1.0)	0 (1.0)	0 (1.0)	0 (1.0)	0 (1.0)	0 (1.0)	0 (1.0)	0 (1.0)	0 (1.0)	0 (1.0)	0 (1.0)	0 (1.0)
protein_motion	162	0 (1.0)	0 (1.0)	4 (0.4554...	0 (1.0)	2 (1.0)	13 (4.053...	16 (0.026...	0 (1.0)	0 (1.0)	1 (1.0)	0 (1.0)	0 (1.0)
wild_type	190	0 (1.0)	0 (1.0)	0 (1.0)	0 (1.0)	2 (1.0)	6 (0.3710...	12 (0.766...	0 (1.0)	0 (1.0)	3 (1.0)	0 (1.0)	0 (1.0)
dynamic_range	242	0 (1.0)	0 (1.0)	0 (1.0)	0 (1.0)	1 (1.0)	2 (1.0)	2 (1.0)	0 (1.0)	2 (1.0)	3 (1.0)	0 (1.0)	0 (1.0)
molecular_dynamics	1553	0 (1.0)	0 (1.0)	23 (1.0)	0 (1.0)	16 (1.0)	11 (1.0)	92 (0.844...	0 (1.0)	17 (1.0)	35 (1.0)	1 (1.0)	1 (1.0)
activation_barrier	1380	2 (1.0)	1 (1.0)	19 (1.0)	0 (1.0)	59 (1.921...	14 (1.0)	94 (0.092...	0 (1.0)	76 (7.8224...	10 (1.0)	0 (1.0)	2 (1.0)
Total	11848	90	32	203	52	221	262	689	78	320	460	235	55

FIGURE 18.8 Cotable of viscosity vs. interaction.

	Count	temperature	denaturation	gelation	betalactoglobulin	heat_induced	ph_values	ph_range	neutral_ph	hydration	solvent_viscosity	quenching
state_fold	127	38 (1.016313...	15 (1.736798...	0 (1.0)	0 (1.0)	0 (1.0)	1 (0.9715...	2 (0.1984...	0 (1.0)	1 (1.0)	0 (1.0)	4 (0.1312...
energy_landscape	387	93 (1.936555...	9 (1.0)	0 (1.0)	0 (1.0)	0 (1.0)	3 (0.9721...	0 (1.0)	0 (1.0)	6 (1.0)	5 (1.0)	1 (1.0)
folding_mechanism	365	53 (1.0)	27 (2.232274...	0 (1.0)	1 (1.0)	0 (1.0)	3 (0.8899...	1 (1.0)	0 (1.0)	5 (1.0)	5 (1.0)	5 (1.0)
secondary_structure	641	109 (1.0)	42 (7.50329E...	2 (1.0)	13 (3.3745724E-5)	2 (1.0)	7 (0.3194...	1 (1.0)	8 (6.35414E-4)	12 (1.0)	6 (1.0)	8 (1.0)
fold_intermediate	408	52 (1.0)	32 (5.861226...	0 (1.0)	9 (2.0536754E-4)	0 (1.0)	3 (1.0)	0 (1.0)	4 (0.06638702)	3 (1.0)	6 (1.0)	8 (0.4589...
fold_pathway	445	89 (0.089044...	16 (0.8396552)	0 (1.0)	0 (1.0)	0 (1.0)	1 (1.0)	0 (1.0)	2 (0.89413494)	4 (1.0)	6 (1.0)	4 (1.0)
chaperone	286	32 (1.0)	6 (1.0)	0 (1.0)	0 (1.0)	2 (0.24221161)	0 (1.0)	0 (1.0)	0 (1.0)	5 (1.0)	6 (0.5366593)	3 (1.0)
native_state	624	116 (0.28616...	57 (7.546983...	2 (1.0)	14 (2.018058E-6)	3 (0.45091814)	6 (0.5513...	4 (1.0)	6 (0.026652006)	11 (1.0)	8 (1.0)	10 (0.862...
folding_rates	247	51 (0.126106...	19 (1.930901...	0 (1.0)	0 (1.0)	0 (1.0)	2 (0.9275...	3 (0.2736...	2 (0.320228)	2 (1.0)	8 (0.045460608)	0 (1.0)
folding_dynamics	147	34 (0.047655...	7 (0.36953187)	0 (1.0)	1 (1.0)	1 (0.42835638)	0 (1.0)	0 (1.0)	1 (0.6056436)	2 (1.0)	12 (3.6637057E...	2 (1.0)
heme_pocket	1031	158 (1.0)	31 (1.0)	0 (1.0)	1 (1.0)	1 (1.0)	18 (1.352...	18 (5.966...	13 (7.5197977...	28 (1.0)	13 (1.0)	12 (1.0)
internal_friction	25	5 (0.6922988)	0 (1.0)	0 (1.0)	0 (1.0)	0 (1.0)	0 (1.0)	0 (1.0)	0 (1.0)	0 (1.0)	14 (0.0)	1 (0.3103...
folding_kinetics	1378	250 (0.24147...	92 (1.585401...	0 (1.0)	9 (1.0)	0 (1.0)	4 (1.0)	5 (1.0)	6 (0.8746365)	16 (1.0)	16 (1.0)	20 (1.0)
fold_rate	482	102 (0.01367...	29 (0.001394...	0 (1.0)	1 (1.0)	0 (1.0)	4 (0.8569...	4 (0.6326...	4 (0.14055403)	6 (1.0)	17 (8.6188124E...	5 (1.0)
folding_reaction	843	102 (1.0)	61 (2.664189...	0 (1.0)	10 (0.078997426)	3 (0.83032024)	5 (1.0)	2 (1.0)	1 (1.0)	14 (1.0)	21 (0.043297704)	16 (0.351...
myoglobin	686	184 (2.01204...	25 (0.744120...	0 (1.0)	1 (1.0)	2 (1.0)	7 (0.4183...	5 (0.8117...	9 (1.3835164E...	45 (4.147...	27 (1.0557136E...	16 (0.073...
unfold	1781	378 (3.12128...	212 (0.0)	9 (1.0)	16 (0.2762139)	12 (0.003478...	23 (0.005...	15 (0.295...	11 (0.13621628)	47 (1.0)	28 (1.0)	42 (0.001...
fluctuations	620	144 (2.45653...	15 (1.0)	1 (1.0)	2 (1.0)	0 (1.0)	3 (1.0)	1 (1.0)	0 (1.0)	41 (1.580...	28 (6.8115478E...	23 (4.672...
protein_dynamics	2253	390 (0.69183...	35 (1.0)	0 (1.0)	0 (1.0)	3 (1.0)	5 (1.0)	6 (1.0)	3 (1.0)	109 (1.16...	39 (0.7038365)	34 (1.0)
Total	11710	1994	401	107	82	37	89	77	48	340	192	178

FIGURE 18.9 Cotable of environment vs. structure.

> Microsecond *folding dynamics* of the F13W G29A mutant of the B domain of staphylococcal protein A by laser-induced *temperature* jump [PMID: 15007169]

This again reveals a physical connection between the two terms from different taxonomies.

These connections can begin to form the basis for creating a relationship annotator that could be used to extract normalized tuples of the form "glycerol increases motion" or "temperature jump causes protein folding." Once all the entities and relationships are in place, it becomes feasible to use them to hone in on the precise text in research articles that are relevant to protein viscosity and to begin to answer complex questions about this domain, such as "what protein properties are related to low viscosity?" (Figure 18.10).

Using this systematic process, it is possible to take any complex scientific corpus and, with the competent aid of domain experts, create an ontology of entities and relationships that allow a computer to ingest research publications and use the knowledge gained from that ingestion to aid in the process of discovery. Text clustering is the engine that makes this endeavor practical in the face of large-scale document collections. But the learning done here is not strictly speaking unsupervised. Instead, a mixed-initiative approach is recommended, allowing the domain expert

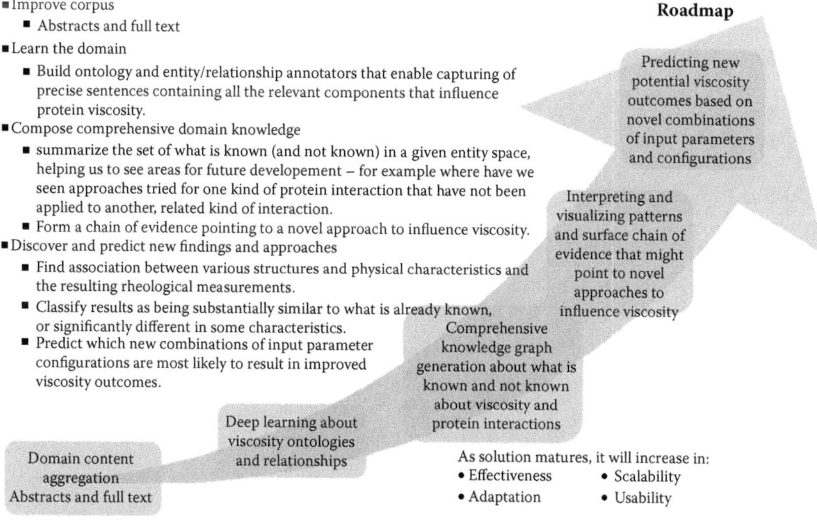

FIGURE 18.10 Process for ontology creation and utilization for discovery.

to direct the process as it unfolds and to ensure that the concepts extracted are not merely artifacts but key features of the domain. Experts can easily recognize an important concept when they see it, but they cannot read research papers very fast. Computers can read fast, but they do not always know what is important. Combining the strengths of each is a requirement for consistently getting good results.

REFERENCE

1. Gao, C., et al. 2006. Plasticization of a protein-based film by glycerol: A spectroscopic, mechanical, and thermal study. *Journal of Agricultural and Food Chemistry*, *54*(13): 4611–4616.

CHAPTER 19

Example: Finding Microbes to Clean Up Oil Spills

Scott Spangler, Zarath Summers, and Adam Usadi

The world is teeming with millions of microbial species in a vast soup of life. Some microbes are "aerobic," meaning they require oxygen for respiration in order to metabolize nutrients. Other microbes are "anaerobic," meaning they use other atoms as electron acceptors during respiration, hence they can live in places that are depleted of oxygen. Furthermore, some of these microbes can metabolize hydrocarbons—the stuff of crude oil. Crude oil can be an environmental pollutant, both through the natural seepage of small amounts that accumulate over time and through occasional large, accidental spills during production, transportation, or refinement. Certain aromatic compounds in these oils can be toxic to macrofauna. However, hydrocarbon-digesting, aerobic microbes are responsible for degrading oil in the open ocean. What about anaerobic environments? Naturally occurring hydrocarbon-digesting, anaerobic microbes might be the answer to biodegrading oil spills in anoxic environments. The trick is to find these microbes, culture them, and introduce them when and where they are needed.

The first step, finding the right microbes, is where Accelerated Discovery comes into play. Anaerobic microbes are actually quite common. Some of them are even living inside your gut right now. Thousands have been studied and hundreds of thousands of papers have been published on their behavior, structure, and properties. Combing through all this literature to find the most likely candidates to culture in the lab is a job for the data scientist.

ENTITIES

The first thing to do is identify the various kinds of entities that exist in communities of hydrocarbon-digesting microbes. The organism itself is the most obvious entity. The basic nomenclature for microbes is *genus species strain*, so for example:

Desulfovibrio desulfuricans ATCC27774

This name refers to the genus *Desulfovibrio* (the most general part of the name), the species *desulfuricans* (more specific than genus, and what we usually think of when we identify an organism), and the strain ATCC27774 (most specific, a variety of organism).

For the most part, organism names are carefully chosen and are used in a consistent fashion across published journals, so this will be the primary entity we use for recognizing, retrieving, and focusing on the text of interest. Beyond the organism itself, there are three major kinds of entities that will help us to determine whether or not a specific organism is interesting for our purposes:

1. Where the organism lives, both in what kind of environment and sometimes, more specifically, the geolocation where it is to be found.
2. What the organism eats; we will refer to this as the "substrate."
3. What the organism breathes; we will refer to this as the "respiration."

Using techniques of text clustering and dictionary perusal, as well as crucial domain knowledge, we were able to come up with the following initial list of terms for each of these entity types:

Environment

aquifer

beach

deep sea

freshwater

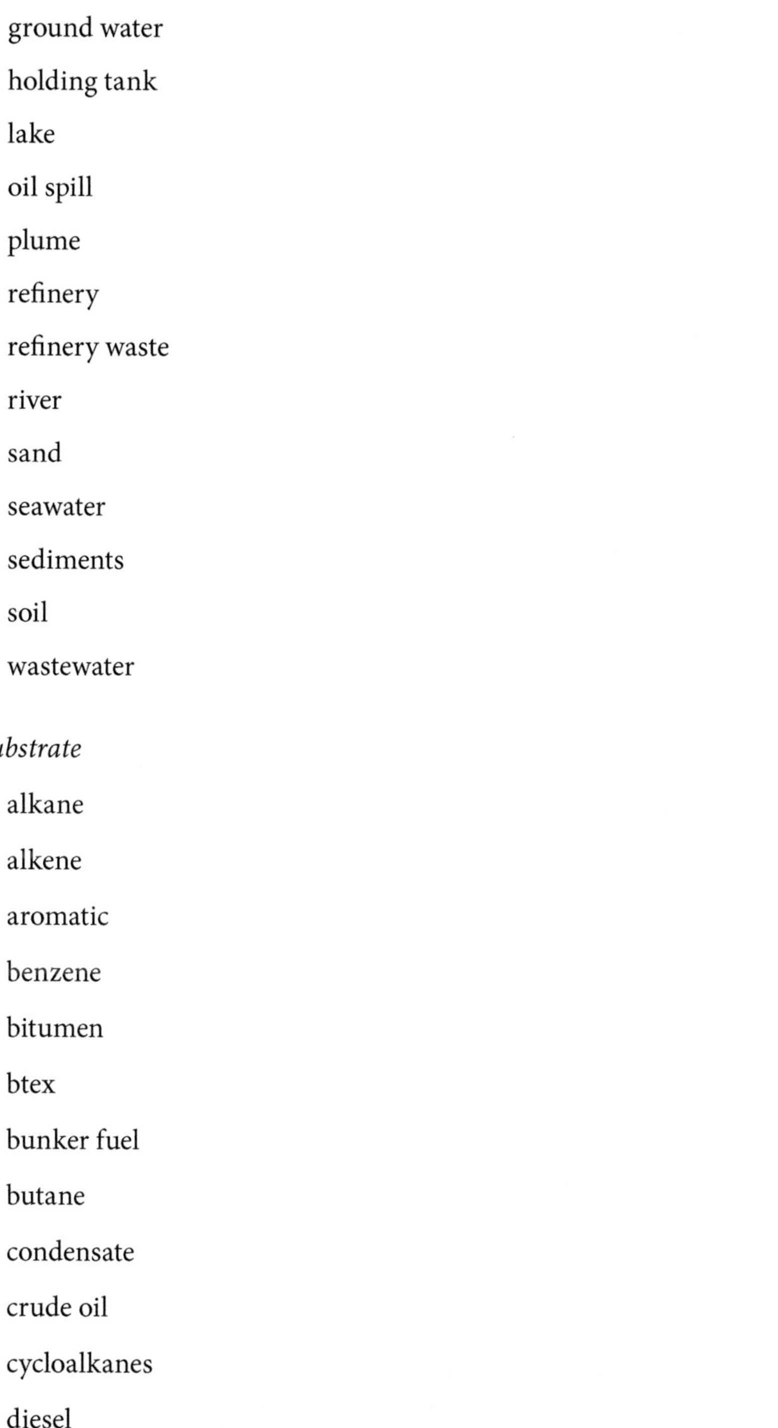

ground water

holding tank

lake

oil spill

plume

refinery

refinery waste

river

sand

seawater

sediments

soil

wastewater

Substrate

alkane

alkene

aromatic

benzene

bitumen

btex

bunker fuel

butane

condensate

crude oil

cycloalkanes

diesel

ethane

gasoline

heavy fuel

heptane

hexane

hydrocarbon

jet fuel

kerosene

methane

pentane

petroleum

propane

toluene

xylene

Respiration

acetogenesis

aerobic

anaerobic

anoxic

fermentation

methanogenesis

nitrate reducing

sulfate reducing

iron reducing

This then becomes our basic dictionary-based ontology, covering all the entities we need to find relevant organisms of interest in the published literature.

USING COTABLES TO FIND THE RIGHT COMBINATION OF FEATURES

The expert microbiologist among us provided us with two lists of organisms. One was a list of candidate species, culled from a few survey papers on the topic. The other was a set of target species, known anaerobes that have been previously observed in oil-contaminated, anoxic environments. This list is reproduced below:

Desulfovibrio vulgaris
Shewanella oneidensis
Methanobacterium thermoautotrophicum
Desulfovibrio desulfuricans
Archaeoglobus fulgidus
Methanosarcina barkeri
Geobacter sulfurreducens
Methanococcus voltae
Methanospirillum hungatei
Geobacter metallireducens
Microbacterium hydrocarbonoxydans
Methanoplanus petrolearius
Desulfovibrio arcticus
Microbacterium oleivorans
Azoarcus toluvorans
Desulfobacterium phenolicum
Geobacter pickeringii

We then created an organism taxonomy by downloading all the Medline abstracts we could find containing both the genus and species name of each organism. This data set ultimately contained 51,799 abstracts. Looking for terms in our respiration dictionary that co-occur with the target organisms in these abstracts leads us to the table in Figure 19.1.

What is interesting here is how well each of the respiration words are correlating with one or more of the target microbes. The substrate and environment dictionaries show far less association (Figure 19.2).

Ultimately, we decided to create a target regular expression pattern that captured the best terms from all of the dictionaries with regard to how well they associated with the known microbes of interest. This target pattern would be as follows:

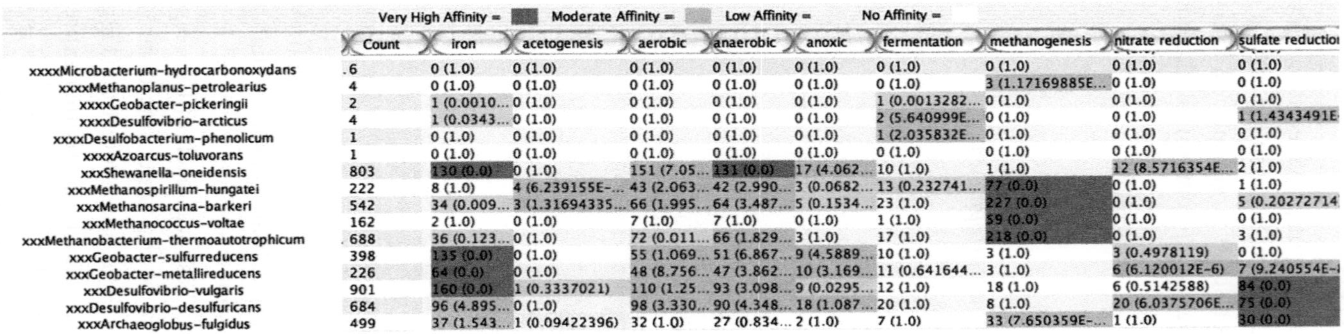

Very High Affinity = Moderate Affinity = Low Affinity = No Affinity =

	Count	iron	acetogenesis	aerobic	anaerobic	anoxic	fermentation	methanogenesis	nitrate reduction	sulfate reductio
xxxxMicrobacterium-hydrocarbonoxydans	6	0 (1.0)	0 (1.0)	0 (1.0)	0 (1.0)	0 (1.0)	0 (1.0)	0 (1.0)	0 (1.0)	0 (1.0)
xxxxMethanoplanus-petrolearius	4	0 (1.0)	0 (1.0)	0 (1.0)	0 (1.0)	0 (1.0)	0 (1.0)	3 (1.17169885E...	0 (1.0)	0 (1.0)
xxxxGeobacter-pickeringii	2	1 (0.0010...	0 (1.0)	0 (1.0)	0 (1.0)	0 (1.0)	1 (0.0013282...	0 (1.0)	0 (1.0)	0 (1.0)
xxxxDesulfovibrio-arcticus	4	1 (0.0343...	0 (1.0)	0 (1.0)	0 (1.0)	0 (1.0)	2 (5.640999E...	0 (1.0)	0 (1.0)	1 (1.4343491E
xxxxDesulfobacterium-phenolicum	1	0 (1.0)	0 (1.0)	0 (1.0)	0 (1.0)	0 (1.0)	1 (2.035832E...	0 (1.0)	0 (1.0)	0 (1.0)
xxxxAzoarcus-toluvorans	1	0 (1.0)	0 (1.0)	0 (1.0)	0 (1.0)	0 (1.0)	0 (1.0)	0 (1.0)	0 (1.0)	0 (1.0)
xxxShewanella-oneidensis	803	130 (0.0)	0 (1.0)	151 (7.05...	131 (0.0)	17 (4.062...	10 (1.0)	1 (1.0)	12 (8.5716354E...	2 (1.0)
xxxMethanospirillum-hungatei	222	8 (1.0)	4 (6.239155E-...	43 (2.063...	42 (2.990...	3 (0.0682...	13 (0.232741...	77 (0.0)	0 (1.0)	1 (1.0)
xxxMethanosarcina-barkeri	542	34 (0.009...	3 (1.31694335...	66 (1.995...	64 (3.487...	5 (0.1534...	23 (1.0)	227 (0.0)	0 (1.0)	5 (0.20272714
xxxMethanococcus-voltae	162	2 (1.0)	0 (1.0)	7 (1.0)	7 (1.0)	0 (1.0)	1 (1.0)	59 (0.0)	0 (1.0)	0 (1.0)
xxxMethanobacterium-thermoautotrophicum	688	36 (0.123...	0 (1.0)	72 (0.011...	66 (1.829...	3 (1.0)	17 (1.0)	218 (0.0)	0 (1.0)	3 (1.0)
xxxGeobacter-sulfurreducens	398	135 (0.0)	0 (1.0)	55 (1.069...	51 (6.867...	9 (4.5889...	10 (1.0)	3 (1.0)	3 (0.4978119)	0 (1.0)
xxxGeobacter-metallireducens	226	64 (0.0)	0 (1.0)	48 (8.756...	47 (3.862...	10 (3.169...	11 (0.641644...	3 (1.0)	6 (6.120012E-6)	7 (9.240554E-
xxxDesulfovibrio-vulgaris	901	160 (0.0)	1 (0.3337021)	110 (1.25...	93 (3.098...	9 (0.0295...	12 (1.0)	18 (1.0)	6 (0.5142588)	84 (0.0)
xxxDesulfovibrio-desulfuricans	684	96 (4.895...	0 (1.0)	98 (3.330...	90 (4.348...	18 (1.087...	20 (1.0)	8 (1.0)	20 (6.0375706E...	75 (0.0)
xxxArchaeoglobus-fulgidus	499	37 (1.543...	1 (0.09422396)	32 (1.0)	27 (0.834...	2 (1.0)	7 (1.0)	33 (7.650359E-...	1 (1.0)	30 (0.0)

FIGURE 19.1 Organism vs. respiration. *Note*: The “xxx” in front of the organism name is simply used to help easily identify the target organisms and cause them to clump together when the full list is sorted alphabetically.

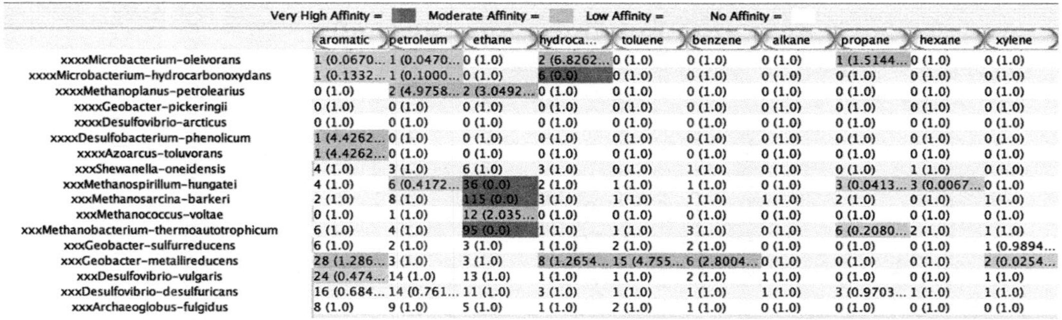

Very High Affinity = Moderate Affinity = Low Affinity = No Affinity =

	aromatic	petroleum	ethane	hydroca...	toluene	benzene	alkane	propane	hexane	xylene
xxxxMicrobacterium-oleivorans	1 (0.0670...	1 (0.0470...	0 (1.0)	2 (6.8262...	0 (1.0)	0 (1.0)	0 (1.0)	1 (1.5144...	0 (1.0)	0 (1.0)
xxxxMicrobacterium-hydrocarbonoxydans	1 (0.1332...	1 (0.1000...	0 (1.0)	6 (0.0)	0 (1.0)	0 (1.0)	0 (1.0)	0 (1.0)	0 (1.0)	0 (1.0)
xxxxMethanoplanus-petrolearius	0 (1.0)	2 (4.9758...	2 (3.0492...	0 (1.0)	0 (1.0)	0 (1.0)	0 (1.0)	0 (1.0)	0 (1.0)	0 (1.0)
xxxxGeobacter-pickeringii	0 (1.0)	0 (1.0)	0 (1.0)	0 (1.0)	0 (1.0)	0 (1.0)	0 (1.0)	0 (1.0)	0 (1.0)	0 (1.0)
xxxxDesulfovibrio-arcticus	0 (1.0)	0 (1.0)	0 (1.0)	0 (1.0)	0 (1.0)	0 (1.0)	0 (1.0)	0 (1.0)	0 (1.0)	0 (1.0)
xxxxDesulfobacterium-phenolicum	1 (4.4262...	0 (1.0)	0 (1.0)	0 (1.0)	0 (1.0)	0 (1.0)	0 (1.0)	0 (1.0)	0 (1.0)	0 (1.0)
xxxxAzoarcus-toluvorans	1 (4.4262...	0 (1.0)	0 (1.0)	0 (1.0)	0 (1.0)	0 (1.0)	0 (1.0)	0 (1.0)	0 (1.0)	0 (1.0)
xxxShewanella-oneidensis	4 (1.0)	3 (1.0)	6 (1.0)	3 (1.0)	0 (1.0)	1 (1.0)	0 (1.0)	0 (1.0)	1 (1.0)	0 (1.0)
xxxMethanospirillum-hungatei	4 (1.0)	6 (0.4172...	36 (0.0)	2 (1.0)	1 (1.0)	1 (1.0)	0 (1.0)	3 (0.0413...	3 (0.0067...	0 (1.0)
xxxMethanosarcina-barkeri	2 (1.0)	8 (1.0)	115 (0.0)	3 (1.0)	1 (1.0)	1 (1.0)	1 (1.0)	2 (1.0)	0 (1.0)	1 (1.0)
xxxMethanococcus-voltae	0 (1.0)	1 (1.0)	12 (2.035...	0 (1.0)	0 (1.0)	0 (1.0)	0 (1.0)	0 (1.0)	0 (1.0)	0 (1.0)
xxxMethanobacterium-thermoautotrophicum	6 (1.0)	4 (1.0)	95 (0.0)	1 (1.0)	1 (1.0)	3 (1.0)	0 (1.0)	6 (0.2080...	2 (1.0)	1 (1.0)
xxxGeobacter-sulfurreducens	6 (1.0)	2 (1.0)	3 (1.0)	1 (1.0)	2 (1.0)	2 (1.0)	0 (1.0)	0 (1.0)	0 (1.0)	1 (0.9894...
xxxGeobacter-metallireducens	28 (1.286...	3 (1.0)	3 (1.0)	8 (1.2654...	15 (4.755...	6 (2.8004...	0 (1.0)	0 (1.0)	0 (1.0)	2 (0.0254...
xxxDesulfovibrio-vulgaris	24 (0.474...	14 (1.0)	13 (1.0)	1 (1.0)	1 (1.0)	2 (1.0)	1 (1.0)	0 (1.0)	0 (1.0)	1 (1.0)
xxxDesulfovibrio-desulfuricans	16 (0.684...	14 (0.761...	11 (1.0)	3 (1.0)	1 (1.0)	1 (1.0)	1 (1.0)	3 (0.9703...	1 (1.0)	1 (1.0)
xxxArchaeoglobus-fulgidus	8 (1.0)	9 (1.0)	5 (1.0)	1 (1.0)	2 (1.0)	1 (1.0)	0 (1.0)	0 (1.0)	0 (1.0)	0 (1.0)

FIGURE 19.2 Organism vs. substrate.

xxxxMicrobacterium-oleivorans	4	3 (0.0015...
xxxxMicrobacterium-hydrocarbonoxydans	6	6 (3.1326...
xxxxMethanoplanus-petrolearius	4	4 (6.2342...
xxxxGeobacter-pickeringii	1	1 (0.0238...
xxxxDesulfovibrio-arcticus	2	2 (0.0013...
xxxxDesulfobacterium-phenolicum	1	1 (0.0238...
xxxxAzoarcus-toluvorans	1	1 (0.0238...
xxxShewanella-oneidensis	594	185 (1.43...
xxxMethanospirillum-hungatei	126	94 (0.0)
xxxMethanosarcina-barkeri	380	249 (0.0)
xxxMethanococcus-voltae	151	63 (3.635...
xxxMethanobacterium-thermoautotrophicum	540	251 (0.0)
xxxGeobacter-sulfurreducens	300	116 (1.35...
xxxGeobacter-metallireducens	114	79 (0.0)
xxxDesulfovibrio-vulgaris	723	297 (0.0)
xxxDesulfovibrio-desulfuricans	503	253 (0.0)
xxxArchaeoglobus-fulgidus	434	100 (1.68...

FIGURE 19.3 Target microbes vs. target pattern.

```
TARGET|hydrocarbon|oil |petroleum|gasoline|anaerobic|c
ontaminat|anoxic|denitrificat|nitrate reduc|sulfate
reduc|sulfate-reduc|SO4 reduc|iron reduc|iron-
reduc|Fe.{0,5}reduc|Fe.{0,5}-reduc|methanogen|propane|
degrad|thermophilic
```

Figure 19.3 shows the results produced by this target pattern when compared to the target microbes.

We seem to have captured the characteristics behind the target microbes very well. Next, we apply these characteristics to the larger candidate microbe list to see which ones rise to the top when sorted by chi-squared probability (low to high) (Figure 19.4).

The result is a list of microbes that tracks extremely well with the expert's opinion about which microbes were the best (most likely targets) from the input list. We can now apply this same formulation to a much wider variety of organisms found in all biological literature to discover the most comprehensive list of species that might be eventually tested in the bioremediation of oil spills.

DISCOVERING NEW SPECIES

We begin by using the target concept to generate a set of queries to apply to Medline abstracts that have the kind of properties present in those that contain microbes of interest. To keep any one query from dominating and to make sure we do not get too much data back, we add a publication year filter to some of the queries so that each query returns at most 10,000 results. Here is the final set of queries we issue:

Very High Affinity = ■ Moderate Affinity = ■ Lo

Term	Count	TARGET
Bacteroides-frag	999	469 (0.0)
Bacteroides-fragilis	995	467 (0.0)
xxxDesulfovibrio-vulgaris	723	297 (0.0)
xxxDesulfovibrio-desulfuricans	503	253 (0.0)
xxxMethanobacterium-thermoautotrophicum	540	251 (0.0)
xxxMethanosarcina-barkeri	380	249 (0.0)
xxxMethanospirillum-hungatei	126	94 (0.0)
xxxGeobacter-metallireducens	114	79 (0.0)
Thauera-aromatica	80	72 (0.0)
Methanosaeta-concilii	58	57 (0.0)
Marinobacter-hydrocarbonoclasticus	43	43 (0.0)
Pseudomonas-stutzeri	793	274 (4.2E...
Methanosarcina-formicicum	37	34 (2.214...
Methanobacterium-bryantii	48	38 (6.496...
Alcanivorax-borkumensis	55	39 (8.228...
Methanothermobacter-marburgensis	37	30 (2.026...
Methanobacterium-Methanococcus	93	53 (3.356...
xxxGeobacter-sulfurreducens	300	116 (1.35...
Methanobrevibacter-arboriphilus	21	21 (3.997...
Aromatoleum-aromaticum	23	22 (9.327...
Alcanivorax-Marinobacter	25	23 (1.663...
xxxShewanella-oneidensis	594	185 (1.43...
Desulfobulbus-propionicus	22	20 (3.523...
Methylomirabilis-oxyfera	19	18 (2.734...
Desulfosarcina-variabilis	19	18 (2.734...
Candidatus-Methylomirabilis	19	18 (2.734...
Desulfomonile-tiedjei	27	22 (6.184...
Desulfococcus-multivorans	20	18 (5.775...
Comamonas-denitrificans	15	15 (2.123...
Syntrophobacter-wolinii	14	14 (2.820...
xxxMethanococcus-voltae	151	63 (3.635...
Azoarcus-tolulyticus	16	15 (6.161...
Methanothrix-soehngenii	27	20 (5.455...
Bacteroides-distasonis	223	80 (3.267...
Methanothrix-soehn	28	20 (3.509...
Thermacetogenium-phaeum	12	12 (5.016...
Syntrophus-aciditrophicus	16	14 (1.511...
Clostridium-barkeri	50	28 (3.680...
Methanoculleus-bourgensis	12	11 (1.834...
Desulfobacula-toluolica	12	11 (1.834...
Acetobacterium-woodii	79	36 (2.321...
Desulfobacterium-autotrophicum	16	13 (2.365...

FIGURE 19.4 Target pattern vs. all microbes.

- pubyear:>2000 AND abstract:(hydrocarbon)
- pubyear:>2009 AND abstract:(oil)
- abstract:(petroleum OR gasoline)
- pubyear:>2009 AND abstract:(anaerobic OR anoxic)
- abstract:(denitrification)

- abstract:(nitrate AND reduce)
- abstract:(nitrate AND reduction)
- pubyear:>1990 AND abstract:(sulfate AND reduce)
- abstract:(sulfate AND reduction)
- abstract:(SO4 AND reduce)
- abstract:(SO4 AND reduction)
- pubyear:>1990 AND abstract:(iron AND reduce)
- abstract:(iron AND reduction)
- pubyear:>1990 AND abstract:(Fe AND reduce)
- abstract:(Fe AND reduction)
- abstract:(methanogenesis)
- abstract:(propane)

We then use a list of 312 genus names culled from the 100 original papers as seed terms to find additional species beyond the original 444, looking for words that immediately follow these genus names and assuming these would be mostly species names. This process discovers over 1000 new species that look like promising candidates. Note that in the long run we would like to build a species annotator that can accurately identify species from context, but this would require a more complete genus dictionary and enough training data to create a classifier that could distinguish organisms from organism-like terms. The time frame for this proof of concept project was too short for that approach, which would have taken a few months. This entire analysis was done in a matter of weeks.

Next we take the new organisms found using this method and create Medline abstract queries to download content specifically around these. Unlike the previous query, this content would not be limited to the target concept but would be generic. This generality is important because it allows us to use statistics to select only those organisms that are most frequently studied in the area of the target concept, regardless of how recent or prevalent the organism is.

At this point, we combine the data sets for new and old microbes (old being those found originally in survey papers). This creates a Medline abstract collection of 163,762 documents containing 1689 microbes. We will use this data set to rank the organisms according to how well they are likely to be of interest for our application.

ORGANISM RANKING STRATEGY

We can think of each organism as being represented by the collection of papers written about it. We can summarize this collection as a centroid vector in word/phrase space as we have described previously. These centroids can then be used to create a distance matrix that describes the difference of every organism from every other organism. Think of this as a fully connected organism network, where the strength of each connection is related to the relative difference of each pair of organisms.

Given that we have a set of known organisms that are considered to have the properties we like, we can use the simplified graph diffusion strategy described in Chapter 7 to give a numeric ranking score to all the other organisms.

The microbiology domain expert eventually ranked 35 organisms as *good*. We ran our simplified heat-diffusion approach to create the following ranked list of best organisms most closely related to the good organisms (Table 19.1).

As a further filter, we add another separate criteria to the ranking that takes into account whether the publications describing the organism are aligned with the target concept. This will help prevent us from ranking too highly those organisms that are similar to good organisms for reasons unrelated to our goal. This creates a ranking that takes a chi-squared probability of less than 0.5 for the co-occurrence value of the organism with the target concept. We then sort first on whether the organism meets the 0.5 or less threshold and second on the heat-diffusion value. This provides the list (the first 35 are original good organisms) in Table 19.2.

This list was validated by the domain expert as being like the target organisms. In order to help visualize the space, we also created a relative neighborhood graph of organisms. This tree labels the known good organisms in green and 100 of the best candidate organisms (using the ranking method) in blue. The full tree in two parts is shown without color in Figure 19.5.

Some more detailed views are shown in the three color blow-ups in Figure 19.6. These similarity trees were deemed to be helpful by the domain expert in finding interesting sets of organisms to investigate further.

TABLE 19.1 Organism Ranking

Azoarcus evansii	0.17672516
Geobacter grbiciae	0.09901544
Desulfovibrio salexigens	0.091102
Methanobacterium formicicum	0.08189709
Geobacter pelophilus	0.08120211
Geobacter chapellei	0.06685753
Marinobacter daepoensis	0.066001125
Pseudomonas nitroreducens	0.053274583
Desulfovibrio idahonensis	0.04951245
Desulfovibrio africanus	0.04882504
Desulfomicrobium baculatus	0.047458537
Stappia stellulata	0.042493194
Neptunomonas japonica	0.04000795
Desulfovibrio gigas	0.03977763
Desulfotalea arctica	0.039483346
Pseudomonas citronellolis	0.033463467
Methanococcus jannaschii	0.03276964
Desulfovibrio aminophilus	0.032080617
Pseudomonas alcaligenes	0.030723322
Methanococcus thermolithotrophicus	0.029223055
Pseudomonas resinovorans	0.027759643
Methanobacterium bryantii	0.027549926
Curvibacter delicatus	0.027284054
Geobacter bremensis	0.026841938
Geobacter bemidjiensis	0.025556587
Pseudomonas marginalis	0.024465652
Pelobacter carbinolicus	0.02391702
Novosphingobium naphthalenivorans	0.023529844
Syntrophobacter fumaroxidans	0.022707168
Methanococcus vannielii	0.022496609
Methanococcus maripaludis	0.021511873
Methanobacterium wolfei	0.02019317
Variovorax soli	0.020018332
Desulfatibacillum aliphaticivorans	0.0196357
Clostridium subphylum	0.01963189

CHARACTERIZING ORGANISMS

For each organism, we wish to discover the set of properties it has. One way to do this quickly, without developing a sophisticated annotator for capturing relationships between organisms and properties, is to use co-occurrence against each type for every characteristic. Our three

TABLE 19.2 Ranking with Probabilities

Organism	Similarity Score	Probability
Geobacter pelophilus	1.068148	2.37E-05
Aromatoleum aromaticum	1.0320061	1.42E-37
Desulfovibrio fairfieldensis	1.0285139	2.93E-05
Methanobacterium thermoformicicum	1.0074619	5.40E-09
Pseudomonas carboxyl	1.0056347	0.100913934
Archaeoglobus fulgidus	1.0039402	8.94E-15
Methanosarcina domination	1.0036249	0.03455271
Nitrosomonas europaea	1.0036187	0.001626533
Novosphingobium lentum	1.0035344	0.03455271
Desulfomicrobium apsheronum	1.0031339	0.002798583
Geobacter psychrophilus	1.0026848	0.24606574
Geobacter toluenoxydans	1.0023046	2.51E-04
Methanothermobacter crinale	1.0013577	0.002798583
Desulfitobacterium chlororespirans	1.0008394	0.002175512
Desulfobacula toluolica	1.0007335	4.86E-11
Desulfuromonas chloroethenica	1.0006719	0.03455271
Methanoculleus bourgensis	1.0005784	4.86E-11
Desulfovibrio baculatus	1.0004449	0.001779489
Campylobacter charcoal	1.0003724	0.100913934
Desulfitobacterium dehalogenans	1.0003626	8.32E-15
Bacillus benzoevorans	1.0002075	0.001218494
Thermus oshimai	1.0001799	4.11E-07
Shewanella possesses	1.0000381	0.03455271
Thauera clade	1.0000316	0.03455271
Azoarcus toluvorans	1.0000159	0.03455271
Methanoregula formicica	1.0000088	0.03455271
Thermus cytochrome	1.0000025	0.100913934
Microbacterium schleiferi	1.0000001	0.24606574

(*Continued*)

TABLE 19.2 (Continued) Ranking with Probabilities

Organism	Similarity Score	Probability
Azoarcus evansii	0.17672516	2.02E-07
Geobacter hydrogenophilus	0.09901544	0.002798583
Desulfovibrio trichonymphae	0.091102	0.03455271
Methanobacterium kanagiense	0.08189709	0.03455271
Geobacter pickeringii	0.08120211	0.03455271
Geobacter chemotaxis	0.06685753	0.03455271
Marinobacter excellens	0.066001125	0.24606574
Desulfovibrio inopinatus	0.04951245	0.002798583
Desulfovibrio aminophilus	0.04882504	4.11E-07
Desulfomicrobium escambium	0.047458537	0.03455271
Nitrosomonas cryotolerans	0.04000795	0.33816776
Desulfovibrio idahonensis	0.03977763	0.002798583
Desulfotalea psycrophila	0.039483346	0.03455271
Methanococcus thermolithotrophicus	0.03276964	9.56E-40
Desulfovibrio baarsii	0.032080617	0.24606574
Methanococcus voltae	0.029223055	1.22E-16
Pseudomonas sensu	0.027759643	0.007248114
Methanobacterium flexile	0.027549926	0.03455271
Cycloclasticus oligotrophus	0.027284054	0.03455271
Geobacter chapelleii	0.026841938	0.03455271
Pelobacter propionicus	0.02391702	3.94E-06
Novosphingobium soli	0.023529844	0.030206043
Syntrophus aciditrophicus	0.022707168	8.65E-14
Methanococcus voltaei	0.022496609	0.030206043
Methanococcus vannielii	0.021511873	3.52E-12
Methanobrevibacter arboriphilicus	0.02019317	2.24E-08
Veillonella dispar	0.020018332	0.007800171
Desulfitobacterium aromaticivorans	0.0196357	0.002798583

TABLE 19.2 (Continued) Ranking with Probabilities

Organism	Similarity Score	Probability
Clostridium subterminale	0.01963189	0.012024043
Geobacter humireducens	0.018167354	0.24606574
Variovorax soli	0.018149748	3.79E-06
Pseudomonas nautica	0.017988844	1.76E-06
Pseudomonas resinovorans	0.01737771	1.35E-13
Desulfovibrio salexigens	0.017269686	1.46E-05
Pseudoxanthomonas mexicana	0.017072655	0.15990137
Geothrix fermentans	0.016802192	3.74E-07
Desulfovibrio aespoeensis	0.016654352	3.94E-06
Methanosarcina dominance	0.015854245	0.002798583
Methanosarcina siciliae	0.015726821	0.003348392
Thalassolituus oleivorans	0.01565854	2.29E-06
Methanospirillum lacunae	0.015637822	0.03455271
Desulfovibrio carbinolicus	0.015589669	0.002798583
Desulfovibrio multispirans	0.015394055	2.51E-04
Desulfovibrio simplex	0.015025029	0.002798583
Methanobacterium wolfei	0.014500944	5.60E-09
Rhodococcus pyridinivorans	0.014363606	4.11E-07
Desulfotignum toluenicum	0.014226441	0.03455271
Desulfovibrio desulfuricansm	0.013339692	0.03455271
Marinobacter maritimus	0.013269075	0.20923875
Desulfuromonas michiganensis	0.012972124	0.24308336

characteristics are substrate, respiration, and environment. With the help of the microbiology domain expert, we define the types within each characteristic area as follows:

Respiration

```
Iron related reduction|Fe.{0,5}reduc|ferrihydrite.
reduc|iron.oxide|iron.reduc|reduction of Fe|reduction
of iron
```

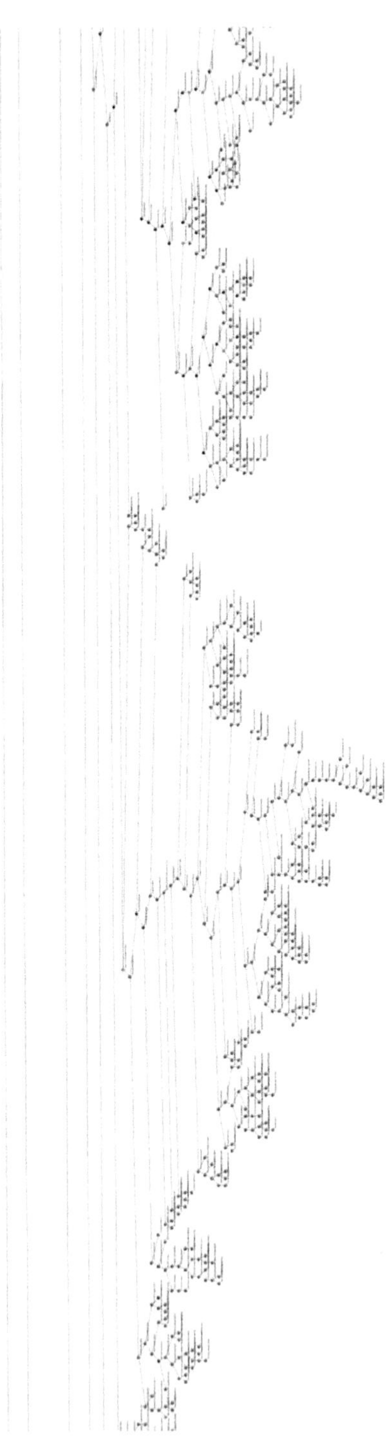

FIGURE 19.5 Relative neighborhood graph of organisms.

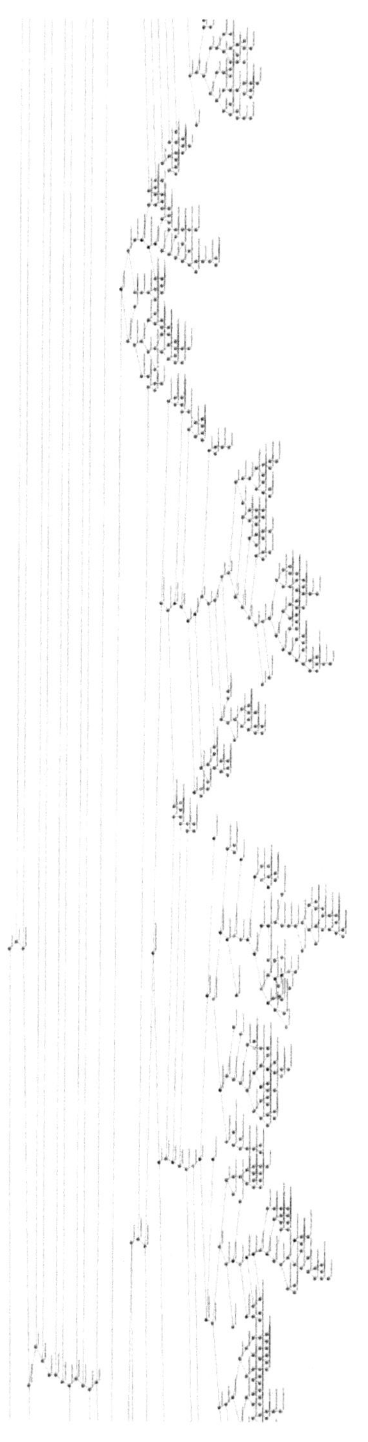

FIGURE 19.5 (Continued)

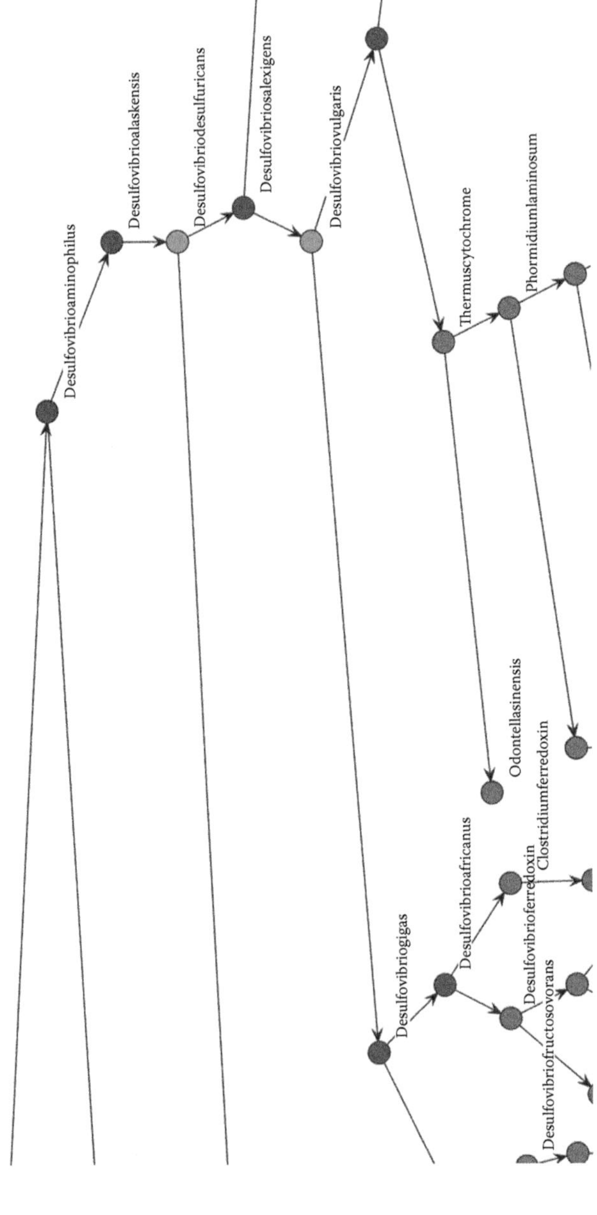

FIGURE 19.6 **(See color insert.)** Blow-up views of interesting areas in relative neighborhood graph of organisms.

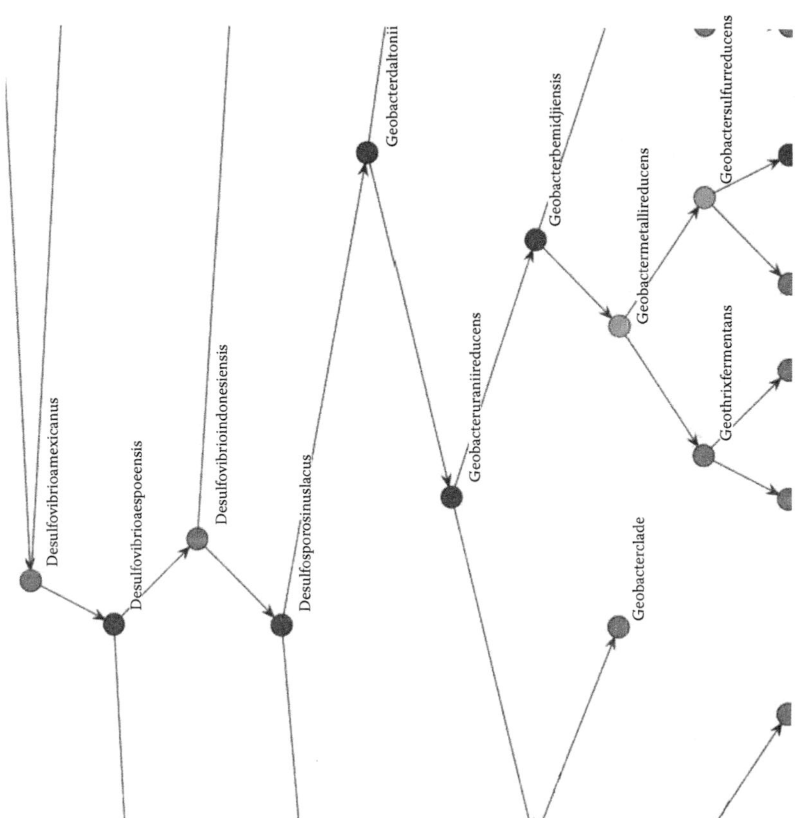

FIGURE 19.6 (Continued)

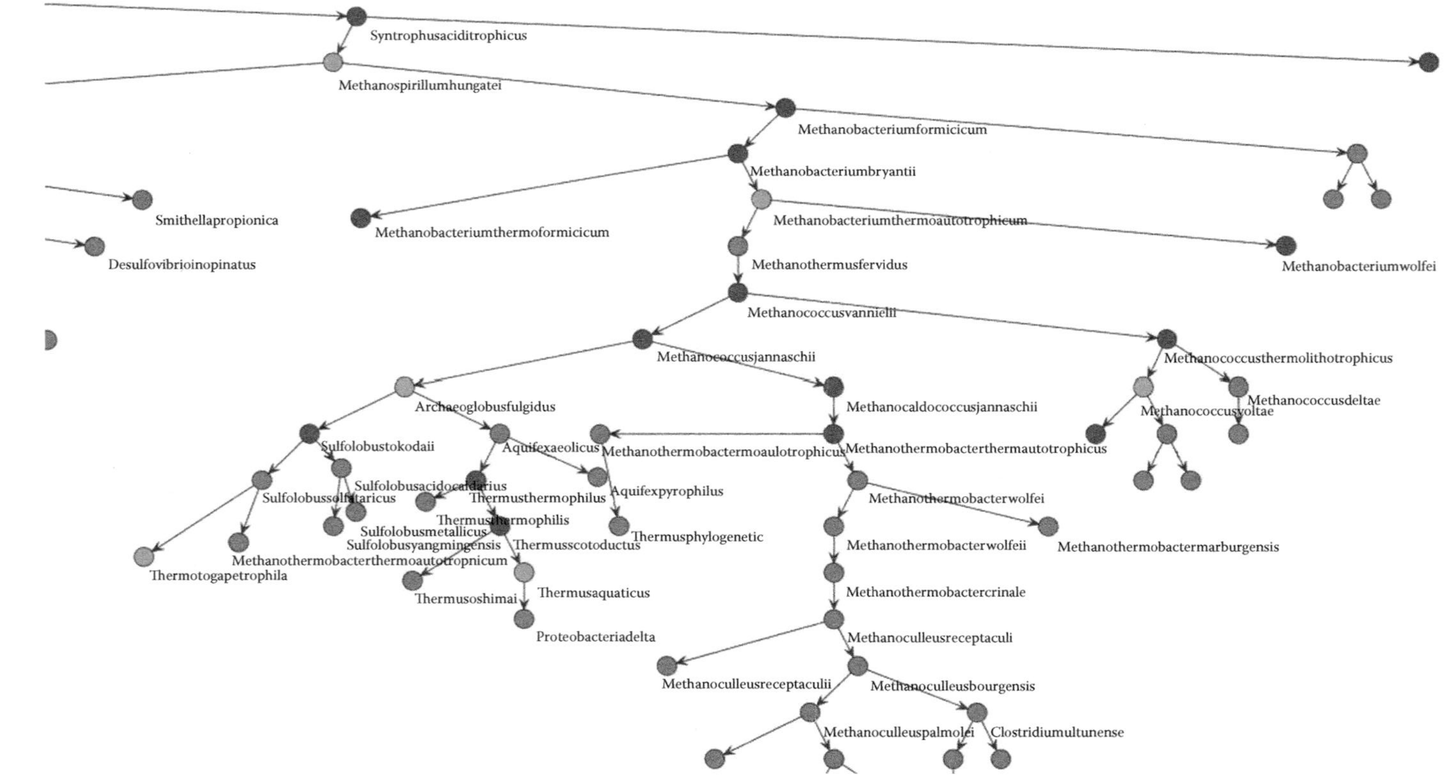

FIGURE 19.6 (Continued)

```
Nitrate related reducution|denitrif|nitrate.reduc|NO3.
reduc
Sulfate related reduction|sulfate.reduc|SO4.
reduc|sulphate.reduc|sulfite.reduc
Methane generating|methanogen
Electron transfer|electron.accept|hydrogenotrophic
Fermentation|ferment
Anaerobic|anaerobic|anoxic|hypoxic
```

Environment

```
Sediment|sediment
Subsurface|subsurface
Aquifer|aquifer
Freshwater|ground.water|lacustrine| lake|fresh.
water|river|pore.water|oilfield water
Seawater|sea water|salt water|marine
Oil reservoir|oil.reservoir|petroleum.reservoir
Polluted soil|OBM|oil based mud|contaminat.{0,10}
soil|pollute.{0,10}soil|oily soil
Soil| soil | soils
Contamination|oil spill|contaminat|broken pipeline|oil
seep|oil sludge|oil.{0,5}shore|oil.{0,5}pollut|plume
|plumes
Desert| desert
Oil production|oil production site|petroleum
system|production well|refinery|refineries|oil well
Energy deposit|energy deposit
```

Substrate

```
TOLUENE|toluene
XYLENE|xylene
ALKANE|alkane| ethane|propane|butane|pentane|hexane|h
eptane|octane|nonane| decane|undecane|dodecane|tridec
ane|tetradecane|pentadecane|hexadecane|heptadecane|oc
tadecane|nonadecane
METHANE|methane
AROMATIC|aromatic
PARAFFINIC|paraffinic
BENZENE|benzene
BTEX|btex|benzene|toluene|xylene
Biodegraded oil|biodegraded oil|biodegraded
petroleum
```

```
Butane|butane
Chlorinated Hydrocarbons|chlorinated hydrocarbon
Fatty acids|fatty acid
Halogenated alkanes|halogenated.alkenes
Hydrocarbons|hydrocarbon|petroleum|crude
oil|diesel|fossil fuel|fuel.oil|gasoline|heavy oil|jet
fuel|JP4|light crude|heavy crude|oil leak|oil
pollutant
Fuel|diesel|gasoline|jet fuel| fuel |fuel oil
Crude oil|crude oil|light oil|heavy oil
TPH
Trioxane|trioxane
```

Next we look for chi-square co-occurrence between each organism and each type for every characteristic. Where we see a chi-squared value of $p < 0.5$, we label that organism as potentially having that characteristic (we err on the side of caution here so that we do not rule out organisms prematurely.

This provides the tables of characteristics for the known good organisms shown in Tables 19.3 through 19.5.

In each case, for these organisms the expert was able to rapidly verify that the properties the method identified were indeed those associated with the organisms.

Next we wanted to apply this same approach to the new organisms that were ranked highly. We discovered that the best way to do this was with a cotable of organisms with organism characteristics/types making up both the row and column headers. This allowed the domain expert to choose frequent and significant combinations of characteristics and types and find exactly those organisms that share the type of interest.

An example of such a cotable of new organisms is shown in Figure 19.7.

To help with interpretation, we created a special characteristic called AnaerobicRespiration (anaerobic and all forms of anaerobic respiration) and another called Freshwater (freshwater and aquifer).

This cotable gave the domain expert an easy way to cue in on organisms of interest, highlighting lesser-known organisms that are capable of hydrocarbon degradation.

CONCLUSION

In this example, we have shown how to use Accelerated Discovery to characterize organisms and find new organisms described by characteristics defined in text. We have also demonstrated how to use the text

TABLE 19.3 Organism Environments

Archaeoglobus fulgidus	Oil reservoir					Subsurface					
Aromatoleum aromaticum					Aquifer		Sediment	Freshwater			
Azoarcus toluvorans											
Bacillus benzoevorans					Aquifer					Soil	
Burkholderia xenovorans			Polluted soil	Desert			Sediment			Soil	
Desulfatibacillum alkenivorans							Sediment				
Desulfitobacterium aromaticivorans			Polluted soil			Subsurface					
Desulfobacterium phenolicum							Sediment				
Desulfoglaeba alkanexedens								Freshwater			
Desulfovibrio arcticus											
Desulfovibrio desulfuricans	Oil reservoir	Oil production				Subsurface	Sediment				
Desulfovibrio vulgaris	Oil reservoir				Aquifer	Subsurface	Sediment				
Geobacillus jurassicus	Oil reservoir										
Geobacter metallireducens					Aquifer	Subsurface	Sediment				Contamination
Geobacter pickeringii						Subsurface					
Geobacter sulfurreducens					Aquifer	Subsurface	Sediment				
Marinobacter aquaeolei	Oil reservoir					Subsurface	Sediment		Seawater		

(Continued)

TABLE 19.3 (Continued) Organism Environments

Methanobacterium thermoautotrophicum											
Methanococcus voltae									Seawater		
Methanoplanus petrolearius											
Methanosarcina barkeri				Desert		Subsurface	Sediment				
Methanospirillum hungatei							Sediment				
Microbacterium oleivorans											
Neptunomonas naphthovorans							Sediment		Seawater		
Novosphingobium aromaticivorans			Polluted soil				Sediment				
Polaromonas naphthalenivorans							Sediment				Contamination
Pseudomonas butanovora											
Pseudomonas mendocina			Polluted soil		Aquifer	Subsurface		Freshwater		Soil	
Pseudomonas oleovorans			Polluted soil								Contamination
Rhodococcus opacus		Oil production	Polluted soil			Subsurface				Soil	
Shewanella oneidensis					Aquifer	Subsurface	Sediment				
Thauera aromatica					Aquifer		Sediment				
Thermotoga petrophila	Oil reservoir					Subsurface					
Thermus aquaticus				Desert			Sediment				

TABLE 19.4 Organism Substrates

Archaeoglobus fulgidus			Fatty acids								
Aromatum aromaticum	Benzene			Aromatic				Toluene			
Azoarcus toluvorans											
Bacillus benzoevorans											
Burkholderia xenovorans	Benzene		Fatty acids	Aromatic	Hydrocarbon						
Desulfatibacillum alkenivorans		Alkane									
Desulfitobacterim aromaticivorans				Aromatic					Methane		
Desulfobacterium phenolicum				Aromatic						Xylene	
Desulfoglaeba alkanexedens											
Desulfovibrio arcticus											
Desulfovibrio desulfuricans							Fuel				
Desulfovibrio vulgaris									Methane		
Geobacillus jurassicus											
Geobacter metallireducens	Benzene			Aromatic	Hydrocarbon		Fuel	Toluene	Methane	Xylene	BTEX
Geobacter pickeringii											
Geobacter sulfurreducens							Fuel				
Marinobacter aquaeolei		Alkane		Aromatic	Hydrocarbon	Crude oil					
Methanobacterim thermoautotrophicum			Fatty acids						Methane		

(*Continued*)

TABLE 19.4 (Continued) Organism Substrates

Methanococcus voltae			Fatty acids						Methane				
Methanoplanus petrolearius													
Methanosarcina barkeri									Methane	Xylene			
Methanospirillum hungatei			Fatty acids			Butane			Methane				
Microbacterium oleivorans													
Neptunomonas naphthovorans				Aromatic									
Novosphingobium aromaticivorans		Alkane		Aromatic									
Polaromonas naphthalenivorans				Aromatic									
Pseudomonas butanovora		Alkane				Butane					Propane		Chlorinated hydrocarbon
Pseudomonas mendocina		Alkane	Fatty acids					Toluene		Xylene	Propane		
Pseudomonas oleovorans	Benzene	Alkane	Fatty acids	Aromatic	Hydrocarbon	Butane	Fuel	Toluene		Xylene		BTEX	
Rhodococcus opacus	Benzene	Alkane	Fatty acids	Aromatic	Hydrocarbon	Butane		Toluene		Xylene		BTEX	
Rhodococcus rhodocrous	Benzene	Alkane		Aromatic	Hydrocarbon	Butane	Fuel	Toluene			Propane	BTEX	
Shewanella oneidensis							Fuel						
Thauera aromatica	Benzene			Aromatic				Toluene		Xylene			
Thermotoga petrophila													
Thermus aquaticus												BTEX	

TABLE 19.5 Organism Respiration

Archaeoglobus fulgidus	Iron reduction		Sulfate reduction				Methanogenic	
Aromatoleum aromaticum	Iron reduction	Nitrate reduction		Electron transfer		Anaerobic		
Azoarcus toluvorans		Nitrate reduction						
Bacillus benzoevorans	Iron reduction			Electron transfer		Anaerobic		
Burkholderia xenovorans								Aerobic
Desulfatibacillum alkenivorans			Sulfate reduction					
Desulfitobacterium aromaticivorans	Iron reduction							
Desulfobacterium phenolicum			Sulfate reduction					
Desulfoglaeba alkanexedens			Sulfate reduction					
Desulfovibrio arcticus			Sulfate reduction					
Desulfovibrio desulfuricans		Nitrate reduction	Sulfate reduction	Electron transfer		Anaerobic		
Desulfovibrio vulgaris	Iron reduction		Sulfate reduction	Electron transfer		Anaerobic	Methanogenic	
Geobacillus jurassicus		Nitrate reduction						Aerobic
Geobacter metallireducens	Iron reduction	Nitrate reduction	Sulfate reduction	Electron transfer		Anaerobic		
Geobacter pickeringii					Fermentation			
Geobacter sulfurreducens	Iron reduction			Electron transfer		Anaerobic		

(Continued)

TABLE 19.5 (Continued) Organism Respiration

Marinobacter aquaeolei		Nitrate reduction	Sulfate reduction	Electron transfer		Anaerobic		
Methanobacterim thermoautotrophicum				Electron transfer		Anaerobic	Methanogenic	
Methanococcus voltae				Electron transfer			Methanogenic	
Methanoplanus petrolearius								
Methanosarcina barkeri			Sulfate reduction	Electron transfer		Anaerobic	Methanogenic	
Methanospirillum hungatei			Sulfate reduction	Electron transfer		Anaerobic	Methanogenic	
Microbacterium oleivorans								
Neptunomonas naphthovorans								Aerobic
Novosphingobium aromaticivorans								Aerobic
Polaromonas naphthalenivorans								Aerobic
Pseudomonas butanovora		Nitrate reduction						Aerobic
Pseudomonas mendocina		Nitrate reduction			Fermentation			Aerobic
Pseudomonas oleovorans					Fermentation			Aerobic
Rhodococcus opacus				Electron transfer				Aerobic
Shewanella oneidensis	Iron reduction	Nitrate reduction		Electron transfer		Anaerobic		Aerobic
Thauera aromatica	Iron reduction	Nitrate reduction	Sulfate reduction	Electron transfer		Anaerobic		
Thermotoga petrophila								
Thermus aquaticus								

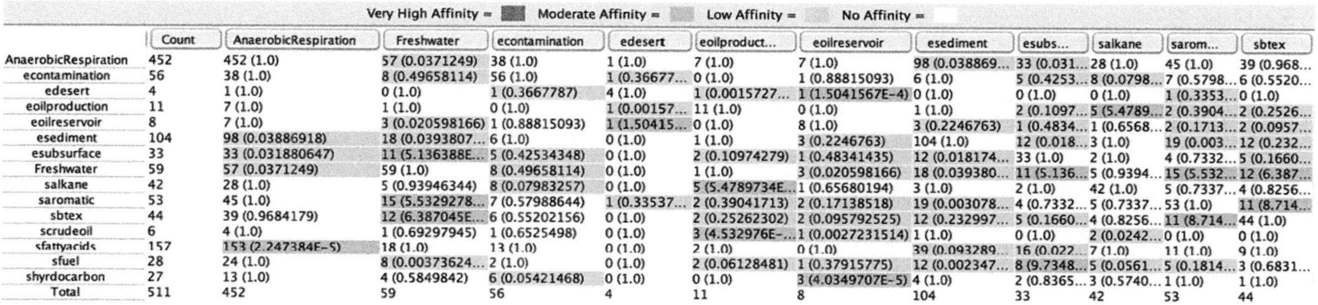

Very High Affinity = Moderate Affinity = Low Affinity = No Affinity =

	Count	AnaerobicRespiration	Freshwater	econtamination	edesert	eoilproduct...	eoilreservoir	esediment	esubs...	salkane	sarom...	sbtex
AnaerobicRespiration	452	452 (1.0)	57 (0.0371249)	38 (1.0)	1 (1.0)	7 (1.0)	7 (1.0)	98 (0.038869...	33 (0.031...	28 (1.0)	45 (1.0)	39 (0.968...
econtamination	56	38 (1.0)	8 (0.49658114)	56 (1.0)	1 (0.36677...	0 (1.0)	1 (0.88815093)	6 (1.0)	5 (0.4253...	8 (0.0798...	7 (0.5798...	6 (0.5520...
edesert	4	1 (1.0)	0 (1.0)	1 (0.3667787)	4 (1.0)	1 (0.0015727...	1 (1.5041567E-4)	0 (1.0)	0 (1.0)	0 (1.0)	1 (0.3353...	0 (1.0)
eoilproduction	11	7 (1.0)	1 (1.0)	0 (1.0)	1 (0.00157...	11 (1.0)	0 (1.0)	1 (1.0)	2 (0.1097...	5 (5.4789...	2 (0.3904...	2 (0.2526...
eoilreservoir	8	7 (1.0)	3 (0.020598166)	1 (0.88815093)	1 (1.50415...	0 (1.0)	8 (1.0)	3 (0.2246763)	1 (0.4834...	1 (0.6568...	2 (0.1713...	2 (0.0957...
esediment	104	98 (0.03886918)	18 (0.0393807...	6 (1.0)	0 (1.0)	1 (1.0)	3 (0.2246763)	104 (1.0)	12 (0.018...	3 (1.0)	19 (0.003...	12 (0.232...
esubsurface	33	33 (0.031880647)	11 (5.136388E...	5 (0.42534348)	0 (1.0)	2 (0.10974279)	1 (0.48341435)	12 (0.018174...	33 (1.0)	2 (1.0)	4 (0.7332...	5 (0.1660...
Freshwater	59	57 (0.0371249)	59 (1.0)	8 (0.49658114)	0 (1.0)	1 (1.0)	3 (0.020598166)	18 (0.039380...	11 (5.136...	5 (0.9394...	15 (5.532...	12 (6.387...
salkane	42	28 (1.0)	5 (0.93946344)	8 (0.07983257)	0 (1.0)	5 (5.4789734E...	1 (0.65680194)	3 (1.0)	2 (1.0)	42 (1.0)	5 (0.7337...	4 (0.8256...
saromatic	53	45 (1.0)	15 (5.5329278...	7 (0.57988644)	1 (0.33537...	2 (0.39041713)	2 (0.17138518)	19 (0.003078...	4 (0.7332...	5 (0.7337...	53 (1.0)	11 (8.714...
sbtex	44	39 (0.9684179)	12 (6.387045E...	6 (0.55202156)	0 (1.0)	2 (0.25262302)	2 (0.095792525)	12 (0.232997...	5 (0.1660...	4 (0.8256...	11 (8.714...	44 (1.0)
scrudeoil	6	4 (1.0)	1 (0.69297945)	1 (0.6525498)	0 (1.0)	3 (4.532976E-...	1 (0.0027231514)	1 (1.0)	0 (1.0)	2 (0.0242...	0 (1.0)	0 (1.0)
sfattyacids	157	153 (2.247384E-5)	18 (1.0)	13 (1.0)	0 (1.0)	2 (1.0)	0 (1.0)	39 (0.093289...	16 (0.022...	7 (1.0)	11 (1.0)	9 (1.0)
sfuel	28	24 (1.0)	8 (0.00373624...	2 (1.0)	0 (1.0)	2 (0.06128481)	1 (0.37915775)	12 (0.002347...	8 (9.7348...	5 (0.0561...	5 (0.1814...	3 (0.6831...
shyrdocarbon	27	13 (1.0)	4 (0.5849842)	6 (0.05421468)	0 (1.0)	0 (1.0)	3 (4.0349707E-5)	4 (1.0)	2 (0.8365...	3 (0.5740...	1 (1.0)	1 (1.0)
Total	511	452	59	56	4	11	8	104	33	42	53	44

FIGURE 19.7 Organism characteristics cotable.

context of organisms to rank them in terms of similarity to a set of target organisms that have desirable properties. We then presented a way to summarize everything we know about a set of organisms as a simple co-occurrence table of organism characteristics.

This approach could easily be reapplied to other groups of biological species to help summarize and discover properties of living things.

CHAPTER 20

Example: Drug Repurposing

CHEMISTRY IS RICH IN variety and detail—the number of different molecules you can create with different combinations of elements in different configurations is practically endless. Biology is extraordinarily complex—each organism is an integrated machine containing billions of parts that act in both regular and irregular ways that are more stochastic than deterministic. Put biology and chemistry together and you have pharmacology: the study of how drugs affect organisms. It is not a discipline for the faint of heart (or mind).

When you think about all that complexity, it is really no wonder that it takes drug companies on average more than a decade to develop each new drug, with a success rate of less than 1%. So many things can go wrong at so many different points, and progress is so difficult to validate before the last hurdle is reached: human clinical trials. So many times, a drug that gets to this last hurdle falls short due to an unforeseen side effect or lack of efficacy at safe dosages.

No wonder, then, that pharmaceutical companies look for any shortcut that can address a market faster than starting all over from scratch. Hence the popularity of drug repurposing: taking a compound that was originally designed for one purpose and looking at another potential application. With this approach, you can start off where the previous drug was abandoned or even reuse a drug that may already be on the market for treating a different disease. In either case, hundreds of millions of dollars and years of time may be saved.

This is a great application area for Accelerated Discovery, because it all boils down to taking lots of old science and experimental results and combining these in new ways to make discoveries that go beyond the literal text of the documentation. The process of discovery consists of connecting the dots in new ways to get from an existing compound to a new disease. This requires creating both the dots (the entities) and the connections (relationships) out of unstructured data that was not really designed for that purpose but nonetheless provides the raw materials we need to point the way to these medical breakthroughs.

Note: The examples of drug repurposing described in this chapter are illustrative. The compounds and diseases are real, but the analysis is retrospective in character and does not correspond to an actual discovery of a new drug treatment via Accelerated Discovery techniques. Research into actual drug repurposing applications is currently ongoing and proprietary.

COMPOUND 1: A PDE5 INHIBITOR

Drugs are typically designed to hit a specific biological target, usually a protein, in order to perform their function. PDE5 is the target of the compound that we wish to repurpose in this exercise. This target was selected originally because of its known importance in regulation of the cardiovascular system. Now we wish to try to connect it to a different disease, outside of that area: osteoporosis. Using the entity annotators we developed for proteins and diseases, we created a protein disease network around these entities to find a connected path that describes how the inhibition of PDE5 could indeed have an effect on osteoporosis. An illustration of that network is shown in Figure 20.1.

Remember that each node in this network represents a protein or a disease occurring in some sentence that describes a relationship in a Medline abstract. Each of the arcs represents a statement that describes a particular regulation or influence that the protein at the beginning of the arc has over the protein at the end of the arc.

This visualization allows us to connect the dots from PDE5, to IL1b, to IRAK3, and finally to osteoporosis. The individual sentences that provide the evidence for these linkages are shown in Figure 20.2.

First, we see that pde5a suppresses normal IL-1 function. This is the first link in the causal chain, and the direction of that link is downward or

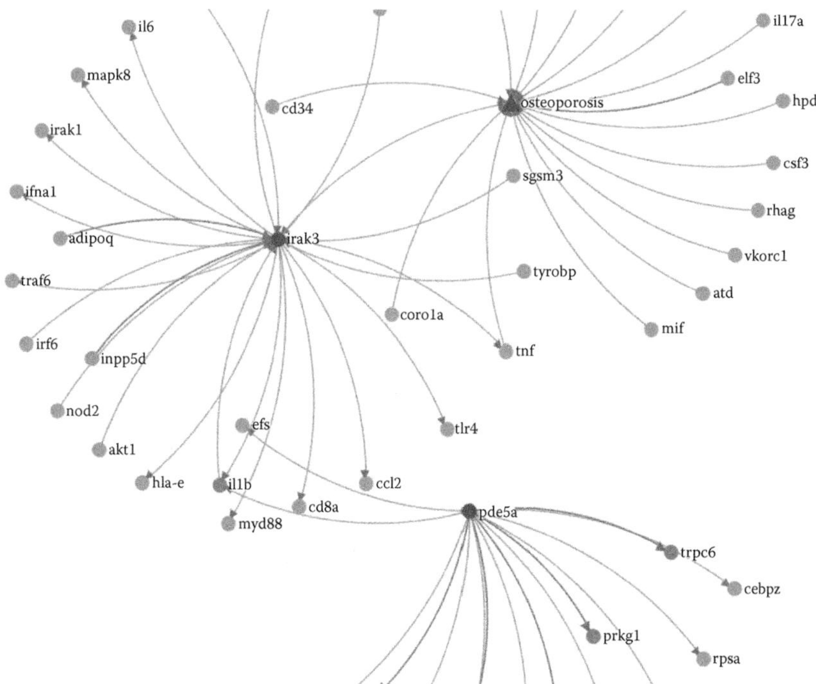

FIGURE 20.1 PDE5A and osteoporosis.

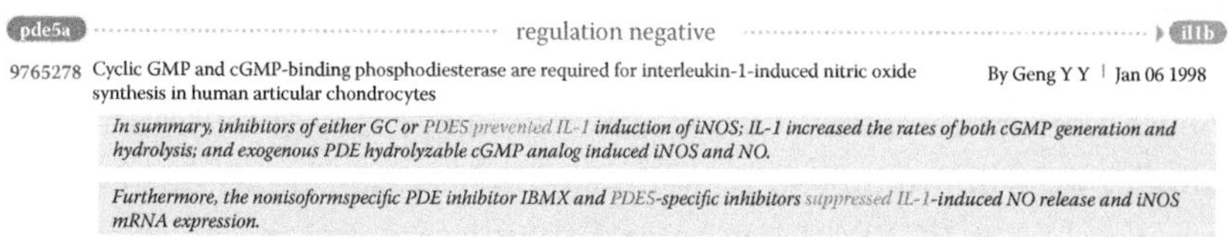

FIGURE 20.2 Evidence.

inhibitory. Since our drug is a PDE5 inhibitor, this means that the effect of the drug will be to maintain normal IL-1 function (Figure 20.3).

Next, we find that IL-1is tightly associated with kinase IRAK-M. So we can assume that maintaining IL-1 function would also help to maintain IRAK-M.

Finally, we see that IRAK-M, when absent in mice, causes the development of severe osteoporosis. This indicates that maintaining the function of this protein could potentially help alleviate that disease.

What is remarkable about the discovery of these connections is that it requires putting together three completely different research articles published over the span of a decade. Even the best experts in the field find this

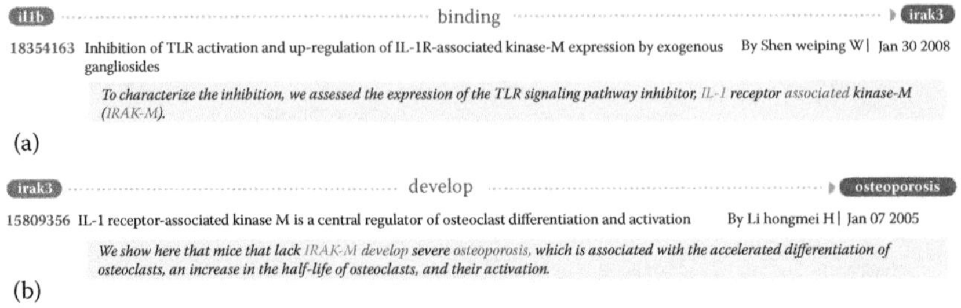

il1b ········· binding ········· irak3

18354163 Inhibition of TLR activation and up-regulation of IL-1R-associated kinase-M expression by exogenous gangliosides By Shen weiping W | Jan 30 2008

To characterize the inhibition, we assessed the expression of the TLR signaling pathway inhibitor, IL-1 receptor associated kinase-M (IRAK-M).

(a)

irak3 ········· develop ········· osteoporosis

15809356 IL-1 receptor-associated kinase M is a central regulator of osteoclast differentiation and activation By Li hongmei H | Jan 07 2005

We show here that mice that lack IRAK-M develop severe osteoporosis, which is associated with the accelerated differentiation of osteoclasts, an increase in the half-life of osteoclasts, and their activation.

(b)

FIGURE 20.3 Evidence.

kind of connection very hard to discover, and it often requires months of research. A system that has read every article and discovered every connection already, instantiating these in a network of proteins and diseases connected by precise indications of which type of interaction is taking place, can theoretically find such patterns in minutes.

The caveat here, of course, is that many apparent causal effects are only true in specific circumstances or conditions, so it requires much greater study to determine if the linkage holds in a manner consistent with an effective drug treatment.

PPARα/γ AGONIST

This compound was originally designed as a treatment for type 2 diabetes. This compound was published as an open challenge to researchers to propose alternative usages. One research group proposed asthma. In this example, we will attempt to recapitulate their reasoning to this conclusion. We start with PPARA gene and the disease asthma as the entity endpoints and look for a way to make a causal connection between these entities.

Here again, using our network of proteins and disease connections found in Medline abstracts, we were able to discover a number of potential connections between the drug target and the disease asthma (Figure 20.4).

In fact, the connection through adiponectin (adipoq) is the one that was uncovered by the experts after much manual labor. Figure 20.5 shows the evidence that the system provided that clearly establishes that connection in medical literature.

Firstly, it is clear that PPAR-gamma is a positive regulator of adiponectin. So the drug in question, being a PPAR-gamma agonist, will tend to also increase adiponectin levels (Figure 20.6).

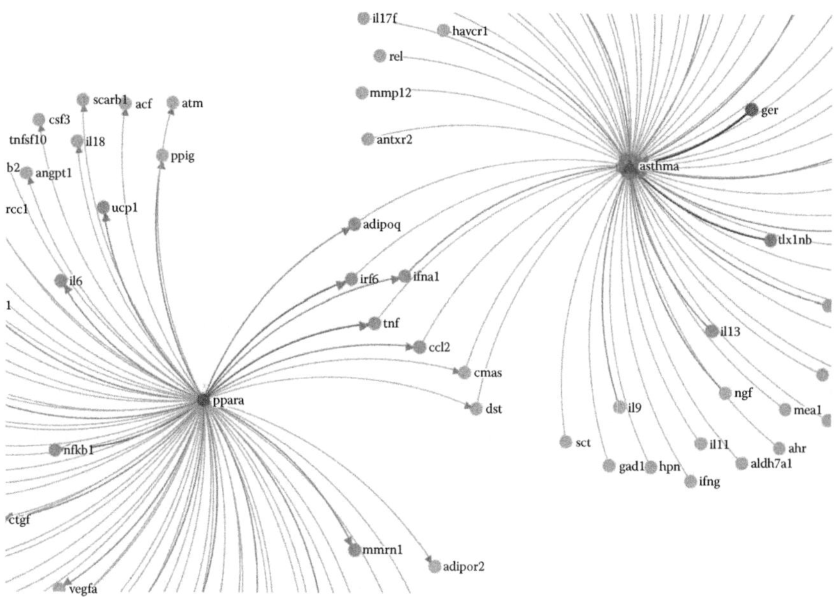

FIGURE 20.4 PPARA and asthma.

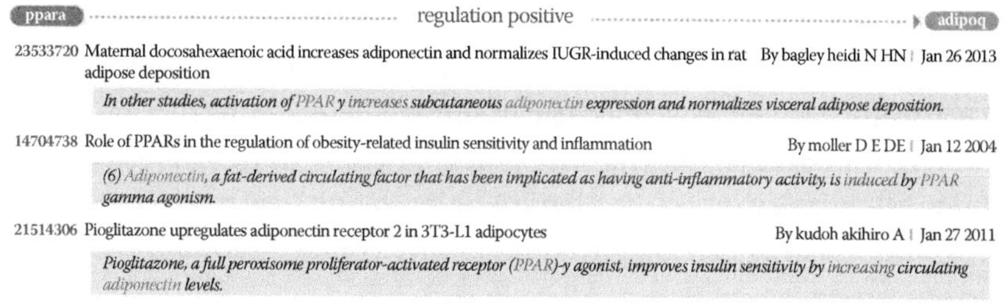

ppara ········ regulation positive ········ adipoq

23533720 Maternal docosahexaenoic acid increases adiponectin and normalizes IUGR-induced changes in rat adipose deposition By bagley heidi N HN | Jan 26 2013

In other studies, activation of PPAR γ increases subcutaneous adiponectin expression and normalizes visceral adipose deposition.

14704738 Role of PPARs in the regulation of obesity-related insulin sensitivity and inflammation By moller D E DE | Jan 12 2004

(6) Adiponectin, a fat-derived circulating factor that has been implicated as having anti-inflammatory activity, is induced by PPAR gamma agonism.

21514306 Pioglitazone upregulates adiponectin receptor 2 in 3T3-L1 adipocytes By kudoh akihiro A | Jan 27 2011

Pioglitazone, a full peroxisome proliferator-activated receptor (PPAR)-γ agonist, improves insulin sensitivity by increasing circulating adiponectin levels.

FIGURE 20.5 Evidence.

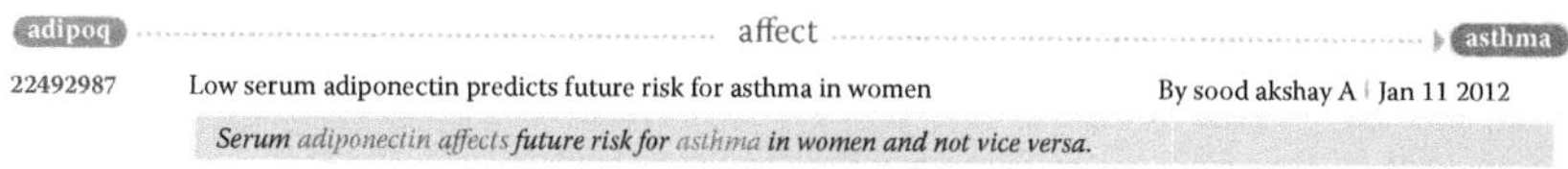

adipoq ········ affect ········ asthma

22492987 Low serum adiponectin predicts future risk for asthma in women By sood akshay A | Jan 11 2012

Serum adiponectin affects future risk for asthma in women and not vice versa.

FIGURE 20.6 Evidence.

Next, we see that low adiponectin seems to be a risk factor for asthma in women. So a drug that increases adiponectin levels ought to have a positive effect on asthma, at least in that population.

Again, this is merely validating a finding already made by human experts, but the remarkable fact is that the Accelerated Discovery methodology was able to find this connection in a manner of minutes, when it took months for the human experts to find the same causal pathway. It turns out to be much more difficult for a human brain to see all the interconnections that might be relevant to a given causal chain, starting from a single node. Computers, on the other hand, are quite good at seeing all the possibilities. The network visualization is a great way to bridge that gap, giving the human expert the power to understand what the computer has uncovered and focus attention on those linkages that are most likely to lead to new discoveries or treatments, while ignoring linkages that are spurious or irrelevant because they do not apply in the context of the disease.

Clearly, the extraction of biological entities and relationships from text shows great promise for accelerating the ability of pharmacologists to discover new applications of existing drugs from articles published in the literature and internal documents indicating connections that exist between the drug targets and other diseases not previously connected directly to those targets. If perfected, through experience and the analysis of the kinds of connections that are most reliable in which situations, it should be possible to make huge advances in finding new treatments for the existing stable of compounds that are already available for rapid development as drugs in the marketplace. There are literally thousands of drugs that have already been approved for use in human beings, affecting hundreds of different molecular targets. The potential gains to be harvested from mining all the relevant connections in order to find new treatments is one of the most exciting early applications of accelerated discovery.

CHAPTER 21

Example: Adverse Events

ADVERSE EVENTS ARE THE unintended consequences or failures of drug intervention. These events needed to be detected, understood, predicted, and, if possible, prevented or ameliorated. Unfortunately, most effective drugs also have some unintended consequences. It is important, therefore, to understand everything the literature is saying about a class of drugs in order to recognize and anticipate downstream consequences of protein modulation, and, if possible, find ways to mitigate the adverse event.

In order to predict adverse events, it is necessary to recognize chemical structures in text and find relevant content. Then, we need to identify possible adverse events and statistically correlate with structural component of chemistry. Then, it is necessary to identify common proteins corresponding to phenotypes and suggest possible modes of amelioration or secondary intervention that might ameliorate the problem.

We analyze a group of similar drugs to better understand how chemical structure potentially relates to known adverse effects and further investigate the biological mechanism that underlies the behavior. The researcher might use that information to propose a new drug that would have less risk of adverse events or suggest a second drug to help counteract the undesirable effect.

FENOFIBRATE

In this example, a drug researcher wants to find what adverse events commonly occur with drugs of the fibrate class, in particular fenofibrate, in order to design better drugs with fewer side effects. Fenofibrate is a drug for reducing cholesterol in order to prevent cardiovascular disease. Fenofibrate is a PPAR-gamma agonist.

PROCESS

We first create an annotator that recognizes all chemical entities, including drugs by their chemical structure. Chemical annotation of text documents is beyond the scope of this book, but processes exist that allow for conversion of drug names and chemical formulas into normalized SMILE strings [1] and InChI keys [2] that can be compared for structural similarity to other molecules (Figure 21.1).

We enter the molecule for fenofibrate (Figure 21.2) into our chemical search across Medline abstracts and retrieve those chemicals with a similar structure. This molecule finds the set of related chemicals shown in Figure 21.3.

We create a new set of molecules that are all known to be in the fenofibrate class. From this starting point, we now want to observe what the conditions are that these drugs are typically either treating or causing.

The conditions associated with all similar molecules (those conditions that co-occur with those molecules in Medline abstracts) are shown in Figure 21.4.

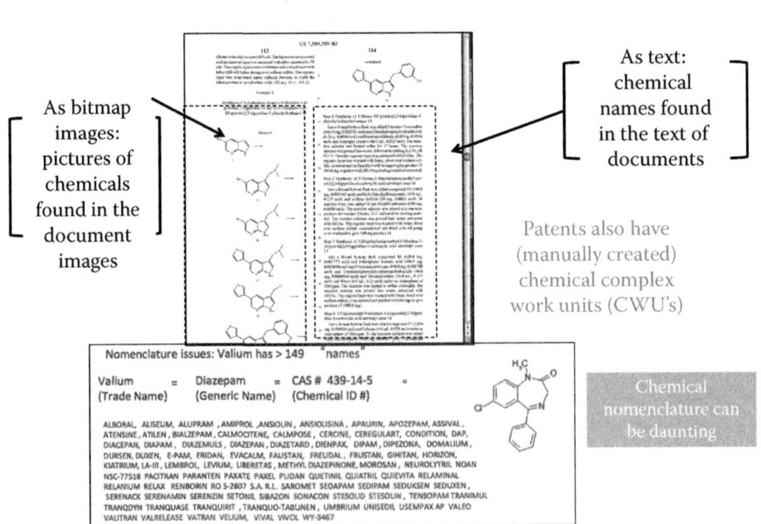

FIGURE 21.1 Chemical entity extraction.

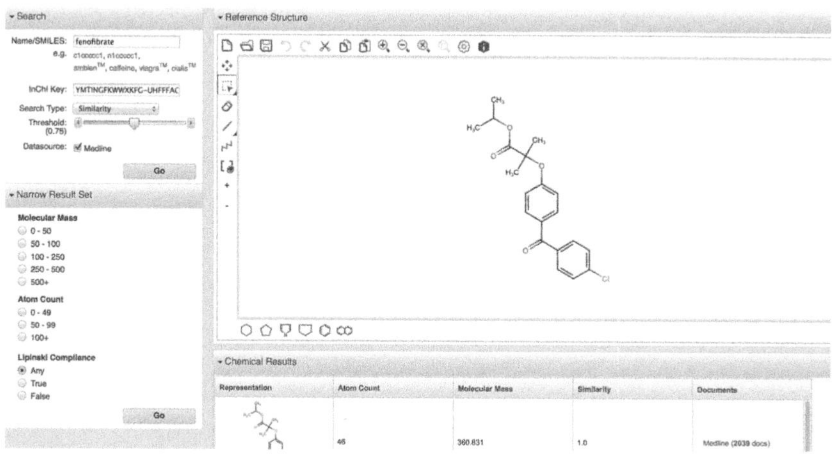

FIGURE 21.2 Chemical search.

The first condition that looks like a potential adverse event is rhabdomyolysis. We can now look for other drugs that exhibit that same effect, whether or not they are in the same class as fenofibrate. Widening the aperture gives us the opportunity to look for structures that are chemically very different. The idea is to find out what structures such chemicals share in common.

Figure 21.5 shows all the connections in text to rhabdomyolysis. This diagram graphs all the known relationships involving rhabdomyolysis, which is a breakdown of muscle fibers that can often lead to kidney disease. The incoming links provide causes of rhabdomyelysis, including many drugs:

flouroquinolones

cyclosporine

fusidic acid

trabectedin

pyrazinamide

olanzapine

Now we find the common downstream causal linkage between drugs and adverse event. We focus on commonalities between two very different drugs: fenofibrate, which lowers cholesterol; and olanzapine, which is an antipsychotic (Figure 21.6).

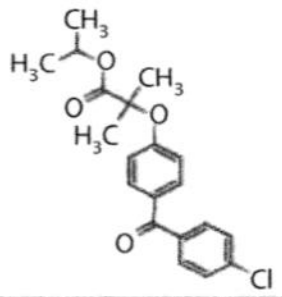	46	360.831	1.0	Medline (**2039** docs)
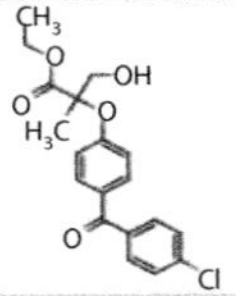	44	362.804	0.9739130139350891	Medline (**0** docs)
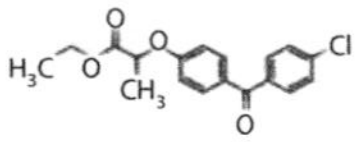	40	332.778	0.9557521939277649	Medline (**0** docs)
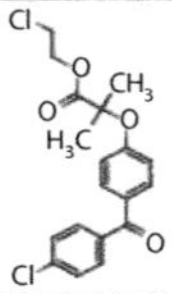	43	381.25	0.9411764740943909	Medline (**0** docs)
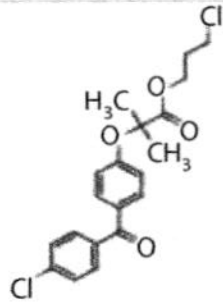	46	395.276	0.9333333373069763	Medline (**0** docs)

FIGURE 21.3 Chemically similar molecules.

Phenotypes of related molecules

Class	Total					
Disease	1531	550	442	308	47	417
Hyperlipidemias	707	231	195	129	27	241
Atherosclerosis	547	220	158	91	23	150
Heart diseases	512	129	194	106	12	151
Dyslipidemias	467	315	134	63	22	30
Hypertriglyceridemia	436	169	150	93	9	80
Coronary disease	432	117	188	94	10	90
Neoplasms	392	105	46	58	55	175
Syndrome	368	166	90	86	7	84
Hyperlipoproteinemias	362	67	48	57	9	224
Cardiovascular diseases	347	193	101	56	11	51
Diabetes mellitus	335	162	90	67	6	49
Hypercholesterolemia	334	101	112	70	11	93
Infarction	278	54	86	108	3	65
Body weight	275	108	26	35	20	110
Coronary artery disease	269	87	95	91	6	37
Insulin resistance	262	142	53	71	4	19
Inflammation	245	152	34	49	5	30
Myocardial infarction	230	50	77	59	2	66
Hypertension	218	84	57	42	7	48
Death	207	49	72	41	8	59
Rhabdomyolysis	201	61	123	42	14	10

FIGURE 21.4 Molecule vs. condition cotable.

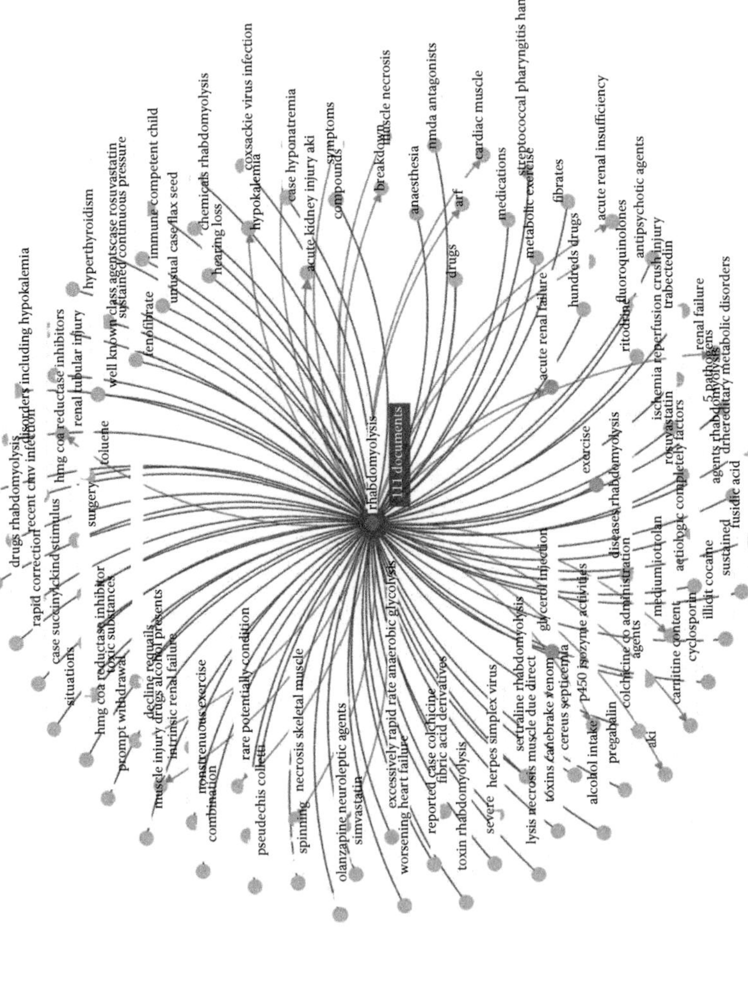

FIGURE 21.5 Relationships to rhabdomyolysis.

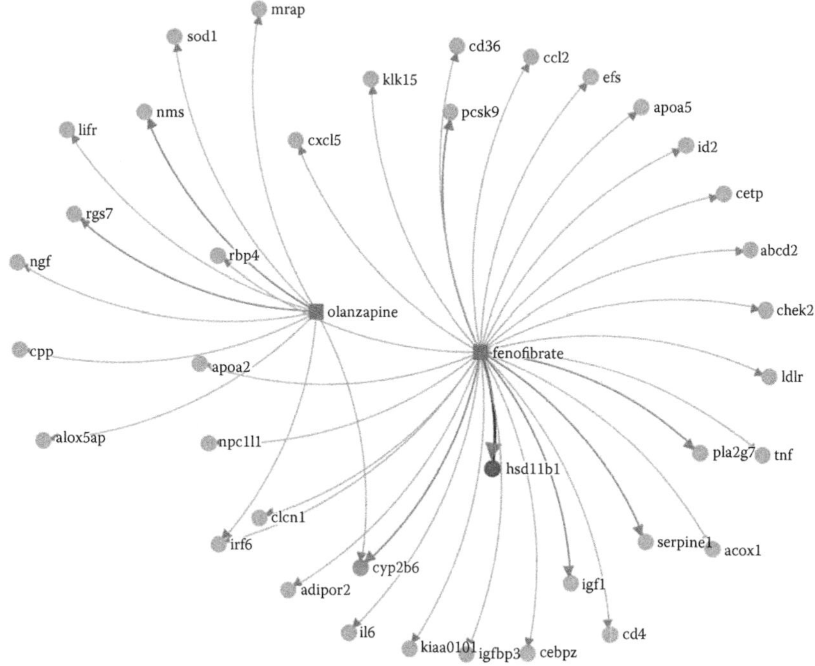

FIGURE 21.6 Proteins affected by olanzapine and fenofibrate.

Note that IRF6 is a protein affected by both drugs. The effect that both of these drugs have on IRF6 might be important. Our hypothesis is that this might be causing the adverse event. IRF6 is a gene that regulates the formation of connective tissue, so that may have some relevance to the breakdown of muscle fiber.

The next step is to find potential mechanisms to avoid or ameliorate the adverse event. We look for drugs that might have an effect on the IRF6 gene (Figure 21.7).

This provides a number of drugs that could affect the IRF6 gene, which could be further investigated to provide a combination therapy or a drug structure similarity approach to find the best chemical structure to avoid the problem. Focusing on the most well supported evidence yields the network shown in Figure 21.8.

CONCLUSION

Understanding all the downstream implications of chemical intervention is essential for creating useful and safe drugs in the marketplace. The more up-front work pharma companies can do in looking out for these

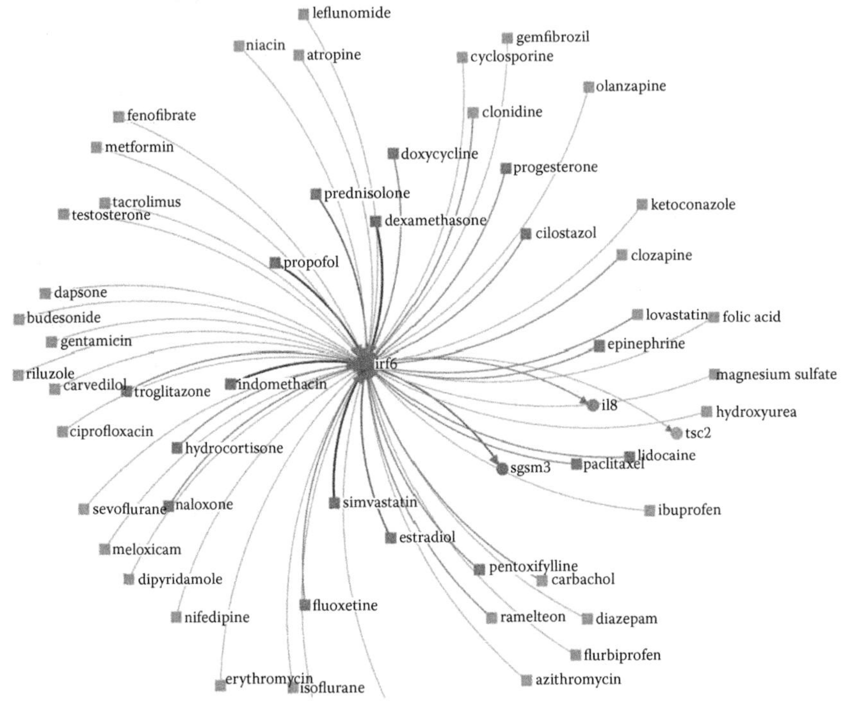

FIGURE 21.7 Drugs affecting IRF6.

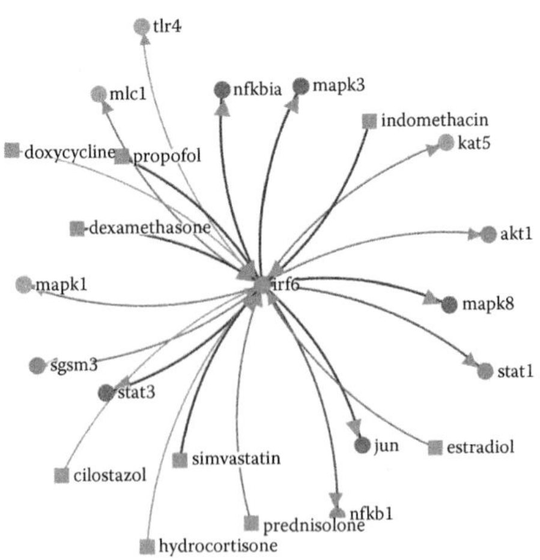

FIGURE 21.8 Drugs with high support.

unexpected consequences, the more likely we are to get drugs to market faster and with better safety and reliability than ever before.

REFERENCES

1. Weininger, D., Weininger, A., and Weininger, J. L. 1989. SMILES. 2. Algorithm for generation of unique SMILES notation. *Journal of Chemical Information and Computer Sciences*, *29*(2): 97–101.
2. Heller, S. R., and McNaught, A. D. 2009. The IUPAC international chemical identifier (InChI). *Chemistry International*, *31*(1): 7.

CHAPTER 22

Example: P53 Kinases

In 2013, a workshop took place that brought together data scientists from IBM who were creating Accelerated Discovery technology and molecular biologists at Baylor College of Medicine. They wanted to see if there was some way to accelerate discovery around the protein P53. The results of that effort were published in a paper in *Knowledge Discovery and Data Mining 2014* (KDD-14) [1]. Here, we describe some of the story behind how we arrived at the result using the Accelerated Discovery methodology described in this book.

The first day of our two-day workshop was spent having Baylor biologists explain P53 biology to the data scientists from IBM. The following extract from the paper gives a good summary of what we learned.

> All human cells throughout an individual's body contain roughly the same genome, that is, the DNA molecules which represent the blueprints of biology inherited from one's parents. These blueprints contain the information necessary to create tens of thousands of different proteins, which are the molecular machines that are fundamental to all of cellular biology, performing a wide range actions such as metabolizing nutrients, allowing a cell to respond to its environment, and even controlling the quantities, or "expression levels," of other proteins. One particularly important protein, p53, is often referred to as "the guardian of the genome" and is implicated in many biological processes and diseases including cancer. As an individual grows and ages, cells

> must repeatedly make copies of their own genomes, which eventually results in degradation of the information contained therein. When enough errors accumulate, it is possible for a cell to enter a broken, cancerous state in which it grows continuously, damaging nearby tissue and causing harm to the organism. The p53 protein is a major player in the cell's natural defense against entering such a state: p53 responds to the detection of genomic problems by increasing the expression of hundreds of other proteins to try to fix the errors, or, if that isn't possible, it can even cause a cell to destroy itself, saving the neighboring cells and the life of the individual. One way that p53 is able to react to such problems is due to signals from a set of proteins that chemically modify p53 in response to different conditions. Each p53 modification, of which there are over 50, acts as an on/off switch, causing p53 to have one response or another. The most common type of modification among all proteins, including p53 in particular, is phosphorylation, in which a phosphate molecule (PO_4^{3-}) is bonded to a specific atom in a protein molecule. The class of proteins that carries out the addition of phosphate molecules are known as kinases, which are increasingly the target of promising cancer treatments for use when these signaling mechanisms. Drugs can affect the behavior of specific kinases, which can produce specific reactions in the proteins they phosphorylate, with the goal being to activate the cell's innate cancer-fighting abilities. Knowing which proteins are kinases is a well-solved problem; however, knowing which proteins are modified by each kinase, and therefore which kinases would make good drug targets, is a difficult and unsolved problem. There are over 500 known human kinases and tens of thousands of possible proteins they can target. Biochemical experiments require months to establish a single novel kinase-protein relationship, and then years to fully elucidate the relationship's biological impact. Only 33 of the 500+ kinases are currently known to modify p53, but it is likely that there are many such relationships that remain unknown.

So this provided us with a well-formed problem. We had a space of entities (kinases) and we had the data to create unstructured information from (published literature in the form of Medline abstracts). We had some known entities that fit the pattern we were looking for (phosphorylate p53).

We needed to extract enough information to derive a prediction model that would extrapolate from the known p53 kinases to some additional kinases that were not yet known to phosphorylate p53. The challenge was that we had very little time to show we could do this. Our funding was only for 6 months.

The second day of the workshop was spent showing the biologists our Accelerated Discovery method.

AN ACCELERATED DISCOVERY APPROACH BASED ON ENTITY SIMILARITY

On the second day, we presented to the Baylor biologists our process for doing Accelerated Discovery. This was essentially the same process described in the 'Form and Function' chapter of this book. They immediately appeared to recognize what we were getting at. They also remarked that it looked very similar to the scientific methods they already used to uncover new properties of proteins. This was encouraging.

Next, we showed them an example of how we could create a centroid representation of a protein that was based on all the published literature (Medline abstracts) that mentioned the protein. We showed them the scatter-plot visualization of six proteins, with p53 being one of them. The large bubble indicates the location of a centroid, the small dots represent documents containing a protein, and the connected lines indicate similarity based on cosine distance (Figure 22.1)

The biologists from Baylor immediately remarked that the associations we were indicating seemed reasonable. Their next question was whether I could do this same thing for protein kinases. We said that we did not see why not. The next excerpt from the paper describes in detail what we did to build this network.

> To approach this problem, we first note that there are over 240,000 papers that mention one or more of 500+ known human kinases in their Medline abstract. An avid reader capable of absorbing 10 papers per day would need 70 years to go through this relevant literature—a completely unrealistic feat. Instead, however, we mine text so as to create a model for each kinase that represents all the terms present in the abstracts of the papers that specifically mention that kinase. In aggregate, and ignoring issues of errors

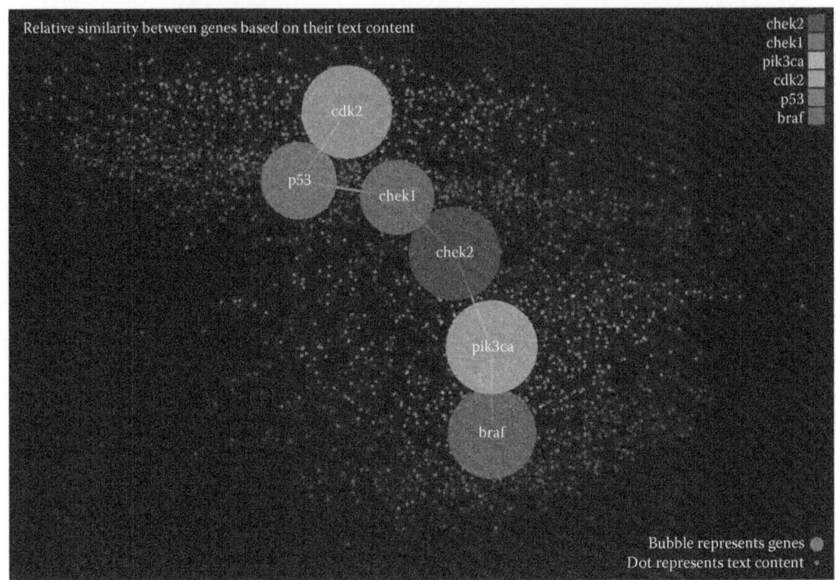

FIGURE 22.1 **(See color insert.)** Gene network based on content centroids.

and uncertainty, the words in these abstracts are assumed to be a useful signature of kinase features, such as details about biological process, molecular function, cellular component and specific interactions.

We collect and label the abstracts to be mined using queries against a text index of all Medline abstracts. There is one OR query for each kinase that includes the kinases canonical name along with its synonyms taken from. We submit the queries and download all abstracts that match each kinase up to query size. (A few kinases have well over 10,000 abstracts, which is far more than is needed to develop an accurate model.). We excluded kinases that had less than 10 abstract mentions. This left us with 259 kinases in all. Of these, 23 were known to be p53 kinases.

Next we create a numeric representation that encapsulates all we know about each kinase relative to every other kinase. To facilitate this process we represent the documents in a vector-space model. That is, each document is a vector of weighted frequencies of its features (words and phrases). We emphasize words with high frequency in a document, and normalize each document vector to have unit Euclidean norm.

The words and phrases that make up the document feature space are determined by counting the number of documents in which each word appears and identifying the words with the highest counts. A standard "stop word" list is used to eliminate words such as "and," "but," and "the." The top N words are retained in the first pass, where the value of N may vary depending on the length of the documents, the number of documents and the number of categories to be created. In our experiments we found that N = 20,000 is sufficient for the categories and documents used in this domain. After selecting the words in the first pass, we make a second pass to count the frequency of the phrases that occur using these words. A phrase is considered to be a sequence of two words occurring in order without intervening non-stop words. We again prune to keep only the N most frequent words and phrases. This becomes the feature space. A third pass through the data indexes the documents by their feature occurrences. We experimented with various methods of weighting term occurrences in this matrix and eventually determined that a Term Frequency–Inverse Document Frequency weighting (TF-IDF) yielded the best overall prediction accuracy.

Once we have a feature space we create a representation of each kinase by averaging the feature vectors of all documents that contain the kinase. This is the kinase centroid. Next we calculate a distance matrix that measures the distance between each kinase and every other kinase in the space. Such matrices are fine for computers to read and calculate properties over, but notoriously difficult for a domain expert to interpret in order to get a sense of the data's underlying validity and meaning. Interpretability is important, because an expert must be confident and insightful when proposing new hypotheses. Thus some way must be found to convert the numbers into a meaningful picture of kinase-kinase relationships.

Now, the strategy we described in the chapter on 'Visualizing the Data Plane' becomes relevant. In this specific instance, the pure network diagram would be mostly unhelpful. Instead, we create a simplified tree diagram that boils down the kinase centroid similarities to their most concentrated essence (Figure 22.2).

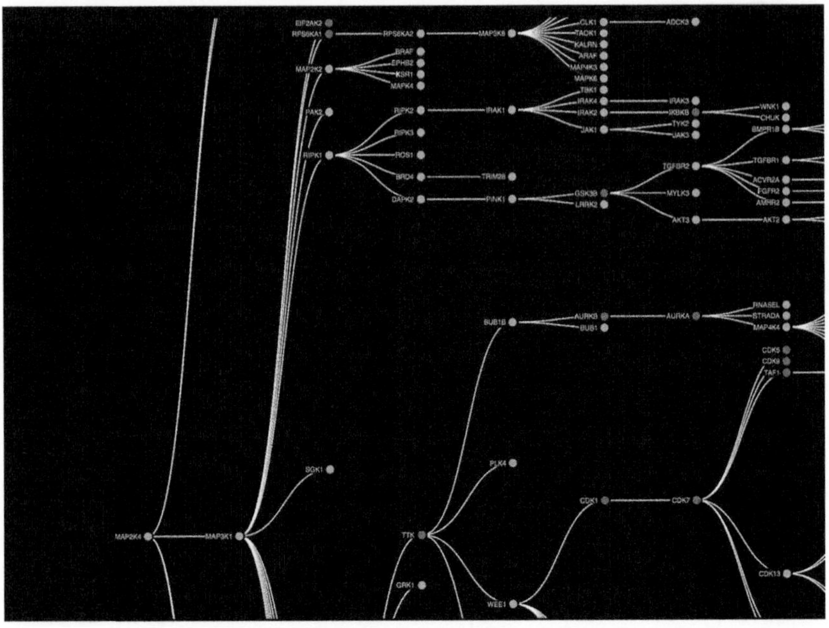

FIGURE 22.2 **(See color insert.)** Kinase similarity network.

Using this approach, we created a graph of all the kinases and then colored them by known P53 associations. The result was immediately striking. The known P53 kinases were occurring together and the other kinases were mostly in other areas of the kinase tree. Moreover, there were a few kinases not known to be P53 kinases that seemed to be in among those that were known. This was exactly what we hoped to find, because it gave us a ready list of potential candidate kinases on which to begin running experiments (Figure 22.3).

In order to validate that our predictions were reasonable, we needed to find a way to test whether the predictive approach we had in mind was indeed able to accurately foreshadow future discoveries. We did this through a time-based taxonomy. Dividing the Medline data by date of publication—either before or after January 1, 2003—allowed us to analyze the data in the older publications in order to try to predict the discoveries that happened subsequently. The retrospective study section of our paper describes what happened.

RETROSPECTIVE STUDY

> One measure of effectiveness is to predict from papers published prior to a given date events that were only discovered after that date. To test this hypothesis, we mined the literature up to 2003,

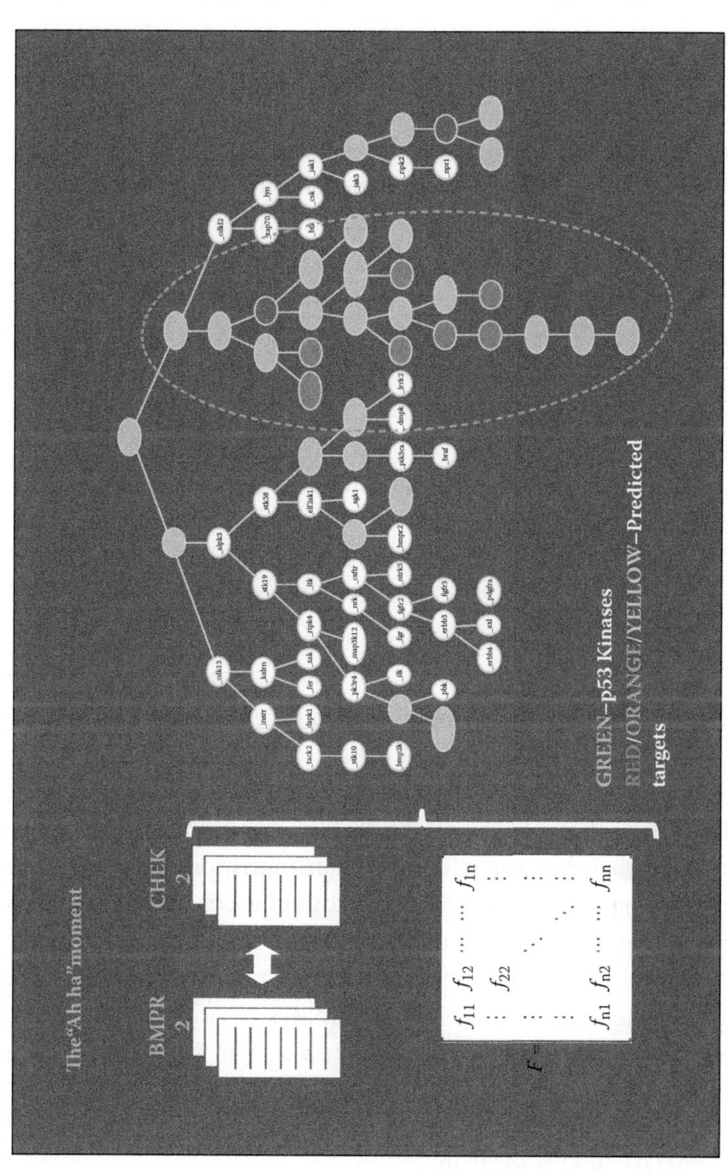

FIGURE 22.3 **(See color insert.)** P53 kinases clump together.

> when only half of the 33 currently known p53 kinases had been discovered. Because we filtered out confusing abstracts that mentioned multiple different kinases and p53, the kinase search space became small: only 74 kinases. But among these 74, ten were known to phosphorylate p53 in 2003, nine were found at a later date, and the remaining 55 are for simplicity assumed to not phosphorylate p53. A kinase distance matrix and a literature vector model was developed for these 74 kinases, the ten p53 kinases that were known prior to 2003 were labeled as such, and these labels were propagated to the other 64 kinases by global graph diffusion from which we could now rank the 64 kinases by the likelihood they targeted p53. Strikingly, an ROC curve shows that seven of the nine true positives are readily predicted with this algorithm (Precision = 0.54 at Recall = 0.77, with an AUC of 0.840). This time-stamped study shows that back in 2003, we could have automatically predicted many of the p53 kinases that were discovered in the subsequent decade by combining text mining with feature analysis and graph-based diffusion. This result is remarkable considering that for simplicity we only used a limited subset of the least ambiguous abstracts, which restricted us to studying only 74 rather than about 500 kinases.

These type of retrospective studies are an excellent way to gain confidence that the predictions we are making are not somehow artifacts of the way people write about P53 kinases. For example, it is conceivable (though very unlikely) that the only reason the P53 kinases clump together in the similarity tree is that the similarity is based primarily on this one property of being a P53 kinase. The retrospective study rules out this mechanism as an explanation for the clumping of the P53 kinases.

Now that we had some confidence that we had a mechanism for prediction, we selected the two most likely kinases on which to being running experiments. The next excerpt discusses what happened in these experiments.

EXPERIMENTAL VALIDATION

> Retrospective analyses are suggestive but never proof of discovery. For the latter it is critical to predict an observation that has never been made and then assess its truth in the laboratory. The

algorithms described above were used to rank 252 kinases (those with at least 20 publications) by likelihood of being p53 kinases. As expected, most kinases known to phosphorylate p53 were near the top of the rankings list. Five kinases on the list not known to phosphorylate p53 were then tested by biochemical and molecular biology experiments for their ability to interact with and phosphorylate p53. Two kinases (PKN1 and NEK2) were chosen from near the top of the list and three kinases were chosen from the bottom half of the list (TNK2, INSRR, and PDGFRA). Two validation assays were used.

In the in vitro kinase assay, p53 is combined with a kinase and a radioactive source of phosphate, gamma-^{32}P-ATP. Then a technique known as electrophoresis is used to separate the components of the mixture by weight to different positions in a gel. Because the weight of p53 is known (53 kilodaltons), we can check for radioactivity of anything that weights exactly that amount. If the predicted relationship is real, the kinase will add the radioactive phosphate to p53, and electrophoresis will move that radioactivity to a specific position in the gel, which is detectable by standard instruments. Top ranked kinase candidates NEK2 and PKN1 exhibit a labeled p53 band, as does a known p53 kinase CHK1 (used here as a positive control). The PKN1 band is faint relative to the others, but in subsequent experiments, the interaction was found to be robust. In contrast, low ranked p53 kinase candidates PDGFRA, TNK2, and INSRR exhibit no 53 kilodalton band, indicating they are unlikely to be p53 kinases (see Figure 22.4a).

For the second validation approach we used a different assay to show that there is a physical protein-protein interaction between p53 and the predicted kinases. This is considered a strong indication that the kinase is likely to target p53. Human cells containing p53 and a candidate kinase are generated and analyzed. Proteins from the cell are isolated and a p53-specific antibody is then added; an antibody is a substance that will bind to and isolate a specific protein, in this case p53, along with any protein that is bound to it, in this case—if the prediction is correct—the kinase being tested. This isolate is then separated by size, and an additional antibody is used to test for the presence of each candidate kinase. Our results show that p53 was indeed bound to NEK2, and that show both NEK2 and the p53 antibody must be present

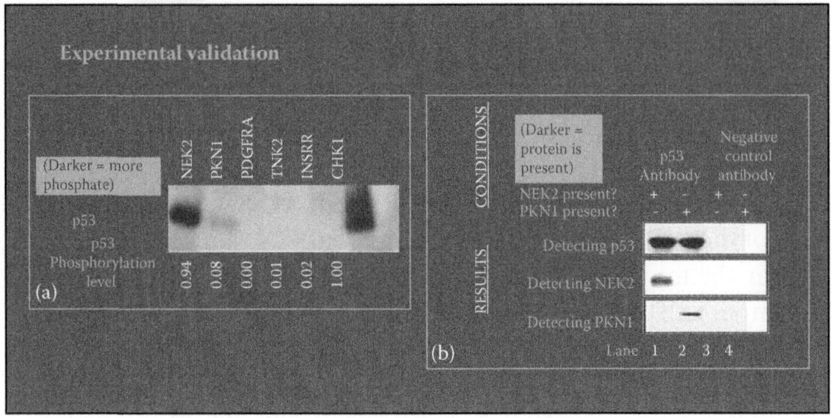

FIGURE 22.4 Experimental validation of predicted P53 kinases.

to achieve this result. Our results also show that p53 was bound to PKN1 (see Figure 22.4b).

These two sets of experiments argue strongly that computationally predicted top p53 kinase candidates PKN1 and NEK1 are indeed true p53 kinases.

What is remarkable about this result is that no single paper or small set of papers could have made this prediction. Even the P53 expert at Baylor was unaware of the connections that were waiting to be discovered between these kinases and P53. If we can do this for P53, why not for other proteins and entities on a much larger scale? This is exactly the direction we are heading. And in fact it can and must be the way all science will be done in the future.

CONCLUSION

Of all the examples given in this book, the P53 kinase experiment is the most compelling. The problem was well chosen and the results went well beyond our most optimistic expectations. Not all engagements are this fortuitous. But it does provide compelling evidence that the methods we are employing have incredible potential to make scientists smarter, faster, and much more productive than they currently are. We have a long way to go, but it is clear we are heading in the right direction.

REFERENCE

1. Spangler, S., and Wilkins, A., et al. 2014. Automated hypothesis generation based on mining scientific literature. In *Proceedings of the 20th ACM SIGKDD International Conference on Knowledge Discovery and Data Mining*. New York: ACM.

CHAPTER 23

Conclusion and Future Work

THIS BOOK DESCRIBES A methodology to address a basic problem that is challenging progress in every field of human intellectual activity: We have become much better at the generation of information than its integrative analysis. This leads to deep inefficiencies in translating research into progress for humanity. No scientist can keep up with the unrelenting flow of new studies and results, even within specialized fields. While intuition and selective reading in a highly narrowed field of work are essential and can certainly lead to breakthroughs, they are also likely to lead most scientists at one time or another toward deeply unproductive hypotheses that might have benefitted from more comprehensive insights into the data that was available but which we could not find an opportunity to learn about. Specialization also inherently limits the opportunities to find common ground at the interface between fields, even though these interfaces are often among the deepest areas of scientific synthesis (Figure 23.1).

The important thing to remember about the process we have described is that it is circular and virtuous in nature. By this I mean that, as you make progress in one area of the cycle, it increases the power and applicability of the other areas.

Our research team, consisting of members in academia and industry, combine talents and technologies in many diverse fields to accelerate scientific discoveries that lead to improved patient outcomes. The example applications described in this book are the first stage in this collaborative

FIGURE 23.1 Process for accelerated discovery.

effort and prove the principle that mining past literature is a viable strategy for predicting previously unknown scientific events. In the future, it should be possible to make many kinds of predictions on a much larger scale as our infrastructure and capabilities ramp up.

We believe this will ultimately accelerate the pace of scientific discovery by an order of magnitude. We also feel that the general approach of mining literature to identify hidden relationships between entities is not confined to biology but is a general tool that can be applied in almost any science. The potential for the dramatic acceleration of discovery in all sciences holds out the possibility of tremendous benefits for human health and for societal progress in the coming years. Given the enormous challenges facing science today on a global scale, with ever-more complex systems of entities and networks of relationships, the acceleration of discovery is not only desirable but also indispensable for human flourishing.

The chart in Figure 23.2 provides a partial list of other industries where Accelerated Discovery may apply.

ARCHITECTURE

By design, we have said little up to this point concerning the architecture for entity annotation, relationship extraction, and reasoning in real time. The diagram in Figure 23.3 represents a broad outline of how an Accelerated Discovery architecture may be implemented.

Since entities, relationships, domain dictionaries, and content may differ from one application to another, it helps to have a layered architecture that allows these elements to be plugged in as needed (Figure 23.4).

A Hadoop type framework allows for scalable data annotation of large content, which is then integrated across many different annotators and content. The analytics layer retrieves information from the indexed

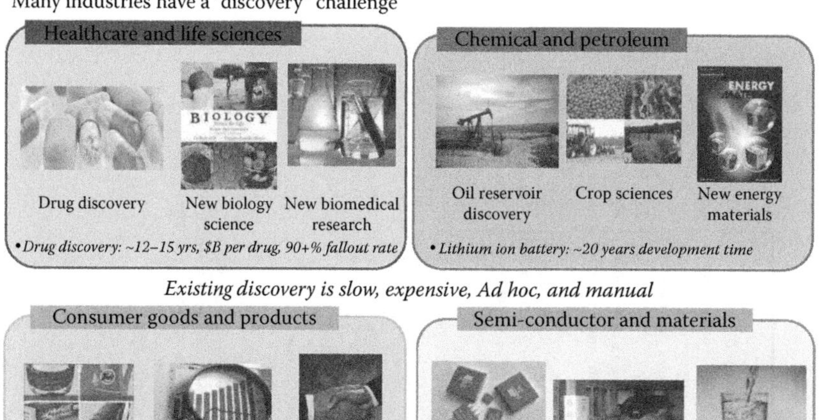

FIGURE 23.2 Industries where accelerated discovery could apply.

repositories and performs discovery and hypothesis generation as well as visualizations of the entities and relationships (Figure 23.5).

The overall workflow starts with unstructured content on the left side, which is annotated, normalized, and indexed through a consistent process that can be improved over time as dictionaries, rule-based annotators, and learning based approaches improve.

FUTURE WORK

We are just at the beginning of this journey, and there are many more areas of research that need to be brought to fruition if Accelerated Discovery is to achieve its full potential. What follows is a partial list. My hope is to encourage students in machine learning and related cognitive science disciplines to take up these problems as worthy of their time and likely to lead to important developments in the near future (Figure 23.6).

ASSIGNING CONFIDENCE AND PROBABILITIES TO ENTITIES, RELATIONSHIPS, AND INFERENCES

Each identification and extraction of entities and relationships from text comes with a possibility of error. To mitigate the consequences of error, it is frequently useful to quantify its degree. By applying statistical learning

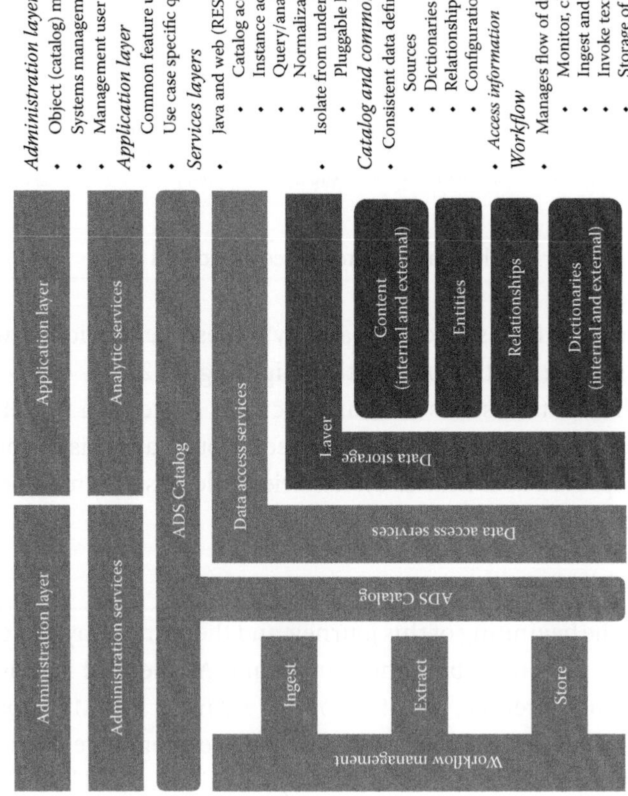

FIGURE 23.3 Systems architecture.

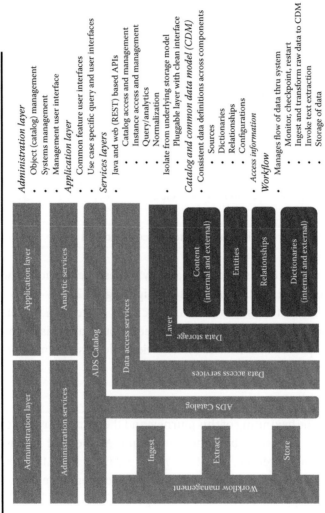

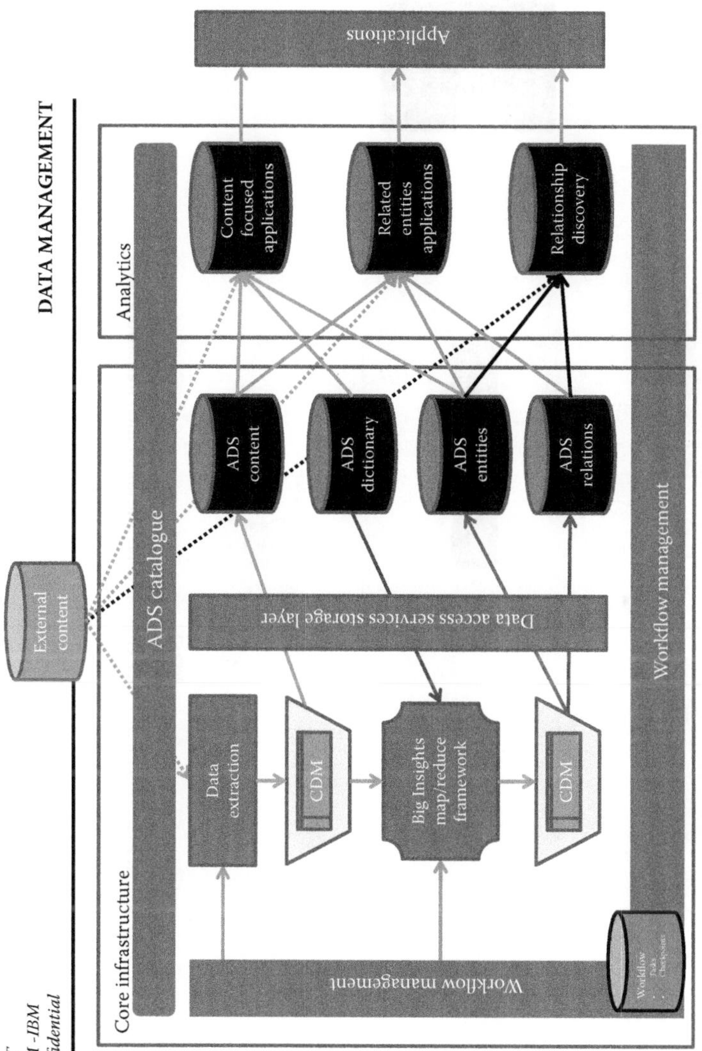

FIGURE 23.4 Data flow.

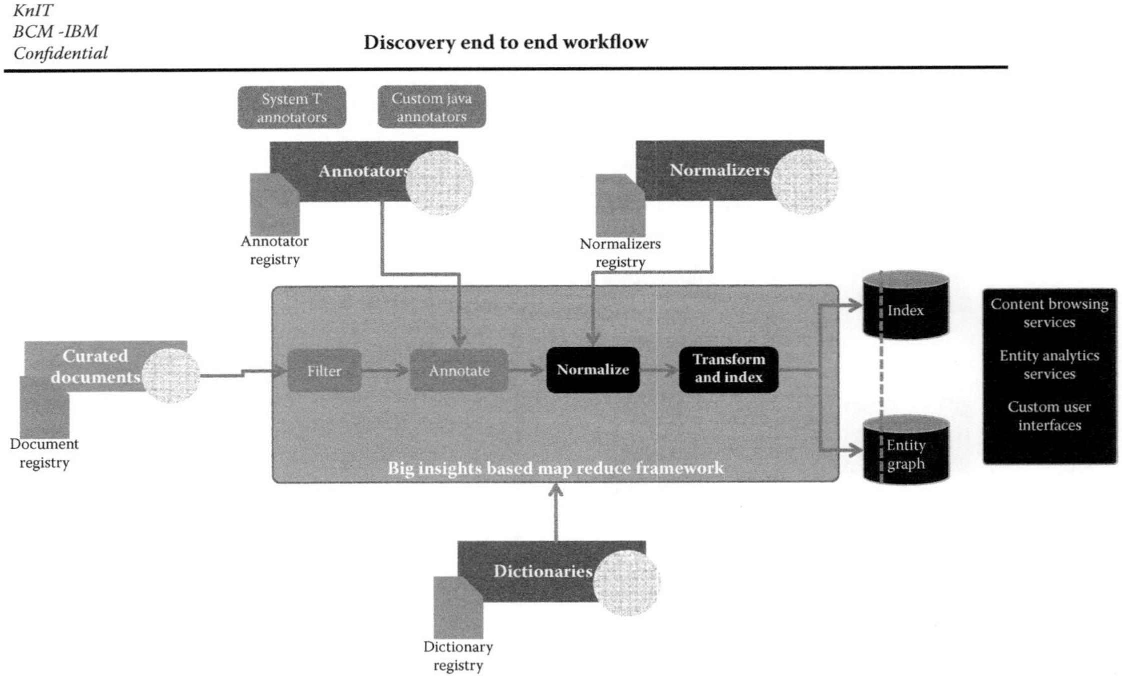

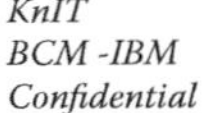

FIGURE 23.5 Workflow for annotation.

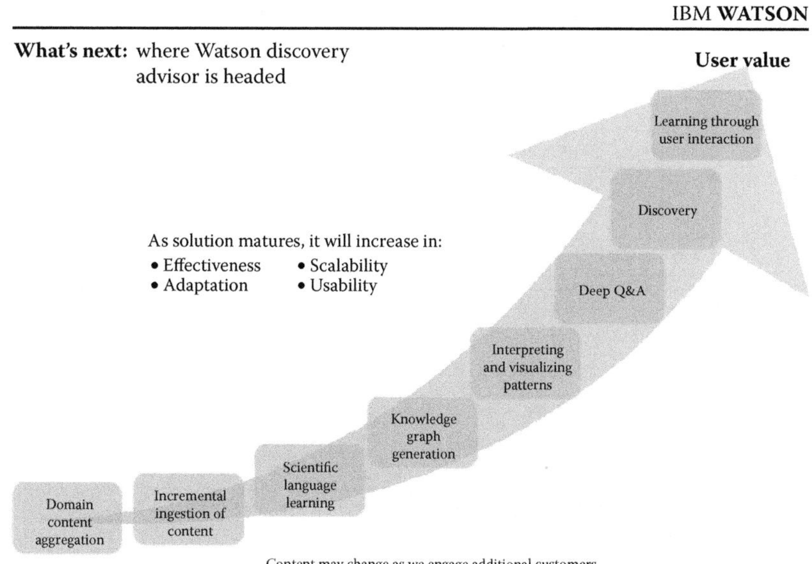

FIGURE 23.6 Future directions.

approaches that focus on features that characterize the situation in which the error is occurring, it should be possible to reliably estimate the probability of error in any given situation. This can then be rolled up to the level of inference or hypothesis generation to give an estimate of likely success. Retrospective analysis can also provide some quantification of how likely predictions about the future are to hold true.

The diagram in Figure 23.7 gives the underlying principles for judging the accuracy of rule-based extraction systems.

The diagram in Figure 23.8 shows how a second learning phase using a ProbIE [1] model will work to produce a confidence score for each prediction.

DEALING WITH CONTRADICTORY EVIDENCE

Often in science, there will be contradictory evidence on a given question before a degree of certainty is obtained. Our system should be able to detect such contradictions and flag them as anomalies to be studied further, or at least bring both positive and negative evidence to the investigator's attention when appropriate.

UNDERSTANDING INTENTIONALITY

When scientists publish an account of their experiments in papers or journals, they frequently couch their results in language that indicates the

Quantifying uncertainty in text annotations (ProbIE)

- Probabilistic information extraction in a rule-based system (SIGMOD 2009)

Annotator	Candidate-generation rules	Rule precision
Person Base annotator	P1: <Salutation><Capitalized word><Capitalized word> P2: <First name dictionary><Last name dictionary> P3: <Capitalized word><Capitalized word>	High High Low
Phone number Base annotator	Ph1: <PhoneClue><\d{3}-\d{3}-\d{4}> Ph2: <\d{3}-\d{3}-\d{4}> Ph3: <\d{5}	High Medium Low
Person phone Derived annotator	PP1: <Person><"can be reached at"><phonenumber> PP2: <"call"><person><0-2 tokens><phonenumber> PP3: [<person><phonenumber>]$_{sentence}$	High High Medium

+ Consolidation rule

Consolidate ("Joe Smith", "Mr. Joe Smith") = "Mr. Joe Smith"

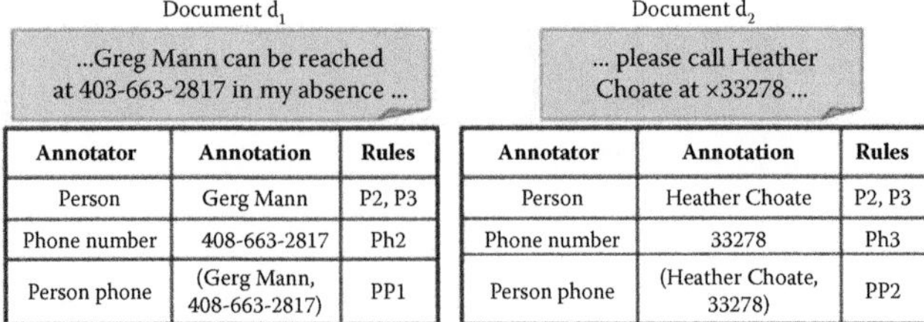

Document d_1

...Greg Mann can be reached at 403-663-2817 in my absence ...

Annotator	Annotation	Rules
Person	Gerg Mann	P2, P3
Phone number	408-663-2817	Ph2
Person phone	(Gerg Mann, 408-663-2817)	PP1

Document d_2

... please call Heather Choate at ×33278 ...

Annotator	Annotation	Rules
Person	Heather Choate	P2, P3
Phone number	33278	Ph3
Person phone	(Heather Choate, 33278)	PP2

Goal: Attach probabilities to annotations in a principled, scalable manner

FIGURE 23.7 Uncertainty. (From Michelakis, E. et al., Uncertainty management in rule-based information extraction systems, *Proceedings of the 2009 ACM SIGMOD International Conference on Management of Data*. New York: ACM, 2009.)

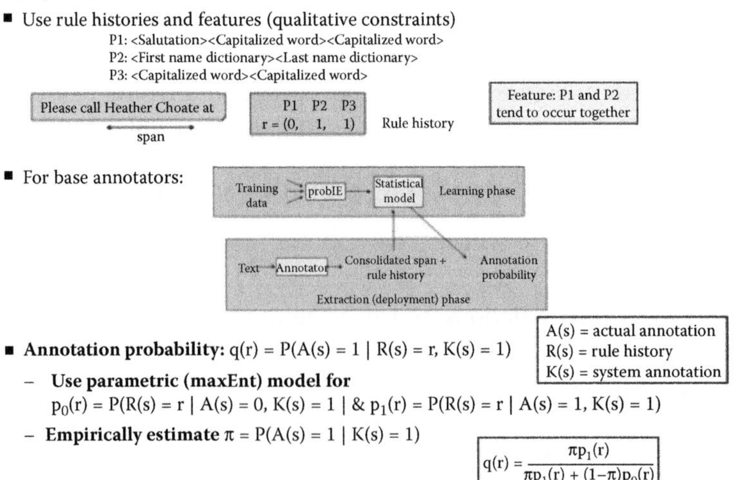
ProbIE, continued
Use rule histories and features (qualitative constraints)
P1: <Salutation><Capitalized word><Capitalized word>
P2: <First name dictionary><Last name dictionary>
P3: <Capitalized word><Capitalized word>
Please call Heather Choate at
span
P1 P2 P3
r = (0, 1, 1)
Rule history
Feature: P1 and P2 tend to occur together
For base annotators:
Training data
probIE
Statistical model
Learning phase
Text
Annotator
Consolidated span + rule history
Annotation probability
Extraction (deployment) phase
Annotation probability: q(r) = P(A(s) = 1 | R(s) = r, K(s) = 1)
A(s) = actual annotation
R(s) = rule history
K(s) = system annotation
Use parametric (maxEnt) model for
p0(r) = P(R(s) = r | A(s) = 0, K(s) = 1 | & p1(r) = P(R(s) = r | A(s) = 1, K(s) = 1)
Empirically estimate π = P(A(s) = 1 | K(s) = 1)
q(r) = πp1(r) / (πp1(r) + (1−π)p0(r))

FIGURE 23.8 A possible approach for calculating confidence.

confidence they ascribe to them. Some statements are background facts that are assumed to be true. Other statements are assertions that may be proved, substantiated, supported, uncorroborated, or disproved by the experimental results reported. Still other statements are hypotheses or suppositions not yet founded on firm experimental results. In a way, this kind of text analysis is similar to sentiment analysis in a social media context. We wish to determine the confidence stance of the author toward whatever factual statement they are recording. This will be an important feature to use as input in calculating the confidence values alluded to earlier.

ASSIGNING VALUE TO HYPOTHESES

The number of predictions that can be promulgated from an entity-relationship network is exponentially related to the number of entities and the different kinds of relationships that may potentially exist between them. This highlights the need for ranking and filtering criteria that will help prune the number of generated hypotheses back to a manageable figure. Confidence calculations are one way to do this, but scientists are not merely interested in the most likely hypothesis. Some hypotheses are worth pursuing even if they are not certain to be true. In some cases, gaining negative knowledge of a hypothesis is valuable in and of itself.

TOOLS AND TECHNIQUES FOR AUTOMATING THE DISCOVERY PROCESS

It is not practical to assign a data scientist to sit at the elbow of every scientist who might benefit from Accelerated Discovery processes. The only scalable solution is to design software that can implement and automate what a data scientist would do in most standard situations. As of this writing, there are many gaps that are currently filled with specialized, ad hoc software and tools that are sort of relevant but do not quite fit. A software system for Accelerated Discovery should really be redesigned from scratch with the entire process in mind to facilitate the gradual evolution of and natural maturation of knowledge extraction and inference in a new domain. This will be no small feat to accomplish, but the rewards would be equally substantial. Imagine every scientist benefitting from the optimum analysis of all relevant literature in her precise discipline. The impact on the rate of technical progress would be staggering.

CROWD SOURCING DOMAIN ONTOLOGY CURATION

Better software is half the battle. The other half is improving the domain taxonomies and ontologies that make up the backbone of the knowledge base. As the open-source movement and projects like Wikipedia have shown, the best way to insure comprehensive coverage is to recruit and maintain an enthusiastic cohort of editors and contributors. The publication and rewards process in science needs to be augmented to reflect the value of such work. This is a big project but one that must happen if we are to ultimately realize the full value of all the information we publish as a scientific community.

FINAL WORDS

I hope this chapter gives the reader a taste of how much important, groundbreaking research there is left to do, and how exciting it is to work in this field at this time. The danger in writing this book at this early stage in the field's development is that it will be seen as speculative or unproven and the methodology outdated as soon as it is published. Personally, I do not think this last possibility is a very likely one. The many examples I have given here, plus many others I have not documented in this book, provide solid evidence that the methods we employ for accelerating discovery are effective. Other methods will certainly be discovered in time to supplement these, but I am convinced the basic approach will remain much the same.

I hope the reader who has gotten this far has been rewarded with a new understanding of and appreciation for the promise of accelerating discovery in science through unstructured data analytics. I have been very fortunate to have chosen such a rewarding profession. I hoped in writing this book to help others who have chosen that profession move a little way forward. Only time will tell if I have succeeded, but for now I am content that I gave it my best effort.

Now go forth, and help science to move forward faster, more accurately, and with greater impact. Good luck!

REFERENCE

1. Michelakis, E., et al. 2009. Uncertainty management in rule-based information extraction systems. In *Proceedings of the 2009 ACM SIGMOD International Conference on Management of Data*. New York: ACM.

Index

U

V

W

X

For Product Safety Concerns and Information please contact our EU representative GPSR@taylorandfrancis.com Taylor & Francis Verlag GmbH, Kaufingerstraße 24, 80331 München, Germany

Printed and bound by CPI Group (UK) Ltd, Croydon, CR0 4YY

08/05/2025

01864341-0001